Pilosity, Prejudice, and Passion in *The Tale of Old Bearded Achbor* by Yaakov ben Elazar of Toledo

Studies in Medieval Literature

Series Editor: Albrecht Classen, University of Arizona

Advisory Board
Werner Schaefke, University of Copenhagen.
Christopher R. Clason, Oakland University.
Andrew Breeze, University of Navarre.
Connie Scarborough, Texas Tech University.
Gloria Allaire, University of Kentucky.
Fabian Alfie, University of Arizona.
Raymond Cormier, Longwood University.
Janina Traxler, Manchester University.
Marianne Ailes, University of Bristol.

Studies in Medieval Literature invites scholars to publish their most powerful, exciting, and forward-looking studies, which will thus become an excellent platform for Medieval Studies at large.

Recent Titles
Pilosity, Prejudice, and Passion in The Tale of Old Bearded Achbor *by Yaakov ben Elazar of Toledo*
   by Tovi Bibring
Criticism of the Court and the Evil King in the Middle Ages: Literary Historical Analyses
   by Albrecht Classen
The Poetry of the Medieval Troubadour, William IX of Aquitaine: The Songs that Built Europe
   by Fidel Fajardo-Acosta
Secrets in Medieval Literature: Epistemology of the Obscure
   by Albrecht Classen
Becoming the Pearl-Poet: Perceptions, Connections, Receptions
   edited by Jane Beal
Incarceration and Slavery in the Middle Ages and the Early Modern Age Cultural-Historical Investigation of the Dark Side in the Pre-Modern World
   edited by Albrecht Classen
Dante Satiro: Satire in Dante Alighieri's Comedy and Other Works
   by Fabian Alfie and Nicolino Applauso

Pilosity, Prejudice, and Passion in *The Tale of Old Bearded Achbor* by Yaakov ben Elazar of Toledo

Tovi Bibring

LEXINGTON BOOKS
Lanham • Boulder • New York • London

Lexington Books

Bloomsbury Publishing Inc, 1385 Broadway, New York, NY 10018, USA
Bloomsbury Publishing Plc, 50 Bedford Square, London, WC1B 3DP, UK
Bloomsbury Publishing Ireland, 29 Earlsfort Terrace, Dublin 2, D02 AY28, Ireland
www.rowman.com

Copyright © 2025 by The Rowman & Littlefield Publishing Group, Inc.

All rights reserved. No part of this publication may be: i) reproduced or transmitted in
any form, electronic or mechanical, including photocopying, recording or by means of
any information storage or retrieval system without prior permission in writing from
the publishers; or ii) used or reproduced in any way for the training, development
or operation of artificial intelligence (AI) technologies, including generative AI
technologies. The rights holders expressly reserve this publication from the text and
data mining exception as per Article 4(3) of the Digital Single Market Directive (EU)
2019/790.

British Library Cataloguing in Publication Information Available

Library of Congress Cataloging-in-Publication Data

Names: Bibring, Tovi, 1973- author. | Jacob ben Eleazar, 1170-1233? Sefer
   ha-meshalim. English.
Title: Pilosity, prejudice, and passion in The tale of Old Bearded Achbor
   by Yaakov ben Elazar of Toledo/Tovi Bibring.
Description: Lanham : Lexington Books, 2025. | Series: Studies in medieval
   literature | Includes bibliographical references and index.
Identifiers: LCCN 2024039695 (print) | LCCN 2024039696 (ebook) | ISBN
   9781666949315 (cloth) | ISBN 9781666949322 (epub)
Subjects: LCSH: Jacob ben Eleazar, 1170-1233? Sefer ha-meshalim. | LCGFT:
   Literary criticism.
Classification: LCC PJ5050.J32 S44335 2025 (print) | LCC PJ5050.J32
   (ebook) | DDC 892.43/2--dc23/eng/20240920
LC record available at https://lccn.loc.gov/2024039695
LC ebook record available at https://lccn.loc.gov/2024039696

For product safety related questions contact productsafety@bloomsbury.com.

♾™ The paper used in this publication meets the minimum requirements of American
National Standard for Information Sciences—Permanence of Paper for Printed Library
Materials, ANSI/NISO Z39.48-1992.

Contents

Acknowledgments		vii
Introduction: Blameworthy Beards, Dangerous Liaisons, and Praiseworthy(?) Maidens		1
1	*The Tale of Old Bearded Achbor*: Translation and Commentary	11
2	Beardly Beloved: Discoursing the Beard in Literature	111
3	A Prutah and a Prusa: Two Fables by Achbor	173
4	A Double Threat to Faith, or Is Achbor a New Balaam?	183
5	"A Remnant of the Flame": Achbor's Black Secret	193
6	Transforming Maidens: Four Women, Three Episodes	209
7	"She Was a Fawn, She Is a Gazelle Now": An Erotic Wine Song in Five Strophes	221
Bibliography		253
Index		265
About the Author		269

וְאִם בִּגְבוּרֹת שְׁמוֹנִים שָׁנָה
Dedicated to my beloved father on his eightieth birthday.

Acknowledgments

I owe a debt of gratitude to far more people than I can possibly acknowledge. A word here, a question there, discussions with students and colleagues—all have sparked ideas and insights that have found their way into these pages. Life itself, with its myriad twists and turns, has played its part as well. I must first offer a special thanks to all those who took part in this voyage and whose names are inadvertently absent—your spirit remains in the book's chapters.

I am especially grateful to Dr. John Levy for his many remarks regarding the numerous Old French translations and for his careful reading of the manuscript. I am deeply obliged to Dr. Ayelet Peer for her invaluable suggestions regarding the Latin translations, to Dr. Hilla Karas for providing me with a quiet office at the beginning of this process, and to Dr. Dafna Nissim for sharing thoughts about artistic imagery.

I extend more thanks than words can express to Prof. Revital Refael-Vivante for her endless patience with my countless questions and for her exceptional generosity in sharing information, listening, and offering encouragement.

I also wish to thank the Center for Ladino, particularly Prof. Shmuel Refael, for their generous funding. Ms. Carolyn Gross-Baruch, your diligent work on language editing has been indispensable. Barr. David Chijner, your unwavering support has been deeply appreciated.

Gramercy! Gramercy! Gramercy to my family for enduring the grand demands that writing a book entails, for tolerating the blurred boundaries between life and work, and for your steadfast support. Adi, Karni, Amir, and Tami, I love you all ad infinitum. And finally, in this epilogue of thank-you notes, the pinnacle of appreciation, my heartfelt praises go to my personal inspirational fairy, my Shani, for teaching me how imagination can transform into interpretation.

Introduction

Blameworthy Beards, Dangerous Liaisons, and Praiseworthy(?) Maidens

Sefer ha-Meshalim [The Book of Tales],[1] a marvelous collection of ten short stories in Hebrew about the art of poetry, philosophy, morality, and, last but not least, love was composed in thirteenth-century Toledo by a Spanish Jew, Yaakov ben Elazar. Of Yaakov, we have very little information.[2] We know that he was a grammarian who wrote a book in Arabic on Hebrew grammar (*Kitab al-kamil*, the Complete Book); a translator who translated sections of *Kalila and Dimna*, the well-known collection of Indian ascendance fables that circulated in Europe in the Middle Ages, from Arabic into Hebrew; a philosopher who composed two moralistic treatises that were never edited; and an author who bequeathed to us an inestimable treasure trove of Hebrew *mahbarot*, the Hebrew parallel of the Arabic *maqamat*.[3]

Christian Toledo was a fervent center of Jewish intellectual and poetic creation. Accomplished writers and poets, headed by Yehuda al-Harizi, excitingly cultivated the Hebrew arsenal of belletristic creation with fictional prose and imaginative poetries. They adorned the Hebrew language and titillated the imagination of the Jewish community with extraordinary adventures written in rhymed prose entwined with sequential poems. Amongst them, Yaakov's *Sefer ha-Meshalim* proposed the freshest and most daring of all the literary works of the Jewish (and perhaps even non-Jewish) writers of the Iberian Peninsula at that time.

The sole existing manuscript opens, conventionally, with a prologue where the historical author Yaakov ben Elazar, presents the circumstances leading to the composition of his book. Alongside the rhetorical elements comprising the prologue of *Sefer ha-Meshalim*, this section offers a narrow glimpse into Yaakov's perception of the world around him. The particular style and subject of the prologue thus separate it from the following tales, which are purely fictional. Here, Lemuel ben Ithiel assumes the role of narrator, guiding the

2   *Introduction*

audience through the ten tales with varying degrees of personal involvement and a number of narrative styles.[4] The allegorical mode, where concepts and virtues are personified; the rhetoric-realistic style, which is centered around a debate that is related to the art of writing, featuring realistic figures; and the mythical style, wherein legendary figures embark on extraordinary and marvelous adventures. Not only are these styles not mutually exclusive, but they are also intricately intertwined, resulting in a rich narratological tapestry.

The tales are dedicated to an array of subjects and narrative styles, personal retrospectives, intellectual debates, and above all, love stories. Traditionally, these tales were divided into two categories. The "rhetoric tales" (tales one, two, three, four, and ten) deal mostly with introspective meditations about philosophical or social matters, including hierarchical dynamics between Reason and Love,[5] conflicts such as those between poetry and prose,[6] between two poets,[7] and between the pen and the sword,[8] and a sober reflection about the predictability of human nature.[9] Tales five through nine are "romance-like tales" and are narratives of extraordinary adventures, often including affairs of the heart.[10]

With a fervent pen, polished humor, and sharp satire, Yaakov invented unique characters and placed them in outstanding situations. While many of his features were inspired by overused stereotypes and nourished by well-known literary traditions, they always appeared invigorating, surprising, and unexpected. He thus vivified legendary territories,[11] such as the Land of the Lions, where a man-lion hunts a lad-fawn, falls in love with him, and almost loses him to a monstrous bearded bald man.[12] The newly anointed king of the exotic Kingdom of Beauty falls in love with a captive from the equally exotic Land of the Arabians, only to find himself battling a giant black horseman.[13] Two maidens from a fantasized market of maidens in Egypt don men's clothing as they vie for the affection of a "tourist" from the Holy Land.[14] An Aleppine princess resides with a shipwreck survivor in an aquatic palace made of glass.[15] Lastly, an exceptionally bearded fraudulent preacher meets his demise at the hands of four fair-skinned maidens because of his love for a black woman. This is Achbor of Mount Tabor, to whom this study is devoted.

The tale begins with the narrator, Lemuel ben Ithiel, reporting that during his travels as a young man, fate brought him to a city where he witnessed an extraordinary scene. At first, he liked the city and wanted to stay there, but soon he found that its inhabitants were corrupt and decided to leave. On the day of his departure, he heard a commotion. Intrigued, he followed the crowd to the public plaza. There he saw a bearded old and lame man, known as Achbor, leaning on one servant and accompanied by another. Lemuel listened to Achbor's sermon, given before a huge audience. With unique eloquence and prodigious rhetoric, in a sermon including two moralizing fables and interlaced with poems, Achbor exhorted and implored his listeners

Introduction 3

to live according to the rules of morality, and especially to perform acts of charity. At the end of the sermon, his servants collected alms, taking not only money but also gold and jewels. As the crowd dispersed, Lemuel became suspicious and decided to investigate the old man's true nature. As Lemuel followed the preacher from a distance, Achbor arrived at a sumptuous palace, and Lemuel's suspicions were confirmed: Achbor led a double life. He was neither lame nor poor, but rather a rich man, who hosted lascivious banquets abundant with wine and delicacies. Four beautiful women served him at the luxurious feast Lemuel witnessed, reciting poems, playing, and dancing with him. Finally, Achbor feigned sleep and the four maidens left. Then, to Lemuel's surprise, a black woman entered the room. While earlier Lemuel assiduously depicted the components of Achbor's excessive life, such as his wealth, his palace, and the feast, it seems he was left almost speechless when the black woman entered. He leaped from his hiding place, hurling insults at the lovers, striking them, and tearing their clothes, leaving them naked. The two men then entered a debate about black and white women. Unable to convince Achbor with his arguments, Lemuel cried out bitterly, and upon hearing his sounds of despair, the four maidens returned to the room. Outraged at discovering Achbor with the black woman, they attacked him verbally, insulted him, and mocked his beard in unprecedented epideictic discourses in the rhetorical model of a parodical encomium, where condemnation replaces the *laudatio* and instead of exaltations "In Praise of the Beard," we read of castigations "In Blame of the Beard." Once they had finished expressing their outrage verbally, the four maidens moved to action. They tore off Achbor's beard, beat him to death, and threw his corpse into a pit. The readers are then told that sometime later, the four maidens entertain themselves in an exquisite orchard, where they are watched by four suitors. The final words of the tale imply that the maidens and their suitors are likely to be wed.

The didactic pattern of the tale is ubiquitous. As we pass from the outside (the public episode) to the inside (the intimate episode at Achbor's home), moralizing pairs guide us through this extraordinary adventure.[16] The poor man is really rich; the lame is actually healthy, although he suffers from a moral sickness, identified metaphorically as a sexual disorder; the two religious mantras preached by Achbor (charity and chastity) become the two sins he commits (greed and debauchery); the two opposite edifying fables that he shared in his sermon at the city plaza correspond to Achbor's two sins.

His vileness is externalized through two signs, the black mistress and the white beard. Yet, here white and black are not opposites, as they usually were in the Pythagorean tradition that enriched medieval didactic and belletrist literature.[17] Rather, in this tale, black and white are complementary. The beard is a physical sign of inner immorality, just like the hideously portrayed black mistress. The expected dichotomy of black and white is ironically replaced by

4 *Introduction*

similarity, a sameness. In other words, on a symbolic level, part of Achbor's hypocrisy is his own physical appearance, as his white beard only covers his "blackness," marking it as the first sign of his inconsistency and duplicity. The beard becomes animated and, to some extent, even personified as a protagonist of sorts. The Hebrew language, which does not differentiate between the feminine (she) and the neutral (it) pronouns,[18] plays on the possible fusion of Achbor and his beard numerous times in the tale.

Schirmann commented briefly on this tale in 1979 and was unable to find Arabic or Christian antecedents in the main plot, other than conventional overtones from the Arabic *maqama,* such as descriptions of Achbor's palace, banquet, and themes from Arabic wine poetry. Therefore, Schirmann assumed that the tale and its main character—Achbor—could have been a pure invention of the writer.[19] While he was not antagonistic to the idea that Christian literature could have also exercised some influence, he did not specifically identify such a source. Jonathan Decter determined that the scene witnessed by Lemuel upon arriving at the ornate palace was a specifically oriental motif, similar to the "scene of debauchery of 1001 nights."[20] Decter also considered the tale's main motif as the Arabic "hypocritical preacher of the maqama."[21] Nevertheless, despite the fact that the image of the hypocritical preacher frequently appeared in the Arabic and Hebrew maqama as representing the anti-clerical satire, it also suggested many variants of the sexual, greedy, and corrupt Christian churchman, and especially the "beggar priest."[22] Achbor, a fraudulent beggar, can exemplify the Arabic hypocrite noted by Decter, but he is also reminiscent of miscreants found in Christian writings. At present, it is an established fact in literary studies that many themes and motif parallels can be found in Christian and Arab texts.[23] What surely differs from the Arabic and the Hebrew maqama tradition is the extensive use of a scatological language. Once his masquerade is revealed, the white beard is verbally blackened, as it is described as covered in manure and excrement.

This book is structured in two parts: chapter 1 is an annotated translation, along with a rich array of commentaries addressing issues of translation and edition, the use of biblical phrases, and references to Jewish sources. Additionally, it evokes themes and suggests analogs from the surrounding literature, thus permitting a broader view of the tastes and interests of medieval readers. The book's second part is composed of six chapters, proposing a series of case studies that cover various matters, including a caricatural hypocrite covered by a prodigious beard, a group of four dichotomic women who are both courtly maidens and murderesses, racist and scatological discourses, and an amalgamation of the carnivalesque and the moralistic.

La raison d'être of chapter 2, "Beardly Beloved: Discoursing the Beard in Literature," is the tale's central leitmotif, the conceptual beard, appearing as a signifier of both merit and worthlessness, starting with the dichotomy

Introduction   5

presented by the magnificence of Achbor's beard. While it inspires reverence for an authoritative figure, worshipped and feared as if it were a holy relic, we cannot overlook the comical, somewhat degrading description of its wildness and dirt. The duality of beards, being the recognizable sign of the "revered community elder," a prophet, a rabbi, a sage, a philosopher, and even a military leader on the one hand, but also an efficient marker for hypocrisy on the other hand, is a long-established cultural dichotomy. The chapter demonstrates the fluctuation of this symbol of masculinity—the beard—from positive to negative. Using Achbor's case as a focal point, I introduce various accounts of virtuous and malevolent beards, concentrating on satires and parodies about hypocrites and impostors ranging from Greek and Roman literature to medieval Latin and vernacular narratives, organized according to seven landmarks. Beyond his beard, Achbor demonstrates considerable talent as an orator. His sermon is extremely passionate, involving meticulous techniques of performance, rhetoric, pathos, and storytelling—all the ingredients needed to manipulate the listeners into giving him money as alms. The pinnacle of this sermon is when Achbor recounts two moralizing exempla, whose analysis is the focus of chapter 3, "A Prutah and a Prusa: Two Fables by Achbor."

"The Fable of the Poor Man" tells the story of a pauper who begged a landlord for some food. After receiving a *prutah* (one coin), he asked the landlord to add some wheat, but the latter refused, claiming that he too is poor and using the name of the Lord in vain. For these three offenses, not giving bread, lying, and speaking sacrilegiously, the landlord was then stricken with three punishments: "blindness, madness, and destruction." In "The Fable of the Two Men Who Lived in the Same District," a rich and drunk man initially refuses to give alms to a poor man, but when the latter threatens him with divine anger, he gives him a banknote. As he was quite tipsy, instead of writing "four shekels" on the bill, he wrote the number "four hundred." Thus, he mistakenly gave all his fortune to the poor man. Such fables illustrate the perils of immoral behavior, especially as almsgiving to the poor is one of the pillars of religious and social solidarity. These fables also warn of two additional severe infractions, blasphemy and drunkenness. The tale's second part reveals that Achbor is the incarnation of the corrupt men described in his fables: a liar and a drunk, abusive of his congregation, exhorting his listeners while using God's name in vain. It is this behavior that will ultimately bring him to ruin.

Many of the numerous biblical phrasings in *The Tale of Old Bearded Achbor* echo incidents where the Hebrews were either in the process of embracing or already practicing pagan ways, inviting the audience to consider that the tale's subtext might be alluding to a similar concern. Does Achbor also incarnate an essential threat to the established order, the threat of enticing the community to forsake its traditions? Chapter 4, "A Double Threat to Faith,

6 *Introduction*

or Is Achbor a New Balaam?.," examines the discourse around hypocritical preachers. I propose the possibility that Achbor himself harbors within him such a peril. I venture to draw a symbolic parallel between Achbor and Balaam, as Balaam stands as an iconic figure who once posed a grave threat to the biblical Hebrews by tempting them with paganism. I also mention Jesus, who defied the Jewish faith and is referred to in the Talmud as the "new Balaam."

The question of cultural assimilation returns in chapter 5, "'A Remnant of the Flame': Achbor's Black Secret," in which I discuss another angle: Achbor's secret black woman, who may also embody the idea of assimilation.

This woman represents the main controversy of the tale, that is, Achbor's lust for a black woman. The tale is nourished by the prejudicial concept that a black person incarnates the threat of religious / moral deviancy, as reflected in various manifestations within medieval didactic and moralistic narratives. Accordingly, she is depicted pejoratively, using debasing stereotyped images. Her adverse portrayal, combined with the fact that she takes no action nor does she ever speak, makes her the externalization of Achbor's immorality. She represents Achbor's sins and depravity. She is a personification, a reflection of the protagonist's sins, rather than an independent character. Like him, then, she also participates in the meditation about assimilation. At first, she is the subject of a distorted theoretical debate about love between Achbor and Lemuel, as Achbor advocates the love of black women, while Lemuel denounces it. On the allegorical level, these two "types" of women signify opposing cultures or religions. Later, in the four maidens' defamatory discourses on Achbor and his beard, she is referred to as a satanic power that has cast its spell on Achbor. This chapter expands on this perspective and examines the broader perception of the Other in medieval culture.

To date, studies of *Achbor* have mostly concentrated on the two salient issues that stand out in a first reading of the text, Achbor's beard and his desire for a black woman. Much less attention has been paid to the four women that accompany the tale in each of its episodes. They were surely noticed by scholars but were viewed mostly as secondary figures. Chapter 6, "Transforming Maidens: Four Women, Three Episodes," purports to see them as a sophisticated poetic tool. I argue that the author used them to present his point of view, each time from a different angle. This is a sophisticated approach on his part since superficially they could be perceived as "active" figures who participate in the plot and are invested in it. A more exhaustive reading reveals that they do not really act subjectively. They remain the same women, but the ideology they convey changes throughout the tale. In their first appearance, they embody Achbor's excessive wealth, which is the first sign of his corruption. They are part of the general overwhelming profusion that reigns in his palace. There is an affluence of everything: food, drinks,

Introduction 7

rooms, silver, and beautiful women, who act as something between servants and entertainers. They are submissive to Achbor's demands; hence they recite erotic poetry and dance with him, but all these actions are mechanical and do not include a single personal subjective statement. When they return to the scene in their second episode, they are much more engaged. Their voice has clearly changed, as now they are no longer Achbor's puppets, but rather his executioners. A circumstantial explanation could clarify this change: Since they had just learned about the black woman, they could be jealous of her. Yet this reading remains superficial, as these four maidens' personalities have radically changed, and the accusations they hurl at Achbor transcend a simple lovers' quarrel. Their brutal discourses reflect and magnify Lemuel's ideology, which he unsuccessfully attempted to convince Achbor to embrace. For their third and last appearance in the tale, they are garbed in yet a new ideological look. The same submissive women who shared (or served) one man, the same brutal murderers who threw their victim's body into a pit, have now become gentle courtly maidens in quest of true monogamic love. With a fairytale-like backdrop, they teach some young lads that premarital sex is not acceptable among noble youth and nor is polyamory, if anachronistic terminology may be applied here. Illustrating the protagonist's debauchery; illustrating the social rejection of such a culprit; illustrating the endeared traditional values regarding relationships—the four maidens continuously follow and reflect the author's perception of the world from within the text.

Chapter 7, "'She Was a Fawn, She Is a Gazelle Now': An Erotic Wine Song in Five Strophes," prides itself on being a close reading of a sensual wine song. Achbor's feast culminates with the four maidens performing a composition, each contributing her own strophe, about wine and love. Drawing upon the immense variety of poetic images and themes found in Arabic poetry, the maidens interweave erotic elements in a somewhat reserved metaphorical language. These four strophes gradually expose the effects of wine as paralleling the evolution of love, blurring the act of love with the act of drinking wine throughout the poem. Drunk on either wine or love, every worry or pain caused by love dissipates.

The maidens' creation arouses desire in Achbor, who adds a fifth strophe. The strophe embodies cups of wine as women and highlights the dichotomy between red cups filled with wine and transparent "white" cups that are empty. The empty cups personify virginal maidens, who after the act of drinking / loving, after wine / bodily liquids are poured, lose their innocence (and whiteness). While this could be construed as referring to Achbor's attraction to his maidens, within the context of the tale, the blatant analogy is clear: Achbor alludes to his favorite cup, the one that is already filled with wine, and therefore not white.

8   *Introduction*

While a quick reading of the interspersed wine poem may give the impression that it is somewhat conventional due to its constant borrowings from the prevailing metaphors descending from Arabic and Hebrew poetry, the thorough decipherment presented in this chapter reveals it to be a sophisticated piece.

The Tale of Old Bearded Achbor is derisive, harboring a variety of carnivalesque motifs such as the subversion of fundamental concepts, epicurean banquets, scatological language, and absurd, vulgar, deformed images of the body, governed primarily by the beard.[24] Overall, the atmosphere is of a barbed and bitter satire, somewhat farcical at times. In its subtext, I believe that *The Tale of Old Bearded Achbor* explores a deeply entrenched, ancient, and universal fear related to culture and religion, specifically the fear of forsaking a cultural community and adhering to another one. Achbor, and the emotions he stirs, incarnate concerns of this kind.

NOTES

1. About this title, see Tovi Bibring, *The Patient, the Impostor and the Seducer: Medieval European Literature in Hebrew* (Oxford: Legenda, 2025).

2. For a summary of Yaakov ben Elazar's biography, see Jefim Schirmann, *The History of Hebrew Poetry in Christian Spain and Southern France,* edited and supplemented by E. Fleischer (Jerusalem: Magnes, 1997), 222–24.

3. On the *maqama* in general, see Charles Pellat, "Makama," in *The Encyclopedia of Islam, Volume 6,* edited by Edmund Bosworth et al. (Leiden: E. J. Brill, 1991), 107–15; H. Nemah, "Andalusian Maqamat," *Journal of Arabic Literature* 5 (1974): 83–92; J. N. Mattock, "The Early History of the Maqama," *Journal of Arabic Literature* 15 (1984): 1–18; Fedwa Malti-Douglas, "Maqāmāt and Adab: 'Al-Maqāma al-Maḍīriyya of al-Hamadhānī,'" *Journal of the American Oriental Society* 105 (1985): 247–58; Jaakko Hämeen-Anttila, *Maqama—A History of a Genre* (Wiesbaden: Harrassowitz Verlag, 2002); Rina Drory, "The Maqama," in *The Literature of Al-Andalus,* edited by María Rosa Menocal, Raymond Scheindlin, and Michael Sells (Cambridge: Cambridge University Press, 2000), 190–210. On the Hebrew maqama, see Dan Pagis, *Change and Tradition in the Secular Poetry, Spain and Italy Jerusalem* (Jerusalem: Keter, 1976), here 199–244 [in Hebrew]. Dan Pagis, "Alternating Faces: On the Rhymed Hebrew Story in the Middle-Ages," in *Poetry Aptly Explained: Studies and Essays on Medieval Hebrew Poetry,* edited by E. Fleischer (Jerusalem: The Magnes Press, 1993), 62–80 [in Hebrew].

4. Fleicher considers that only in two tales, the third and the tenth, the narrator, Lemuel, is "the real hero of the story" and that in the tales whose subject is love he "does not even have the role of the voyeur; in these [stories] he is only an insignificant narrator. His role ends with the opening sentence . . ." Schirmann, *The History of Hebrew Poetry in Christian Spain and Southern France,* 226, note 18.

Introduction 9

5. Tale One, "Body and Soul," is studied in Tova Rosen, "Eros and Intellect in the First Maqama by Jacob Ibn Eleazar," in *Studies* in *Hebrew Literature of the Middle Ages and Renaissance in Honor of Professor Yona David*, edited by Tova Rosen and Avner Holtzman (Tel-Aviv: Tel-Aviv University Press, 2002), 191–212.

6. Tale Two.

7. Tale Three studied in Bibring, *The Patient.*

8. Tale Four.

9. Tale Ten.

10. There is, however, an interplay between the rhetorical and Romanesque elements within the tales.

11. On the landscapes in *Sefer ha-Meshalim*, see Jonathan Decter, *Iberian Jewish Literature: Between al-Andalus and Christian Europe* (Bloomington: Indiana University Press, 2007).

12. Tale Five, "Sapir, Shafir, and Birsha," studied in Decter, *A Sodomite Tale*, a forthcoming translation and study of this tale is due to begin in 2025.

13. Tale Six, "Maskil, Penina, and Cushan," is studied and translated in Tova Rosen, "Love and Race in a Thirteenth-Century Romance in Hebrew with a Translation of the Story of Maskil and Peninah by Jacob Ben El'azar," *Florilegium* 23, no. 1 (2006): 155–72. and Bibring, *The Patient.*

14. Tale Seven, "Yoshpe, Yefefiya and Yemima." A forthcoming translation and study of this tale is due in 2025.

15. While this tale has not yet been translated into English, it was studied in David A. Wacks, *Double Diaspora in Sephardic Literature: Jewish Cultural Production Before and After 1492* (Bloomington: Indiana University Press, 2015) and Tovi Bibring, "Fairies, Lovers, and Glass Palaces: French Influences on Thirteenth-Century Hebrew Poetry in Spain—the Case of Ya'akob ben El'azar's Ninth Mahberet," *The Jewish Quarterly Review* 107, no. 3 (2017): 296–321; "A Medieval Hebrew French-Kiss: Analyzing the Love Story of Sahar and Kima by Yaakov ben Elazar Through Courtly Love Ideals," *The Jewish Quarterly Review* 109, no. 1 (2019): 24–37.

16. Jonathan Decter also saw dualities in this tale, which he divided into two parts, containing mirroring episodes. See Decter, *Iberian Jewish Literature.*

17. On such dichotomies, see, for example, Tovi Bibring, "Juif ou français? Berechiah ha-naqdan au carrefour culturel: Nouvelles considérations sur *Souris et Grenouille*," in *Berechiah ben Natronai ha-Naqdan's Works and Their Reception*, edited by Tamas Visi, Tovi Bibring, and Daniel Soukoup (Brepols: Turnhout, 2019), 29–50.

18. Yaakov ben Elazar bases himself here on the vernacular languages (and not on Hebrew), and the beard is referred to with female pronouns. See Tova Rosen's discussion of the "She-Beard" in this tale: "The Beard as Spectacle and Scandal in a Thirteenth-century Hebrew *Maqāma*," *Intellectual History of the Islamic World* 9, no. 1 (2021): 1–24, here 16–17.

19. Jefim Y. Schirmann, "A Tale of an Old Hypocrite," in *The History of Hebrew Poetry and Drama: Studies and Essays* (Jerusalem: Mosad Bialik, 1979), 375–88 [in Hebrew].

10 *Introduction*

20. Decter, *Iberian Jewish Literature.*

21. Decter, *Iberian Jewish Literature.*

22. On the hypocrite in the Hebrew maqama, see Revital Refael-Vivante, "Religious Hypocrisy in Medieval Hebrew Rhymed Prose," *Hispania Judaica* 6 (2009): 5–51. On the Christian tradition of the motif, see, among others, Daron Burrows, *The Stereotype of the Priest in the Old French Fabliaux: Anticlerical Satire and Lay Identity* (Lausanne: Peter Lang, 2005).

23. All the tales in the book are deeply enrooted in the literary traditions of Arabic poetry and reflect the world of Spanish Jewry. Yet, alongside the intrinsic elements of such Andalusian cultural heritage, the flourishing secular Christian literature of the time is constantly echoed, re-codified, adapted, and interpreted in the tales. Dan Pagis, Haim Schirmann (with Ezra Fleischer's additions), and Raymond Scheindlin established the foundations for thematic examinations of this work, exploring possible influences from Christian literature, though never identifying a specific source. Schirmann, *The History of Hebrew Poetry*; Pagis, "Alternating Faces"; Scheindlin Reuven [Raymond], "Love Stories by Ya'akov ben Elazar: Between Arabic and Romance Literature," in *Proceedings of the World Congress for Jewish Studies, Division III* (Jerusalem, 1994), 16–20 [in Hebrew]. The acknowledgment that the two streams of influence, Arabic-Andalusian and Vernacular-Latin, are simultaneously put in motion in Yaakov's book is continued in the works of Tova Rosen. On French influence on the first tale, see Rosen, "Eros and Intellect." On "the shift to the allegorical mode" in the sixth tale, see Rosen, "Love and Race." Further below, I will refer to Rosen's recent publications on the eighth tale. Jonathan Decter continued this orientation and expounded on three aspects of the influence of Romance literature: the love model, the development, and the allegory. Decter, *Iberian Jewish Literature,* especially 113–24. David A. Wacks defined Yaakov ben Elazar as "a diasporic writer," adapting literary conventions (Arabic and Christian) for his own purpose in order to discuss issues relevant to his community. Wacks, *Double Diaspora.* On how the ninth tale shares affinities with French and Latin vernacular literature, see Bibring, "Fairies"; "A Medieval Hebrew French-Kiss."

24. The most prominent study of medieval carnivalesque notions remains that of Mikhail Bakhtin, *Rabelais and His World*, trans. Helen Iswolsky (Bloomington: Indiana University Press, 1984). In her recent study about Achbor, Tova Rosen offered a strongly oriented Bakhtinian analysis of the tale. Rosen, "The Beard as Spectacle."

Chapter 1

The Tale of Old Bearded Achbor
Translation and Commentary

The translation of *The Tale of Old Bearded Achbor* purports to be as accurate, fluent, and modernized as possible. I aimed to stay as close to the text as I could, but at times a literal translation yielded its place to a more interpretative one, which I felt gave better meaning and ease of expression to the new text that was born in English. Endeavoring to provide as precise a translation as I could, I preferred a non-homogeneous translation approach, which is dynamic and acknowledges that each scriptural reference should be dealt with according to its particular function. In most cases, therefore, I reduced the citation of the biblical verses to a bare minimum, preferring to translate the obvious biblical quotes in my own words rather than using established biblical translations. This translation strategy blurs the intentional margins of both obvious linguistic levels, Yaakov ben Elazar's narrative and the quoted narrative that is intertwined within it. It is, however, logical to assume that medieval Hebrew had more common denominators with biblical and Talmudic Hebrew than modern Hebrew, and that medieval audiences were more proficient in biblical texts than their modern counterparts. In other words, the transition between the two linguistic levels was much more fluid and natural in the Middle Ages than it is today.

The Tale of Old Bearded Achbor was composed in rhymed prose, into which several poems were integrated. Regarding the art of rhyming, the difference between the two poetic styles found in the tale lies in the prose sections. In these sections, every pair of sequences (and sometimes three sequences) rhymes, with the rhyming words usually changing from pair to pair. For example:

ואומר: כי ראיתי מטי משפט לוקחי שוחד עתה אספה יום אחד כי דרכם משוכת חדק וחתחתים. אין לי
טוב כי אם הימלט אל ארץ פלישתים

12   Chapter 1

Some sections contain two or more rhyming pairs, thus intensifying and
dramatizing the episode. For example:

עַל כֵּן תַּשְׁפִּילִי גְאוֹנֵךְ / וְהַרְחִיקִי זְדוֹנֵךְ / וְאַל תַּתְנִי עַל בִּצְעֵךְ עֲווֹנֵךְ / וְאַל תִּבְטְחִי בַּהוֹנֵךְ / כִּי הוֹנֵךְ
מוֹנֵךְ / וּבְצְעֵךְ בּוֹצְעֵךְ / הֲלֹא בְּיוֹם פְּקֻדַּת עֲווֹנֵךְ / הַרְבֵּה יִרְבֶּה עִצְבוֹנֵךְ.

Regardless of their length, the apodosis of all the poems rhyme among
themselves, but not with the protasis. For example:

וְלִבִּי זָע וְגַם חָרַד	וְרָאִיתִי זְקַן עַכְבּוֹר
וְהִנֵּה הוּא בְּצוּר מֶרֶד	חֲשַׁבְתִּיהוּ לְאִישׁ תַּמִּים
כְּשֶׁלֶג שָׁב וְכָבֵד	וְאִם הַזָּקֵן זְקַנוֹ עָשׁ,
הֲלֹא אַךְ אֶל שְׁאוֹל תּוּרַד.	וְאִם הוּשְׁקָה בְּמֵי חַטָּאת,

I chose to entirely abandon any attempt to reconstruct the rhymes in
English in the sections of rhymed prose[1] and challenged myself to use rhymes
or phonetically close words in some of the poems, albeit inconsistently. I
did not follow the form of apodosis rhyming but rather rhymed between the
protasis and the apodosis. I did not wish to imitate the text's rhyming, nor can
I compete with Yaakov ben Elazar's unique talent. Rather, I undertook this
challenge hoping to transmit some of the different types of ambiance that the
prose and rhyme intended to create.

As a rule, I followed the two existing editions, written by Jefim Schirmann
and Yonah David.[2] I also constantly consulted the sole extant manuscript
containing the text,[3] occasionally modifying the text established in these
two excellent editions according to my own reading of the manuscript.
These modifications are explained and elaborated upon in the commentaries.
To facilitate the reading of this text, I divided the tale into six sequences
according to the tale's subjects: "Prologue," "Achbor's Preaching in the City
Plaza," "Feasting with the Four Maidens," "The Black Mistress," "In the
Blame of the Beard," and "A Fairy Tale Ending," referred to accordingly in
the commentary.

The commentary pages that follow the translation attempt to illuminate *The
Tale of Old Bearded Achbor* and thoroughly discuss select translation decisions,
along with the exquisite compounded and recursive puns and double entendres
found in the text. This is not based merely on the particular features of Hebrew,
but also on the gap between biblical and medieval Hebrew. I also strove to
accompany my close reading of the tale with a comparative approach,
suggesting possible Christian and Arabic sources of inspiration that circulated
in Europe at the time. Yet, much of my work is focused here on the Source of
Sources, the omnipresent biblical phrasings that repeatedly embellish the text,
granting it endless interpretative possibilities.[4] Hundreds of biblical phrasings,

known as *shibutzim* (שיבוצים), a term borrowed from the fine craft of the goldsmith setting gemstones in a piece of jewelry, are interpreted in the commentary section. Translating medieval Hebrew texts into a modern language presents significant challenges, particularly due to the complexity of translating biblical or Talmudic phrasings. An even greater challenge lies in deciding the extent to which these references can be relied upon to impart meaning to the fictional text. This task is complicated further when the translation strategy is not homogeneous but dynamic, requiring each scriptural reference to be treated according to its particular function and the limitations of the target language. This is only part of the complexity. It is difficult to delineate between enhancing interpretation and over-interpreting the biblical source in relation to the tale. The temptation to understand the literary text through its affinity with the biblical source is immense, yet this can lead to unnecessary deviations. My hope is that I have not gotten carried away with my interpretations of the biblical phrasings in the commentaries and the following chapters.

The entries in the commentary are of different lengths and nature: At times they are merely informative, while at other times they are much more interpretative. Some are technical, while others are meditative. Still, others merely explain a term, or note a required departure from a literal translation, while in other instances I delve into the network of biblical connotations and associations, when such remained unexplained in the book's subsequent chapters.

The English quote above each entry is taken from the translation. The Hebrew quote is taken, unless otherwise mentioned, from David's edition, though without the diacritics (*nikud*), as I adapted David's punctuated text into modern orthography instead using plene spelling (*ktiv male*). For the sake of clarity, I use the term "verse" to refer to the verses of the biblical phrasings, and the terms "lines," "sequences," or "stanzas" to refer to the verses of the tale. For comparisons with the biblical texts, I mostly quote the JPS 1917, as opposed to the translation itself, which is my own, and not based on formal sources.[5]

PROLOGUE

These are the words of Lemuel ben Ithiel: From my youth, I used to wander the earth and roam upon it,[1] from people to people and from one kingdom to another nation. At times I have slept in the desert and in the forests,[2] other times in the mansions of aristocrats,[3] as is the custom of wanderers and travelers. Sometimes outside [the city walls], at other times on the streets. There were nights when I slept on sumptuous ivory beds [hosted by the rich] who sleep well in their beds, who loll on their couches.

Chapter 1

Other nights, [I slept with the poor who have] no nightcaps on their heads,[4] who sleep naked without clothes. And I had days when I wandered exhausted, on my last legs,[5] having no bread and no water. Such and such is the fate of wayfarers.

Sometimes pampered, sometimes disgraced, sometimes like villains, sometimes like kings.

And I declaimed my poem, and so I said:[6]

The state of a man stands not still	it changes and it always will[7]
There is a time[8] when he rises up and a time he lies down[9]	a time that he journeys and a time that he lingers around
A time he shall grow strong and a time he shall weaken	a time he is wealthy and a time poverty-stricken.[10]
A time he laughs and a time he aches	a time he builds and a time he wrecks.
A time he rejoices and a time he trembles	a time he does justice, a time he embezzles.
At dawn he worships his Creator,	at dusk he turns into an idolator.[11]
It may be that he relies on his fortune	but the master shall be betrayed by Fortune![12]
It may be that he leans on worldly glory indeed	yet his staff is of broken reed.[13]
And it may be that he toils to attain richness	yet he only achieves heart sickness.
Would the episodes of a human being's entire life be enumerated	would they be calculated?
And through his different ages	ten times change his wages![14]
You seek for him after all this,	and lo, there is no voice, no one answers!!

Likewise, I have seen marvels, extraordinary and awesome. I have met [rich] men and poor, villains and noblemen.[15] [Once I had arrived in a city][16] whose inhabitants were rich, its merchants—princes—they do not spare their gold, and they squander their silver.

This city pleased me, and all my sorrows dissipated.[17] Once I saw it, I decided: "I shall settle here, this is my desire."[18]

And I declaimed my poem, and so I said:

Therefore, choose to abide in a place on earth,	whose inhabitants are of noble birth.
Rich and content with their treasure,	men of reason and good measure[19]
They will always greet you with approbation,	with benevolence and no exasperation!
Should one of them become unfortunate,	they reach out to him, their hearts compassionate.[20]
With these people you shall abide intact,	and among them, your soul shall delight.

The Tale of Old Bearded Achbor   15

I woke up early in the morning, [and went] to observe its people, its inhabitants, its streets and its fields. Lo and behold! They were all men of deceit and children of guilt! When I saw their wickedness, I said: "I shall go to their elders and I will speak with them, for they are those who teach laws and morals," but these ones had already broken their yokes and had torn off their reins.[21]

I saw that their judges were false judges, nocturnal wolves, who leave no bones for the morning.[22] All the swindlers gather around them, and all those who speak lies. A man deceives and sins against his brother! The righteous fall before the treacherous who become fattened like a laboring heifer[23] while they persecute those who publicly rebuke them.[24] All you could find were perverse and sinful men. The city was filled with iniquity.

And I declaimed my poem, and so I said:

So many trails have I ambled![25]
I explored the earth's edges[26]
I wandered deep into the woods,
Sometimes with a trembling soul
Sometimes my companions were rapscallions,
Sometimes my lodging was in a pile of waste,
Sometimes I groped [my way] without candlelight,
To seek and explore places[27]
People of truth, lovers of virtue,
Hither [I] follow my wishes
I met people whom I thought sinless
Hither you desire to go, my heart,[28]
Thither, if any misfortune bites me,
I then investigated—lo and behold,

Because it was filled with men of perjury,
All over it grow thistles
Worshipers of the queen of the heights[31]
Their food is the venom [of vipers],[32]
Their hands are tainted by exploitation and theft
Their share of the land shall be cursed
They shall be quickly eradicated

The spears bent in their hands
Yet men of faith and justice,
Then, they will rejoice merrily,
I shall leave, seek a better neighbor[33]

I strolled, I walked along the ways.
until I reached the end of the tracks.
encircled long roads!
and perplexed thoughts.
sometimes princes were my companions.
other times in homes of good taste.

I was lost, drifting in the dark of night.

where men rely on their senses.
bereft of vanity and sin.
thither my longing takes me!
and brimming with innocence.
to the city of virtuous kings.[29]
here the bitten shall live![30]
here it was the opposite of what I thought.
with scoundrels and men of intrigue.
like tangled thorns.
pouring libations unto her.
their wine is the oblation of violence!
and by bloodshed.

in a moment they shall be crushed.
and the candles lighting them, shall be suffocated.
shall be stuck in their hearts.
they shall be blessed by their Creator
those who now weep and cry bitterly
amongst a people whose youth are well educated.[34]

16   *Chapter 1*

A people who will judge the poor and the orphan [equitably],	[one law] for the destitute, the rich, the unfortunate.
They shall not favor the poor in feuds,	they shall not prefer the poor and the miserable.[35]
They anticipate the will of their Creator	and they hope and wish for His grace.[36]
They dwell under the protection of the Almighty,[37]	shielded by the wing of mercy.
They are not concerned by the day of Wrath[38]	because they are protected from wrath and anger.

And I said [to myself]: "for I have seen those who wrest justice, who take bribes. Surely I shall perish here one day, for their way is thorny and dangerous.[39] It would be better for me to flee to the land of the Philistines."

ACHBOR'S PREACHING IN THE CITY PLAZA

Before I even finished speaking in my heart,[40] I heard a tumultuous noise, a noise of war. I wondered: why is the city all agitated? And lo, an old man enters the city's street, heading toward the city's central plaza.[41] Every single man, young and old, was screaming.[42] And this one walks slowly, at his own pace, leaning on his stick, it seems that his legs are not moving,[43] looking like an innocent man, chaste, without fault. And I said: finally, justice will germinate, evil will be eradicated, the city will be ready for salvation![44]

His name was Achbor of Mount Tabor.[45] He had a beard,[46] branches were spreading out from it, and they were divided here and there, as [the beard] scattered its stems and its stalks and its limbs and its wings.[47] A calf grazed there, it was sprawled there, destroying all its fronds.[48] Its sight amazed and frightened all who looked at it. The entire congregation came there and gathered to see it. People approached it but withdrew, [wanted to] touch it, but feared. Under its heaviness, he walked stooped, as if he could no longer hold on. He walked among this multitude of people, bent under his burden,[49] for the crowd surrounded him like the countless sands of the sea. Until he reached the street where the crowd gathered, and all those who came there stood still.

I was watching, and lo and behold, [the congregation] staged a setting for him, they had prepared a chair in the street[50] upon which he could climb on the day of his preaching. He approached it, standing as [if he were] an angel[51] [of God], leaning on his servant. And I said [to myself] now [the Lord] shall be doing you good, sending you this [divine] messenger.[51] He arranged his garment on his shoulders, whistled, and shook his head. I was terrified, I was astonished, I was amazed by the vision.

The Tale of Old Bearded Achbor

And I declaimed my poem, and so I said:

If his beard is the beard of truth,[52]	he shall awaken them from their sinful sleep.
If their crimes are numerous like sand,	surely with his righteousness he will atone for them.
Should they rebel or be corrupt,	he shall chasten them like his own sons.
If they become lost or err,	he will guide them like a shepherd.[53]
Should they transgress or be corrupt,	he will announce their absolution.
Defiled by sins,	he will sweep the sins into the middle of the sea.
For He will conceal them in His tent	He will hide them in His shelter.[54]

And the crowd around him, some were talking, others were silent. Some whistled and others whispered. Achbor ordered his servant boy and his clerk, upon whom he was leaning,[55] and [one of them] said reproachfully: "if you are here gathered to whistle and whisper, turn and be gone!" When they realized that he had become very angry, they stood still and spoke no more. Then Achbor began to speak with words of faith and admonishing statements. He raised his voice, lifted his right hand and his left, and then said mellifluously, with tearful eyes: "Blessed is the man who has purified his heart, is worried about his sins and saddened by his crimes.[56] He shall abide in the shelter of the Most High, and shall wait for His mercy, there he shall pitch his tent!" [57]

And he declaimed his poem and so he said:

My heart implores the Creator,	always it cries out to its King.
His name is luscious on a man's tongue,	His memory is honey-sweet on his palate.
I shall jeer at drought and flood,	for He shall conceal me in His Pavilion.
Hope for His salvation and wait,	blessed is the man who awaits Him.

I will clarify my words, beginning with an extolment, a praise that is befitting of Him.[58] He created the heaven and the stars with the power of the word, and He hung the earth on nothingness, and created mankind on it to be His own treasured possession. Ergo, hear the praise. I beseech you, [my daughter], incline your ear, and listen, be chastised and succumb. Come into the temple, and set your heart on the right path, purge yourself, purify yourself, defend yourself, safeguard yourself, lest those who bear hollow beards of ignominy and impiety, blighted by evil, carry you astray, and branches of deception and dissimulation lead you close to them.[59] Those who seduce with words of books and promises[60] can easily soothe the pains of the daughter of my nation.[61] They sigh and moan, and deliver [to my people] vain and delusive presages. Surely you know what is said of the beard of ignominy, which is blighted by evil: I shall judge you like adulteresses are judged![62]

18   *Chapter 1*

And he declaimed his poem and so he said:

Beard and oldness, neither should terrify,	do not trust them though before you verify.
For too often you may think you found wheat,	still you only found thistle, this is no feat![63]
Likewise, you may think that a man is charitable	but he abuses the poor and the miserable.
He craves to eat the bread of the poor,[64] as a glutton dog	he is avid to gorge himself on his own vomit.[65]
Do not say: "He shall thus act, and be exonerated."	No, he shall not be forgiven, he shall not be vindicated![66]

Hence! Diminish your pride, banish your malice, do not make greed your crime and do not trust your fortune; for your fortune is your oppressor and your executioner is your silver![67] Surely on the day that your crime is judged, your agony will increase more and more. Embrace charity and banish pride, and do not follow lust, lest you shall be scarred and burnt![68] Wash wickedness from your heart, hear this out, and let your soul live. How long shall your oppressed cry, and your abused lament? Would you roll [dice] for the orphan ['s fate], and dig [a pit] for your companion?[69] Hear me out, assembled congregation, come, allow me to give you counsel and you shall atone for your crime with your abundance, and the fruit of your disgrace with your fortune, for if you will indeed give to the poor, you shall be entrenched in righteousness, and if indeed you dispense your bread to the hungry, the Lord will bless your bread and your water. And you shall not castigate the unfortunate and the pauper, and you shall not suppress the poor at the gates, and may it be that the oppressed shall not return shamed [by you]. Do not ignore your kin, you shall open up [your hand] to the poor amongst you, and you shall grant them from your granary and your winery. Do not trample the poor, giving alms covertly soothes wrath.[70]

And he declaimed his poem and so he said:

If you wish your gain to be hundredfold,	offer a present to the people of the Lord.[71]
To the poor, you shall surely donate,	open your hand to the begging unfortunate.
Then the Lord shall say: "Endless blessings	take for yourself, by all means!"
And He shall redeem you from [your] sins,	He shall carry your crimes and you shall be saved.

I adjure you in the name of the Most High, to pity the pauper and the indigent,[72] and not scorn the name of God when you are adjured in His name by a beggar. As in the fable of the pauper who, at the threshold, asked for bits of food.[73] The Landlord gave him a *prutah* (penny). He adjured him, in the name of the Most High, "Add here a little wheat because I have young boys

The Tale of Old Bearded Achbor

19

tormented by hunger and thirst." Then the landlord, in his own court, sinned and lied, and committed an act of heresy, as he said: "How dare you adjure me in the name of the Most High? Can you not see that I am a pauper and indigent?" And it came to be that even before he finished speaking, he was seized by pain and agony. His Creator struck him with blindness, madness, and annihilation. A voice passed over then: "So will be done to those who scorn the name of the Most High!" And you, my brothers, be warned. Perhaps on the day of [the Lord's] fury and wrath, you shall be protected in the shelter of the Most High.

And he declaimed his poem and so he said:

Blessed is the man who prays and is answered,

his Creator's shadow hangs over him like a crown.

He shall be assured, and shall not fear the day of anger,

for God's shadow shall be his shelter.

He will be saved from those who draw the bow

on the day that on their string they adjust their arrow.

Saved, he shall flee to the depth of the sea,

without a sailor nor someone to row.

But the man who scorns and despises the name the Most High,

shall be decomposed by his sin just as if dissolved by lye.

Lo! Just as light transcends darkness,

the sheltered is supreme to the serpent.[74]

I dream of abiding in the shelter of the Most High,

only my Savior my dream shall clarify!

I shall make a covenant with His Mercy,

I shall sacrifice a calf and will adhere to this alliance.[75]

I shall praise and sing, and say:

Blessed is the man who prays and is answered.

So he spoke all that is innocent and pure, and no one replied. He then told them: "My brothers, why do you desire profit, and why do you harden your hearts? Have you not heard the fable about the two men who lived in the same district?[76] One was rich and the other was poor. The rich man was a merchant; he used to [drink] every day till dawn. The poor man afflicted his soul with a three-day fast, sunrise to sunset. There was almost no breath left in him, from hunger and thirst. On the fourth day, in his distress, he took his stick in his hand and went, grieving and leaning upon the Lord's graces,[77] until he arrived at the merchant's. He told him: 'Please comfort your servant's heart, do not tarry!' [The merchant] scolded him, and thought he was a good-for-nothing, because he was tipsy from wine. He told him: 'Why did you come here so early?' And he replied: 'Because my heart was starving.' He prostrated himself at his feet and went and sat on the other side. Then he scolded him again and told him: 'You are seeking but your own shame! I know your evilness! Why are you standing here? What are you plotting against me? What are you thinking about?' And the guest replied to him: 'Would I count on your

20   *Chapter 1*

fortune? It is the All-Mighty that I trust. He impedes the thoughts [of the wit-
ted], and He will turn your heart around.' While the merchant was hearing
this, God converted his heart into another.[78] He had a friend whom he made
his clerk, who took care of all his treasure. He wrote an order [for the clerk]
to give the poor man four shekels, but his hand wandered and his heart was
inattentive. He meant to write to him: 'Give him four shekels and nothing
more,' but he wrote: 'Give him four hundred silver shekels.' The pauper took
the document from his hand and came to the clerk. The latter weighed the
money, and [the poor man] put it under his clothes and returned home. Then
the merchant came [there] and demanded the money and the order, and said
to the poor man: 'Is it not so that you inherit what your Lord bequeaths you?
He made my hand wander, to give you my fortune and fame. He is the One
who enriches and impoverishes, who sows and uproots,[79] who preserves the
faithful and silences the [false] preachers.[80] All are His lowly and haughty,
He is the Redeemer of all, the deceivers and the faulty.'"[81]

A man may think of himself as having a wise heart,	yet he is not right.
There is a wise man who may become impoverished	and a fool who will have flourished.
There is a righteous [man] who will find himself erring	and one who is wealthy but he is suffering.
There is one who begs for food and clothes	upon every mountain and every valley,
another one shall be satisfied with the Lord's plenty;	he shall thrive and enjoy prosperity.
There is one who rejoices initially	but at his end, he shall sigh bitterly.
God will be the One who judges,	He shall lift the downtrodden, and lower the haughty.
The One for Whom every human awaits,	and to Him, he yearns and anchors himself.

Once he had finished orating the fable, a man rose from among the elders
that gathered in the city plaza and said:[82] "Do you not know? This man is
eighty years of age, he is old and venerable. Humble yourself before the
length of his beard and the abundance of its branches, upon each frond the
whelps crouch.[83] Now be charitable with him, each of you give him the best
of your treasures."[84]

As he was standing amongst the crowd,[85] so he spoke, not once nor twice,
and the heart of the people melted and became like water. The man called
Achbor's two valets, and they wandered among the people to collect money.
The peoples' hearts had overturned, it had softened and was impressed,[86] and
they gave him—one a coin, another his clothing and his scarves, each according to his means. The two valets carried their gold and silver. Achbor bowed

The Tale of Old Bearded Achbor

and blessed them and thus he spoke: "I told you that I never ask of you, other than the generosity of your hearts."

And he declaimed his poem and so he said:

The Creator of hearts,[87] He alone will	turn them pure, according to His will.
He hardens, toughens, indurates them	and then draws them towards His want.
He toughens then redresses them and at his decree,	He pours them like the water of the sea
So, [subject] your soul to me and	commit your spirit in my hands.

Thus, may it be that He inclines your hearts towards His pleasure and leads your desire toward His will. And thus, He shall wait [for He may have] mercy on you, and He [should be] exalted so [He may have] compassion for you and may He bind your souls in the bond of life.

Achbor bowed before them, and departed, and continued on [his way], and the people dispersed, and each returned to his home.

Feasting with the Four Maidens

I then said in my heart: "I shall follow this old man,[88] and know whether he is a prophet or a seer, whether he is honorable or despicable." Achbor departed with his two valets, and where he goes, I am right behind. He arrived at his home, removed his shoes, threw his stick, and put all his goods in his dwelling.[89] His residence had ten entryways just like the homes of emperors.[90] I would have told you all about its shapes and courts and turret, had I had enough words to articulate all that my eyes saw there. Who could ever recount the streams of water and the pool, the birds and the enclosures,[91] the types of trees, and flowers and the buds, the skillets and the utensils[92] and the wine goblets to drink from, and different kinds of garments for wearing, and the vessels of silver, gold, and copper?!? I then said in my heart: "Did your tributes come from villains or from gentlemen?"[93] He made a fortune and much wealth! Surely, he was not ashamed to collect from the praiseworthy and the despised alike, and thus he created for himself all this opulence. I then knew that he was from among the sons of the villains, and a mean man of evil acts.[94]

There is one who profits from theft	and becomes rich from the tears of the oppressed.
There are men whose hoariness and beard look respectable,	yet men painted upon the wall would be preferable.[95]
There is a beard whose hairs are remarkable,	yet hairs all covered with tar would be preferable.[96]

There is a beard so lengthy, but not healthy,	in its sin, its inhabitants rot.[97]
Do they not nurture their beards with their bones' marrow?	Yet their brains, like their heads, are narrow![98]
There are men who in their own eyes are brilliant,	yet from brilliance they are quite distant!
There are men prosperous as the sand of the seashore,[99]	they subjugate men of reason.
There are men who oppress the wise,	like thorns in his side and splinters in his eyes.
There is a beard whose bearer is a man of deceit,	to his palate, the destitute's sustenance is so sweet.
His sustenance comes from the poor man's deprivation	he has become rich, and devours sourdough, bread, and sweet confections.[100]
They did not remember He who listens to the shouts of the poor,	hears the cry of those who moan,
since they were filling their sackcloth with booty.	Before the morrow, their bags are empty.

Shortly thereafter, four maidens came out,[101] walking bright as the moon. They kissed his hands,[102] undressed him from his clothes, sat him at the table, and placed before him plenty of food and a profusion of delicacies,[103] with tableware and goblets and floral braided ornaments, with old wine and buds and lilies, and [chalices of] running water, it was a splendor worthy of kings. Achbor sat at his table and with a merry heart said to his maidens: "Awake, perform a song!"[104] In their hands, they held harps, lyres, sistra, and cymbals.

The first sang and so she said:[105]

Wine, like lightning, like flames	the heart of those who drink it, with its spark enflames.
Bitter, yet sweeter than honey,	its fragrance invigorates as its splendor is like myrrh.
Shall it find sorrow in any man's heart,	it releases the regiment of joy to stamp it out.
It renders the miser's heart like the heart of a generous man.	Under its effect, the tight-fisted shall open his hand.
Wine's spark, like lightning, like a flame	Shall ignite its drinkers' heart the same
Bitter, yet sweeter than honey, that's true	its scent vivifies, like myrrh's is his virtue.
Shall it find sorrow in any man's heart,	it releases the regiment of joy to tear it apart.
It renders the miser's heart like the heart of the grand.	Under its sway, the tight-fisted shall open his hand.

The second sang and so she said:

Wine that within cups glows, resembles deep waters that froze.
But its appearance is not concealed by you see well the spark through its covers.
the cup,
And I shall say, when they despair of resolving the secret of the cup and the
wine's glare, impenetrable to them:
Just as the sunbeams glow, and then hide under the clouds.

The third sang and so she said:

A fawn covered her cheek with scarlet, her hand holds a cup as if filled with the
blood of thee slain.
The redness of the two rendered the beloveds' faces, garments and vessels.
everything red
So much, that [even] the night is covered the stars in the sky envy the radiance of
by [their] glow, their face.
With the fawn's apparel and her cup, the lights up and the shadows flee.
most obscure darkness

The fourth sang and so she said:

When the vineyard's daughter is poured (together) with the tears of the graceful
out gazelle when her beloved sways,
she kills all worries at once, as if in her she holds a sword, to put every [sorrow]
hand to an end.
She turns a fearful heart into a lion's and by her splendor, she awakens lust.
heart,
Should you say: "How would her light sparkle through the cup and all her
secrets be in plain sight?"
Can you not see that a doe is charming Similarly, imagine that the cup is her
under her mantle? mantle.
Now then, get up, as this is a time for my friend, in her bountiful treasure(s)!
drinking, find pleasure

Then Achbor said: "Lo, your mouth [sang] very well and your hands played admirably,[106] and by the quality of your poetry you multiplied your slain! As you have awakened my desire, I shall also reply with my part."

And he declaimed his poem and so he said:

Crystal cups empty of wine are pure, and white and they do shine!
Once they are filled with the vineyards' I see them [bloody] red and glowing.
tears
Small sparks dance within them, growing larger, into flames.
Did they glow or blush or did they not? Is the appearance of the full the same as
the appearance of the empty?

It is indeed the gazelles' way the moment they meet their beloved,	the faces and the cheeks with red are covered!
Reddened from the blood of the desirers' hearts	because they oppress and rob the love of the sweethearts.
Get up, graceful gazelle! Let me drink them all,	the big cups after the small.
Would that it be that my cup be the lip of a beloved,	as it is sweeter than any goblet.
For the way of the desirers is to sip	—these are their rules—from a beautiful gazelle's lip!

The maidens told him, "You have done very well! Your poems are more delightful than many other great poems!" He then rose toward them, and he regaled them, he seemed to be bouncing from lap to lap. They all rose to play, and in his heart's gladness, he was dancing because he was burning like fire. And so it was until he became fatigued, and he lay down, closed his eyes, covered his face, and fell into a deep sleep. The maidens exited toward the patio, and [he remained as if] he did not see, keeping silent and feigning [sleep].[107]

The Black Mistress

The minute they were gone, he called quietly. From the [other] room a woman exited,[108] utterly Cushitic.[109] She had a lip similar to a firebrand, a remnant of flames, her eyes were like blazes, and her nostrils were flared.[110] Then I said, "Nothing but adulteries!"[111] I was outraged by the evil of their exploits; I beat them and removed their clothes, leaving them naked and barefoot, because I was furious with these lechers.[112] And Achbor said:[113] "Withdraw your hands! Why do you act this way towards your servants? Evidently, the ardents' hearts are not drawn[114] to vile figs."[115]

And he declaimed his poem and so he said:

Would that my waist was sick,	then the figs I will trick.[116]
Since only rot is my antidote,	learn the remedies, you dolt![117]

I castigated [him] for his foolishness and offense, but he continued his verse:

You despise the Cushitic. Why?	Is she not the pupil of your eye? [118]
I would prefer a blackish [woman] over the bright,	because for me she is the light![119]
Her dark shins for me glow	open to me whenever I'm low.[120]

The Tale of Old Bearded Achbor 25

I retorted to his senselessness: "Answer the fool, according to his silliness!"[121]

What shares the blackish, whose stench shall stir	With the maiden perfumed with myrrh?[122]
In the hand of a lover, a lily so bright,[123]	to every eye, beauty and delight.[124]
But every black [girl] is heartless,	tantalizing, vociferous and devious.[125]
I shall say the word of the Eternal to every Cushitic maid:	"Turn back, return to where you were made!"[126]

Then I said to him: "Achbor, what is wrong with you? Why are you drinking from such murky water?"[127] He retorted and so said: "Surely, all those who like fair girls are riders of white she-asses."[128] To that, I raised a bitter cry. The maidens returned because I raised my voice and called out. I told them about Achbor's affair, and they insulted him, and they slandered him using tremendous taunts and they mocked the hairs on his beard that had lengthened and whitened. They did not know and they did not understand,[129] [how] the bright seemed to him as black and the black as the light.[130] Who could reverse his lust for black women? For they are tenebrous.[131]

In Blame of the Beard

The first said: "The crushed testicle,[132] he dug in the darkness![133] Well, I saw that his beard engendered awe and reverence in the hearts of those who saw it. [But] it reaches until the lowest hell.[134] Its invigorated branches are a refuge for conies. Between one section and another is a hideout where foxes wander, and the fleas have fallen asleep within it, as they have been there for a long time."[135]

And she declaimed her poem and so she said:

Achbor's beard is the beard of the fools' pastor,[136]	its branches stretch to every part and sector!
It has grown so long it now brushes his hellhole,	doing so vigorously until it has no strength at all![137]
In it, little animals march, and I had wondered: inside	are these apes that hide?
I have seen some creatures flying into it like birds,	and fleas have taken possession of it and set up their nests there, undeterred.
I was answered: Achbor's beard is like a forest,	where [live] wild animals and little foxes.
There, the night-owl nested and laid eggs,	and there, it is also a refuge for the conies.
There they reside safely and with peace of mind,	each complacent under their vines.
And each under their fig tree abound,	under Achbor's beard's shadow, invigorated and safe and sound! [138]

26 *Chapter 1*

The second spoke: "Lo, I have seen Achbor whitened by his old age, not one single black hair.[139] I thought he was innocent of any crime. But he made his bed in the darkness, he fornicated with the daughters of Ham, and he has worked in the coal [mines].[140] That is why I call his beard the beard of villainy. Alas, the sordid, the soiled! And though I did previously think that it was the beard of wisdom and reason, lo, it is the beard of shame and disgrace."

And she declaimed her poem and so she said:

Achbor's beard is the beard of a man who can heal,	so I believed, from any ill!
A beard of justice, a beard of honesty,	a beard of honor, a beard of security.
And lo, it is a beard of ignominy,	a beard of disgrace, a beard of infamy!
Pleasant on the blackness of his face like muck	upon of a pile of junk.
With no razor, it shall be shaven away,	it shall be eradicated by a shard of dry clay.[141]
Satan stood at his side,	causing so that in his eyes, black is beautified.
So much so till darkness he deems as light,	and beauty and grace he puts to slight.
Over the scented he chooses the smelling,	and over a girdle, a swelling!

The third said: "Lo, I have seen Achbor's beard, impressive and admirable, abundant and dense. I believed its hairs were pure and innocent. [The beard] yielded boughs and sent out shoots. They lengthened till the fringes [of his clothes], and touched his feet. The [facial] hairs reached the hairs of his branch, wing to wing they touched each other.[142] Then I said to myself: I thought—and how could I have thought this—that his beard's hairs were hairs of reason and righteousness, yet they all lead downhill to Little Hole."[143]

And she declaimed her poem and said:

What man is like Achbor, praised among his kinship?	As if his beard glows with kingship?
My heart was seduced because I saw his beard so lengthy.	Well, there is nothing about it that is healthy!
I have investigated it and there it is, planted in junk,	stuck in muck.
Indeed, its root is on his cheek, but its edges extend,	all the way down to Little Hole they descend.
Its branches are gnarled,	every single hair snarled
It has enough fleece for [two] mules' saddlecloth	and a covering for the net [encircling] the flock's fold![144]
It would be a blanket upon your privy	and you shall cover your excrement with this blanket.[145]

The Tale of Old Bearded Achbor 27

The fourth spoke: "Would that he wash it, which is filled with filth and [thus] remove the excreta from its plumage. For as much as its hairs are sinners and malicious, they are a delusion, and useless. Withal, it has grown old and futile and has whitened as hail, it would only descend to hell."

And she declaimed her poem and so she said:

I saw Achbor's beard,	and my heart trembled and also feared.
I believed he was an innocent man,	and behold, he rebelled against the Sovereign!
And even if he aged and his beard filled with blight,	as snow and hail it became white.
And even if it were irrigated with the water of purification,[146]	it would still only be thrown down to Perdition!

The four of them came forward and beat him and plucked [his hairs]; they judged him as adulteresses are judged![147] This one pulls his beard, and that one plucks it. They tormented him and did not let go, and he died from the blows of those who beat him. For indeed, they killed him. They bound him in ropes and threw him into one of the pits. Hence, they said: "Such a despicable man shall not be amongst us, for the shame would be on us!"

A Fairy Tale Ending

So it came to pass, they entered the vineyards to stroll in the gardens and pick lilies. They promenaded in the orchards, paced among the myrtle trees,[148] wearing colorful garments, telling stories and riddles and fine poetry about the blossoming flowers, the vines, and all sorts of buds. They spoke of the trees, of lilies and blossoms.[149] Then at noontime, they sat at the pools of water, sitting in the shadows, playing psalteries and harps.

Lo and behold, four lads heard their singing, listened to their chants and melodies, and, exulted by the sound of the string music, they observed them [surreptitiously] from behind the windows. They perceived this and said: "Who is it who listens to our voices, hiding behind our walls?[150] Are you an ally or a foe?"[151]

Then, at eventide, they rose from their ambuscade, stepped out and came closer and when they approached them, they nodded and bowed. [All] were seated, each person in their place, and each person within their camps.[152] [The lads] looked at one another, marveled at their [the maidens'] beauty and allure, and the glow of their faces, and they said, whispering: "would that you were our wives!"

[The maidens] heard that and said: "We heard your discourse, now let your words be verified. How can it be proven that you have spoken the truth? How

28 *Chapter 1*

could we know that you are not betrayers? Why did you come here to glance at us naked, are you not ashamed? And why did you not say: If thus far we remained concealed from their sight,[153] let us speak to them before we are revealed, and if they tell us: come to us—then we shall come."

One of them declaimed her poem and so she said:

Were they committing a crime, the lovers who knocked on the fawns' doors?
Ah! Would they be mindless, or fatuous, or imbeciles—or would they be amorous?
Lovers, it is forbidden to approach a fawn just because you are smitten.

The oppressed should not oppress,[154] with their mouth they should caress.
If they are desirers,[155] they shall behave as a model and an example, a day shall come, their reward will be ample!
If they are supporters of Amor, a friend should control his passion and not want more.

Desirers' hearts are always in anguish, in flames they languish.
They murmur, they ululate from heartache they vociferate.
If you are desirers, where are the tears that should streak down on your cheek?
Where are the lovers' implorations? Where are the sweet declarations?
Where are the great desirers gone, those who insist [on wooing] the fawns?
The admirers whose craving on the tablets of their hearts are engraving.[156]

They are no more! Look for them everywhere Outworn they have become, if mighty they [once] were!
Lovers, you shall be tested as follows: do not engage yourselves in quarrels.
[rather] Get up and hurry, accelerate, the reins of wandering you should amputate![157]

Choose yourself each man a mate, among you decide your fate!
Because from his father and mother a man shall go, and cleave to a graceful doe![158]
Then they hastened to pick, and each lad, was holding now the wife he had.

And there it was that their youth was flourishing. with their beloveds they were relishing[159]

COMMENTARY

The following commentary does not aim to provide an exhaustive listing of all the existing biblical phrasings (*shibutzim*) in the tale. Rather, it glosses over or expounds on those of specific interest, which are not discussed in the subsequent chapters. For a systematic list of the biblical phrasings, see David's edition (1992-3) and Rosen's translation (2020).

The Tale of Old Bearded Achbor 29

Prologue

1. wander the earth and roam upon it

מתהלך בחוצות וסוחר

The word "חוצות" refers both to streets (Jer. 5:1), and markets (1 Kings 20:34). The verb סוחר initially meant moving about the earth (to circulate, to walk, to roam; Jer. 14:18), later evolving into meaning "the exploitation of natural resources" and, by extension, to trade. Thus, another possible translation could justify "wandering" in the sense of "I was circulating in the markets and doing business [. . .]." Since nowhere else in *Sefer ha-Meshalim* is it hinted that Lemuel is a merchant, I prefer to consider Lemuel as a traveler or explorer, as travel is a main topos in this book.

2. At times I have slept in the desert (Ps. 55:8) and in the forests (Ezek. 34:25)

פעם אלין במדבר וביערים

The locution במדבר אלין (slept in the desert) serves as a bridge to a decisive biblical chapter, the first of several chapters that resonate regularly within the tale. In Psalm 55 the biblical poet describes a theoretical escape he wishes to undertake to flee a corrupt city, full of moral and physical adversaries who are "אנשי דמים ומרמה" (men of blood and deceit, 55:24). For that, he prays "הנה ארחיק נדד אלין במדבר סלה" (Lo, then would I wander far off, I would lodge in the wilderness, Selah. 55:8). The reference to this psalm seems, at first, merely ornamental. It is quoted as part of what may be perceived as a travel journal, and the specific allusion to sleeping in the desert is not associated with a negative experience, but only with the nature of adventurers. We will soon learn, however, that Lemuel is also about to arrive at a corrupt city from which he will desire to flee for reasons similar to those quoted in Psalm 55.

The psalmist also complains about his greatest adversary, an old companion to whom he was close, and with whom he used to pray. This companion became hateful, since, like all depraved men "כי רעות במגורם בקרבם" (for evil is in their dwelling, and within them, 55:16). The psalmist continues to describe his violations: "שלח ידיו, בשלמיו; חלל בריתו. חלקו, מחמאות פיו וקרב-לבו: רכו דבריו משמן; והמה פתחות" (He hath put forth his hands against them that were at peace with him; he hath profaned his covenant. Smoother than cream were the speeches of his mouth, but his heart was war; his words were softer than oil, yet were they keen-edged swords, 55:21-22). He then asks: "ואתה אלהים תורדם לבאר שחת אנשי דמים ומרמה לא יחצו ימיהם" (But Thou, O God, wilt bring them down into the nethermost pit; men of blood and deceit shall not live out half their days, 55:24). Lemuel will soon encounter these exact

30   *Chapter 1*

topoi, of an evil, hypocritical man who will end up in the nethermost pit. Thus, while the power of this reference is only revealed at the end of the tale, its first seeds are planted in the prologue.

3. *mansions of aristocrats (Lev. 25:31)*

בתי החצרים

Schirmann considered this to mean "open villages," that is, villages that are not surrounded by walls. This corresponds to the literal meaning of the biblical phrase "בתי החצרים אשר אין להם חומה סביב" (the houses of the villages which have no wall round about them, Lev. 25:31) and its context. it should be noted, though, that the main motif at the beginning of the tale is the random fluctuation of the vagabond's living conditions, presented through a series of significant contrasts: inside a city and outside of it, with the rich and the poor and so forth, and thus I believe that this description should also be contrasted. As Lemuel had been obliged, at times, to sleep in the deserts and forests, in his case the opposite of the unprotected outdoors would be the medieval castle. In this vein, the word "חוצות" would construe a play on words with the word "חצרות", courts, that is, the homes of the courtly people.

4. *no nightcaps on their heads (Jon. 2:20)*

ולילה סוף לראשם חבוש

While there is no explicit mention of either rich or poor hosts, this is implied by the text. Within the context of the contradiction motif implemented in the prologue, another way of understanding this statement is that sometimes he would stand next to the marshes, along with poor people who had no clothes.

5. *I wandered exhausted, on my last legs (2 Sam. 4:4)*

ויום יהלך יעף ונכה רגליים

While literally this refers to a cripple, the meaning here is metaphorical and was replaced by an English idiom to keep the notion of the word "leg."

6. *And I declaimed my poem, and so I said:*

ואשא משלי ואומר

The biblical formula "וישא משלו," employed several times in the biblical Numbers, became a conventional locution in medieval Hebrew literature when

The Tale of Old Bearded Achbor   31

introducing a poem within the narrative rhymed prose. Different Bible translations considered the various possible senses that the word "משל" conveys, especially a parable, message, or discourse. For this translation, I embraced the Holman Christian Standard Bible's translation (declaimed his poem, e.g., Num. 23:7), which perfectly corresponds to the poetic convention.

Without entering here too deeply into the theoretical aspects of the poetic intermissions in the maqama genre, I would argue that in *Sefer ha-Meshalim*, a clear distinction exists between the narrative, that is, the rhymed prose descriptions of events and plots, and the lyrical, that is, the poems inserted between the narrative parts. The prose sections narrate the protagonists' actions as they occur, and while they can include confessions, thoughts, meditations, and dreams, these are just reports of what the protagonist is experiencing in the sequences of events. The poems uphold the sequences. Time freezes for a moment within a certain sequence, and the character who recites the poetry has the chance to express relevant issues poetically, theoretically, and philosophically. For example, in the ninth tale, *The Love Story of Sahar and Kima*, Kima does not wish to engage in sexual relations with the very disappointed Sahar. Their rhymed prose dialogue about kissing, being part of "what happens" in the tale, is interrupted when Kima poeticizes her insights about how aristocrats should behave when in love. The poetry is not detached from the plot, it is part of it, because one of the things that the lovers most enjoy doing is exchanging love poems. But the content reflects reformulations and meditations on actions that were either taken or should be taken (or not taken).[6] This is also the case in *Achbor*, where Lemuel the narrator, Achbor the protagonist, and the four maidens engage frequently in poetry to emphasize their perceptions and thoughts, sometimes with personal discourses, and other times in a more theoretical way.

In this inaugural poem, Lemuel poeticizes general ideas about the hazards of time, while later he will compose poems about his personal experience. The most significant poem, however, is yet to come, and is the wine poem declaimed by the four maidens and answered by Achbor during the feast at his home.

7. The state of a man stands not still (Lev. 13:5), it changes and it always will (Lam. 4:1)

דבר אדם בלי יעמוד / בעינו, יד ליד ישנא

Literally "ליד יד" (hand to hand), this is a formula of a pledge, perhaps close enough to the modern "hand on heart" (Prov. 11:21, 16:5). Schirmann suggested reading the meaning here as "from phase to phase" or "from time to time."

32   *Chapter 1*

8. There is a time

ועת

In this first poem, Lemuel rewrites the beginning of Ecclesiastes 3, although none of the biblical contrasts are used here. After Psalm 55, Ecclesiastes is the second substantial source to which Yaakov ben Elazar returns often throughout this tale, in different contexts.

9. a time he lies down (Num. 2:34)

עת ישכב

In David's edition, this is translated as "ישב" (sits), while Schirmann understood this as "ישכב" (lies down). The manuscript is unclear, and both options are plausible as both echo biblical idioms. In Psalm 139:2, the psalmist refers to God as knowing all of man's positions or, by abstraction, his actions, "אתה ידעת שבתי וקומי" (Thou knowest my downsitting and mine uprising). The three verbs are tied together in Deut eronomy 6:7, indicating the principle that whatever a man does, he must remember God's orders: "בשבתך בביתך ובלכתך בדרך ובשכבך ובקומך" (when thou sittest in thy house, and when thou walkest by the way, and when thou liest down, and when thou risest up). I was more inclined to agree with Schirmann, as the formula בשכבך ובקומך (when you lie down and when you rise) became a fixed notion indicating the times for קריאת שמע (*kriyat shma,* reciting the "Shema Israel" prayer) and recalls the commentary written by Shlomo Yitzchaki (known by the acronym Rashi) "זמן שכיבה וזמן קימה" (the time for laying down and the time for rising), which is linked to the main idea here, referring to the different times in a person's life.

10. A time he shall grow strong and a time he shall weaken, a time he is wealthy and a time poverty-stricken.

ועת יגדל ועת ידל / ועת יעשיר ועת יענה

In this stanza, the protasis is doubled by the apodosis: יעשיר (literally: will become rich) repeats יגדל (literally: will grow), and both terms describe various forms of prosperity. יענה (literally will become poor, the root is ענה) repeats ידל (will become meager, the root is דלל) and these two words depict numerous ways to describe misery. The specific juxtaposition of ידל and יענה resonates with Psalm 116, where, in verse 6, the psalmist expresses the idea that he becomes weak, tormented, or poor by using the verb דלותי (דלל), and repeating it in verse 10, using the verb עניתי (ענה).

The Tale of Old Bearded Achbor   33

11. At dawn he worships his Creator, at dusk he turns into an idolator (Deut. 32:21)

ושחר יעבוד צורו- / וערב לא לאל יפנה

In Deuteronomy 32, the Hebrews are accused of arousing the Lord's ire by worshipping other deities: זרים (strange gods; 16), תועבות (abominations; 17, also meaning idolatry), שדים לא אלוה (demons, no-gods; 17), אלהים לא ידעום (gods that they knew not; 17), חדשים (new gods; 17), and אל בלא (no-god; 21), the latter synonymous with idol worship.[7] While here Lemuel speaks in generalizations, this sentence also has a "prophetic" power, as we will soon meet the dangerous religious hypocrite who is guilty of what can be interpreted as enticing innocent people into *avoda zara*.[8]

12. It may be that he relies on his fortune (Isa. 50:10) but the master shall be betrayed by Fortune!

ויש נשען עלי הונו / והונו[9] על בעלו יזנה

Literally, this sequence translates as: "It may be that he relies on his wealth but his wealth shall betray (literally prostitute against) its own master (or owner)." The verb זנה (prostitute) frequently describes forsaking the Lord and choosing to worship idols. The Hebrews had done just that, worshiping any number of pagan deities with various designations,[10] but in Judges 8:33, they are said to have gone astray (verb זנה) after the ba'alim (ויזנו אחרי הבעלים). The word "בעל" refers to both the god Ba'al and the owner or master of something. Since the tale of the impostor develops the idea of the dangers inherent in following another religion, and since the subject of greed is also consistently alluded to in this tale, as will become apparent in the following pages, it is plausible to see here a manipulation of the verse from Judges. Lemuel talks about the ephemerality of riches, echoing a text discussing the pursuit of idols, both main themes of the tale.

In my translation, I paid tribute to Yaakov ben Elazar's possible fascination with mythologies. While he does not specifically refer to the goddess Fortuna or her wheel, the personification of wealth as turning the tables captures this motif, which was recurrent in medieval Europe.[11] Achbor uses a similar notion, warning his congregation in his sermon: "For your fortune is your oppressor and your executioner is your silver." In the fable he is about to share in his sermon, he also recounts to his listeners a story about a rich man whose fortune betrays him, which will be studied below. Last but not least, the possible pun created by the phonetic similarity of הון (wealth) and און (vigor, including sexual vigor), should be considered.

34 Chapter 1

13. It may be that he leans on worldly glory indeed, yet his staff is of broken reed (Isa. 36:6, 2 Kings 18:21).

ויש נשען בהוד תבל / ומשענתו רצוץ קנה

For the translation of this verse, I am inspired by the well-known phrase "sic transit gloria mundi," found in the writings of thirteenth-century Etienne de Bourbon and believed to be a meditation upon I John 2-15. While I cannot be entirely sure that Yaakov ben Elazar had one of these sources in mind, I think it is safe to say that he conveys here a similar idea, the vanity and fragility of worldly splendor.

14. And through his different ages ten times change his wages! (Gen. 31:41)

ומשכורתו בעת ועת / עשרה יחליף מונה

This seems to be a disruption of מעת לעת, which in modern Hebrew means "from time to time," that is, occasionally. In medieval (and earlier) Hebrew, however, this referred to a period of 24 hours, an entire day. Yaakov is alluding to his namesake, the biblical Jacob, who complained that Laban modified (i.e., decreased) his wages ten times, or considerably (Gen. 31:7 and 41), over a period of twenty years. The translation here thus depends on our interpretation. If we assume that Jacob's salary was cut on an average of every two years (and considering the modification of the locution בעת ועת and not מעת לעת) it is possible to understand this as meaning that a man's salary is modified from time to time, even decreasing ten times, or, more generally, that a man's salary is considerably modified over his lifetime. According to the general idea that life is inconsistent, it can be understood that such changes may happen to a man over his lifetime. It can also be understood as I translated here, based on the idea that a man's wage changes over twenty years.

15. I have seen marvels, extraordinary and awesome (1 Chron. 17:21), I have met (Exod. 5:20) [rich] men and poor, villains and noblemen.

וראיתי נפלאות גדולות ונוראות ופגעתי אנשים ורשים נבלים ונדיבים

This sentence is somewhat problematic, as it seems that the two sequences should have rhymed, that is, ורשים should rhyme with ונדיבים.[12] This may be the reason that Schirmann replaced רשים (poor) with רבים (many), which somewhat ameliorates the rhyme רבים / נדיבים. If we remain with the manuscript's reading of אנשים, we may postulate that the word is used to indicate "rich men" to create a harmony with the other three nominal adjectives (poor, villain, noble (or generous), and two balanced dichotomies (rich / poor villain / generous).[13] It may also be that the word "rich" was omitted for the sake of the rhythm, either intentionally or erroneously (i.e., the text was meant to be עשירים ורשים). Men, that is, the city's inhabitants, are the subject of all the nominal attributes.

16. [Once I had arrived in a city . . .]

[וּבָאתִי לעיר]

The line is edited in square brackets as it does not appear in the manuscript, but it is essential to the tale. Lemuel's following disclosure about an idealized desirable city is reminiscent of Lucian's city of Virtue in his *Harmonides* (see lines x and a where a city is referred to as the City of Kingly Virtue),[14] though, as we shall see, this is possibly parodical. Such a depiction, in turn, is somewhat analogical to Plato's *Republic*.[15] The disillusion after discovering that the city is depraved and its inhabitants are corrupt is a topos. We find it, among others, in two texts that share affinities with *Achbor*. First, the *Misopogon*. In this redaction, Julian returns numerous times to describe the frivolous city that he is about to leave. Moreover, at a certain point he tells the anecdote about Cato the Roman, who "once visited this populous and luxurious and wealthy city." Instead of greeting him, the courageous Roman, they were eager to welcome Demetrius "a freedman of Pompey, who had acquired a very large fortune" (p. 477). To this "Cato answered not a word, but only cried aloud like a man stricken with madness and out of his senses, 'Alas for this ill-fated city!' And took himself off" (p. 479). It is also evocative of the narrator's impressions regarding Ireland in the tale *Moriuht*, a text with which, as we shall see, *Achbor* shares several affinities.[16]

17. whose inhabitants were rich, its merchants—princes (Isa. 23:8), they do not spare their gold, and they squander their silver (Isa. 46:6). This city pleased me, and all my sorrows dissipated.

יושביה עשירים וסוחריה שרים / ועל זהב לא יחמולו וכסף בקנה ישקולו

There is a paradox in the depiction of the idealized city to which Lemuel arrives and where, at first, he desires to stay: What is emphasized is the disproportionate wealth of its habitants, whereas materialistic concerns are usually dichotomic to moral aspirations.

The biblical phrasing used here, "הזלים זהב מכיס וכסף בקנה ישקלו" (Ye that lavish gold out of the bag, and weigh silver in the balance; Isa. 46:6),

36 *Chapter 1*

mocks pagans who spend their gold and silver on constructing useless idols to worship. Exegetes understood that measuring the silver in the manner described meant that the measuring was imprecise, emphasizing the idea of the gold and the silver dripping freely from their pockets. Based on this interpretation, I slightly changed the literal text.

One way this paradox can be explained is that the wealth here is, in some way, beyond materialism, metaphorically expressing the inhabitants' lack of interest to gain more, or even care for gold and silver, as they are happy with the wealth (materialistic or as a metaphor for spiritual) they possess.[17] Another, possibly ironic, explanation is that these words hint at the upcoming disillusion, as the corruption of the inhabitants will become clear to Lemuel, and it is then that the quoted biblical phrasing will be at its most powerful. Like in the book of Isaiah, these men will be discovered to be not righteous, but sinners.

18. I shall settle here, this is my desire (Ps. 132:14).

כי איוויתיה

Literally, "I desire it," that is, the city (see below, "You desire my heart"). If we accept that this text might have an affinity with Lucien's City of Virtue, than this remark might also be an echo of sorts (perhaps in a distorted fashion) to Lucian's work (in whatever way Yaakov could have known the text or its themes). The movement here is reversed. Lycinus confesses that when he was young, he refused the invitation of an old man to be a citizen of Virtue: "I would not listen at that time through folly and youth," but now, fifteen years later, "I myself am in love with the same things [being the city's utopic principles]" and that "If the city had been near at hand and visible to everyone" there is nothing he would have loved more.

19. Rich and content with their treasure / men of reason and good measure

עשירי הון שמחים בו / מתי שכל וטוב טעם

This description is similar to one uttered by Lycinus in *Harmonides*: "Virtue then seems to me like a city whose inhabitants are happy . . . outstanding in their wisdom, all of them brave, just, prudent, almost gods."[18] For Lucian however, in the ideal city there is no consideration for a person's rank. On the contrary, "all the inhabitants were aliens and foreigners, not one was a native; there were even many barbarians among the citizens, as well as slaves, cripples, dwarfs, and paupers." This perspective depicts the ideal city's citizens as noble men.

The Tale of Old Bearded Achbor   37

20. Should one of them become unfortunate (Job 21:17), they reach out to him, their hearts companionate.

ואם בא איד לאיש מהם / יבואוהו בלב נפעם

In the Scriptures, לב נפעם refers to a soul that has been troubled by surprise. In the twelfth century, Moshe Ibn Ezra used the verb פעם to describe emotional excitement.[19]

21. "I shall go to their elders (Jer. 5:5) and I shall speak with them, for they are those who teach laws and morals," but these ones had already broken their yokes, and had torn off their reins (Jer. 5:5)

אלכה לי אל הגדולים ואדברה עמם כי המה יורו חוקות ותורות אך המה שברו עול ניתקו מוסרות

The word "גדולים," literally "the big" or "the great," refers here to the people's most respected men, who are regarded as such because of their social status, fortune, profession, or erudition. I used the word "elder" for the translation, as it conveys the traditional aura of the honored senior members of the tribe. Chapter 5 of the book of Jeremiah, which is quoted here, is the third momentous biblical source used in the tale. The prologue reverberates its prophecy, which relates to the corruption that has spread in Jerusalem, emphasizing, as in our tale, the question of iniquity. This particular segment in the tale rewrites Jeremiah 5:5, and I italicized the cited element to distinguish it from the new wordings inserted within: "אלכה לי אל הגדולים, ואדברה אותם- כי המה ידעו דרך ה', "משפט אלהיהם; אך המה יחדו שברו על, נתקו מוסרות" (*I will get me unto the great men, and will speak unto them; for they* know the way of the Lord, and the ordinance of their God. *But these had altogether broken the yoke, and burst the bands*). The phrase "יורו חוקות ותורות" (teach laws and morals), which replaces "ידעו דרך ה', משפט אלוהיהם" (know the way of the Lord, and the ordinance of their God), introduces the relevant subject matter. In Jeremiah, the prophet asks to see the community's elders, believing that they, as opposed to the poor and foolish (5:4), are still pious and will be able to understand the prophecy that he will shortly pronounce. He is therefore frustrated to discover that they have all become ungodly. Similarly, Lemuel asks to speak with the men he believes to be responsible for meting out justice and teaching it to the people. Like the prophet Jeremiah, Lemuel is also disillusioned, discovering that the people have lost the most important virtue according to the prologue, the virtue of justice, a loss that is a supreme sign of immorality.

On the biblical phrasing "שברו על נתקו מוסרות" ("broken the yoke, and burst the bands") as an allusion to assimilation, see chapter 4. Yaakov could have possibly used this quote for the phonetic connection between mosser (plur. mosserot, reins) and moussar (מוסר, morality) to emphasize the judges' lack of morals.

38   *Chapter 1*

The prophecy described in Jeremiah 5 continues with the following commentary.

22. I saw that their judges were false judges, nocturnal wolves, who leave no bones for the morning.

שופטי שקר, זאבי ערב לא גרמו לבוקר

Like Jeremiah 5, Zephaniah 3, referred to in this sequence, also tells of a prophecy that begins with a description of the corruption of the city of Jerusalem, described as מוראה ונגאלה (filthy and polluted), a phrasing that will be used later to describe Achbor's beard. Despite appearing in two different biblical books, these chapters are connected. Jeremiah predicts that the corrupt men of Jerusalem, both rich and poor, who turned their back on God, will be prosecuted by "על כן הכם אריה מיער זאב ערבות ישדדם" (the lion from the forest and the wolf from the desert, Jer. 5:6), among other animals. Similarly, Zephaniah compares Jerusalem's corrupt ministers and judges to "שריה בקרבה אריות שאגים שפטיה זאבי ערב לא גרמו לבקר" (Her princes in the midst of her are roaring lions; her judges are wolves of the desert, they leave not a bone for the morrow, Zeph. 3:3).[20] Considered a sublime sign of moral degeneration, discriminatory judges are frequently referred to as exemplifying general corruption in didactic literature, as they have the power over human lives, perhaps more than any other authority. This is the first of a series of fierce images used by Lemuel to describe the perversion and depravation of the avaricious judges of the city. The judges are so materialistic that instead of representing all that is humane, reasonable, just, and moral, and fulfilling their educational role, they are presented as the most horrible and bloodthirsty of creatures, the evening wolves, whose hunger is insatiable and who live only according to their basic instincts. Therefore, they voraciously eat all their kill, including the bones, and do not even leave one bone for the morning. According to Abraham Ibn Ezra, "since they did not keep a bone to the morrow, lo, they are starving in the evening."[21] David Kimhi (known by the acronym Radak) likened this to "the judges who grab the bribe and devour it."[22] A similar image will return in Lemuel's poem, where he will once again describe the rich and corrupt men of the city, who extravagantly spend all the money they steal from others, leaving nothing for the next morning.

23. The righteous fall before the treacherous (Prov. 25:26) who become fattened like a laboring heifer (Jer. 50:11)

וצדיק מט לפני רשע וכעגלה דשה יפושון

The Tale of Old Bearded Achbor

The fattened heifer image is borrowed from Jeremiah, ironically describing the short-lived joy of the Babylonians responsible for the exile of the Jews, as according to the prophecy they will be destroyed (Jer. 50:11). Like the Babylonians in the biblical source, the corrupt men of the city are described as rejoicing and benefiting from the suffering of others. The biblical phrasing hints at the fact that such behavior will not remain without divine punishment. Medieval commentators explained this peculiar metaphor based on the fact that while the heifer tramples the soil, it eats as much produce as it desires and thus becomes fat or content.[23] The use of this simile is remarkable because it simultaneously creates a concordance and dissonance with a previous metaphor, comparing the false judges to hungry wolves. On the one hand, the transgressors are compared to gluttonous animals who feed themselves at the expense of those who are weaker. On the other hand, the juxtaposition of the voracious adult wolf and the newly born heifer, the carnivore and the herbivore, to describe the same group of people, is a blatant oxymoron.

24. while they persecute those who publicly rebuke them (Isa. 29:21).

ולמוכיח בשער יקושון

Lemuel literally cites Isaiah's prophecy of destruction for the cruel tyrants who, amongst their other crimes, "lay snares for him that reproveth in the gate" (Isa. 29:21), meaning, in public.

25. So many trails have I ambled!

כמה אהלך נתיבות!

Lemuel's third poem resumes in three parts, repeating what he has said so far. In part one, he tells of his habit of traveling long distances; in part two, he shares that he once arrived at a city that seemed to him utopic, but was disillusioned; in part three, he shares his decision to leave that city.

26. I explored the earth's edges (Hab. 3:6)

קצוי אדמה אמודד

Literally, "I measured the earth's edges."

27. To seek and explore places (Eccles. 1:13)

לדרוש ולתור מקומות

40   *Chapter 1*

Kohelet, one of the names attributed to King Solomon, says in the first chapter of Ecclesiastes "ונתתי את לבי לדרוש ולתור בחוכמה על כל אשר נעשה תחת השמים" (And I applied my heart to seek and to search out by wisdom concerning all things that are done under heaven, 1:13). This relates to his personal and social attempts to understand humanity, from which he was mostly disappointed, concluding that "הכל הבל הבלים" (all is vanity of vanities, 1:2). Lemuel is inspired by the king's philosophy and turns King Solomon's ideological experiment to find answers in "wisdom" into a real quest, hence the word "wisdom" (חכמה) is replaced by "places" (מקומות).[24] Exploring the human experience may thus be the initial reason for his journeys.

28. Hither you desire to go, my heart,

הן תאוותך לבבי -

A poetic personification of the heart, whose wishes are to find the glorious city (see the following note), which also ornamentally doubles Lemuel's previous statement about the city he had reached.

The personified heart, or, more precisely, the heart as embodying the most intimate part of a human being, is an archetype common to different cultures and languages. In our tale, the motif will culminate in Achbor's melodramatic sermon, which ends in a poem dedicated to the heart as symbolizing human beings.

29. to the city of virtuous kings (Eccles. 2:8)

היא עיר סגולת מלכים

In the biblical source quoted here, סגולת מלכים refers to material wealth, כנסתי לי גם כסף וזהב וסגולת מלכים והמדינות (I gathered me also silver and gold, and treasure such as kings and the provinces have as their own; Eccles. 2:8). But in the specific context of the tale, it seems that Lemuel is referring to a different meaning of the word סגולה (segula). Here, Lemuel might be referring to virtue, as we know that he does not pursue riches, but is searching for an honorable place to settle in, a place whose leaders / kings are righteous and just. The biblical excerpt, however, is not without significance. We have already seen above that the main idea of Lemuel's first poem derives from Ecclesiastics. This specific phrasing will be quoted again later, much more literally, to describe Achbor's excessive wealth in a passage that parallels the excessive wealth that Kohelet attests to having accrued. Yet, the Ecclesiast despises all the earthly profusion he holds, treating all of it as הבל ורעות רוח (vanity and a striving after the wind, Eccles. 2:11). By using the same phrase twice in completely different contexts and in contradicting senses,

The Tale of Old Bearded Achbor   41

Lemuel differentiates himself from Achbor. Through his quest for סגולת מלכים
Achbor seeks earthly pleasures, which are another sign of his immorality and
insignificance, while Lemuel seeks a spiritual environment, the peculiar virtue
worthy of kings.

30. Thither, if any misfortune bites me, here the bitten shall live!

הן אם זמן ינשכני / פה יחיו הנשוכים

Lemuel creates a symbolic parallel between his wanderings and the children
of Israel who wandered in the desert after their exodus from Egypt (Num.
21:4-8). The rough conditions of their voyage made them speak against God
and Moses, and as a punishment God sent poisonous snakes to bite them, killing many of the insurgents. After they had repented, God instructed Moses on
how to heal the bitten who had survived. The bite is thus a divine punishment
for skepticism and is associated in the biblical context with degeneration,
but simultaneously also with contrition. Whereas in the biblical episode the
snake bites are real, Lemuel uses them only metaphorically, weaving them
into his new framework. He believes that the city he has reached is free of
immorality and that its people are so virtuous that if he is bitten, meaning that
if he ever slightly deviates from the true path, he will be cured and restored,
as the elders of the city and its judges, responsible for the spiritual guidance
and education, will redress him and all those who transgressed moral norms.
As we will soon discover, the situation will turn out to be just the opposite of
these expectations.

31. the queen of the heights (Jer. 7:18; 44:17, 18, 19, 25),

מלכת מרומים

A distortion of מלכת השמים, the false goddess, probably Ishtar, that the
Hebrews are accused of worshipping in the book of Jeremiah.

32. Their food is the venom [of vipers] (Deut. 32:33; Job 20:14, 16)

כל מאכלם פתנים

The addition of the word "venom" is inspired by Deut. 32:33 and Job 20:14,
16, though I replaced the common translation of פתנים as "asp" or "cobra"
with the more flowery "viper."

33. I shall leave, seek a better neighbor (Prov. 27:10)

אלך אבקש שכן טוב

42   *Chapter 1*

This marks the beginning of the poem's third part, in which Lemuel shares his disenchantment with what he saw in the city, and describes his desire to leave the city so that he may find a better place for his soul.

34. youth are well educated (Prov. 22:6)

תוך עם ומנערים חנוכים

Schirmann edited this as תוך עם מצעורים חכוכים, while David edited it as תוך עם ומנערים חנוכים. Neither understood the meaning of this problematic line. I suggest that this line be perceived as echoing the proverb "חנוך לנער על פי דרכו" (Train up a child in the way he should go, Prov. 22:6) in the sense that Lemuel prefers to go and seek a civilized society, where good morals and education are taught to children from a young age, and justice rules, rather than corruption. This corresponds with Lemuel's earlier use of the metaphor of instruction while referring to the false judges.

35. They shall not favor the poor in feuds (Exod. 23:3), they shall not prefer the poor and the miserable (Lev. 19:15)

לא יהדרו דל בריב, לא / ישאו פני דל ודכים

This verse of Lemuel's poem emphasizes the importance of justice to him. So far, he mainly focused on condemning the discriminatory judges. Here, by alluding to two different biblical sources, he refers to the other extreme, stating that poor people should not be favored in judicial procedures just because they are poor. The first reference echoes a passage from Exodus 23, where the Hebrews receive a handful of instructions and warnings on the subject of justice (Exod. 23:1-9). The specific principle that is described here is "ודל לא תהדר בריבו" (neither shalt thou favor a poor man in his cause, Exod. 23:3). This directive was understood by the sages of the Mishnah and the Talmud and by medieval exegetes to mean that justice must be impartial. Thus, although the rich should give alms to the poor, when justice is meted out a judge should not take a person's financial situation into account while handing down his verdict, and should not find in favor of a poor person just because of their financial status.[25] The second source refers to the same directive, that is, the only criterion in court is justice, and the poor should not have an advantage because they are pitied, nor should the rich enjoy an advantage just because of their wealth: "לא תעשה עול במשפט לא תשא פני דל ולא תהדר פני גדול בצדק תשפוט עמיתך" (Ye shall do no unrighteousness in judgment; thou shalt not respect the person of the poor, nor favor the person of the mighty; but in righteousness shalt thou judge thy neighbor, Lev. 19:15). The Pentateuch emphasizes this principle, which is also found in Deut. 1:17 and 16:18-20.

The Tale of Old Bearded Achbor   43

36. They anticipate the will of their Creator and they hope and wish for His grace (Ps. 37:32)

צופים רצון בוראם ול / חסדו מקווים וחוכים

A pun reversing the psalm "צופה רשע לצדיק, ומבקש להמיתו" (The wicked watcheth the righteous, and seeketh to slay him, Ps. 37:32).

37. They dwell under the protection of the Almighty (Ps. 91:1)

יושבים בסתר שלומים

A variation of the designation of God, whose shelter and protection will become a leitmotif in the tale.

38. They are not concerned by the day of wrath (based on Isa. 13:9 and Zeph. 2:2)

לא יראו יום חרון אף כי אף וחרון שכוכים

A pun based on changing the order of the words, which unfortunately cannot be translated. חרון אף literally means "the ire of the nose."

39. their way is thorny (Prov. 15:19) and dangerous (Eccles. 12:5)

דרכם משוכת חזק וחתחתים

An allegorical description of the path of the corrupt people who walk on roads hedged by thorns and cracks.

Achbor's Preaching in the City Plaza

40. Before I even finished speaking in my heart (Gen. 24:45)

אני, טרם אכלה לדבר אל לבי

This is an "orphan" sequence that does not rhyme with any other. It is possible that the scribe may have omitted a sequence that was there originally.

41. towards the city's central plaza (1 Sam. 17:20)

אל המעגלה

44 Chapter 1

The city's plaza, the central place, the town square, which in Hebrew is referred to as a circle.

42. *Every single man, young and old, was screaming (2 Kings 3:21)*

ויצעקו מכל חוגר חגורה ומעלה

The biblical context (2 Kings 3:21) refers to all the men who may participate in a war. The literal translation is "from each who strap a sword upwards," but there are several ways to understand this choice of words. For example, they might be referring to the simple men who merely have a strap for a sword, as opposed to the higher-ranking commanders, who wear upper armor. According to Gersonides (1288–1344), this means "כל מי שראוי לחגור חגורה ולמעלה מהם" (anyone worthy of a strap and above), or as translated here, from the youngest to the oldest.

43. *it seems that his legs are not moving*

ורוח לא יבוא בין פשע לפשע

Literally, the sentence says: "There was no air (according to Schirmann, no gap) penetrating between one step and another." This is intended to convey the idea that Achbor plays his role as old and lame admirably, walking so slowly and with such small steps that they do not even leave a gap for air to pass through. The play on words is also apparent, as without the vocalization signs, "pessa" (a step) and "pesha" (a crime) are written identically: פשע. This comical description is thus presaging, since Achbor will shortly prove to be a man who passes smoothly from one crime to another. The orthography פשע for step, instead of the more common one, פסע, is already extant in the Pentateuch, for example in 1 Samuel 20:3 and Isaiah 27:4.

44. *the city will be ready for salvation! (Isa. 45:8)*

תפתח הארץ ויפרה ישע

The context required a manipulation of the biblical citation, as the original text is: "let the earth open, that they may bring forth salvation."

45. *His name was Achbor of Mount Tabor*

ושמו עכבור מהר תבור

The mention that Achbor is from Mount Tabor carries significant implications, especially given Mount Tabor's associations with pagan idolatry and

The Tale of Old Bearded Achbor

its exclusion as the chosen site for the giving of the Torah in Midrashic literature. Moreover, Mount Tabor is significant in Christian tradition as the site of the Transfiguration. Against this backdrop, Achbor's character is cast in doubt as soon as he is introduced. His name, derived from one of the kings of Edom as mentioned in Genesis 36:38, further underscores his connection to paganism and suggests a dubious nature. For a more comprehensive discussion of the significance of the name "Achbor of Mount Tabor" as a clue of Achbor's dangerous Otherness, which symbolizes the threat of assimilation, see chapter 4.

46. He had a beard

ולו זקן

The Tale of Old Bearded Achbor includes three central discussions about beards. Achbor's beard is described in detail by Lemuel while recounting his general appearance, and he even composes an entire poem about it. Further on, Achbor himself refers to beards in his sermon, portraying them as signs of morality and immorality. Finally, and most extensively, the beard is the subject of a virulent satirical account. These episodes are commented upon as they arise, in the spirit of this chapter, that is, I emphasize here the biblical phrasing and linguistic issues, enhanced sporadically with some thematic considerations. A more thorough discussion of beards as a literary topos, as well as an interpretation of the specific significance of Achbor's beard, which conveys, I believe, a message about assimilation, can be found in chapter 2.

47. branches were spreading out from it, and they were divided here and there, as [the beard] scattered its stems and its stalks and its limbs and its wings.

וענפים יוצאים ממנה ויחצו הנה והנה כפרוש מברחיה ואגפיה ואברותיה וכנפיה

This image of a man-tree is commented in Atlas in chapter 2.

48. A calf grazed there, it was sprawled there, destroying all its fronds (Isa. 27:10).

שם ירעה עגל ושם ירבץ וכילה סעיפיה

The biblical reference relates to the destruction of the enemy city, which shall be so ruined, that instead of the fortified city it used to be, it will become a deserted wilderness where calves will gather and feed until no branches remain, even for shade: "שם ירעה עגל ושם ירבץ וכילה סעיפיה" (there shall the

46 *Chapter 1*

calf feed, and there shall he lie down, and consume the branches thereof, Isa. 27:10). I manipulated the prophetic biblical quote into the practical present, to fit the vivid returning image of the fantastic beard harboring a variety of beasts and birds, which is reminiscent of the satirical account known as *Misopogon* (*the Beard-hater*), written in the fourth century by Emperor Julien, and discussed further in chapter 2.

While it is plausible to view Yaakov ben Elazar's words as a development of the satirical topos of the *Misopogon*, the allusion to Isaiah's prophesy cannot but hint at the bitter end awaiting Achbor.

49. Under its heaviness, he walked stooped (Psa. 10:10) . . . bent under his burden (Exod. 23:5)

ובכבדותה ילך שחוח. . . / רובץ תחת משאו

In Byzantium, Theodore Prodromos (fourteenth century) wrote a mocking poem against Thoukritos' beard. Just like Achbor, Thoukritos is an old man, with a beard "huge in all its dimensions." In almost the same way as Achbor, he is "Oh, the enormous burden of that beard! / How long it is, how wide, / quite simply, how huge in all its dimension / That is why you're stooping down, old man. / And you wear your bulge and you bend your back! / For that beard is pulling your neck, / As it is quite big, and of immoderate weight."[26]

50. lo and behold, [the congregation] staged a setting for him, they had prepared a chair for him in the street (1 Sam. 15:12, 1 Chron. 18:3)

והנה מציב לו יד, כי הכינו ברחוב כסא

The phrase להציב יד is often used in biblical sources to indicate setting up a monument intended to exhibit a king's dominance: "והנה מציב לו יד" (and, behold, he is setting him up a monument, 1 Sam. 15:12); "ויך דוד את הדדעזר מלך-צובה, חמתה, בלכתו, להציב ידו בנהר-פרת" (and David smote Hadarezer king of Zobah by Hamath, as he went to establish his domination at the river Euphrates, 1 Chron. 18:3). In this case, the verb's subject is not clearly evident. Schirmann and David thought the assembly gathered at the city plaza to be the subject and understood this sequence as if the people prepared a stage for Achbor, upon which they also set a kind of a seat or a chair (*cathedra*) where he would sit while presenting his sermon.[27] It is also possible, however, that it is Achbor who is establishing his (spiritual) domination with his pompous presence and dramatic appearance, which has obviously garnered him some respect, as it seems that the chair was prepared for him in advance.[28] In addition, Lemuel might be playing on the homonyms

The Tale of Old Bearded Achbor 47

יד (monument) and יד (hand) and thus we can imagine Achbor taking control of the situation by lifting his hand for silence or saluting his congregation.

51. as [if he were] an angel [of God] / (e.g., 1 Sam. 29:9, and 1 Chron. 21:15) . . . [divine]messenger

כמלאך . . . אשר מלאך

The word "מלאך" means both an angel and a messenger, two semantics with which Yaakov ben Elazar plays in these two instances. The additions in brackets capture, I believe, the intended irony.

52. If his beard is the beard of truth

אם זקנו זקן אמת

This is the first poem devoted to the beard. Lemuel enumerates seven moralizing actions that a bearer of a "beard of truth" executes in order to bring the sinners to redemption: awakens, atones, chastens, guides, heralds their forgiveness, sweeps their sins, protects and guides them to the Lord's shelter. Lemuel is cautious about the persona that he sees preaching in the corrupt city, and later we will learn that his skepticism was justified, as we will discover that the beard belongs to a religious impostor. The recurring structure "beard(s) of" followed by a moral or immoral attribute (truth, ignominy, villainy, wisdom, shame, justice, honesty, honor, security, disgrace, infamy) serves as a poetical signature. This pattern undoubtedly enhances the personification of the beards and their synecdochical relation to the character of their bearers. An interesting parallel can be drawn here with a Christian theological concept regarding the external beard as a reflection of the inner beard. Constable explored this notion, demonstrating that beards' "hairs were compared to thoughts and especially to evil thoughts and sins which grew involuntarily in the mind."[29]

53. lost or err, he will guide them like a shepherd (Esther 3:8)

נפרדו או יפוזרו / זה כרועה יפקדם

This is another comical turn of the biblical situation. In the book of Esther, Haman uses the same verbs to describe the Jewish people: "ישנו עם אחד מפוזר ומפורד בין העמים" ("there is a certain people scattered abroad and dispersed among the peoples," Esther 3:8). Haman uses these words to state that the Jews remain in segregated communities, disassociating themselves from others and transgressing the king's laws. Here, the meaning is the

48   *Chapter 1*

complete opposite. In his poem of admiration, Lemuel wants to believe that Achbor will assume the role of a true preacher, one that, upon seeing that his flock of believers is lost and erring, will gather them together and guide them back to the righteous path, as a shepherd would.

54. For He will conceal them in His tent, He will hide them in His shelter (Ps. 27:5)

כי בסוכו יחביאם גם בסתרו יסתירם

The metaphorical image of the superior God as sheltering his believers in His concealed shelter, somewhere in the heights is a leitmotif with a certain blurring between the shelter itself (seter, sitro), and the designation of God as the "highest hiding" (seter elyon) translated as "Most High." It is borrowed from the book of Psalms, where the concealed shelter, in the form of a tent, appears several times (e.g., 18:12; 27:5; 31:20-21; 61:5; 91:1). Here Lemuel ascribes a divine action, protecting the righteous in a metaphorical tent, to Achbor, the alleged spiritual leader who will heal the nefarious congregation. On the leitmotif of the Lord protecting the just in His shelter, see further below.

55. his servant boy and his clerk, upon whom he was leaning

לנער משרתו ופקידו אשר עכבור נשען על ידו

Achbor was initially described leaning on one servant, and we may deduce from this sentence that the boy accompanying him is both his servant and his clerk. Later, it will become clear that Achbor has two boys in his service, and therefore I refer here to two men. Achbor was only leaning on one of them, but the second man must have accompanied them.

56. Blessed is the man (Ps. 1:1) who has purified his heart (Prov. 20:9), is worried about his sins (Ps. 38:19) and saddened by his crimes (Isa. 13:5)

אשרי האיש אשר לבו זכה ודאג מחטאתו ומעוונותיו מדוכא

Achbor begins his discourse with the same words that open the book of Psalms, "אשרי האיש" (Blessed is the man, Ps. 1:1), a quite ironic repetition as the words in the book of Psalms applaud those who "אשר לא הלך בעצת רשעים ובדרך חטאים לא עמד ובמושב לצים לא ישב" (hath not walked in the counsel of the wicked, nor stood in the way of sinners, nor sat in the seat of the scornful, Ps. 1:1), whereas Achbor will turn out to be a wicked, sinful and scornful man.

The Tale of Old Bearded Achbor 49

By using the first two praises, "purified his heart" and "afraid of his sins" alternatively, Yaakov may have been presenting here a double reverberation. First, this refers to the idea he explicitly quotes from Psalm 38, "אדאג, מחטאתי" (I am full of care because of my sin, Ps. 38:19). Second, it can be another allusion to Proverbs 20:9, which he quoted a little earlier: "זכיתי לבבי" (I have made my heart clean), and which continues with "טהרתי מחטאתי" (I am pure from my sin).[30]

57. He shall abide in the shelter of the Most High (Ps. 91:1), and shall wait for His mercy, there he shall pitch his tent! (Jon. 4:5)

וישב בסתר עליון ולרחמיו חיכה / וישם לו שם סוכה

The phrase "abide in the shelter of the Most High" is borrowed from Psalm 91:1, where God's conventional appellation as the upper one or the supreme, the Most High, עליון (elyon), is combined with His shelter (seter). Seter can be understood as God's high seat, hidden from mankind. Alternatively, it can metaphorically refer to the man sitting next to Him, who is thus protected by Him, since the Most High shelters him from any danger. This idea will be repeated in the following poem ("for He conceals me under His tent").

58. an extolment, a praise that is befitting of Him (Ps. 33:1).

בהלל לו נאוה תהילה

Achbor preaches to the crowd gathered around him straightforwardly. While he mostly uses the imperative form, he changes from the neutral address, conjugated alternatively in the plural and singular second masculine person, to the personification of the crowd as a young maiden, addressing them in the singular second feminine mode. The transitions from the masculine to the feminine and from the plural to the singular create dramatic effects that must have had performative power, unfortunately lost in the translation into English, where the imperative is identical for all pronouns. For the first transition from the plural "ergo hear the praise" (על כן שמעו נא תהלה) and the feminine singular "I beseech you, lend your ear" (הטי נא אזנך) Schirmann suggested the addition of the word "עדתי," which could be translated as: "I beseech you [my congregation], lend your ear." The children of Israel are commonly personified as a woman in prophetic biblical discourses. Further in his sermon, Achbor refers to the crowd as his daughter and as his people, using a biblical phrase from Lamentations and Jeremiah: בת עמי, the daughter of my nation.

50   *Chapter 1*

*59. lest those who bear hollow (Gen. 41:6) beards of ignominy and impiety,
blighted by evil, carry you astray, and (Gen. 41:5, 22) branches of deception
and dissimulation lead you close to them*

פן ישיאוך בעלי זקן חרפות ומרדים שדופות קדים ואצלינה ילוך ענפי כחש ופחד עולות בקנה אחד

Schirmann did not make sense of the line, ילוך ענפי כחש ופחד, and apparently
neither did David, who followed the amendment that Brody suggested in his
unpublished version, which David had at his disposal. Brody corrected the
manuscript's reading ילוך ענפי כחש וכחד (literally, branches of deception and
dissimulation will accompany or escort you) into ואל יבהלוך אנשי כחש וכחד
(literally: let not men of deception and dissimulation terrify you).[31] My choice
to stick with the manuscript here is based on the idea I believe this statement
conveys. The beard splitting into branches is a leitmotif in the tale, and thus
the modification of "branches" by "men" compromises an important topos.
Moreover, the segment "עולות בקנה אחד" (a biblical phrasing depicting the
corn ears that "burst from one stalk," upon which I will shortly comment) is
hardly comprehendible when referring to "men." Not merely is the botanical description of branches spreading out of a stalk completely coherent, it
plays a role in the bawdy representation of the phallic beard. Branches that
"are elevated in one direction" are an image that perfectly integrates, in vivid
literary tradition, the branches being a metaphor for an erect penis. For further
discussion, see the Segment on penis erectus in chapter 2).

   Another problematic word in the manuscript is what Schirmann and David
read as אבליגה (I shall restrain or I shall control myself, e.g., Ps. 39:14; Job
9:27). This interpretation is not supported in the text, as it is Achbor who is
speaking and it is unclear in what way he would conquer his desire.[32] I suggest that the word should be אצלינה, a plural feminine form of אצל, meaning
"at their place," the subject being, more logically, the branches.[33] Conjugated
with the verb ילוך (accompany, escort), and reverberating with ישיאוך (carry
astray) this conveys the idea that bearers of bad beards would "carry you
astray" by "lead[ing] you close to them," that is, close to corruption, or, as I
argued in chapter 4, to idolatry.

   Hence, the warning expressed in this passage is composed of two images
doubling one another. Each segment is set up as a warning against an action
(ישאוך carry astray; ילוך lead) that bearded imposters (בעלי זקן bear . . . beards;
ענפי branches) can potentially implement upon the innocent victim. In the
two segments the beard is triply debased: First, by two nouns in an adjectival
role (זקן חרפות ומרדים beards of ignominy and felony; ענפי כחש וכחד branches
of deception and dissimulation), and then reinforced by the attribution of a
biblical phrase describing it, creating in the Hebrew text a rhyme:

(שדופות קדים blighted by evil; / עולות בקנה אחד standing firm).

The Tale of Old Bearded Achbor 51

In my translation, the biblical phrasings were replaced by adjectives (worthless;[34] robust).

The two biblical phrases that were lost in the translation are interconnected. They are both quoted from Pharaoh's double dream about the seven fat cows and seven skinny cows who were devoured by the seven bad cows, followed by the seven good corn ears swallowed by the seven bad corn ears (Gen. 41). In contrast to the good corn ears, described as robust (בריאות), good (טובות) and whole (מלאות), the bad ears of corn are depicted as thin (דקות), empty (רקות), lean (צנומות) and blighted (שדופות). While the good ears burst from one stalk (עולות בקנה אחד), which is precisely the phrasing that Yaakov uses to describe the branches of deception in the second section (here translated as robust) symbolizing their richness and prophesizing the plentiful cereals from which Egypt prospers in the following seven years, the bad pieces of corn are damaged by the hot weather caused by the eastern wind (שדפות קדים) (27, 23, 41:6), which is precisely the phrasing that Yaakov uses to describe the beards of ignominy in the first section (here translated as worthless). The beards here are thus analogous to the two types of ears. They are both שדפות קדים (blighted by the east wind) like the bad ears and עולות בקנה אחד (emanate from one stalk) like the good ones. In Achbor's discourse about beards there is no dichotomy, as the two descriptions convey a negative image of the bearded impostors. I believe the first one expresses the idea of hollowness as it is found in Moses Ibn Ezra's (twelfth century) "זרעיו יעשו מגדי מליצה ושבולת תנובתם שדופה"[35] Unlike Yaakov ben Elazar, who kept the reference to the east wind (שדופות קדים), Ibn Ezra dropped it (שדופה). I believe that it is not implausible to argue that Yaakov promoted here the idea of a worthless beard (i.e., illusive, artificial, superficial, hollow[36]) and that while sticking to the biblical phrase in order to preserve prosody and rhyming, the word "kadim" is not crucial.[37] Similar to the biblical phrasing שדופות קדים, whose literality faded to convey the idea of hollowness, the phrasing עולות בקנה אחד also became metaphorical. The biblical idea of the full ears that spread out from a single stalk symbolizes the forthcoming seven years of prosperity for Egypt. Starting in the Middle Ages, this phrasing took the meaning of something that is consistent or compatible with another. As I have shown above, it can be read as a bold image relating the impressive aspect of dense, flowing beards or to the *penis erectus*.

60. Those who seduce with words of books and promises

המפתים בדברי ספר ומילה

A reference to the double seduction, "words of books" may be referring to forbidden books belonging to other cultures, while "promises" may allude to

52 *Chapter 1*

sexual seduction. On the issue of assimilation and idolatry and a fuller explanation of this line, see chapter 2.

61. daughter of my nation, for example, Isaiah 22:4,

בת עמי

On the personification of Achbor's congregation as a daughter, see chapter 4.

62. I shall judge you like adulteresses are judged!

ושפטתיך משפטי נואפות

On the way "the adulteresses are judged," see commentary no. 147.

*63. you may think you found wheat, still you only found thistle (Job 31:40;
Prov. 26:9), this is no feat! (Prov. 21:10)*

תחשוב למצוא / חיטה—ותמצא חוח ולא יוחן

When Achbor's preaching is read out of context, the ideas that unfold in the
powerful demonstrations seem to be genuinely benign. It can be argued that
the sermon itself is not misleading and the messages reflect basic morals.
Nevertheless, as the tale continues and Achbor's transgressions (the same
ones that he warns of in his sermon) are revealed, Achbor's words lose their
gravity. What do sublime words mean when they are uttered by a fraud? What
can the significance of a call to perform charitable acts be, when people who
follow Achbor will be led to a life of debauchery, like the four maidens?

The metaphor of the wheat and the thistle are evocative of the corn-ears
metaphor we saw above, and the passage is also linked to the image of the
gluttonous dog that will soon be referred to.

64. He craves to eat the bread of the poor

יתאב אכול פת דל

This sequence can be translated in two contradictory ways since the verb יתאב
has two contradictory semantics, namely "detests" and "desires." The word
"דל" can be read as either an adjective (poor, meager) or an adjectival noun
(the poor man), both possible interpretations of this verse in Achbor's poem.
We can thus read here "he detests eating a meager bread," or, as appears here
"he craves to eat the poor man's bread." The first option is justified, since the
verse's apodosis prophesizes the abundant feast that Achbor (who will soon
be discovered to be the depraved man that he is now criticizing) is about to

The Tale of Old Bearded Achbor 53

have and contains a vivid description of its delicacies, which is compatible with disliking eating meager bread.

Despite this, the second option, the theme of the immoral man who eats the poor man's food and generally abuses him, is more appropriate here. This theme is reiterated not only throughout Achbor's sermon, but reappears in Lemuel's poem. In addition, we know that Achbor himself has become rich by deceitfully profiting from the townspeople's donations to charity. Perhaps, by using an ambivalent metaphor, Yaakov ben Elazar wanted to combine the two ideas, stating that corrupt men are simultaneously gourmands and takers, and the bread of the poor here is to be understood in the larger sense, as the bread of others.

65. as a glutton dog he is avid to gorge himself on his own vomit (Prov. 26:11, Isa. 28:8)

ככלב שב / אל קיא ומקיא יערוך שולחן

The literal translation of this would be: "as a dog returning to its vomit, and from vomit he draws a feast!" see a detailed consideration of this image in chapter 4.

66. he shall not be vindicated!

ולא יוחן

A repetition of the formula ולא יוחן, which was first used to describe the ungraceful aspect of finding thistle instead of wheat. While the morphology is identical, Lemuel obviously plays on the meanings. The first appearance of the word is derived (per the biblical source) from the word חן (grace), the second derives from the word חנינה (mercy, pardon).

67. for your fortune is your oppressor (Isa. 49:26) and your executioner is your silver!

כי הונך מונך ובצעך כספך

This is the manuscript reading. In David's edition it appears as כי הונך מונך ובצעך בוצעך, which would be translated as "for your fortune shall be your oppressor and your greed, your executioner."

68. Embrace charity (Prov. 1:2) and banish pride, and do not follow lust, lest you shall be scarred and burnt! (Lev. 13:28).

קחי מצווה והרחיקי גאווה ואל תלכי אחרי (התאניה ו) התאווה פן תורישכם צרבת המכווה

54   *Chapter 1*

This flowery passage required some distancing from its literality in the translation. קחי מצוה literally translates as "take or receive a commandment" (mitzvah) and, based on Proverbs 2:12, could have also been translated as "receive [my] commandment." I preferred to translate this word as "charity," as it symbolizes one of the most important social commandments, and the didactic order to perform acts of charity and alms is referred to frequently in Achbor's sermon. As for the word "lust," its graphical presentation in the manuscript is unclear. In his edition's commentary, David suggests that it stands for התאוה. In the manuscript, the word is followed by these two words (ותה והתאוה). The first word is quite blurred but begins and ends with the letters of the word "pride." The second word is quite clearly "pride." Therefore, he edited the word "pride" only once.

While it is logically possible that the inscription ותה could be an error, I believe that the writer did intend to include two different notions by choosing the two words that he chose. One is clearly "and pride" (והתאוה), and while the other is blurred, it was meant to create a harmony with the previous set: מצוה and גאוה. Furthermore, based on the sentence's structure, it is obvious that the writer wanted to insert another duo of notions by using the two manifest definite articles and the conjunction "and" before the second one. Since "ואל תלכי אחרי" (do not go after) appears immediately before, it is apparent that the two notions of the second duo are not dichotomic, as opposed to the first couple. I believe that there must have been four notions: (1) מצוה; (2) גאוה; (3) ?; and (4) התאוה.

It also seems that Yaakov ben Elazar designed a sophisticated graphical analogy between the two couples. We see that (2) *גאוה* and (4) *התאוה* are identical except for their first respective letters and definiteness, and it seems that this should have been the case for (1) *מצוה*, and the unclear (3), as well. In my opinion, the letters seem to form the word *התצוה*, which creates quite an impasse, because התצוה does not have any sense in the context, nor does a double use of the word התאוה (which, in any case, might not be the word written there). This must be a scribal error. I therefore suggest a reconstruction of the word התאנוה, or התאניה.[38] התאניה means a cry of mourning or grief,[39] and is reminiscent of a series of words that are pejoratively used later in the tale: תאנים, תואנה, תאנה, תאונים. This is not an ideal option, as it does not create a perfect analogy of the letters, but it can at least be imagined as referring to a certain negative notion of something that, along with lust, the congregation should avoid. Here I chose "malice," to contradict it with "charity."

Finally, "*צרבת המכוה*" (the scar of the burning, Lev. 13:28) literally means the scars that remain on the body after the inflammations of leprosy. A literal translation is "lest you will inherit the scar of the burning." The meaning is allegorical, hinting that moral transgressions leave their marks, and it is to this sense of the word that I am referring to in the translation.

The Tale of Old Bearded Achbor

69. Would you roll [dice] for the orphan['s fate], and dig [a pit] for your companion? (Job 6:27)

אם על יתום תפילו ותכרו על רעכם?

This is a dramatization, based on Job 6: "אף על יתום תפילו ותכרו על רעכם" (Yea, ye would cast lots upon the fatherless, and dig a pit for your friend, Job 6:27). It alludes to the practice of heartless creditors who toss dice or cast a lot when selling children into slavery, in order to pay off their parents' debts.

70. giving alms covertly soothes wrath (Prov. 21:14)

מתן בסתר יכפה אף

Some biblical commentators (e.g., Joseph Kimhi, Moses Kimhi, Isaiah di Trani, Gersonides) understood this phrase, מתן בסתר (giving a gift in secret, Prov. 21:14), as referring to giving bribes to appease the judges or the leaders. I think, however, that in the tale's context it actually means "giving a charitable donation secretly," following other commentators (e.g., Rashi, Radak).

71. If you wish your gain to be hundredfold (Gen. 26:12), offer a present (Job 6:22) to the people of the Lord (2 Sam. 14:13)

ואם תרצה מצוא מאה / לכל בצע שחד עם אל

While שחד is the common verb used to indicate giving bribery, here it should be understood as giving alms, and we can consider it to be the continuation of the sentence ending the last sequence, מתן בסתר יכפה אף (giving alms covertly soothes wrath). It echoes Proverbs 21:14, where מתן and שחד can be either synonyms or antonyms: "מתן בסתר יכפה אף ושחד בחק חמה עזה" (my emphasis. A gift in secret pacifieth anger, and a present in the bosom strong wrath). In his commentary on this verse, Rashi perceived שחד as synonymous with מתן. See also Job 6:22, where שחד means ransom. This somewhat demagogical statement resonates with "The Fable of the Two Men Who Lived in the Same District," which Achbor is about to tell his congregation. A rich man who initially refuses to offer a present to the pauper, ends up losing a hundredfold: when he changes his mind and is ready to give the poor man four shekels after all, his hand trembles and inscribes on the bill the sum of four hundred shekels, leading to his ruin. A study of this fable can be found in chapter 3.

72. I adjure you in the name of the Most High, to pity the pauper and the indigent

ואני משביעכם בסתר עליון שתרחמו עני ואביון

56 Chapter 1

On the epithet "seter elyon," see chapter 3.

73. As in the fable of the pauper who, at the threshold, asked for bits of food

משל העני ששאל על דלת לפתי מכולת

Here begins Achbor's first fable, commented and studied in chapter 3.

74. the sheltered is supreme to the serpent (Amos 9:3),

נסתר עלי נחש יהי יתר

This sentence is somewhat obscure, and Schirmann did not understand it. David attributed it to Numbers 23:23, where the word נחש means enchantment, and perhaps he saw this as advice to reject things related to paganism, such as magic. Another possible interpretation relates to a previous line from this same poem, "ניצל וימלט בלב ימים" (Saved, he shall flee to the depth of the sea) as well as to Amos 9:3. In the biblical source, it is said that the evil people will not be able to hide from the Lord's fury, and if they try to hide at the bottom of the sea, a monstrous creature will be sent to bite them. Thus, I believe the word נחש is used here in its more common semantic meaning, a snake, or, in the context of the sea, a whale, or a metaphoric creature. This intertextuality allows the line to be understood as prefiguring a symbolic confrontation between those who are "concealed" (נסתר), for example, sheltered in the shadow of the Most High, which in this case is located in the depths of the sea, and those who "hide (from God) in the sea will be bitten by a snake." The former, those who are concealed, represent believers trusting in the Lord. The latter, in contrast to those who trust in the Lord and for whom the sea acts as a shelter, will be deserving of spiritual punishment, administered through the sea snake. These nonbelievers also represent a threat to the devout, ready to entice them at any moment, and are a sort of נחש as the word is interpreted by David, that is, an enchantment or a hint at idolatry. Hence the line affirms that the believers, crowned by Lord's protection, will have the upper hand in their encounter with the "snakes" (i.e., the immoral), just as the light surpasses the darkness, which is another repetitive motif in our tale.

75. I dream of abiding in the shelter of the Most High, only my Savior my dream shall clarify! I shall make a covenant with His Mercy, I shall sacrifice a calf and will adhere to this alliance

אחלום עלי שבתי בסתר אל / אך צור ישועתי יהי פותר

עם רחמיו אכרות ברית עגל / אכרות בתווך אעבור בתר

The Tale of Old Bearded Achbor   57

Achbor becomes somewhat cryptic in these two lines, as he applies intense religious symbolism to emphasize his extreme devotional conviction. First, he describes a spiritual vision, in which he sees himself abiding in God's shelter, to which he is constantly referring. Achbor borrows the idea of dream interpretations from the well-known dreams in Genesis, but the meaning is slightly different here. The Lord is referred to here as צור ישועתי (the rock of my salvation), an epithet for the Lord found in Ps. 89:27. This implicitly conveys the idea that the Lord accepts Achbor under his protection. In this sense, the line is close to the modern notion of "making dreams come true," though this meaning is not conveyed in biblical or medieval Hebrew.

Second, Achbor uses a doctrinal statement, literally "עגל אכרת בתוך אעבר בתר", echoing Jer. 34:18: "אשר לא הקימו את דברי הברית אשר כרתו לפני העגל אשר כרתו לשנים, ויעברו בין בתריו" (. . . that have not performed the words of the covenant which they made before Me, when they cut the calf in twain and passed between the parts thereof). This recalls the sacrificial ritual performed while establishing a covenant: a calf was divided into two pieces vertically, and the parties to the covenant passed between the two parts of the slaughtered animal, symbolizing their commitment. The process described above also echoes Abraham's alliance with the Lord, known as "The Covenant of the Pieces" (ברית בין הבתרים), though then only God passed through the animals sacrificed by Abraham as a symbol of His promise that Abraham's descendants would inherit the Land of Israel (Gen. 15). This is the source to which David is referring here, though the immediate reference is to Jeremiah and the direct meaning is the speaker's affirmation that he is engaged in the alliance he has made with the Lord.

76. Have not you heard the fable about the two men who lived in the same district?

הלא שמעתם משל שני אנשים שהיו באחד מגרש?

This is the beginning of Achbor's second fable, also commented on and studied in chapter 3.

77. leaning upon the Lord's graces (Ps. 68:5)

נשען על חסדי רוכב ערבות

Literally "רוכב ערבות" (He who overlaps the wilderness) a picturesque reference to God, based on Psalm 68:5.

78. God converted his heart into another (1 Sam. 10:9)

ויהפוך לו אלוהים לב אחר

58   *Chapter 1*

The personified heart is presented as the reflection of the protagonists. It represents the pauper's hunger and the rich man's intentions. The words "סעד נא לבב עבדך" usually refer to a meal comprised of a morsel of bread. It can therefore be deduced that the poor man is merely asking for some bread, as found in the same biblical context a few verses earlier (Judg. 19:5 and Gen. 18:5). The phrase "היה לבבי סחרחר," literally, my heart was fluttering (Ps. 38:11), indicates hunger in this context. Another creative epithet for the Lord is "הופך לבבות" (He who turns the hearts over) and Achbor will compose an entire poem about human hearts, describing the Lord as "בורא לבבות," He who creates hearts, or as translated, "The Creator of Hearts." With these words, Achbor lays the foundations for the idea that follows in the next two stanzas, that the rich man's heart was turned around and his initial refusal to give money to the poor man is replaced by his donation.

79. who sows and uproots

הנוטע והמשריש

This is a distortion of Jeremiah 12:2, where משריש means "takes root." The root שרש, however, simultaneously denotes the opposite, that is, uproot, which is the obvious meaning here, as the verse opens with a series of contradictory actions that God can perform.

80. who preserves the faithful and silences the [false] preachers (Job 12:20)

מסיר שפה לנאמנים

Literally, "מסיר שפה לנאמנים" (He removeth the speech of men of trust). The idea in Job is that God can rearrange the order of the world, including depriving the spiritual leaders of their ability to speak. I think that in the tale's context this line should be read as an ironic reference to Achbor himself, the dramatic preacher who is about to be silenced.

81. All are His lowly and haughty (Isa. 2:12, Ps. 138:6). He is the Redeemer of all, the deceivers and the faulty (Job 12:16).

ולו כל נישא ושפל וכל גואלו שוגג ומשגה

While the recurring formula "וישא משלו ויאמר" is missing, the apodosis' ending "ומשגה" confirms that Achbor's last poem begins here (all the lines end with גה).

82. a man rose from among the elders that gathered in the city plaza and said:

ויקם איש מזקני המעגל, ויאמר

The audience member who speaks to the crowd is old, and the way he encourages the mob to respect and donate to Achbor, raises the question of whether he could have been Achbor's accomplice. The dichotomy of beards, which we already noticed both in Lemuel and Achbor's discourses, emerges here again as the man treats it both with reverence "Humble yourself before the length of his beard" and scorn "upon each frond the whelps crouch."

83. upon each frond (Ps. 80:12) the whelps crouch (Ezek. 19:2)

אשר בכל פארותיה רבצו גוריה

See the discussion on the *Misopogon* theme in chapter 2.

84. the best of your treasures (Judg. 8:24, Prov. 31:11)

נזם שללו

According to Judges 8:24, this means "the ear-ring of his spoil," referring to the spoils collected by the Hebrews from the Ishmaelites, the ear-ring being the symbol of their idolatry. In the tale, this phrasing is used as an overstatement, encouraging the audience to be generous and donate the best of their possessions.

85. amongst the crowd (Judg. 5:16)

בין המשפתיים

Literally "among the herds," referring to the herds of people in the city plaza.

86. The people's heart had overturned, it had softened and was impressed

ויהפוך לבב העם ורך ונחת

The image of a melting or softened heart as the expression of fear in general, or God-fearing specifically, is quite common. The verb נחת refers to the way of warriors "ונחת קשת-נחושה" (bend a bow of brass, 2 Sam. 22:35; Ps. 18:35), or the way an arrow penetrates (Ps. 38:3), that is, the hearts of the people do not remain indifferent to the words spoken by both Achbor and the elder. The emphasis on the crowd's hearts that are touched may be due to the fact

60 Chapter 1

that just before the sermon begins, Lemuel has the impression that all of the city's inhabitants are sinners and hopes that Achbor will instruct them to correct their ways.

87. *The Creator of hearts*

בורא לבבות

Achbor's final poem, dedicated to the heart as the poetic emblem of a human being, begins with another reference to the picturesque designations of God, the creator of the human heart.

Feasting with the Four Maidens

88. I shall follow this old man

[אלך] אחר הזקן הזה

Hebrew permits a comical pun that functions as a metonymy. Without the diacritics, "old man" (zaken) is read exactly like "beard" (zakan). Thus, Lemuel could have also been saying here: "I shall follow this beard," especially since the beard becomes a major component of the tale.

89. *put all his goods in his dwelling (1 Sam 17:54)*

וכליו שם באוהלו

The biblical phrasing, "he put his armor in his tent" (1 Sam. 17:54), refers to Goliath's weapons, which were brought back from the battlefield by David after he decapitated him. Goliath's armor, described in unprecedented details (see vv. 5-7) indicating its magnificence, was brought to David's tent, though exegetics disagree as to whether this refers to a tent literally, such as his tent at the army camp, or to David's dwelling in Bethlehem (e.g., Radak). In our context, the objects referred to by the word "כלים" are precious pieces of jewelry, gold, silver, and any other expensive items collected by Achbor's valets after his sermon. As we will soon see, Achbor uses these priceless objects to decorate his home.

90. *the homes of emperors*

כבתי שרי צבאות

The term "שרי צבאות" is commonly translated as "captains of the hosts" (Deut. 20:9; 1 Kings 2:5). I believe that the idea here was to emphasize Achbor's

The Tale of Old Bearded Achbor

excessive wealth. The poetic embellishment the Hebrew language gives to this antiquated biblical phrase does not pass to modern English in a literal translation, and I feel the word "emperor" is more suitable here.

91. the birds and the enclosures (1 Kings 7:17)

העוף והשבכה

Schirmann wondered if when using the word "שבכה," Yaakov imagined a שובך, a dwelling place for the birds. David confirmed this was Yaakov's intention, highlighting the similarity to the Arabic word "subach." The image of birds inside an enclosure indeed makes more sense than the common meaning of the word "שבכה," ornaments constructed of nets, and creates a poetic analogy with the image that precedes it. Only in the richest mansions would we have found gardens with water in basins or pools and birds in special enclosures. It is, however, important to recall that the word "שבכה" also means "a trap" (see Job 18:8). This suggests that Yaakov was, in fact, hinting at the corrupt manner in which Achbor had gained all his riches, and is reinforced by "ככלוב מלא עוף, כן בתיהם מלאים מרמה, על כן גדלו ויעשירו" (As a cage is full of birds, so are their houses full of deceit; therefore, they become great, and waxen rich, Jer. 5:27).

92. The skillets and the utensils (1 Kings 7:50)

והכפות והמחתות

These instruments are two of the objects made of gold by King Solomon for use in the Temple (1 Sam. 7:48-50). Here, they refer to any kind of luxurious tableware (see also: Exod. 25:38; Num. 7:26).

93. Did your tributes come from villains (Ezek. 13:3) or from the gentlemen?

המשאתך מנבלים או מנדיבים?

In the manuscript the word appears as משאתך, but was changed by David into משאלתך. Despite that the modification is unnecessary, as משאתך means "gift," often used when relating to offerings and donations (see Ezek. 20:9). This is an exact description of the situation: Lemuel is disgusted to discover how the alms collected by Achbor are used.

94. I then knew that he was from among the sons of the villains, a mean man of evil acts (1 Sam. 25:3)

ואדע כי הוא מבני הנבלים והאיש קשה ורע מעללים

62 *Chapter 1*

This is a somewhat comical use of the biblical reference. In 1 Samuel 25 we read of Nabal the Carmelite and his wife Abigail. Nabal was an extremely rich man, known to be "והאיש קשה ורע מעללים" (but the man was churlish and evil in his doings, 25:3), words that are also used to describe Achbor. Here this serves as a pun, as the Hebrew pronunciation (and orthography) of the name Nabal, that is, נבל (Naval) is homophonous with the word "villain".

95. yet men painted upon the wall would be preferable (Ezek. 23:14)

וטוב מהם בקיר אנשי מחוקים

This reference is studied in depth in chapter 4.

96. yet hairs all covered with tar would be preferable (Isa. 34:9).

וטוב מהם במו זפת דבוקים

The image here doubles the one that precedes it. Here it is tar, whose attributes, being black, sticky, and odorous, are used metaphorically in a pejorative manner.[40] This is reminiscent of Isaiah 34, a chapter that deals with the destruction of Edom, whose land will remain cursed forever: "ונהפכו נחליה לזפת, ועפרה לגפרית; והיתה ארצה, לזפת בערה. לילה ויומם לא תכבה, לעולם יעלה עשנה; מדור לדור תחרב - לנצח נצחים, אין עבר בה" (And the streams thereof shall be turned into pitch, and the dust thereof into brimstone, and the land thereof shall become burning pitch. It shall not be quenched night nor day, the smoke thereof shall go up forever; from generation to generation it shall lie waste: none shall pass through it for ever and ever. Isa. 34:9-10). It recalls descriptions of Gehenna, where pitch, sulfur (גפרית), or blaze (לבה) run in the rivers instead of water, and where there are constant fire and smoke. The biblical source is relevant here for two reasons. First, Achbor's beard, and his punishment, will soon be associated with hell. Second, the following biblical verses of Isaiah 34, 11-16, evoke the wild voracious birds that will inherit the land from human beings, a sign of humanity's annihilation. Achbor's beard will be later described as a harbor for similar birds.

97. There is a beard so lengthy, but not healthy, in its sin, its inhabitants rot (Ezek. 33:10)

ויש זקן ארוכה—ואין ארוכה / בחטאתה, שכניה נמקים

Literally "there is a long beard but there is no cure," the meaning of these words is perhaps related to the apodosis, according to which all the beard's inhabitants die because of the beard's sins.[41] Here, I replaced the pun ארוכה

The Tale of Old Bearded Achbor 63

(arouka, long) and ארוכה (aroucha, cure) with the rhyme "lengthy / healthy," which is not an exact translation but conveys the idea that is now being repeated for the third time in the poem, that is, that the beard's appearance does not reveal its true nature. It is also possible that there is a bawdy hidden meaning here, referring to sexual impotence.

98. Do they not nurture their beards with their bones' marrow (Job 21:24)? Yet their brains, like their heads, are narrow! (Nah. 2:3)

במחיהם הלא ישקו זקנם / וראשיהם במו מוחם בקוקים

A literal translation would be that their brains and heads are "empty," but I modified this to "narrow" to support the rhyme.

The protasis is based on a metaphorical image from Job, according to which a prosperous man is exaggeratedly described as "עטיניו, מלאו חלב; ומח עצמותיו ישקה" (His pails are full of milk, and the marrow of his bones is moistened, Job 21:24). The idea here is that the vain men irrigate their beards with their marrow, meaning that they focus all their efforts on vainly nurturing their beards. This image works in Hebrew because of two literary devices: The artificial modification of the passive form ישקה (will be moisturized) into the active form ישקו (will irrigate), and, more substantially, the pun based on the phonetic similarity between מחיהם (their marrows) in the protasis and מוחם (their brains) in the apodosis.

99. There are men prosperous as the sand of the seashore (Job 6:3)

ויש אישים כחול ימים כבדים

Literally, heavy as the sea sand, the word "heavy" here refers to prosperous or mighty, that is, in a position to abuse other people.

100. devours sourdough, bread, and sweet confections

ויבלע כל שאור מצות רקיקים

These words provide an exalted image of the voraciousness of the venal and deceitful man, who indiscriminately devours whatever he can get his hands on, including leavened and unleavened pastries. This image resonates with Achbor's previous description in his sermon, when he refers to a man who became wealthy by abusing the poor.

101. Shortly thereafter, four maidens came out (Exod. 15:20)

ויהי עד כה ועד כה—ותצאן ארבע נערות

64 *Chapter 1*

At this point, the four maidens join the tale. Initially, they appear as subservient participants, perhaps servants, in the decadent feast, behaving in a submissive manner. They take care of the practical details, fulfilling all of Achbor's wants; removing his clothes, serving food and wine, playing music and, last but not least, composing poems at his behest. They animate the banquet entirely but automatically, without the filtration of any emotion. They express no subjective will, they do not say anything besides the strophes of the poem that they perform. Even then, the poem does not concern them individually but is a theoretical piece describing the extraordinary power of wine and love. The maidens will appear two more times in the tale, behaving in an entirely different manner. Their contribution to the tale is studied further in chapter 6.

102. They kissed his hands

ותישקנה בידיו

It is important to note that it is never directly indicated that the maidens are Achbor's servants. Yet, this action is a sign of subordination that plausibly implies that they indeed are.

103. profusion of delicacies

כל מאכליו ופרי מעדניו

Both Schirmann and David correctly edited the form found in the manuscript, which undoubtedly reads "פרי מעדניו" (pri ma'a'danav), and which can mean here literally "his delicious fruit" or simply "all his delicacies." Neither scholar noticed, however, the artful biblical references that this phrase echoes. I am referring here to two biblical references, in particular. In chapter 4 of the Song of Songs there are two mentions of the "sweetest fruit" (פרי מגדים, pri megadim) found in the closed garden, which is an erotic metaphor for the Shulamite's body. In verse 16 the beloved Shulamite wishes that her lover would come to "his" garden and eat the garden's "sweetest fruit." "Pri megadav" could have worked admirably here, as it resonates phonetically with "begadav" בגדיו (his clothes, which the maidens had just removed). The second reference I have in mind is the locution "פרי מעללים" (pri ma'a'lalim—the fruit of doing, the results of actions). It appears twice in the possessive form "פרי מעלליו" (pri ma'a'lalav) in the book of Jeremiah, meaning that each man will be rewarded according to his doings, but the word "מעלל" (ma'a'lal) is often used in the context of wrongdoings. "Pri ma'a'lalav" could also work well here, forming a much better rhyme with "מאכליו" (ma'a'chalav, his food). It is precisely with the word "ma'a'lalim" that Achbor was described

The Tale of Old Bearded Achbor 65

in the sequence before ("a mean man of evil actions"). The form "his delicious fruit" may also be a scribal mistake, as the two biblical expressions are so obvious here. Yet, this may also be the author's intentional manipulation, preferring to leave both options valid: the sensual idea conveyed by "the sweetest fruit," that is, an allusion to sexual relations, or "the fruit of his ruses," that is, Achbor's wealth is the result of his hypocrisy.

104. "Awake, perform a song!"

התעוררנה ושיר [ת]דברנה!

The wine song that begins here, including linguistic issues, biblical phrasing, and translation decisions, is covered extensively in chapter 6; therefore, the corresponding verses do not appear here.

105. The first sang and so she said (Exod. 15:21)

ותען האחת ותאמר

The usual introductory line before a figure composes a poem in the maqama is, as we have seen so many times in our tale, "וישא משלו / וישא משלי / ותשא משלה" The formulation ותען va'ta'an is less frequent and here it plays on the two semantics of the verb, ותען sang (e.g., Exod. 15:20-21, which tells of Miriam playing, dancing, and singing with the women after the crossing of the Red Sea. See also Num. 21:17; Ps. 147:7) and answered (e.g., Gen. 31:14; 1 Sam. 1:15; Esther 5:7). It is also important to note that the idea of subordination may be slightly hinted at here, as the maidens are responding to Achbor's demand to engage in singing, which may reflect the hierarchy between them. In their next declamation of poetry, right after their disenchantment from Achbor, the verb introducing the act of enouncing the poem changes from the somewhat submissive (in this context) "replied" into an authoritative "said" (ותאמר, va'tomer).

106. your hands played admirably (2 Chron. 29:31)

ובידיכן מילאתן

The usual meaning of the phrase "למלא יד" (literally to fill one's hand) is "to be consecrated to fulfill a holy function." In our context, the reference to the maiden's hand can only imply her musical talent.

107. keeping silent and feigning [sleep] (Gen. 24:21).

מחריש ומשתאה

66   *Chapter 1*

In the midst of what seems to be the beginning of a bacchanalic celebration, Achbor suddenly falls asleep. This is quite peculiar. Why would a man who is the incarnation of lechery behave in a manner that clearly reflects his lack of desire? We will shortly learn that this is only a lack of desire for the maidens. Achbor very much desires the black Mistress, for whom he "awakes" the minute the four exit.

Men falling asleep as a way of avoiding sexual relations, voluntarily or involuntarily, is a known topos in medieval literature.[42] In Jean Bodel's fabliau *Li Sohaiz desvez* (the dream of pricks), for example, after the merchant's wife prepared an exquisite dinner for her husband and gave him much wine, the merchant fell asleep, neglecting to satisfy her as she had hoped. The wife then falls asleep herself and is taken away by an erotic dream. She is in a market full of penises of all sizes and shapes, and after having chosen the biggest, she reaches out her hand to the seller to conclude the deal, and thus slaps her husband, waking him up. The merchant is awakened literally and sexually, as once he is woken from his sleep, he insists on hearing about the dream. Aroused by the subject matter, he asks his wife how much she would have paid for his organ. Feeling sexually neglected because of her husband's nap, she retorts with a deriding answer: If his penis was placed in a market, it would have never found a client to buy it, being so small. With such provocation, there was surely no more sleeping that night, as the tale ends with the couple having intercourse seven times in a row.[43] While the hurtful words hurled at her husband are spontaneous, they denote the wife's sexual frustration. I chose to mention this example (one of many) in the context of our tale, in order to emphasize the pattern of the topos: women who experience sexual frustration caused by a drunken man's neglect. While at first the women accept the situation (the merchant's wife goes to sleep, and the maidens exit the hall), they end up (in different circumstances) taking revenge on the neglecting man. In *Achbor*, the maidens' violence is not simply due to sexual frustration, but is a circumstantial and comical addendum to the more important issue: Their disgust with the corrupt man.

The Black Mistress

A thorough study of the black Mistress is the focus of chapter 5.

108. From the [other] room a woman exited,

ותצא מהחדר אישה

"A woman exited" is the only time that the Mistress is ever referred to as a human being, with the attribution of the noun "woman." From now on, she

The Tale of Old Bearded Achbor 67

will only be referred to by demeaning adjectives and metaphors. Dehumanized, she is demonized.

109. utterly Cushitic.

כלה (כולה) כשית

The wit of the combination כלה כשית, is somewhat lost in translation. כלה Can be read as either a bride, or as "utterly." As noted by David, this is the manuscript's reading (כלה כושית), and a bit further the word "all" is used again when Lemuel reacts to what he has seen (ויאמר: לכל ניאופים). Schirmann modified the two uses of ה / כל into the word "old" (בלה), editing "אשה בלה כושית" (an old black (or Cushite) woman) here and "לבלה ניאופים" (the old [woman]'s adulteries!) later (see more on that in the corresponding note below). He bases this on Ezekiel 23:43: "ואמר לבלה נאופים" (Then said I of her that was worn out by adulteries). Graphically, בלה / לבלה are quite close to כלה / לכל, and it seems that both interpretations, "old black woman" and "all-black woman," are equally conceivable. On the other hand, the redundant emphasis of her blackness is the aim of the tale, and therefore it seems that a correction of the manuscript is not appropriate here. Moreover, I believe this wording presents us with a parodical echo of two sources. The first is one of the most poetic descriptions of beauty in the Song of Songs, "כלך יפה רעייתי" (Thou art all fair, my love, Song of Sg. 4:7). This echo is ironic, since the beloved referred to in the Song of Songs is also black, as we learn from the well-known verse "שחורה אני ונאוה" (I am black, but comely, Song of Sg. 1:5).[44] By the same token, see the distortion of the erotic image of the fig "התאנה חנטה פגיה" (the fig-tree putteth forth her green figs, Song of Sg. 2:13) in the discussion of the "vile figs," below.

The second source is Numbers 12:1. Miriam and Aaron admonish Moses for having taken a Cushite woman "ותדבר מרים ואהרן במשה, על-אדות האשה הכֻשית אשר לקח: כי-אשה כשית, לקח" (And Miriam and Aaron spoke against Moses because of the Cushite woman whom he had married; for he had married a Cushite woman). According to Rashi however, Moses's black wife was beautiful: "האשה הכושית – מגיד שהכל מודים ביופיה כשם שהכל מודים בשחרוריתו של כושי... כושית בגימטריא יפת מראה... האשה הכשית על שם נויה נקראת כושית כאדם הקורא את בנו נאה כושי כדי שלא תשלוט בו עין" (The Cushitic woman means that all admit her beauty the same way that all admit the blackness of a Cushitic man. Cushit in gematria means good looking, . . . the Cushitic woman is called Cushit, for her beauty, as a man who calls his handsome son Cushi, against the evil eye).

Chapter 1

110. She had a lip similar to a firebrand (Amos 4:11), a remnant of flames, her eyes were like blazes, and her nostrils were flared (1 Kings 6:4; 7:4).

ולה שפה כאוד מוצל משריפה ועיניה כרשפים ואפיה שקופים

This demeaning portrait of the Mistress includes three conventional descriptions used in medieval narratives to refer to demons, often depicted as black characters: the smoky mouth or nostrils and the red eyes that look like flaming fire. Numerous examples illustrating this depiction are discussed in chapter 5. Based on such descriptions, I somewhat modified the literal wording כאוד מוצל משריפה, which would literally read "She had a lip like a *firebrand snatched from a blaze*" (Amos 4:11).[45] In the literary context, it seems plausible that the still-smoking firebrand would be depicted as a smoking mouth or lips.[46]

As for the Mistress's nostrils, Yaakov uses a somewhat cryptic noun, שקפים, rather than an adjective, to describe them. This word is used in 1 Kings (6:4; 7:4), in the context of the Temple's architecture, in order to illustrate the magnificence of its windows, referring either to the frames, the lintels, or the glass that, according to medieval commentators, was transparent from the inside and opaque from the outside. Here it is used as a caricature, meant to emphasize what Lemuel perceives as awful facial features.

111. "nothing but adulteries!" (Ezek. 23:43)

לכל ניאופים

The word "ניאופים" (adulteries) refers to "different types of unauthorized sexual behavior,"[47] but is mostly used to indicate married people having extra-marital sexual relations. Since Achbor is not married, the word here is meant to denote what Lemuel considers to be Achbor's debauchery. It is interesting to link this scene, in which Lemuel lurks and captures the two lovers in action, specifically to conjugal adultery, because it is a subversion of the topos of *flagrante delicto*, capturing an adulterous wife with her lover in the act. The literary topos, which goes back to Homer, postulates that "captured in the act" refers to an infraction of a sexual order, usually the violation of a husband's conjugal rights.[48] In such a situation, it is acceptable for the husband to react impulsively and kill the transgressing adulterers. Another important feature of *flagrante delicto* is the husband's cry, summoning witnesses and ensuring that there is indisputable evidence of the act, that is, it must be clearly witnessed. Like so many other features of our tale, the topos' conventions are distorted here. Under the guise of moralism, Lemuel takes upon himself the role of the cuckold husband and feminizes Achbor, since it is Achbor and not his mistress who is accused, and later judged, as an

The Tale of Old Bearded Achbor 69

adulterer. This is the reason I dismissed Schirmann's suggested amendment of "לבלה ניאופים," which addresses only the Mistress. Later, when Achbor undergoes the "trial of the adulteresses," I will develop this topos further.

112. because I was furious with these lechers (Ps. 73:3)

כי קינאתי בהוללים

The verb used here, קנאתי, has a double meaning. On the one hand, as we saw above, it is symbolically linked to the (symbolic) jealousy of the husband who catches the adulterers.[49] On the other hand, the word indicates Lemuel's true role, to castigate Achbor for his attraction to a foreign culture, embodied in the black woman. Here, the verb refers to the anger felt by the moralistic Lemuel toward one who has abandoned the ways of God.

113. And Achbor said

ויאמר עכבור

Here begins an atypical exchange of words between the narrator and the protagonist. It should be noted that the Mistress has, by now, ended her short-lived role in the tale. She does not participate in the conversations in which she is discussed, nor in the debate about to take place between Achbor and Lemuel. She also does not take part in the following sequence, where the four maidens attack Achbor, precisely because she is a theoretical principle rather than an active figure.

114. The ardents' hearts are not drawn

כי אין לב לבוערים

Achbor refers to Lemuel as representing the "ardent," signifying zealous moralists. It is a somewhat sarcastic use of the word, as "ardent" concurrently denotes promiscuity, referring therefore to people alight with the fire of desire. Hence, Achbor could be easily labeled as ardent himself, yet he ironically casts that adjective on Lemuel, who has beaten him severely, verbally and physically, in the name of morality, thus including him in the group of ignorant zealots who seem to understand nothing about love, but, more profoundly, repudiate any kind of Otherness. This can be compared with בערים in commentary n.117.

115. vile figs (Jer. 29:17)

תאנים שוערים

70 *Chapter 1*

The adjective "שוערים" (vile) is a biblical *hapax legomenon* and its meaning is uncertain. It is related to corruption, spoiling, and abomination, and the same root gave words such as שערוריה (biblical Hebrew, abomination, modern Hebrew scandal) and שערורה (corruption). Here, the adjective depicts black women, but the question is whether this is a positive or a negative depiction. Decontextualized, it would seem to belong to the arsenal of a derogative language suggesting that the women's black color is a sign of their immorality, as are "bad figs with a dark colour," in David's words p. 152. But of course, it is Achbor who celebrates the love of black women, when he refers to them as such. For him, the infamous hypocrite, one should be happy to eat spoiled fruit. See more on that term in chapter 7.

The objectification of the female body and its comparison to fruit is not new. The Shulamite's body in the ultimate song of love, the Song of Songs, is described as such: "קומתך דמתה לתמר, ושדייך לאשכולות. אמרתי אעלה בתמר, אחזה בסנסניו ויהיה נא שדיך כאשכולות הגפן וריח אפך כתפוחים" (This thy stature is like to a palm-tree, and thy breasts to clusters of grapes. I said: "I will climb up into the palm-tree, I will take hold of the branches thereof; and let thy breasts be as clusters of the vine, and the smell of thy countenance like apples," Song of Sg. 7:8-9). As hinted earlier, it seems that Yaakov ben Elazar has chosen to parody the Song of Songs as a means in his ironical discourse. Similar to the modification of "כלך יפה" to "כלה כושית," the vile fig metaphor may be seen as a contrast to the sensual metaphor of the enticing ripe fig and the grapes, whose fruition is a sensual invitation to lovemaking: "התאנה חנטה פגיה והגפנים סמדר נתנו ריח" (The fig-tree putteth forth her green figs, and the vines in blossom give forth their fragrance," Song of Sg. 2:13).[50]

Fruit is a universal sexual metaphor, because of "the intrinsic sexuality of fruit itself. Fruit is the reproductive part of the plant—its sexual organs."[51] More specifically, the fig has been extensively associated with sexuality in the classical languages. In ancient Greece "the figure of the 'fig' served primarily as a metaphor for sexuality. . . . The fig tree with its pendant fruit (suke, suka) represented the male reproductive organs; the single fig (sukon) represented the female genitalia."[52] It is probably the source of the Latin sexual metaphor ". . . late popular Latin *ficus* may have taken on the same 'female pudenda.'"[53] Yaakov ben Elazar may also have associated the word for figs, te'e'nim (תאנים), with the word denoting an act of felony, té'u'nim (תאונים), as both are written identically without the vowel signs.[54] Another possibility is that he associated the word for the single fig, te'e'na (תאנה), not only with the similarly written "in heat," ta'a'na (תאנה), see Jeremiah 2:24 but also as "an excuse to do wrong," to'a'na (תואנה).[55] The role of the figs in the context of our tale and the pun hidden in the word "שוערים" (rotten) will be discussed further in the following commentaries.

The Tale of Old Bearded Achbor

116. Would that my waist was sick, then the figs I will trick. (Ps. 83:4)

יום יחלו מותניי אזי / סוד על תאנים אערים

This concise miniature poem is somewhat obscure because of a series of double entendres and puns. The first is the contrast between two types of figs, embodying two types of women. If earlier "vile figs" was a term with which Achbor referred to black women as an incarnation of rotten (i.e., immoral) women, then by contrast "figs" (סוד על תאנים), that is, regular, good figs, denote fair women.

A second double entendre is based on the contrasting facets of what the "waist sickness," mentioned here, might be. It is obviously a euphemism for Achbor's sexuality, as it is a well-established metaphor for the sickness of his loins.[56] But does it refer to lechery or to its exact opposite, impotence? The third double entendre, by abstraction, is between the cause of the malady and its cure, embodied again in the women-figs. "Good" figs were sometimes used as a remedy, and dried figs were specifically mentioned as an ingredient used in an ointment to heal boils (2 Kings 20:7; Isa. 38:21). "Bad" figs, like other rotten food, can cause indigestion and other stomach maladies. Since we are in a carnivalesque world, everything is blurred and thus everything is possible. Achbor's malady could be the result of either the good or the evil figs. In other words, Achbor's sickness may be his excessive lust for his Mistress, or the opposite, his lack of desire toward the four maidens, a possibility that will be implied again soon, when one of the four fair maidens will refer to him as "crushed testicles." Is Achbor desperately aroused or entirely impotent? Either way, it is only the Mistress who can cure him, either by laying with him as a cure for the first possible condition or by sexually awakening him as the cure for the second. Therefore, the entire matter must be concealed from the four maidens, and that is why I believe the word "סוד" (secret) should be read here as a ploy or a trick, a scheme to maneuver his four maidens into believing that he had fallen asleep, thus curtailing their erotic games.[57]

117. Since only rot is my antidote, learn the remedies, you dolt! (Ezek. 21:36; Ps. 94:8)

אך שעריהן לי צרי, / למדו רפואות, בערים

A fourth double entendre can be found in the cure for that lack or abuse of desire with Yaakov's use of the word "שעריהן," the meaning of which varies according to the selected vocalization. Sha'a're'hen means "their gates," and would be a wanton, though common, innuendo referring to vaginas.[58] This reading would mean that Achbor's loss of sexual drive can be cured with

72   *Chapter 1*

sexual relations. We may further assume, however, that only the "gates" of the black woman can remedy this malady, since the text is ambiguous and does not clarify whether the subject of "their gates" are the vile figs' or the "regular" ones. This is a result of the fact that שעריהן may also be vocalized as sho'a're'hen (though this would be a comical neologism), and, based on the previously discussed שוערים (sho'a'rim, rotten), would be referring to the rotten figs. By wittingly implying a possible transformation of the adjective "vile" into the noun "gates," the two ideas intermingle in this one word and practically become synonymous in this context. Achbor finds a cure to the condition afflicting his loins in either a rotten, that is, vile and therefore black woman, or in her "gates." In other words, the lack of lust caused by a fair woman, or the libido awakened by a black woman, are both assuaged by having sexual relations with a black woman, and even impotence transforms into virility, which is perceived by Lemuel's moralistic eye as lechery.

Finally, there is a play on words in this part of the poem, when Achbor offers a piece of advice to Lemuel and others like him. Earlier, he called these men בוערים, "ardent." Now he calls them בערים, "dolts," encouraging them to learn something about "love cures."[59] The pun Yaakov uses is, once again, based on the phonetic and graphic similarities between the plurals of בוער bo'er (ardent) and בער ba'ar (ignoramus or dolt), whose plural forms sound the same: בוערים (bo'a'rim).[60]

118. You despise the Cushitic. Why? Is she not the pupil of your eye?

מה תמאסו כושית ועינכם לא / תיכון בלי הדרת שחרחורת

In order to properly understand the first stanza in this strophe, we must depart from a literal translation. הדרת שחרחרת literally means "the glory of the blackish," but here it is a personification of the eye's pupil.[61] Decontextualized, this stanza would say "Why do you despise the blackish when your eye cannot function without the existence (literally the glory) of the eye's pupil (literally the blackish)?" This could have been a satisfying translation, closer to the Hebrew literal text. I believe, however, that the meaning conveyed here is slightly different, as it corresponds with a stanza that will shortly be declaimed by Lemuel in his replying poem. While Lemuel speaks of the "good" maiden, he describes her as: "מחמד לכל עין ותפארת" (delight and beauty to all eyes). The literal meaning is a delight and beauty to all eyes, but the pun is based on the deconstruction of the idiom מחמד עין (e.g., 1 Kings 20:6; Ezek. 24:16; Lam. 2:4), which means the thing, or the person, most cherished and treasured. The idiom מחמד עין is synonymous with בבת עין (Zach. 2:12), which means the pupil of the eye, that is, the element with which one is able to see, and by abstraction, it also refers to the most precious thing.[62] Achbor

The Tale of Old Bearded Achbor

did not use the specific term בבת עין, but rather chose another metaphorical image for the pupil of the eye, which also echoes the idea of a precious and beautiful thing. Thus, when we juxtapose the two stanzas it seems that Lemuel repudiates Achbor's images by suggesting an alternative from the same metaphorical field. For Achbor, it is incomprehensible that a man is not fond of black women, and he believes it to be as crucial as the pupil is for seeing, emphasizing the fact that the pupil is also black. For Lemuel, it is just the opposite that is incomprehensible (note the same questioning adverb "מה"): how can a man prefer a black woman over a white one?[63] He replaces the blackness of the pupil in the eye with the radiance of the lily in the hand of a lover ("ברה כשושנה ביד חושק"), but echoes the second-degree sense of the "pupil of the eye" by using a close term, מחמד עין, to suggest that it is not the black, but rather the fair maiden who is the radiant pupil of every eye.

119. I would prefer a blackish [woman] over the bright, because for me she is the light! (Lev. 13:4)

אבחר שחרחורת ואל ברה / כי אחשבנה לי לבהרת

While the protasis of this stanza is quite clear, its apodosis is open for interpretation. First, the two women, the black and the fair, may be the grammatical subject of אחשבנה בהרת ("ba'heret") is a biblical medical term for any white spot appearing on the skin, known in modern terminology as vitiligo, and is phonetically very close to בהירה (be'hira, bright), or ברה (bara, beautiful) which is the qualificative used describing the light-skinned woman. By referring to a fair woman as בהרת, Achbor could be intending it to be an insult, alluding to her unattractiveness by stating that "she looks like a wound."[64] Thus, another possible translation would be: "Prefer a blackish over fair, that I would! Because for me she is like a whitened wound."

Furthermore, it is possible to read the word "לי" either as reemphasizing אחשבנה, that is, in my eyes, for me, or as an indirect object, implying that the malady is Achbor's, that is, "I consider her as my 'white spot,'" hinting again euphemistically to his loin illness, i.e., "she causes me my sickness."[65] Thus, Achbor would be using another image based on a pun from his arsenal of medical associations. The pun is established since the dichotomy between black and white receives its power from the name of a pigmentation malady, and Achbor outsmarts Lemuel once again. For him, the color white is a synonym for a disease, as opposed to Lemuel, who sees it as synonymous with innocence.

I have selected here a third possibility, suggesting that the Mistress is the subject, she is the "baheret." In this case, the term serves not to denote a malady but rather as a phonetic pun, meaning that in Achbor's eyes the black

74 *Chapter 1*

woman is ironically bright, that is, she is glowing. I preferred this reading, as it corresponds with other instances in the text where we are presented with the idea that the Mistress can be perceived by Achbor as glowing (e.g., "הדרת שחרחרת," and later "והשחורה כאורה").

120. *Her dark shins for me glow, open to me whenever I'm low*

כתמו בשוק צלמה וחתולה / אל יד שערים או לפי קרת

The last stanza is the most arcane. In the manuscript, the protasis's detectable words כתמו בשוק צלמה וחתולה, are incomprehensible, and both Schirmann and David transcribed the letters and left them without vowel diacritics to mark that they were unable to decipher their meaning. Perhaps the image כתמו בשוק צלמה could be referring to the external signs of the malady evoked in the previous stanza. כתמו, "its mark," would be the medical white spot, and here it is found on the שוק, the shin, which echoes the sensual body. Since צלמה is a word describing darkness,[66] it would support the earlier assumption that "baheret" refers to the Mistress.[67] Appearing together and edited, this can be translated as "its mark is on her dark shin." The specific word used here, כתם, is usually ascribed to the glow of gold, hence the image is clarified by connotation. The white spot "glows" on her black body, meaning that the source of the symbolic (sexual) malady is the desire for a black woman.

The word "חתולה" poses a problem. It could be referring to the cure, that is, the dressing applied to the afflicted zone by the Mistress, found in the place described as "אל יד שערים או לפי קרת," which I will discuss shortly. In this case, however, I suggest we return to the assumption that it is Achbor who has the "baheret" and he is the one seeking a dressing or a cure. We must therefore conclude that either the scribe missed something or made a mistake when copying the text, or perhaps the writer intentionally left the text blurred to allow for varied readings.

In any case, the place where the dressing or cure is to be found, "אל יד שערים או לפי קרת," is a biblical phrasing found in Proverbs: "ליד-שערים לפי-קרת" (Beside the gates, at the entry of the city, 8:3, see also Prov. 1:21), describing two of the many dwelling places of divine wisdom, frequently personified in Proverbs as a good wife.

Based upon the previous mention of the Mistress's gates, and combined with the word פי (entrance, opening, also mouth),[68] this may be a duplication of the idea that the lower section of the Mistress's body is a cavity that offers a cure for Achbor's infamous sickness. This is also befitting her representation as a prostitute, as Lemuel will soon imply in his upcoming castigation. As we shall see, this castigation borrows from the parable of the foreign seductress described in the book of Proverbs, who is contrasted with

The Tale of Old Bearded Achbor 75

the personification of the divine wisdom as the good wife and who speaks ליד-שערים לפי-קרת. Achbor is on the verge of desacralization when he modifies the symbol of divine wisdom, using the verses attributed to her to refer to the questionable Mistress.

It should also be noted that without vowels, שוק could also be read as "the marketplace," or the streets, the path that is taken by the foolish man on his way to the foreign woman (see Prov. 7:8). Thus, it is also possible that the reference to streets and the entrance to the city are meant to link this passage to the upcoming depiction of the Mistress as a prostitute.

While this translation is far from literal, I hope to have captured in it the different elements composing the stanza, relating them to the entire tale.

121. I retorted to his senselessness: "Answer the fool, according to his silliness!" (Prov. 26:5)

ואענהו על חסרון דעתו: / "ענה כסיל כאולתו!"

Once again, Lemuel portrays Achbor's adherence to the Mistress as proof of his lack of reason. and His supposed foolishness embodies his deviance from the divine wisdom, and by extension from the ways of God, as Lemuel's repeated allusions to the book of Proverbs suggest. The Mistress, as we will see, is thus the reflection of the beguiling aspects of any moral transgression, which may lead to assimilation and paganism.

122. What shares the blackish, whose stench shall stir / With the maiden, perfumed with myrrh? (Song of Sg 3:6)?

מה לשחרחורת אשר תבאש / ולנערה במור מקוטרת?

Reacting to his bold poem, filled with bawdy justifications regarding his attraction to black women, Lemuel answers with a poem of his own, composed as a didactic admonishment. Continuing Achbor's essential dichotomization of the black and the white, Lemuel emphasizes the exact opposite. Lemuel's poem is broadly analyzed in chapter 5. I include here some complementary considerations and needed amplifications.

123. In the hand of a lover, a lily so bright

ברה כשושנה ביד חושק

The metaphor "like a lily," is found in Hosea "אהיה כטל לישראל, יפרח כשושנה ויך שרשיו, כלבנון" (I will be as the dew unto Israel; he shall blossom as the lily, and cast forth his roots as Lebanon, 14:6), and once again in the Song of

76 *Chapter 1*

Songs "כשושנה בין החוחים" (as a lily among the thorns, 2:2). I develop on this issue in chapter 5.

Positioning this lily "in the hand of a lover" reverberates as a complementary image of the maiden holding a glass full of red wine or a sword in her hand, as depicted in the wine poem.[69] Now, in what Lemuel considers the good, normative way of loving, the worthy man is presented as holding in his hand the charming flower, reminiscent of the flowers that the beloved of the Song of Songs gathers in his hands, "דודי ירד לגנו, לערגות הבשם לרעות, בגנים, וללקט, שושנים. אני לדודי ודודי לי, הרעה בשושנים" (My beloved is gone down into his garden, to the beds of spices, to feed in the gardens, and to gather lilies. I am my beloved's, and my beloved is mine, that feedeth among the lilies, 6:2-3). The flower is conventionally a metaphor for the innocent maiden, a flower that is about to be deflowered, but in a courtly manner. This idea is best represented in medieval literature by the allegorical *Roman de la rose*, written initially in the first half of the thirteenth century by Guillaume de Lorris, which tells of a lover who falls in love with a rosebud, and his metaphorical quest to pick it.

The biblical occurrences of the combination "in the hand of . . ." are innumerable, referring, for example, to arrows in the hand of a competent soldier (see Ps. 127:4, "כחצים ביד גיבור," as arrows in the hand of a mighty man). The matching allegorical image can be associated with, for instance, a verse from Isaiah "והיית עטרת תפארת ביד ה" ("Thou shalt also be a crown of beauty in the hand of the Lord"). I specifically refer to this verse because of its use of the word "beauty," encountered in the verse's apodosis. The biblical context refers to the allegorical relations of Zion and God as bride and groom.

124. to every eye, beauty and delight (Ezek. 24:25)

מחמד לכל עין ותפארת

מחמד עין is a common idiom, meaning a thing that is precious and adored, and is similar to בבת עין, the pupil of the eye. Although it is found several times in the scriptures, I think the occurrence closest in meaning is found in Ezekiel 24:25, where it extends, like here, the word tif'e'ret: "משוש תפארתם; את מחמד עיניהם" (the joy of their glory, the desire of their eyes). See also commentary 118.

125. But every black [girl] is heartless, / tantalizing (Hosea 7:11; Prov. 9:13), vociferous and devious.

כי כל שחורה היא בלי לבב / פותה והומייה וסוררת

These four demeaning attributes: heartless, tantalizing, vociferous, and devious, form three pairs, evoking three biblical sources: heartless / tantalizing;

The Tale of Old Bearded Achbor

tantalizing / vociferous; and vociferous / devious. In Lemuel's eyes, the Mistress represents Achbor's folly, blindness, and deviance from the right path. The menace of assimilation that Lemuel confers on the black woman is manifested by a series of reverberations to biblical verses concentrated in his chastising words and requires a hermeneutic reading.

Heartless / Tantalizing: The combination of the two first attributes, בלי לבב פותה, is reminiscent of a verse from the book of Hosea, dealing with the tribe of Ephraim's assimilation to paganism "אפרים בעמים הוא יתבולל" (Ephraim, he mixeth himself with the peoples, Hosea 7:8). The entire tribe is compared to a brainless bird: "ויהי אפרים כיונה פותה אין לב" (And Ephraim has become like a silly dove, without understanding, Hosea 7:11) and its members are mocked for being unable to understand the consequences of their errancy from the ways of God. Achbor is accused of a similar transgression. Lemuel refers (or: previously referred) to Achbor's adherence to the woman, symbolizing the "other," as stemming from his lack of reason.[70] Yet, I argue that the words "בלי לבב פותה," referring here to the Mistress and not to Achbor, serve as an ideological, rather than a semantic, association to the biblical source. What was earlier insinuated, namely that the black woman represents the fear of assimilation, is reinforced by the allusion to one of the tribes of Israel that had done just that. I would not, however, apply the same semantic meaning for the words "בלי לבב פותה" as in Hosea. For בלי לבב, I prefer "heartless," and for פותה, "tantalizing," two words to which I shall return shortly.

Tantalizing / Vociferous: The combination פותה והומייה echoes the manner in which the allegorical personification, Folly, is presented in the book of Proverbs: "אשת כסילות המיה פתיות ובל ידעה מה" (The woman Folly is riotous; she is thoughtless, and knoweth nothing, 9:13). The word "פתיות" means nonsense and is from the same root as פותה. Folly is personified as a prostitute, and medieval exegetes understood פתיות as the object of הומיה, that is, the words that Folly shouts to entice her victims. The foolishness that Folly represents is the deviation from the divine wisdom, and hence for Radak "The foolish woman, she speaks words of nonsense and yearns in a loud voice, words of derision, and you cannot understand what she puts forth out of her mouth, if it is good or evil."[71] Gersonides, on the other hand, understood the verb פתה to mean "to seduce or entice," thus explaining this quote as "the woman Folly raises her voice to say [words of] seduction, to seduce the men."[72]

Lemuel's words direct us toward an interpretation of a sexual nature. The Mistress is a bad woman: she is the pagan from Hosea and the prostitute from Proverbs. As such, פותה should be read as מפתה, that is, to seduce sexually or to a sexual act. If we prefer to remain with the same verbal stem (pa'al),[73] פותה also means to open her mouth or her lips negatively,[74] that is, to gossip, betray a secret, or mislead.

78 *Chapter 1*

The idea of heartlessness returns in the book of Proverbs in a reference to Folly, who is said to entice he who lacks a heart, that is, a senseless man (9:16) "חסר לב," into behaving sinfully "מים גנובים ימתקו ולחם סתרים ינעם" (Stolen waters are sweet, and bread eaten in secret is pleasant, Prov. 9:17). In addition, he who follows Folly "ולא ידע כי רפאים שם בעמקי שאול קראיה" (He knoweth not that the shades are there; that her guests are in the depths of the netherworld, 9:18). As we have seen, Lemuel emphasizes Achbor's lack of reason. He is the type of man to whom Folly calls to suggest her body "מי פתי יסר הנה וחסר לב ואמרה לו" (Who so is thoughtless, let him turn in hither; and as for him that lacketh understanding, she saith to him, Prov. 7:16). As the biblical source warns, Achbor will soon be doomed to the depths of the netherworld as his cadaver will be thrown unburied into a pit.

Vociferous / Devious: Finally, the combination הומייה וסוררת recalls another chapter from Proverbs. In fact, the Folly mentioned in Proverbs 9 can be seen as a development of the foreign woman described in Proverbs 7 as "המיה היא וסררת" (She is riotous and rebellious, 7:11).[75] Here, הומייה is consistent with the meaning we saw above. It is used pejoratively to refer to the stereotyped female boisterousness, or to the uttering of flattering words intended to lead to sexual commerce.[76] סוררת literally means rebellious, but in the context of the foreign woman discussed in Proverbs, the rebellion is of a sexual nature, a revolt against her husband, to whom she is unfaithful.[77] It can also be perceived allegorically, as deviating from the right path.[78] The word "devious" seemed a better choice here to transmit what I believe to be Lemuel's meaning, emphasizing her scandalous, disgraceful, and outrageous nature. While stressing the fact that she is a foreigner, thus alluding to her paganism and Otherness, she is also conceived, like Folly, as a whore or an adulteress, which are quite interchangeable in the sense that as either a prostitute or an unfaithful wife, she is clearly an abhorred seductress.

The boy who follows her and succumbs to her fatal seduction, is, too referred to as, חסר-לב (void of understanding, Prov. 7:7). His "heartlessness," that is, foolishness and naiveté, is contrasted by the heart of the seductress, which is present but unseen: "והנה אשה לקראתו שית זונה ונצרת לב" (And, behold, there met him a woman with the attire of a harlot, and wily of heart, Prov. 7:10). The meaning of ונצרת לב was understood in exegetics as shameless ("who is not ashamed of what she does," Radak) or senseless (according to Gersonides, the harlot uncovers her body to seduce her victims, but covers her heart, that is, her mind).[79] In a way, then, both the boy and the seductress lack a heart. The pagan, the whore, the foreign adulteress, all represent, according to Lemuel, the same fatal danger. The man who is vulnerable to such threat is the man who lacks a heart (אין לב and חסר-לב), a man that has no reason, whose faith is feeble. More globally, taken as an emblematic organ the meaning of the heart may alternate between denoting the organ of emotions and faith, wisdom and sense, and

The Tale of Old Bearded Achbor   79

sincerity and faithfulness. In sum, the heart is synonymous with everything that is positive about human beings. Consequently, its lack bespeaks symbolic inhumanity, a lack of consciousness and sense. All these options are befitting of Lemuel's perception of the heartless, בלי לבב black woman.

126. I shall say the word of the Eternal (Judges 3:19) to every Cushitic maid: / "Turn back, return to where you were made!" (Ezek. 21:35).

אמר לכל כושית דבר סתר: / "שובי, לכי במקום אשר נבראת!"

This stanza is reminiscent of exorcism formulas. In that sense, דבר סתר can be seen here as referring to "the word of the Eternal," since exorcism is conventionally implemented in the name of religious devotion. In addition, as has already been discussed numerous times, the word "סתר" is frequently used in the tale as referring to the divine. Furthermore, even in the biblical source, the "דבר סתר" (secret thing, Judg. 3:19) that is about to be told to the king, is actually דבר אלהים (God's message), as the following verse reveals.

127. Then I said to him: "Achbor, what is wrong with you? Why are you drinking from such murky water?" (Jer. 2:18)

ואומר לו: "מה לך עכבור לשתות מי שיחור?"

See chapter 7 for a discussion of this question.

128. He retorted and so said: "Surely, all those who like fair girls are riders of white she-asses" (Judg. 5:10)

ויענני לאמור: "הלא כל אוהבי נערות ברות, רוכבי אתונות צחורות"

This, too, is considered in chapter 7.

129. They did not know and they did not understand (Ps. 82:5)

ולא ידעו ולא הבינו

According to Schirmann and David, ולא ידעו ולא הבינו is the predicate of the beards' hairs. It expresses the total oneness of Achbor and his beard. Metaphorically, the hairs, which represent Achbor, cannot discern the black from the white and, by extension, moral from immoral. The biblical phrasing here concerns the false judges, who do not hear nor understand the biblical poets' instructions about justice, and therefore wander in darkness: "לא ידעו ולא יבינו בחשיכה יתהלכו" (they know not, neither do they understand; they go about in darkness, Ps. 82:5).[80] The biblical apodosis is not part of

80 *Chapter 1*

the quote, but it is certainly referred to contextually. Upon recognizing the citation, the medieval reader was surely led to make the association between the immoral judges who walk in the darkness of ignorance, and the immoral Achbor (or his beard), entirely ignorant and blind to his immoral actions with the Mistress. Another allusion to this apodosis will be discussed below.

It is also possible that the maidens are the subject of these verbs. This explanation would imply that the maidens did not understand how, for Achbor, "the bright seems as black and the black as the light."

130. the bright seemed to him as black and the black as the light (Ps. 139:12)

והברה כנגדו כשחורה והשחורה כאורה

In Psalm 139, the biblical poet praises the omnipresent God from whom no one can hide, not even under the darkness of night, for to the Lord "ולילה כיום יאיר כחשיכה כאורה" (but the night shineth as the day; the darkness is even as the light, Ps. 139:12). In terms of poetic means, Yaakov ben Elazar duplicates, in a subversive manner, the same structure of the biblical verse, by repeating the same idea using different words and condensing the number of words. The protasis ולילה כיום יאיר becomes והברה כנגדו כשחורה and the apodosis כחשיכה כאורה becomes והשחורה כאורה. The first subversion is implemented by substituting three out of the four nouns denoting notions (night vs. day, darkness vs. light,) with the qualifying (and therefore subjective) adjectives, denoting mostly the two kinds of women. The second subversion is manipulated by minimizing the poetical vigor, reducing the four elements of comparison into three, and using the word "black" twice. The third subversion is the replacement of the elements' order in the protasis. The biblical synonymous parallelism becomes a chiasmus (it is almost a perfect antimetabole). It is not merely a technical distortion, but also inserts the idea of divine order and mastery into the chaotic nature of "the world upside down," which characterizes the tale. With the closing sentence of this sequence, Lemuel reminds us of the well-established symbolic distinction between these essentially opposing elements. In Job 30:26, "כי טוב קויתי ויבוא רע, ואיחלה לאור, ויבא אופל" (yet, when I looked for good, there came evil; and when I waited for light, there came darkness). The biblical source emphasizes the literal meaning of the opposing elements (night vs. day, darkness vs. light), implying that the Lord is both omnipresent and omnipotent. Night and darkness are archetypally negatively associated in the human imagination, hence the biblical poet wrongfully thought that they would be his only chance to hide from the Almighty, but for God there is no hierarchization. He can see alike in both light and darkness. Lemuel ironically manipulates this verse, implying that just as night and day and darkness and light do not have an influence on the Lord's greatness, that is, they are equal, in Achbor's eyes a black woman and

The Tale of Old Bearded Achbor   81

a fair one are equal. As opposed to the divine impartiality which celebrates
God's supremacy, though, Achbor is denounced for his moral weakness,
since, according to the tale's context, not knowing "black" from "white" corresponds to not knowing wrong from right, immoral from moral.

*131. Who could reverse his lust for black women? (Jer. 2:24), For they are
tenebrous*

ותאוותו מהשחורות מי ישבינה כי אפלות הנה

This is Lemuel's last sentence before he puts an end to his exceptional intru-
sion into the plot, and returns to his position as an external narrator who, for
the rest of the tale, will limit himself to providing descriptions. In his final
words in his role as part of the story, Lemuel corrects Achbor's misconcep-
tion that "black can be seen as white" with his somewhat redundant repetition: "they [black women] are tenebrous." The word "אפלות" appears in Isaiah
in another example, demonstrating the fundamental opposite qualities of dark
and light, as seen above: "נקווה לאור והנה חושך לנגוהות באפלות נהלך" (we look for
light, but behold darkness, for brightness, but we walk in gloom, Isa. 59:9).

This repetition plays with the Mistress's skin color and its symbolic meaning of moral darkness. Moreover, the specific form אפלות is closely related
to the notion of hell and death, notions that will be discussed below. They
are also connected to the image of the foreign woman we discussed earlier,
who traps her victims "באישון לילה ואפלה" (in the blackness of night and the
darkness, Prov. 7:9)

In Blame of the Beard

One leitmotif in the tale is the vacillation between the positive and negative
images reflected by the beard. The first occurrence of this motif is when,
astounded at the sight of this beard, Lemuel wonders if "his beard is the
beard of truth," in which case Achbor, so he believes, will inspire the crowd
to renounce their sinful behavior. Once he realizes that Achbor is not the poor
and pious man he presents himself to be, he refers to the beard as "a beard
whose bearer is a man of deceit."

The next section contains four discourses that keep us in the binary rhythm
of the whole structure, as they are set as two pairs of two. The first two maidens perceive the beard as a referent of aberrant sexuality, and the second pair
of maidens as a referent to a scatological attack.

132. The crushed testicle (Lev. 21:20)!

מרוח אשך

82 *Chapter 1*

"Crushed testicle" is a biblical term referring to a physical condition (an innate infirmity or mutilation) that is used here metaphorically as an offensive sexual insult against Achbor.[81] As we have seen earlier with the reference to Achbor's "loin / waist illness," "crushed testicle" can also be understood in two complementary ways. It may imply a provocative allegation of impotence meant to undermine Achbor's manhood. Since earlier, after frolicking with the four maidens, Achbor pretended to be falling asleep, it is plausible that, in her anger, the maiden would call him impotent. The term "crushed testicles", however, may imply the opposite, referring to the carnal behavior displayed by Achbor upon being joined by his Mistress.[82]

Addressing Achbor with such furious words, the maiden may have been expressing her jealousy as a rejected woman.[83] Yet, I believe that her expressed offense at Achbor's so-called unfaithfulness to her and her friends is superficial, merely a cursory mimesis of a jealous mistress compatible with the "materialistic" embodiments of the situation. If we only look at it literally, we indeed see a woman who was expelled from the palace of delights, along with the other three maidens, because Achbor had fallen asleep. But beneath the surface the Mistress represents much more than another woman, she embodies Achbor's substantial transgressions of *avoda zara*, and the maiden's fierce anger is not about love, but rather about the much worse immoral behavior that Achbor displays.[84] In sum, the maiden may be voicing both a personal (her immediate displeasure) and a general (the tale's main intention) offense.

133. he dug in the darkness (Job 24:16)

חתר בחושך

A sequence in Job 24 considers sinful people, stating that the murderer kills his victims, the poor and the miserable, in the morning, while the thief steals at night (14). Likewise, the adulterer secretly fornicates during twilight: "חתר בחשך, בתים: יומם חתמו למו לא ידעו אור" (In the dark they dig through houses; they shut themselves up in the day-time; they know not the light, 24:16). Such villains build their homes in the dark, metaphorically meaning that they perform their evil deeds under the darkness of night. Yosef Kara interpreted this verse to mean that the adulterer "sleeps the entire day, and in the dead of night he awakens and seeks adultery."[85] Though for Kara the term "adultery" refers to procuring the services of prostitutes, this description is also reminiscent of Achbor's pretended slumber, from which he "awoke" to meet his Mistress. The appearance of the phrase "סתר פנים" in this stanza is also noteworthy. Previously, I discussed in depth the repetition of the word "seter" as describing God or God's protection. Here, it appears in a more literal meaning, related

The Tale of Old Bearded Achbor 83

to the adulterer covering himself while perpetrating his sinful act. However, a reader versed in the Scriptures would not miss the sarcastic layer added by the context of the words. Achbor had previously implored his listeners vigorously to aspire to the divine hiding place. Now the maiden reminds us, indirectly, that he himself hides his transgressions. Another interesting reference is found in Job 24:17 "כי יחדו בקר למו צלמות כי יכיר בלהות צלמות" (For the shadow of death is to all of them as the morning; for they know the terrors of the shadow of death). In his commentary on this verse, Rashi writes that the transgressor knew the "terrifying demons but was not afraid of them" (שדים המבהילים, ולא היה ירא מהם). Rashi also stresses that according to the Sanhedrin tractate, such transgressors hid fruit in the homes they wished to rob (or to fornicate) so they could find them later by following the smell. Similarly, as we have seen previously, the Mistress is referred to as demoniac and odoriferous. Finally, medieval biblical commentators associated Job 24:16 with Amos 9:2 "אם יחתרו בשאול" (Though they dig into the nether world), which seems to be relevant here, since hell is also a leitmotif in the maidens' current discourses. In sum, this example demonstrates how deeply the hermeneutic reading of the biblical phrasings can go. The maiden merely uses a sequence from one verse, turning it into a debasing image of sexual intercourse (i.e., dug in darkness), but subconsciously the unquoted context of the biblical source is evoked to echo several of the tale's main features.[86]

As we can deduce from the last verse quoted by the first maiden, it seems that Achbor incorporates all the various sinners mentioned by Job: He abuses his congregation during the day and fornicates during the night. Night, however, is merged with the Mistress, and the Mistress is merged with her sexuality, as all of them (the night, the Mistress, and her body) are referred to, pejoratively in this context, as "darkness." There is thus a double meaning to the maiden's allegation. Achbor had offended her by betraying her in the darkness, that is, secretly, but this betrayal goes beyond individual infidelity as, shockingly, he was fornicating specifically with a dark woman, representing general moral errancy.[87]

134. engendered awe and reverence in the hearts of those who saw it (Ezek. 26:17) [But] it reaches until the lowest hell (Deut. 32:22).

נתנה בלב רואיה מורא וחיתית ותיגע עד שאול תחתית

The new topos introduced here is the coarse association of the beard with the anus, and, by extension, of the rectum with hell. [88] The beard will be described several times by the four maidens as covering Achbor's nether body,[89] and they also repeat that Achbor is heading toward the Netherworld. The literal sense of the nether region, that is, the Netherworld, is fused with

84   *Chapter 1*

its figurative sense, as a common metaphor for the anus. This is both a
scatological provocation aimed at caricaturing Achbor and an annunciation
of Achbor's approaching end as conceived by the maidens, which is his sure
journey to hell.

*135. Its invigorated branches are a refuge for conies. Between one section
and another is a hideout where foxes wander, and the fleas have fallen asleep
within it, as they have been there for a long time. (Ps. 104:18)*

וענפיה רעננים מחסה לשפנים, בין פוארה ופוארה מחבוא שועלים
הילכו בו ופרעושים שם נרדמים, כי ארכו להם שם הימים

Here, and throughout her subsequent poem, the maiden manifests a comical
talent by developing a fantasized discourse, reminiscent of the *Misopogon*
by Julian, describing the beard as a wild forest in which animals and insects
dwell peacefully. See below commentary 138 and, in more detail, chapter 2.

136. Achbor's beard is the beard of the fools' pastor

זקן עכבור—זקן רואי (רועי) אווילים

I chose to follow here Schirmann and David's amendment of רואי (the manuscript reading) to רועי, the shepherd, or by abstraction the pastor, the spiritual
shepherd, of the foolish, based on "רעה אוילי" (a foolish shepherd, Zech.
11:15). Here too the meaning is allegorical, as the flock are the people and the
shepherd is their spiritual leader, though the adjective describing the shepherd
has transformed into the noun describing those who follow him. This correction is not essential, as staying closer to the manuscript would have resulted in
"seers of the fools." The two ideas are quite close to one another, presenting
Achbor as a false spiritual authority who causes people to deviate from the
right path. Two other biblical sources are also relevant in this context. First,
shortly after using the metaphor of the foolish shepherd in Zechariah, we
find רעי האליל (worthless shepherd, Zech. 11:17) meaning incompetent shepherd, or, as was the common reference in the Middle Ages, pastors of idols
(or pastors of the believers of idols). By abstraction, this refers to impostors.

    There is yet another way of deciphering the meaning of these words, as it is
possible that the letter פ was accidentally dropped (or deleted) from the manuscript. This would give us רופאי אלילים (physicians of no value, Job 13:4), col-
loquially translated as "witch doctors," and would mean that Achbor is being
referred to here as a charlatan. This possibility, of a missing letter that should
be restored, is quite plausible, since it is most likely that medieval Spanish
Jewry distinguished phonetically between א and ע, as in Arabic. More importantly, the image of Achbor as a charlatan posing as a doctor is repeated in

The Tale of Old Bearded Achbor 85

the second maiden's discourse. In any case, "impostor" and "charlatan" are entirely interchangeable here, just as a good preacher can be metaphorically referred to as a healer. It is also quite possible that Yaakov ben Elazar had both sources, Zechariah and Job, in mind. Comparing Achbor to either an impostor or a charlatan, the first maiden thus inaugurates an ironic circle of alternations between Achbor's true state of moral illness, and his presentation as a false physician or pastor.

137. so vigorously (Isa. 40:26) until it has no strength at all! (Isa. 7:13; Ezek. 24:12).

ברב אונים עדי הלאות תאונים

This sentence is attributed to Achbor's beard, perhaps intending to communicate its heaviness. In the context in which it is found in the poem, it may mean that the beard is so long and dense that it causes its bearer complete exhaustion. These words, however, include an intentional pun that echoes the larger context, referring to Achbor's general carnality as reflected by the beard. אונים means both "strengths" and "evil deeds," and the common denominator between the two meanings is male sexual virility.[90]

Similarly, the word "תאונים" also presents a play on words. The form in the manuscript is somewhat problematic, as it reads, תאונים תאומים but the closeness of הלאות תאומים with Ezekiel 24:12 "הלאת, תאנים," (It hath wearied itself with toil) quoted later by the fourth maiden, permits us to believe that this was the intended form. תאונים is probably a form derived from און / אונים in the sense of evil deeds. As we have seen earlier, though, it phonetically resembles both the word referring to women as a sexual object, figs, תאנים, and female sexual desire, תאנתה. Hence, the two rhyming elements אונים / תאונים abstractly juxtapose male sexual desire with that of women, and while the first exhausts the latter, both are associated with transgression.

138. Achbor's beard is like a forest

זקן עכבור כיער

This description is reminiscent of Moriuht's hirsuteness: "that in the vast forest of his groin a stork could build its nest and a hoopoe could have a place of his own." See chapter 2.

139. not one single black hair (Lev. 13:31)

ושיער שחור אין בו

86   *Chapter 1*

This is a phrasing from Leviticus 13:31, which discusses people who are infected with leprosy. According to this verse, if black hair stops growing around a laceration it is a sign that the disease has reached an advanced stage, requiring seclusion and confinement. In the Middle Ages, every disease, and leprosy specifically, was directly linked to immorality and sexuality.[91] Leprosy was perceived as sexually transmitted and divine punishment for immoral and licentious behavior. Thus, just as a leper is contagious and must be isolated, it was believed that the spiritually ill should also be removed from society.[92] As argued above, all the references to diseases in the text should be understood metaphorically, as signifiers of immorality. The opposite is also true: every reference to Achbor as a healer or a doctor should be understood as a supplementary reflection of his hypocrisy. After implying in her poem that he suffers from an immoral sickness, the second maiden presents Achbor as a false healer, declaring that "I believed that Achbor's beard was the beard of a healer." The third maiden will ironically continue this idea, stating that she "found no cure in it."

Like her predecessor, the second maiden also initially presents Achbor as sick, and then as a charlatan. In her rhymed replica she describes his beard, which has "not one single black hair."

140. But he made his bed in the darkness (Job 17:13) he fornicated with the daughters of Ham (Gen. 10:6; 10:20), and he has worked in the coal [mines] (Isa. 44:12)

ובחושך ריפד יצועיו זנה את בנות חם ופעל בפחם

Yaakov ben Elazar's source of inspiration is Yehuda al-Harizi's *Book of Takhkemoni*. In its sixth maqama, the protagonist discovers that his newlywed wife is as ugly and rancid as if Satan, symbolically her creator, "פעל בפחם עד חשבתיה מבנות חם" (labored in coal, until I thought that she was one of Ham's daughters). This resonates strongly with the people of Israel, who "began to commit harlotry with the daughters of Moab" (Num. 25:1).

Doubling the first maiden's "dug in the darkness," the second one also sarcastically presents the notion of darkness as referring to both Achbor's duplicity and lechery and to the despised Mistress' sexuality, stating that "he made his bed in the darkness." Here too, the context of the quoted biblical phrase mingles with the tale's abstract ideas, evoking the blurring of light and dark, death and hell.[93] As for her statement that "he fornicated with Ham's daughters, worked in the coal," according to the biblical tradition, Ham's son is Cush, and this is the name of the land given to him and his descendants.

The Tale of Old Bearded Achbor

141. With no razor, it shall be shaven away, it shall be eradicated (Isa. 7:20)
by a shard of dry clay (Job 2:8)

תגולח אך בלי תער / במו חרש תהי נספה

Literally, this stanza refers to Achbor's forthcoming torture—his beard's removal without a razor—which may be alluding to beard-flaying.[94] It is with the flowery metaphor of shaving (killing), with a razor (a sword) of the head (the king), the legs (his simple warriors), and the beard (his generals), that Isaiah prophesizes Sennacherib's fall in his attack on Hezekiah: "ביום ההוא יגלח אדני בתער השכירה בעברי נהר במלך אשור את הראש ושער הרגלים וגם את הזקן תספה" (In that day shall the Lord shave with a razor that is hired in the parts beyond the River, even with the king of Assyria, the head and the hair of the feet; and it shall also sweep away the beard, Isa. 7:20).[95]

Based on this verse, it becomes clear that Achbor's punishment represents much more than the elimination of his beard. It heralds the extermination of the enemy that he is, the word "נספה" corresponding with both the beard and Achbor, the impostor. Interestingly, as opposed to the echoed source, the maiden insists that the punishment will be executed without the razor, thus blurring the metaphorical image of the razor as a sword (alluding to a heroic death on the battlefield) and the practical humiliation of being plucked by women.[96]

In Jean Froissart's famous fourteenth-century chronicles, the Duke of Anjou warns captain Raymonnet de l'Espée, who is under siege, to leave and never turn back: ". . . car si vous vous y boutez et je vous tiengne, je vous delivreray à Janselin qui vous fera vos barbes sans rasoir" (because if you will turn back, I will deliver you to Janselin who will shave your beard without a razor).[97] As in *The Tale of Old Bearded Achbor*, the threat that one will be shaved without a razor is proverbial, using derisory euphemistic language to convey a man's decapitation (in the French source) or execution in general (in the Hebrew). From this, we may deduce that such a diction about the beard might have existed in medieval slang.

Another text that discusses the shaving of a beard is *Culhwch and Olwen*, which tells of a bizarre ritual.[98] The giant Ysbaddaden, Olwen's father, challenges Culhwch with a list of impossible tasks he must accomplish before being allowed to marry his daughter. Many of the tasks are related to the way he, the giant, must be shaved for the wedding (obtaining specific grooming instruments, a shaving lotion made from the blood of a witch, etc.).[99] Like *Achbor*, here too not only does the tale use scatological discourses, it ends with Ysbaddaden being violently shaved, killed and his body thrown away, three actions that describe Achbor's fate, as well:

88   Chapter 1

And then Culhwch set out, and with him Goreu the son of Custennin and those
who wished ill to Ysbaddaden Chief Giant, taking the rare and difficult things
with them and heading to his court. And Caw of Pictland came and shaved the
giant's beard—the flesh and skin to the bone, and the two ears completely . . . .
And then Goreu son of Custennin seized him by the hair of his head and dragged
him after him to the refuse mound and cut off his head and put it on the post of
the castle yard . . . . And that night Culhwch slept with Olwen. And she was his
only wife as long as he lived.[100]

I included the last two sentences, referring to the marriage, because after
Achbor's beard is torn off and he is killed and his body thrown into a pit,
the four maidens find young "desirers" and pair up with them. While I am
not claiming that an affinity exists between these two texts, I am suggesting
the existence of a pattern, which frequently appears in passing in medieval
literature: the liberation of an innocent victim from its monstrous, sometimes
incestuous, keeper. In *The Tale of Old Bearded Achbor*, once the monstrous
Achbor is defeated, the maidens are free, and they can leave behind them the
immoral palace where they entertained a depraved father figure.

*142. The [facial] hairs reached the hairs of his branch, wing to wing (1 Kings
6:27) they touched each other*

והגיע שיער לשיער ענף נוגעות כנף אל כנף

A limb is both a body part and a branch. Literally "the branch hairs," "branch"
being a metaphor for the male organ, interchangeable, I believe, with the limb
metaphor. It is with this bawdy, mocking description, that what was only
hinted at previously, that is, Achbor's beard is a euphemism for his sexuality,
becomes explicit. Achbor's facial hairs are assimilated with his pubic hair.
Such ribald interchangeability between a man's two manes is also a common
locus in literature, as I discussed in this chapter.

*143. Then I said to myself: I thought—and how could I have thought this—
that his beard's hairs were hairs of reason and righteousness, yet they all
lead downhill to Little Hole*

אחשוב—ואיך אחשוב? שערות זקנו שערות דעת וכשרון—והן במורד בית חורון

From sexuality to scatology, the maiden now compares Achbor's head
to his buttocks, his beard possibly fusing with his rectal hair.[101] The hair
that grows on the face, the body's upper part, can easily be linked to
wisdom, spirituality, or even royalty, as the maiden will soon state in
her poem "כאילו על זקנו הוד מלוכה" (as if his beard reflects the splendor of

The Tale of Old Bearded Achbor 89

majesty). Yet, their descent to the buttocks area cannot but represent an abomination. It may suggest that the beard would be used to wipe excrement, as it is also suggested by stanza: "It would be a blanket upon your privy / and you shall cover your excrement with this blanket,"[102] creating an association between facial and rectal hairs.[103] In the final words of this stanza, the maiden refers to the biblical city of Bet-Horon, which literally means the house of Horon (the Canaanite name for the god Horus). Here it is used as a parodical theophoric name for Achbor's anal orifice, both metaphorically (the house of the little hole) and phonetically (sounding like the word "hara," excrement).[104]

Thus, by first metaphorically changing the facial hair into pubic hair, and now to rectal hair, the maiden echoes Achbor's essential hypocrisy, which divides the tale between the public and the intimate. Facial hair is public, it is within the consensus. In the tale's first part, everyone sees and admires Achbor's outstanding beard. However, pubic and rectal hair are not supposed to be seen at all, nor admired or even mentioned; it is a taboo.

144. It has enough fleece for [two] mules' saddlecloth / (2 Kings 5:17) and a covering for the net [encircling] the flock's fold! (Num. 32:16).

ובה צמר למרדעת פרדים / ומסכה, לגדרות צאן שבכה

This is an allusion to 2 Kings 5:17, where Naaman, a pagan army commander who had just been healed of leprosy due to the efforts of the prophet Elisha, asks the latter if he may take holy soil in order to build an altar to the Hebrew God whom he will worship from now on. He asks for a quantity that can be loaded up on צמד פרדים (two mules). The words "צמד" (a pair) and "צמר" (fleece) are phonetically close, and based on the biblical source, I believe that it is safe to translate "the fleece for two mules." Although once צמד is changed into צמר the text loses its reference to quantity, such a translation supports both the plural form of mules and the comical exaggeration of the beard's dimensions. Besides its comical effects, however, these words also convey a peripheral message. The two biblical mules are covered with holy soil as a token of Naaman's healing, not only physically, but more importantly, spiritually.[105] Achbor's mules are metaphorically covered by a load of an excremental beard.

The use of the word "מסכה" here denotes a covering (see Isa. 25:7; 28:20), doubling the word "saddlecloth" and extending the exaggerated caricature of the beard's length, thus suggesting that the beard itself can serve as a form of disguise. The perception of the beard as a mask varies. For Gellius in the second century, it is the attire of hypocrisy, as he states that he "hate[s] base men who preach philosophy . . . disguised with beard."[106] For the writer

90   *Chapter 1*

of the fourteenth-century Occitan epic poem, *Daurel et Beton*, beards can provide camouflage for good people when they need not or wish not to be recognized. This is exemplified by Daurel, who grows a beard and does not shave for seven years: "Gran ac la barba, qu'om nol poc albirar / Ben a vij. ans no lais laissetz ostar" (he left his beard long, so no man would be able to recognize him: indeed, seven years he did not let it be shaven).[107] Similarly, satirical accounts such as *Le blason de barbes* share that "The bearded man who did wrong, immediately grows his beard and becomes completely unrecognizable. But the one who has a bare chin, razed as a priest, is much easier to be recognized."[108] These examples are random; in the intervening years that separate them from one another, dichotomic considerations of the beard as a symbolic mask proliferate throughout the literature. The notion of the beard's dual essence as both concealing and revealing persists pervasively across texts and eras. Finally, it is worthwhile to remind ourselves of a theme explored in this chapter, the barboire, a facial mask intended to intimidate with its oversized beard.[109]

A second meaning of מסכה renders this word somewhat of a pun in this context, and cannot be overlooked, as it refers to a molten image used in pagan rituals. This secondary meaning is significant given that the main implicit accusation against Achbor is his deviation from the Lord's path. While numerous biblical verses discuss such pagan idols, 2 Kings 17:16 seems to be most appropriate in the context of the religious assimilation of the children of Israel and their adherence to pagan cults. The chapter deals with the fallen Hebrews forsaking God's ways. They create a molten image of two calves, which correlate, conceptually, with the pair of mules. Another extension of the same idea is in the peculiar image of the sheepfold. The maiden has either provided another example of the length of the despicable beard, which could easily cover the area of the flock's enclosure, or she might be referring to a net large enough to capture a large number of sheep and goats. Either way, she describes the image of Achbor's beard as a piece of fabric so long that it can cover his bestiality (implied by the references to beasts, mules, and sheep, and perhaps calves). In the following stanza, she brings this idea to a climax, by mentioning a fourth type of textile, a blanket.[110]

145. It would be a blanket upon your privy (Deut. 23:14) / and you shall cover (Judg. 4:8) your excrement (Deut. 23:14) with this blanket.

שמיכה תהיה לך על אזנך

The blanket is another fabric to which the beard is compared. The meaning of the word "אזן" (azen) is unclear and was subject to several interpretations,

the two prevailing ones being either "quiver" or a weapon of some sort. It is
mentioned in a quote from Deuteronomy 23:14 "ויתד תהיה לך על אזנך" (And
thou shalt have a paddle among thy weapons), as part of the instructions
given to the Hebrews to eradicate evil. Here they are instructed on how to
keep their camp pure when they find themselves going to war. The two first
instructions concern body waste, that is, semen and excrement. In case of
nocturnal emissions, for example, the soldier must exit the camp until the
evening, at which time he should wash and return to camp the next morning. The men are also ordered to keep a spade "among thy weapons,"[111] and
if they wish to defecate, they are required to exit the camp, dig a hole, and
after defecation "turn back and cover that which cometh from thee" (23:14).
Purity, virtue, holiness, and lack of evil are thus found in places devoid of
human waste. By the same token, such filth is the décor of unholy places, first
and foremost Gehenna.

146. the water of purification (Num. 8:7)

מי חטאת

Numbers 8:7 instructs the Levites on their purification before they enter their
sacred service: "וכה תעשה להם לטהרם הזה עליהם מי חטאת והעבירו תער על כל בשרם
וכבסו בגדיהם והטהרו" (And thus shalt thou do unto them, to cleanse them: sprin-
kle the water of purification upon them, and let them cause a razor to pass
over all their flesh, and let them wash their clothes, and cleanse themselves).
Two of the prerequisites (the sprinkling of water and the razor) are echoed in
the accusations hurled at Achbor. In the Bible these actions indicate a ritual
of physical purification that the privileged Levites should undergo as they are
about to become spiritual leaders. In the tale, however, similar actions denote
the transformation of one who had been a spiritual leader and is now stripped
of his holy position as part of his fatal punishment.

Previously, I suggested that the description of Achbor being "shaved," that
is, killed, *without* a razor is reminiscent of a metaphorical epic battle where
an army will be defeated by the Lord's razor (i.e., sword), and was intended
as a means of disparaging of his execution. Perhaps it can be combined in
some way with the idea that while the razor was used in purifying the Levites,
Achbor's shaving has no elements of purification and therefore it will not be
done with a razor. In any case, the reference to the purifying water here tells
us that Achbor's beard, a personification of Achbor himself, is so corrupt,
that even if it or he were to be sprinkled with purifying water, neither can be
saved from hell. Such a gloomy message reminds us of Achbor's own predic-
tion "Do not say: 'he shall thus act, and be exonerated,' No, he shall not be
forgiven, he shall not be vindicated!"

92   *Chapter 1*

147. they judged him as adulteresses are judged! (Ezek. 16:38, 23:45).

ומשפט נואפות שפטוהו

The biblical parable refers to two adulterous sisters, אהלה (Ohala, the personification of the city of Samaria and thus representing Israel) and אהליבה (Ohaliba, the personification of the city of Jerusalem and thus representing Judea). Ezekiel explains that both will be judged "as adulteresses are judged" (23:45) and then stoned to death. The fact that Yaakov ben Elazar uses here the word "adulteresses" in its feminine form is significant. This is not simply for the sake of respecting the quoted source, as we know that Yaakov did not refrain from manipulating biblical verses in other instances. This choice of words is intentional and a symbolic part of Achbor's humiliation, as he is symbolically effeminized: he is verbally insulted by the maidens and beaten by them, symbolically castrated by them by the removal of his beard,[112] and finally executed as an adulterer in a manner that seems to have been more typically reserved for women rather than men.[113]

This overwhelming scene presents the four maidens not merely in the typically masculine role of orators as before, but also as judges and executioners, which are also strictly masculine roles. Women working together to exact punishment or revenge on a transgressive man is a literary topos. Whether it appears in comical or non-comical narratives, it always conveys gender blurring, because of its unusual feature of women exercising violence, an act that is traditionally associated with men.[114]

A Fairy Tale Ending

In an extreme contrast to the previous part of the tale, Yaakov ben Elazar takes us from the macabre scene of Achbor's execution to an enchanting atmosphere of a fairy-like *locus amoenus,* or "pleasant place." The literary theme consists of a delightful outdoor scene, in which "minimum ingredients comprise a tree (or several trees), a meadow, and a spring or a brook. Birdsong and flowers may be added."[115] Such *loci* provide the perfect setting for courtly love adventures, which take place amidst abundant trees and flourishing gardens. The references to the Song of Songs only augment the erotic atmosphere that Yaakov ben Elazar describes in this charming depiction, which provides the beloveds with a setting for lovemaking: "נשכימה לכרמים" (let us get up early to the vineyards, Song of Sg 7:13);[116] "אל גנת אגוז ירדתי" "לראות באבי הנחל, לראות הפרחה הגפן, הנצו הרמונים" (I went down into the garden of nuts, to look at the green plants of the valley, to see whether the vine budded, and the pomegranates were in flower, Song of Sg 6:11). The setting is

The Tale of Old Bearded Achbor   93

that of an erotic *locus amoenus,* an orchard full of beautiful flowers and fruit, put at the service of young maidens in their quest for love.

148. they entered the vineyards (Song of Sg 1:6; 2:15; 7:13), to stroll in the gardens, and pick lilies (Song of Sg 6:2). They promenaded in the orchards, paced among the myrtle trees (Zech. 1:8, 10, 11)

ותצאנה אל הכרמים לרעות בגנים וללקט שושנים מתהלכות בפרדסים מתנהלות בין ההדסים

Vineyards, gardens and orchards are three emblematic landscapes that invite lovemaking, and all appear in the Song of Songs as metonymies for the sexual body. A third location mentioned in this section, the orchard, reinforces this idea, as it is yet another eroticized embodiment of the sensual female body "שלחייך פרדס רימונים עם פרי מגדים" (Thy shoots are an orchard of pomegranates, with precious fruits, Song of Sg 4:13). The word "שלחייך" translates as shoots and thus could be a metaphor for the limbs of the body. Within the context of the blossoming orchard, though, the more likely meaning of the word is the one used in the *Mishna*: artificial channels or pools dug for irrigation purposes. "Your pools irrigate an orchard of pomegranate with the sweetest fruits" easily corresponds to the varied sensual metaphors presented here. The specific visualization of the Shulamite's body as a pool in Song of Songs is linked by abstraction to the fourth outdoor area mentioned in Yaakov's *locus amoenus,* the pools of water where the maidens bathe, which will be discussed below.

The myrtle, the sacred plant of both the Greek and Roman goddesses of love (Aphrodite and Venus respectively), with its alluring perfume and white flowers, is associated with erotic love. It is reported that in ancient women's rituals (the Veneralia, for example) women used to bathe wearing diadems braided with myrtle,[117] and brides have worn this flower as a hair ornament from antiquity until the present. The myrtle appears as one of the trees in the *locus amoenus* described by the roman poet Tiberianus (fourth century) "Amnis ibat inter herbas valle fusus frigida / Luce ridens calculorum, flore pictus herbido / Caerulas superne Laurus et virecta myrtea" (Through the fields there went a river, down the airy glen it wound, smiling mid its radiant pebbles, decked with flowery plants around dark-hued laurels waved above it close by myrtle greeneries).[118] Upon describing his vision of the horses as god's emissaries, the prophet Zechariah shares that he saw a man, perhaps God's angel, who had stopped the horse he was riding "ראיתי הלילה והנה איש רכב על סוס אדם והוא עמד בין ההדסים אשר במצלה" (I saw in the night, and behold a man riding upon a red horse, and he stood among the myrtle trees that were in the bottom, Zech. 1:8). The myrtles have no particular role except that they are associated with divine miraculous power

94   *Chapter 1*

that can transform desolate deserts into flourishing places, as demonstrated, for example, in Isaiah 41:19: "אתן במדבר ארז שטה והדס ועץ שמן" (I will plant in the wilderness the cedar, the acacia-tree, and the myrtle, and the oil-tree, Isa. 41:19), a parenthetical allusion that contributes here to the enchanted, magical atmosphere of the garden where fairies-mistresses sojourn.[119]

149. wearing colorful garments (Gen. 37:7) telling stories and riddles (Ezek. 17:2) and fine poetry about the blossoming flowers, the vines, and all sorts of buds (Song of Sg 7:13, see also Song of Sg 2:12). They spoke of the trees (1 Kings 5:13), of lilies and blossoms.

מספרות משלים וחידות ושירות חמודות על הסמדר והגפנים ועל כל מיני הניצנים
ותדברנה על העצים ועל השושנים והציצים

This picture extends the ideal description of the Edenic place, where the maidens, liberated from Achbor, are free to practice all the delicate activities of the pastoral idyll. Their grace is emphasized by their rich garments[120] and the erotic atmosphere is reiterated by the subject matter of their riddles and poetry, emphasizing the sexual symbolism of vines and flower buds. We should also note the reference to the maidens' wisdom and finesse. They are first juxtaposed with Ezekiel, the prophet renowned for his use of fables: "בן אדם חוד חידה ומשל משל אל בית ישראל" (Son of man, put forth a riddle, and speak a parable, Ezek. 17:2), and then with King Solomon, who "וידבר שלשת אלפים משל ויהי שירו חמשה ואלף. וידבר על העצים" (spoke three thousand proverbs; and his songs were a thousand and five. And he *spoke of trees*, 1 Kings 5:12-13, my emphasis).

150. they observed them [surreptitiously] (Song of Sg 2:9) from behind the windows. They perceived this and said: "Who is it who listens to our voices, hiding behind our walls (Song of Sg 2:9)?"

משגיחים מן החלונות ותדענה הדבר ותאמרנה:
"מי הוא אשר יקשיב לקולנו ועומד אחר כותלינו?"

Literally, "they observed them from the windows" and "Who is it who listens to our voices, hiding behind our walls?" This episode takes place outdoors, where the maidens are bathing or paddling in the water pools in the gardens and the orchards, and it is suggested that they are naked. The windows from which the lads peek at the maidens, and the walls behind which they stand, are therefore metaphorical (i.e., the lads are behind trees, for example), just like the "fawns' doors" upon which the lovers knock in the first stanza of the final poem that follows. Another option is that this indicates that the orchard

The Tale of Old Bearded Achbor 95

where the maidens are sitting is enclosed by walls (as would probably be the case in the homes of aristocratic families), and it is through such walls that the lads watch. In erotic discourses, the window is the quintessential site for both forbidden gazing and stolen moments of a lovers' tryst.[121] Walls are a common metaphor for the protected, unachievable body, and uphold their gates or doors, which are, as we have seen, metaphors for the vagina.

151. Are you an ally or a foe (Josh. 5:13)?

הלנו אתה - אם לצרינו?

A rhetorical question dramatizing the moment: what is the nature of the person peeping at the maidens? The dramatic reference to two possible manners of conduct by a man finding unprotected "game" is the main subject of the following poem. The singular form used here is rhetorical and applies to the four lads.[122]

152. [All] were seated, each person in their place (Gen. 41:13, Dan. 11:20) and each person within their camps (Num. 1:52)

והושיבום איש על כנו ואיש על מחנהו

Literally, "each man sat at his place and with his own camp." I interpreted "camp" to be each man's intended wife.

153. If thus far we remained concealed from their sight (Job 18:3)

אם עד כה בעיניהן נטמינו

In its biblical occurrence, "נטמינו בעיניכם" ("reputed dull in your sight," Job 18:3) mainly conveys the idea of seeming stupid in their eyes. Schirmann explains this passage thus, based on Rashi's commentary on Job. Nevertheless, here, I believe it would be much more logical to see this verb, נטמינו (from טמה, tama), as phonetically associated with טמן (taman, conceal). Such a translation supports the following stanza, where the subject is a revelation.

A Didactic Love Poem

This poem can be read as a didactic reply to the erotic wine / love poems the maidens sang at Achbor's feast. It deals with the way that lovers should behave, adhering to the rules of decent and moral "good love," also quite reminiscent of *fin'amor*, rather than allowing their physical impulses to control them.

96   *Chapter 1*

154. *The oppressed should not oppress*

אִם עֻשְּׁקוּ, אַךְ לֹא לַעֲשׁוּקִים לַעֲשׁוּק

The verb עשק, usually used to express the idea of oppression and abuse, becomes in love poetry a metaphor for the torments of love afflicted by the maiden, intentionally or not, on her "desirer." The semantic *glissage* intended here is significant. According to the rules of honorable love, the tormented "desirer" should humbly accept, and even cherish, such persecutions as part of their path toward Love, the incarnation of Amor (the medieval name for Eros / Cupid). They should suffer mentally by restraining their desires and refining them. They should not, however, torment the maidens, as here the semantic conveys the idea of physical torment, that is, physical.

155. *desirers*

חוֹשְׁקִים

On the use of the word "desirer" for חושק, see chapter 7.

156. *The admirers whose craving, on the tablets of their hearts are engraving (Jer. 17:1, Prov. 3:3)*

הַכּוֹכָבִים חֲשָׁקָם עֲלֵי / לוּחַ לִבָּם חֲקָקוּ

The word "כוכבים" (stars), which is in the manuscript, is somewhat puzzling here. Schirmann replaced it with נובבים, in the sense of expressing (from the root נוב), and David concurred with him. This correction is not implausible, as it implies that the stanza is an amplification of the preceding one "Where are the great desirers gone, those who insist [on wooing] the fawns?" The two stanzas could have been translated, for example, as "Where are the great desirers who entreat the fawns [for their love], who express and engrave their desire on the tablets of their heart." I preferred however to place a noun here, as the fourth parallel in a series of questions addressed to the four young lads, depicting them each time by using a poetic synonym (חושקים, אוהבים, חושקי עולם, כוכבים) and asking them about required deeds of love:

> If you are desirers, where are the tears that should streak down on your cheek?
> Where are the lovers' implorations? Where are the sweet declarations?
> Where are the great desirers gone, those who insist [on wooing] the fawns?

To complete this series, let us return to the manuscript's noun, כוכבים. Stars can embody lovers perfectly, usually as a metaphor for their beauty

The Tale of Old Bearded Achbor   97

and glamour. To refine this idea, I preferred "admirers" as a synonym for "suitor," or "desirer" keeping in line with the nouns used in the three previous lines.[123]

157. Get up and hurry, accelerate / the reins of wandering you should amputate!

קומו וחושו מהרו / מוסרות נדודים נתקו

These last words, suggesting that the reins of wandering be cut (based on Jer. 2:20), refer to a metaphorical wandering, embodying the idea of the long and lonely quest a lover undertakes until he finds true love, who, from a more moralistic perspective that may be hinted here, will also become his wedded wife. The image of the reins is quite interesting in this context, as it is more often connected, often comically, to the burden of marriage, while bachelorhood is presented as a symbol of freedom. Then the maiden poet continues: "Choose yourself each man a mate, among you decide your fate! (e.g., Num. 33:54) / Because from his father and mother a man shall go (Gen. 2:24) / and cleave to a graceful doe (Prov. 5:19)."

158. Choose yourself each man a mate / among you decide your fate! / Because from his father and mother a man shall go / and cleave to a graceful doe!

התנחלו איש רעיה / אכן בגורל תחלקו
כי יעזוב איש אב ואם / וביעלת חן ידבקו

The reference to drawing lots, for example, conveys the idea of the permanent bond that can be established between the four couples, as it echoes the divine order that the tribes of Israel inherit the land and the respective territories that will belong to them permanently.

The echoed biblical sources deal with drawing lots and inheriting lands. Picking a wife or a beloved by choosing lots should be read here symbolically and not literally. As part of the enchanted atmosphere, the perfect locus, and the rules of Love, which encourage each man to find his one true beloved, each lad will "naturally" be led to pick his perfect mate. In biblical and medieval Hebrew, the word "רעיה" was used to designate a beloved rather than a wife. We might wonder if these couples would legally wed. This question remains unanswered. On the one hand, there is no mention of a legal, formal matrimonial ceremony, as is found in the *Tale of Sahar and Kima*. The formation of the couples may just be a mimetic, conceptual marriage of love, where the lovers obtain their mates in a "civilized" way, after proving themselves deserving. On the other hand, the two last stanzas sealing the entire tale imply that these

98   Chapter 1

four couples may indeed possibly wed[124]: "And there it was that their youth was flourishing, with their beloveds they were relishing."[125]

The stanza "Because from his father and mother a man shall go / and cleave to a graceful doe," includes the most popular quote defining the concept of marriage. Although this was written in reference to Adam and Eve long before the constitution of marriage, the idea is clear: the couple is formally bound for life. It is quite possible that Yaakov may have been intending to impart a moral message here, implying that love should only be consummated within the institution of marriage. The combination of courtly love and a religious context climaxes with the stanza "Because from his father and mother a man shall go, and cleave to a graceful doe." The graceful doe embodies the image of erotic poetry par excellence, while "from his father and mother" provides the image of leaving the family home in order to enter into a legal marriage. This is an exquisite image with which to conclude the maiden's poem.

159. And there it was that their youth was flourishing, with their beloveds they were relishing.

ויהי נעורים חדשו, על אוהבים התרפקו

The vocabulary and sources used to refer to the success of the matches in the final verse of this poem allow the reader to assume that the couples will indeed marry.

NOTES

1. Regarding the matter of rhymed translation in popular songs, Peter Alan Low notes that "Since rhyme is in essence a phonic device, rhyme is of limited use in a text intended only for silent reading," Peter Alan Low, "Translating Songs that Rhyme," *Perspectives: Studies in Translatology* 16, no. 1–2 (2008): 1–20, https://doi.org/10 .1080/13670050802364437.

2. Jefim Schirmann, "The Love Stories of Jacob ben Elazar," *Yedi'ot haMakhon leHeker haShirah halvrit* 5 (5699 [1939]): 211–66; Yonah David, *The Love Stories of Jacob Ben Eleazar (1170–1233?): Critical Edition with Introduction and Commentary* (Tel-Aviv: Ramot Publishing, Tel-Aviv University, 1992–93).

3. Bavarian State Library Munich Germany Cod.hebr. 207. This was made possible thanks to the Israeli National Library's project "Ktiv—The International Collection of Digitalized Hebrew Manuscripts," which generously enabled access to the manuscript online. From the collections of Bayerische Staatsbibliothek, München.

4. Bibring, Tovi, "Blood Matters, Matters of Blood—Fable 81 by Berechiah ha-Naqdan: Study and Critical Translation," in *"And Wisdom Shall Flow from the*

Wise": Wisdom and Morals in Medieval Literature, edited by Tovi Bibring and Revital Refael-Vivante (Jerusalem: Misgav Yerushalayim, 2022), 59–86.

5. https://www.mechon-mamre.org/p/pt/pt0.htm.

6. On this tale, see Bibring, "A Medieval Hebrew French-Kiss," 24–37.

7. David also refers to לאל אל as a modification of Deut. 32:21 (see also Jer. 5:7).

8. On the idea that Achbor encourages idolatry, see chapter 2.

9. I follow here the manuscript's reading, while David replaced והונו with הונו.

10. E.g., שעירים (satyrs, Lev.17:7); מלך (molech, Lev. 20:5); אלהי נכר (foreign gods, Deut. 31:19); אלהים אחרים (other gods, Judg. 2:17); גילולים (idols, Ezek. 6:9); צלמי זכר (images of men, Ezek. 16:17).

11. Although the goddess Fortuna originates in Pagan culture, Christianity embraced the motif through allegory. The use of the *Rota Fortunae* in literary and didactic texts is recurrent, brought to medieval popular and theological culture mainly through Boethius' magistral work, *Consolatio Philosophae.*

12. It should be noted that אנשים ורשים create an inner rhyme between them, and such inner rhymes are characteristic of medieval Hebrew poetry.

13. It could also have been considered redundant. Support for this postulation is found, for example, in Prov. 13:8 "כפר נפש-איש עשרו ורש לא שמע גערה" (The ransom of a man's life are his riches; but the poor heareth no threatening) where the word "man" refers to a rich man who is contrasted with a poor man. See also 2 Samuel 12:4.

14. Lucian, *Harmonides. In Lucian, Volume VI,* translated by K. Kilburn. Loeb Classical Library 430 (Cambridge, MA: Harvard University Press, 1959), 301.

15. George Bragues, "The Market for Philosophers: An Interpretation of Lucian's Satire on Philosophy," *The Independent Review* 9, no. 2 (2004): 227–51, 245.

16. "Where the sun sets lies an isle, called Ireland, a fertile (land) though not well tended by its habitants. Many people say that if this island was occupied by a nation of any skill, it would surpass Italy in its riches. Regrettably, though this (land) affords a view of life in paradise from all sides, it rears and fosters Irishmen who lack refinement . . . under the frame of their bodies, their mind is crashed . . . . How much they run after prostitutes with their bodies . . . Phew! They defile beds . . . . It is immoral to record them and it shames (me) to recount (them)." 75. The English translations of *Moriuht* are from Christopher J. McDonough, ed., *"Moriuht": A Norman Latin Poem from the Early Eleventh Century.* Studies and Texts 121 (Toronto: Pontifical Institute of Mediaeval Studies, 1995), here 121.

17. And compare to the inhabitants of Lucian's ideal city, Virtue "They do not any longer look on gold."

18. Lucian, *Harmonides.*

19. See in his poem "ממרום קול עובר" (from high a voice passes): "וכי אתיצב למולו / אני נפעם במהללו" (And that I will stand before him / I will be moved by his praise), quoted from Moshe Ibn Ezra, *The Liturgical Poems of Moshe Ibn Ezra, A Critical Edition,* annotated and introduced by Israel Levin and Tova Rosen (Tel-Aviv: Tel-Aviv University Press, 2012), 425.

20. זאב ערבות can be read either as "the wolf from the plains," or just like in Zephaniah, the "evening wolf," who only hunts at night (the Hebrew plays on a phonetic resemblance created by the use of the same letters in a different order, "erev" for evening, and "ra'ev" for hungry).

100   *Chapter 1*

21. שלא שברו עצם לבקר, והנה בערב רעבים

22. כן השופטים חוטפים השוחד ואוכלים

23. The verb was understood either as getting fat or as rejoicing. In his exegetic on the subject, Rashi wrote that the Babylonian will become fat like the heifer "הדשה ואוכלת תמיד" בתבואה (who treads grain and constantly eats). Similarly, Joseph Kara (eleventh-twelfth century) wrote: "כעגלה הרבוצה בנאות דשא ורועה במרעה טוב, שמשתמנת מתוך מרעה הטוב" (as a heifer laying in the meadow and grazing in rich pasture, and fattening from this rich pasture). Menachem ben Shimon from Pousquières (twelfth century) and Isaiah di Trani (twelfth–thirteenth century) linked the abundance of food to pleasure and joy: "שהעגלה תרבה בתענוג כאשר היא דשה בעבור שיכולה לאכל מהתבואה כרצונה" (the heifer shall have great delight when it is treading since it can eat from the grain as much as it wishes); Isaiah said this in different words: "לשון תענוג הוא... והעגלה כשהיא דשה אוכלת שיבולים הרבה" (the meaning of pleasure... the heifer when it is treading eats many stalks).

24. Kohelet attempts to understand the meaning of the human experience based upon his own experiences and acquired knowledge and wisdom, seeking examples from history. For Rashi, the "wisdom" means the Torah.

25. Sanhedrin 20:4. See Rashi's commentary "לא תחלוק לו כבוד לזכותו בדין ולומר: דל הוא זה אזכנו ואכבדנו" (you shall not honor him by acquitting him in justice [proceedings] and say this one is poor, I will acquit him and honor him). Abraham Ibn Ezra (twelfth century) emphasized that the rich and the poor are equal in the eyes of the law: "כאשר הזהרתיך שלא תעזור העשיר, גם כן אל תעזור הדל בריבו" (Just as I've warned you not to aid the rich man, you shall not help the poor man in his trial). See also their commentaries on Lev. 19:15.

26. Janek Kucharski and Przemyslaw Marciniak, "The Beard and its Philosopher: Theodore Prodromos on the Philosopher's Beard in Byzantium," *Byzantine and Modern Greek Studies* 41, no. 1 (2017): 45–54.

27. Note though the transition from the singular מציב to the plural הכינו, both conjugations of verbs relating to the same subject.

28. Of course, the text remains quite obscure, and it is also possible to think that all of these preparations occur spontaneously.

29. Giles Constable, "Introduction," in *Apologiae duae*, edited by R. B. C. Huygens, with an introduction on beards in the Middle Ages by Giles Constable (Turnhout: Brepols, 1985), 47–150, 77–78, here 70.

30. See also Psalm 73:13.

31. It is plausible to think that Brody corrected this line relying on a verse in the poem that immediately follows this excerpt, which clearly reads "זקן ושיבה אל יבהלוך". Repetitions, developments, and variations of phrases from the text in the poem are current and hence Brody's amendment, considering that the manuscript's reading is hard to decipher, is justifiable.

32. David, *The Love Stories*, 148.

33. The graphic representation of the word in the manuscript is unclear, but it is hard to believe that the letter before the obvious ה is ג. As for the suggested feminine form for branches: Yaakov ben Elazar, influenced by the vernacular languages, conjugates branch in the feminine form.

34. For Schirmann, the subject of the first section is the ignominies, maybe since the verb is conjugated in the feminine form of the plural that corresponds to the noun (i.e., ignominies vs. beard). Schirmann referred to the impasse as follows: "it is hard to guess why the author writes that 'ignominies' are 'blasted with the east wind.'" I, however, see the beard as the subject of this sentence: it is the beard that is blasted, or, as I translated, worthless. While the word "beard" appears here in the singular, in biblical and medieval Hebrew it may refer more generally to the beard's hairs, or in Yaakov's text it may even imply "beards." The verb's feminine form is justified in any case. "Hairs" take the feminine form and, influenced by the vernacular languages (which lean on Latin), "beard" is usually referred to in the feminine form in medieval Hebrew texts (as opposed to its masculine form in modern Hebrew). With the beard as the grammatical subject, it corresponds to the image of impostors' beards, which, by connotation to the biblical bad corn ears, are empty, rotten, and vile, and not without irony in our case, also blackened (as a result of the blight that dries their grains, making them inconsumable, the ears become black. Some Bible translations translate שדפות as "scorched"). All of these attributes constantly circle back in one way or another to Achbor the impostor and his black Mistress. In any case, since in the entire tale the beard is metonymic to the person who wears it, the grammatical subject whether it is the beard or the ignominies in this sentence means the same thing.

35. Note that the tautology that is present in this sentence, using the words "קדים" and "שדופות" to form an adjectival combination is attested in modern Hebrew "רב לנו דבר מהתלות יבשות ושדופות קדים" (Abraham Mapu).

36. This is reminiscent of Plutarch's metaphor of the full and empty grain, where the latter represents the immature student of philosophy's beard, discussed in chapter 2.

37. A literal translation would be "lest those who bear beards of ignominy and felony, blighted by the east wind . . ."

38. Is it possible that what is actually written is the word "הזימה"?

39. In the scriptures, the word only comes in the fixed locution תאניה ואניה.

40. The tar metaphor is also somewhat ironic, as it resonates with the stereotyped portrait of the Mistress, hated for her blackness and her stench. Only here, once again, Lemuel refers to tar as something superior to some of the superficially magnificent beards.

41. As we recall, the beard appears several times in the tale as a harbor for different kinds of animals.

42. As opposed to the case of women who are often subject to rape while they sleep, as I demonstrated in *The Patient*. This is most probably related to the prevalent medieval conception that women should be passive in sexual relations, while men are active.

43. Jean Bodel, "Li sohaiz desvez," in *Nouveau recueil complet des fabliaux (NRCF)*, edited by Willem Noomen, *Volume 6* (Assen and Maastricht: Van Gorcum, 1991), 259–72, notes on 354–56.

44. On the black woman described in the Song of Songs, see Jacqueline de Weeber, *Sheba's Daughters: Whitening and Demonizing the Saracen Woman in Medieval French Epic* (New York: Garland Publishing, 1998).

102 *Chapter 1*

45. In Rashi's commentary on כאוד מצל משרפה, he interprets this to mean that survivors of divine ire remained "שחורים וחשוכים וקדרים" (black and dark and gloomy). Schirmann, "The Love Stories of Jacob ben Elazar," 279.

46. The smoky firebrand in Isaiah 7:4 also provided some inspiration. Although in this source the smoky firebrand is a symbol of weakness, the visual aspect is similar. In a different context, it is the Lord who is described as emitting fire or smoke from his nostrils or his nose as an expression of his ire.

47. Maureen J. Alden defines the word in this manner, referring to the word used to describe transgressions committed in Homer's *Odyssey*, which is usually translated and referred to as adultery. Maureen J. Alden, "The Resonances of the Song of Ares and Aphrodite," *Mnemosyne* 50, no. 5 (October 1997): 513–29, 516.

48. Bloch, *Medieval French Literature and Law* (Berkeley: University of California Press, 1977), 55. The *flagrante delicto* scene surely derives from medieval Western interpretations of classical mythology. With endless variants and variations, the main ingredients of the topos postulate an infraction of a sexual order (usually adultery, but can also refer to the unfaithfulness of lovers). See Demodocus' song about Aphrodite and her lover Ares, caught naked in bed with a net that Aphrodite's lame husband, Hephaistos, threw on them (book 8, 266–76). When, in Homers' *Odyssey*, Demodocus sings of the capture of the adulterers Ares and Aphrodite, he describes how the lovers were surprised in Hephaestus' (Aphrodite's husband) bed with an invisible cage that he crafted, and how the latter raised a cry, summoning the male gods to see and humiliate the caged lovers. Varied scenes of ambushes (tainted sometimes with voyeurism) abound in medieval literature. The most notable lovers captured in flagrante delicto include Tristan and Iseut, Lancelot and Guinevere, Muldumarec and his lady in Marie de France's *Yonec* and the king and the seneschal's wife in her *Equitan*.

49. See the passage in Numbers 5:14 about the adulterous women, specifically concerning her husband "ועבר עליו רוח קנאה וקנא את אשתו" (and the spirit of jealousy come upon him, and he be jealous of his wife).

50. See Rashi's commentary "כל העניין הזה, לפי פשוטו – לשון חיבת פיתוי, שבחור מרצה את ארוסתו לילך" (Literally, all this matter—is the language of affectionate wooing with which a lad would solicit his fiancé to follow him).

51. Ronald A. Veenker, "Forbidden Fruit. Ancient Near Eastern Sexual Metaphors," *Hebrew Union College Annual*, 1999, 57–74, here 58.

52. Danielle S. Allen, *The World of Prometheus: The Politics of Punishing in Democratic Athens* (Princeton: Princeton University Press, 2000), 160.

53. J. N. Adams, *The Latin Sexual Vocabulary* (Baltimore: Johns Hopkins, 1990), 113.

54. Shulamit Elizur notes that the difficulties a modern reader would have encountered while reading poetry regarding the appropriate vocalization of the word would have been non-existent in the Middle Ages, as the poems were not read but rather performed, and the words were heard. See Shulamit Elizur, *Hebrew Secular Poetry in Muslim Spain* (Tel-Aviv: Tel-Aviv University Press, 2004), 44. Nevertheless, one cannot completely overlook the graphic resemblance and phonetic potential with which even the medieval author worked.

The Tale of Old Bearded Achbor

55. The use of the overly ripe fig as a metaphor for the black-skinned person may also recall the metaphor of the overly ripe blackberry in the description assigned to the wild boar in *Baudouin* de Flandre, which is a prefiguration of the black she-devil that is about to marry the count: *"Et il trouva ung sanglier qui c'estoit endormy qui estoit grant et fourny et estoit plus noir que meure"* ("he saw a boar that was asleep and was big, fat, and blacker than a blackberry," *Baudouin de Flandres,* edited by Elisabeth Pinto-Mathieu [Paris: Librairie Générale Française, 2011], 52). Of course, we must also mention the part that the fig leaf played in the story of Adam and Eve, who used these leaves to hide their nakedness after eating from the forbidden fruit.

56. Compare to castrations referred to as a thigh injury in medieval literature (see for example *Guigemar* or *Chaitivel* by Marie de France). Decades later, Shakespeare would ironically use the term "colt-evil" to refer to such pains.

57. The word "סוד" (sod), here meaning ploy or trick, has an entirely different meaning than its semantic use in the wine poem's second strophe (see chapter 7), but still echoes it. While "sod" there referred to the riddle's mystery, to the love enigma to be deciphered, here it refers to the crafted plan Achbor executes in order to avoid the maidens' love. The use of the same term links ironically between the two quite different secrets. While Achbor was competent when solving the poem's secret about love, he avoids the theoretical love offered to him by the maidens, and uses a different kind of secret against them. The biblical source refers to Israel's enemies, conspiring to destroy them: "על-עמך, יערימו סוד ויתיעצו על צפוניך" (They hold crafty converse against Thy people, and take counsel against Thy treasured ones, Pss. 83:3-4).

58. This was suggested by Melamed, who interprets תאנים שוערים as "fig-like gates," and שעריהן as "their gates" and concludes: "'The gates' here is a euphemism for the female sex organ, a balm that cures." Abraham Melamed, *The Image of the Black in Jewish Culture: A History of the Other*, translated by Betty Sigler Rozen (London: Routledge, 2010), 164. It is Melamed's comment about the balm that seems incongruous: "The same is true for the metaphor 'the fig-like gates', where the female organ is described in terms of a sweet, ripe fruit, whose taste brings great pleasure" (p. 164). צרי (a balm) is indeed a sensual cure, concocted from fragrant oils, and as shown by Deborah Green, can be a euphemism for the liquid secreted by a woman's sexual arousal. Deborah Green, *The Aroma of Righteousness: Scent and Seduction in Rabbinic Life and Literature* (University Park: Penn State University Press, 2011). Figs are also a common metaphor for the vagina, as depicted by Raphael's "Garland of Vegetation". This, however, does not seem to be the meaning here, as the pun with שוערים manipulates the biblical term that is explicitly and traditionally connected with rotten figs (and not ripe figs) and turpitude, and should be read as Achbor's sarcastic affirmation that he is attracted to corruption, and cannot be confused with any positive association to sweetness. It is the stench of a rotting fruit that would normally cause illness rather than a cure, and not the sweetness of a ripe fruit that heals Achbor. This will reverberate in Lemuel's castigations, as he is about to use a very specific synonym to describe the Mistress's stench and rot: תבאש. See Adams, *The Latin Sexual Vocabulary*, 89.

59. This possibly alludes to Ovid's *Remedia Amoris*, which had much influence over medieval literature, including the advice to cure oneself of the disease of love by having several mistresses.

104   *Chapter 1*

60. In the manuscript they are spelled differently (בוערים, בערים) which could have been the scribe's intention to mark the semantic difference between the two phonetically identical terms, or a simple lack of attention. The pun, in any case, is clear.

61. The personification of the pupil as a black person, in this case as a token of beauty, is a common image in Arabic and Hebrew love poetry, and is also found in the maqama. See, for example, in *Sahar and Kima*: "וירא והנה פנים נוצצים ועיניים מתלוצצים ושם שני בני כושים חלוצים" (and he saw there were glowing face, and jesting eyes, and within them two Cushites' sons exposed!).

62. On this expression in Hebrew and Latin see Bibring, "Blood Matters, Matters of Blood—Fable 81 by Berechiah ha-Naqdan."

63. The word "white" is not uttered, but it is an obvious *sous entendre* in the context.

64. Perhaps the choice of evoking skin conditions specifically is an ironic statement vis-à-vis the Mistress's skin color.

65. Melamed attributes the malady to the white woman, "whose skin color he rhymes with 'blight,' i.e. with ugliness and illness." Melamed, *The Image of the Black*, 164.

66. It could echo another reference to her body, not without irony. The world צלם (tzelem, idol, image), would be an inference to the black woman's paganism and the danger of assimilation that she represents, but also to her carnality. The images are associated with orgiastic cults and phalluses.

67. As a double entendre. In the previous stanza "baheret" would have been a play on words and intended to mean "behira," and here "baheret" plays on its meaning as a wound, a physical mark on the body. However, in the carnivalesque spirit of the tale, it is a metaphorical wound, and does not repulse Achbor, but rather entices him, specifically since it is positioned on the shin.

68. The relevant biblical verse includes a third synonym of the idea that the divine wisdom is waiting at the city's threshold: "מבוא פתחים תרנה" (at the coming in at the doors, she crieth aloud).

69. See "interspersed wine poem."

70. "I retorted to his senselessness: Answer the fool, according to his silliness."

71. השוטה היא מדברת דברי פתיות, והומה בקול רם דברי לעג, ואין לה הבנה במה שמוציאה בפיה, אם הוא טוב ואם רע.

72. שאשת הכסילות מגבהת קולה לאמר פתיות לפתות האנשים

73. Seducing is usually in the nif'al verbal stem.

74. The similarity to the word "פות" (vagina) cannot be overlooked.

75. There are four such allegories in the book.

76. See, for example, Gersonides on this verse: הנה היא משמעת קולה בהפך חק האשה הצנועה והיא נוטה מבית בעלה

77. See, for example, Radak: בעלת תרעומת ומורדת לבעלה, והיא יוצאנית ואינה מתעכבת בביתה, כדרך הנשים קלות הדעת

78. See, for example, Rashi סרה מן הדרך; Moses Kimhi (twelfth century) רוצה לומר סרב ונוטה ללכת; Menachem Meiri (thirteenth century) דוברת סרה למוכיחים; ארחות עקלקלות ... הנה והנה

The Tale of Old Bearded Achbor 105

79. הלב מכוסה בזה הפועל כי לא יוכל השכל לעשות פעולתו עם ההמשך אל התאוות.

80. This is also associated with a source from Hosea that we encountered earlier, "אכלו זרים כחו והוא לא ידע גם שיבה זרקה בו והוא לא ידע" (Strangers have devoured his strength, and he knoweth it not; yea, gray hairs are here and there upon him, and he knoweth it not, 7:9).

81. On the signification of the term "crushed testicles" in the Scriptures and the Mishna, see Julius Preuss, *Biblical and Talmudic M edicine*, translated and edited by Fred Rosner (Northvale: Jason Aronson, 1993 [1911 for the original German text]), 330–31.

82. Although the two sicknesses are not synonymous, neither is really evoked to denote a real pathology. Rather, they both function here as metaphors for a sexual disorder, referring to Achbor's genitalia, and it is in that sense that they are interchangeable.

83. This is how Melamed read the scene.

84. Similar to the superficial mimesis of Lemuel as a cuckolded husband when he first sees Achbor and his mistress.

85. ישן לו כל היום, ובאישון לילה הוא ניעור ורודף אחר הניאוף.

86. The comical tone aside, let us note that in the Middle Ages, sexual allegations could have caused accusations in court and severe sentences in the case of adultery, and annulled marriages in the case of impotence. As was shown by two important studies of late medieval English courts, women were more often the target of sexual insults and defamation than men. See L. R. Poos, "Sex, Lies, and the Church Courts of Pre-Reformation England," *The Journal of Interdisciplinary History* 25, no. 4 (Spring, 1995): 585–607; Ruth Mazo Karras, *Sexuality in Medieval Europe: Doing unto others* (New York and London: Routledge, 2017), 180.

87. I am less inclined to accept the possibility, suggested by Melamed, that the maiden's fury could be the expression of her own feelings of humiliation as a rejected woman. Indeed, minutes earlier she was expelled from the palace of delights with the other three maidens because Achbor had fallen asleep, and here she discovers him with another woman. Yet, I am not convinced that she would be offended by Achbor's so-called unfaithfulness to her (and her counterparts) as physical mistresses. As I have shown in chapter 2, there might be here a superficial mimesis of a jealous mistress, equal to the superficial mimesis of Lemuel as a cuckolded husband when he first sees Achbor and his Mistress. Generally, Achbor is a seemingly devout hypocrite *secretly* leading an immoral life while preaching for moral behavior. The way he treats his four maidens-servants, *secretly* keeping another woman, is just another reflection of how he treats his congregation. From this perspective, the insult "crushed testicles" may be alluding, ironically again, to his fake public appearance as a lame man. We have here a perfect *Mise en abyme* of Achbor's hypocrisy. Hence, when the servant says: "the crushed testicle labored in the darkness," she may be voicing both a personal (her immediate displeasure) and a global (the tale's main subject) offense. Whether "crushed testicles" stands for impotent, effeminate, or zealot, the maiden insults him by undermining his manhood, regardless of the truth of this statement. This "love immorality" is the micro expression of the general immorality. In fact, it is almost its synecdoche.

106   *Chapter 1*

88. On the term "she'ol" as referring to hell, see Samuel J. Fox, *Hell in Jewish Literature* (Northbrook: Merrimack College Press, 1972), 7–9. The reference to she'ol is also developed in the fifth tale, relating immoral actions to a predestined fatal punishment. Birsha's beard, like Achbor's, is an externalization of his immorality, and it too is depicted as a beard from hell. These themes are substantially studied and developed in chapters 2 and 3.

89. A bearded anus appears as a mockery in Aristophanes' *The Acharnians*, in which Dicaepolis hurls at one of the ridiculous ambassador's eunuchs: "O shaver of a hot and horny arsehole, with such a beard, you monkey, do you come before us apparelled as a eunuch?" Aristophanes, *Acharnians Knights,* edited and translated by Jeffrey Henderson. Loeb Classical Library 178 (Cambridge, MA: Harvard University Press, 1998), 71. See also the description of Moriuht's lower body.

90. See Psalm 78:51.

91. Saul Nathaniel Brody, *The Disease of the Soul: Leprosy in Medieval Literature* (Ithaca: Cornell University Press, 1974); Danielle Jacquart and Claude Thomasset, *Sexualité et savoir médical au Moyen Age* (Paris: Presses Universitaires de France, 1985), 242–57.

92. Metaphorical sicknesses are a leitmotif in our tale. See, for example, Achbor's self-depiction as having caught a "loin illness," and the first maiden's description of him as a "crushed testicle," as discussed above.

93. See Job 17:12-16.

94. The practice of "to tear off (a man's beard) together with the skin" as an act, though certainly noteworthy for its viciousness, was more than mere punishment: since the beard can serve as a marker of masculinity, its removal shames him whose beard is torn off—shaved—against his will, see Michael Livingstone, "Losing Face: Flayed Beards and Gendered Power in Arthurian Literature," in *Flaying in the Pre-Modern World*, edited by Larissa Tracy (Woodbridge: Boydell & Brewer, 2017), 308. On coerced shaving as punishments see Constable, "Introduction."

95. On the link between this stanza and Num. 8:7, see below.

96. Job used the pottery shard to scrape himself when he was suffering from boil sores.

97. *Chroniques de J. Froissart, troizième livre, Volume 2* (1356–1388), edited by Léon Mirot (Paris: Champion, 1931), 44.

98. The existing manuscripts are from the fourteenth century, but it is likely that the text is much older and goes back to the eleventh century.

99. For a vibrant study of the barbering theme in this tale, see Sarah Sheehan, "Boar-hunts, and Barbering: Masculinity in 'Culhwch ac Olwen,'" *Arthuriana* 15, no. 3 (2005): 3–25. And also an important treatment of the theme in Livingston "Losing Face," specifically on Culhwch ac Olwen, 312–14.

100. "Culhwch and Olwen," in *The Romance of Arthur: An Anthology of Medieval Texts in Translation*, edited by Norris J. Lacy and James J. Wilhelm (Abingdon: Routledge, 2013), 28–57 (translation quoted from this book). For a critical edition, see Rachel Bromwich and D. Simon Evans, *Culhwch and Olwen. An Edition and A Study of the Oldest Arthurian Tale* (Cardiff: University of Wales Press, 1992).

The Tale of Old Bearded Achbor 107

101. Scatological discourses are common in Latin and vernacular medieval literature: ". . . [These] are everywhere in medieval culture: in sermons, in saints' lives,
in histories and chronicles, in Biblical commentaries, in fables and moral tales, in
accounts of heresy and witch trials, in pious poetry, in religion plays, in depictions
of hell, in manuscript illustrations, in paintings in Cathedrals and houses and both
in learned and popular stories. For the medieval world, excrement and dung were
powerful moral and theological material." Martha Bayless, *Sin and Filth in Medieval
Cultures: The Devil in the Latrine* (New York: Routledge, 2012), xviii.

102. Which is also a literary motif. See, for example, this colorful image quoted
from *Le blason des barbes de maintenant,* presented in the Introduction:

Les barbes des prothonotaires,
Des chicaneurs et des dataires
Ne serviront à maistre nul,
Sinon que pour torcher le cul.

(The beard of solicitors / Of ushers, and of officers / Shall not serve for any
task / Other than for to wipe their asses! p. 168). This is also the text that was printed
in Rouen in 1602 (edition accessible on Gallica: file:///C:/Users/314/Downloads/Le_b
lason_des_barbes_de_[. . .]_bpt6k83479q.pdf). Interestingly, an incognito edition
accessible on Googlebooks was published in the nineteenth century "with permission" according to the publisher, where this passage was modified as follows: Les
barbes de ces chaimans, / Des enchanteurs et telles gens" (The beard of these preten-
tious men, Of liars and fellows of this kind). https://books.google.co.zm/books?id
=0JlOAAAAcAAJ&printsec=frontcover#v=onepage&q&f=false

103. See Bakhtin, *Rabelais and His World,* 373.

104. See Isaiah 36:12.

105. First, since leprosy is viewed as a punitive malady resulting from immoral
behavior. Second, Naaman's healing, consisting of a ritual immersion in the water of
the Jordan river, brings the Aramean commander to recognize the superiority of the
Hebrew God.

106. Gellius, *Attic Nights, Volume II: Books 6-13,* translated by J. C. Rolfe. Loeb
Classical Library 200 (Cambridge, MA: Harvard University Press, 1927), 431 (see
chapter 2).

107. *Daurel et Beton, chanson de geste provençale,* edited by Paul Meyer (Paris:
Firmin Didot, 1880), 64, lines 1922–1923, 64, vv. 1922–1923.

108. *Le blason des barbes de maintenant,* 163. See fn. 97.

109. See chapter 2.

110. See the discussion of the giant's coat of beards in chapter 2.

111. The biblical word "weapon" in this context can thus become "privy" in
the translation. See the discussion above regarding the sword held by the beautiful
maiden in the love song.

112. See Rosen, commenting on Achbor's bearding by the four girls (in episode
3), by verbally ridiculing his beard as well as by physically plucking it, as an overt
act of castration. "The Spectacle of the Beard," 6.

113. In her comments on *Culhwch,* Sheehan sees the violent acts of shaving and
killing as a symbolic emasculation, stating that "the scene of excessive shaving as

108   *Chapter 1*

a prelude to execution . . . comes very close to literalizing the threat of castration." Sheehan, "Boar-hunts," 17.

114. On *Lai d'Ignauré*, a thirteenth-century tale by Renaut, and its relevance to the discussion about *Achbor*. See Tovi Bibring, "Violent Women and the Blurring of Gender in some Medieval Narratives," in *Blurred Boundaries in Pre-Modern Texts and Images: Aspects of Audiences and Readers-Viewers Responses,* edited by Dafna Nissim and Vered Tohar (Berlin and Boston: Walter de Gruyter, 2023).

115. Ernst Robert Curtius, *European Literature and the Latin Middle Ages*, translation Willard R. Trask, Bollingen Series (Princeton: Princeton University Press, 1973 [1948]), 195.

116. On the symbolic level, the gardens are synonymous with the vineyards and are regularly juxtaposed as analogous, even interchangeable, in the Bible. For example, "ונטעו כרמים ושתו את יינם ועשו גנות ואכלו את פריהם" (and they shall plant vineyards, and drink the wine thereof; they shall also make gardens, and eat the fruit of them (Amos 9:14). See also the story of King Ahab coveting Navot's vineyard, which he wishes to turn into an herb garden (1 Kings 21:2). The orchard is another interchangeable synonym: see Kohelet, 2:5. Ironically, the figs are also used in the Bible as synonyms of gardens and vineyards (Amos 4:9), though used here as the place of "criticized" love.

117. See Elaine Fantham's commentary on Ovid's *Fasti*, IV:133 in Ovid, *Fasti Book IV* (Cambridge: Cambridge University Press, 1998), 116.

118. Text and translation by J. W. and A. M. Duff are quoted from Tiberianus, in Ernst Robert Curtius, *European Literature and the Latin Middle Ages*, translated by Willard R. Trask, Bollingen Series XXXVI (Princeton: Princeton University Press, 1953), 196.

119. This may echo the number symbolism, as the myrtle tree is one of the four species mentioned in the Torah in the context of the Jewish holiday of Sukkot, and the number four recurs throughout the tale.

120. They wear a very specific garment usually associated with tragedies, the כתנת פסים (coat of many colors). It was the luxurious coat that Jacob offered his youngest and most beloved son Joseph, leading to his brothers' jealousy and their terrible actions (Gen. 37). This is also the clothing worn by King David's virgin daughters, and was worn by Tamar, the king's daughter, and torn thereafter, when she was raped by her brother Amnon (2 Sam. 13). I believe that here Yaakov uses this cloth first as a sign of the maidens' beauty and nobility. Yet, the obscure past these maidens had shared with Achbor makes me wonder if we cannot indirectly link this to the biblical garment given to a chosen child, though in a reversed manner, since here the outfit is related to an optimistic ending.

121. Can we even attempt to count the number of perfumed letters and enticing apples that were thrown out of windows in the medieval maqama (e.g., the ninth tale in *Sefer ha-Meshalim*)? The clandestine trysts of loving neighbors meeting at the windows or climbing therein (e.g., Pyramus and Thisbe, or Marie de France's Laustic)?

122. In chapter 4, the possibility of perceiving the four maidens as metaphorical "doubles" of a single figure. The fact that only one of them sings the final poem supports this claim.

123. The stars are also sometimes personified in biblical language. See, for example, Judges 5:20, Numbers 24:17.

124. These lines are clearly written as poem verses. Yet they seem not to be part of the maiden's poem, but rather a general concluding miniature poem transmitted by the narrator, as they refer to the way the lads act after hearing the instructions conveyed to them by the maiden's poem.

125. ויהי נעורים חדשו, על אוהבים התרפקו

Chapter 2

Beardly Beloved

Discoursing the Beard in Literature

ושערות זקנו עד טבורו האריכה

The hairs of his beard were so long, she reached his navel[1] (Yehuda al-Harizi)[2]

There is not a single person in Israel who grew up in the eighties and is not familiar with Maestro, the leading character of the series *Il était une fois . . . l'Homme* (Once upon a Time . . . Man),[3] which made its debut in 1979. In each episode, Maestro traveled through time and incarnated diverse manifestations of the cultural, positive man, the authoritative elder, the reasonable leader, the wise philosopher, the genius inventor, or the passionate artist. Above all, Maestro was distinguished by the white beard that covered him entirely, from head to toe. Moving from one century to another, from discipline to discipline, the spectacular beard remained. Although his figure was comical and somewhat clumsy, he incarnated all that was positive in a civilized society and showed what could be achieved by the human mind. While the children watching this animated history show might deduce that geniuses were all male and bearded, Maestro was never sexualized and was always presented above the men and women of his community. He did not have a wife or family, yet his most distinct trait, his beard, a symbol of manhood, affirmed, again and again, a historical stereotype: Philosophy, wisdom, spirituality, morality, and leadership are all characteristics that are archetypically linked and often accompanied by a physical, emblematic trait—the white or gray beard of old age.

The beard is on everyone's lips in *The Tale of Old Bearded Achbor*, but mostly on the author's, who seems to relish continuously exploring it through his imagination, offering elaborate descriptions of beards. This discursive enthusiasm with the beard was noticed by Jefim Schirmann: "Yaakov Ben

112   *Chapter 2*

Elazar discusses it [the beard] with exaggerated prominence, returning to it time and again until it seems to have become a fixation. There is no doubt that Yaakov ben Elazar did not like people who grew ostentatious beards to serve them as a certificate of honor and integrity."[4]

The author's apparent rhetorical pleasure while describing the wonders of singular beards extended also to the description of abundant hirsuteness, a fascination that Yaakov ben Elazar shares with numerous writers throughout history, such as the portrayal of the inhumanly old holy man in the French fifteenth-century masterpiece, *Perceforest*,[5] who appears to Alexander the Great and his men and is a prefiguration of the Christian ideal. He was described as wise and spiritual and exemplifying goodness:

> Adont veyrent passer ung homme de tresgrant aaige et voient appertement que sa barbe estoit sy grande et sy longue qu'elle luy venoit jusques emmy la jambe et sy estoit sy treslee qu'il en estoit pardevant tout vestu et sy estoit sy tresblanche que c'estoit une beauté a regarder. Et sy avoit les faitures du viaire sy plaisans selon son aaige qu'on se delictoit ou regarder, car il avoit les yeulx vairs et aussi beaux et aussi clers et aussi netz que ung homme de .XV. ans. Et le viaire avoit il d'une couleur brune et pale, les soucilz luy estoient grans et longz aussi blancz que neige et se recerceloient en montant. Et avoit le viaire a merveilles appert et hardy par semblant selon son aaige. Ses deux grenons luy lançoient aux .II. lez de la bouche sy avant qu'on boutast son puing parmy la recerceleure qui luy descendoit aval sur la poitrine. Après regarda le roy et ses compaignons au passer qu'il fist qu'il avoit sy grant plenté de cheveulx qu'il en estoi tout vestu par derriere et sy estoient sy longz qu'ilz luy venoient rez a rez des talons et en avoit sy grant foison car ceulx de devant, qui luy venoient par derriere descendans, se rassambloient par les costez a la barbe qui l'acouvroit pardevant, sy l'acouvroient sy plainement qu'on ne veoit de tout son corps de nu que le viaire et les bras, qui couvers estoient d'unes manches larges de blanchet, et les piez, qu'il avoit aussy blancs que neige. Et sachiez tous certainement que sa barbe et ses cheveulx, qui acouvroient le corps, estoient aussi netz et aussi desmellez que chacun poil fust ung fil d'argent brun. Et estoit advis a ceulx qui le regardoient qu'on les oïst fourmier entour luy ou il aloit. Et estoient sy blancz a tous lez que ce sembloit de luy chose celestielle.[6]

Then they saw, passing by, a man of very old age, and they clearly saw that his beard was so immense and so lengthy that it descended till the middle of his leg and that it was so abundant that from the front, he was entirely covered by it, and it was also so very white that it was a beauty to contemplate. And his facial features, despite his age, were so pleasing, that one enjoyed gazing upon him because he had fair eyes and likewise beautiful and likewise bright and likewise shiny, just like a man fifteen years of age. And his face was of burnished and somewhat radiant color, his eyebrows were thick and long and also white as snow, and they were curling upwards. And his face was marvelously brave and

Beardly Beloved 113

courageous as it seemed for his age. The two [parts] of his whiskers, spread so far from the two sides of his mouth, that one could capture with one's hand the curling that went down straight on his chest. As he was passing by, the king and his companions noticed that he had such a huge affluence of hair that he was entirely covered from behind and that they were so lengthy that they reached not an inch higher than his heels, and that he had such an abundant mane: hairs from the front side, which came from the two parts of the beard that covered him from the front, joined those that descended from behind and so they covered him entirely that one could not see any of his entire body exposed, except his face and the arms that were dressed with large sleeves of white fabric, and his feet, which were as white as snow. And know for sure that his beard and his hair, which covered his body, were so resplendent and groomed that each hair looked like a burnished silver thread. And it appeared to those who watched him that they were scintillating around him wherever he went. And they were so white from all the parts, that it seemed to be that he was a celestial creature.

It would not be improbable to believe that this approach to the beard echoes an Augustinian tradition admiring Aaron's beard as the pinnacle of holiness based on Psalm 133.[7] Contrarily, like any number of dichotomic archetypes, beards also suffered from a bad reputation. Grown naturally, anyone could have cultivated one effortlessly. Beards were perceived as a superficial mask concealing hypocrisy, deceitfulness, and charlatans who attempted to take advantage of innocent victims. For example, in one of his letters, Hieronymus (*c.* 345–420) described the figure of the shady religious man, suggesting that one should:

Avoid those men also whom you see loaded with chains and wearing their hair long like a woman's, in contravention of the apostle's precept; and with all this a shaggy goat's beard, a black cloak, and bare feet braving the cold. All these things are plain signs of the devil. . . . Such men as these make their way into noble houses, and deceive silly women laden with sins, ever learning and never able to come to the knowledge of the truth. They put on a mournful face and pretend to make long fasts, which for them are rendered easy by secret nocturnal banquets. I am ashamed to say more, lest I should seem to be using the language of invective rather than of admonition.[8]

Schirmann mentioned the beard as a literary motif, referring to the sorcerer Chernomor's beard in Pushkin's poem, *Ruslan and Ludmila*. Presumably, the nineteenth-century magician epitomized a longstanding tradition of heavily bearded men, with the sorcerer archetype evoking the legendary figure of Merlin the Enchanter. Merlin is often depicted as a beggar, clad in tattered garments, bearing a wild appearance characterized by his unkempt beard, as exemplified in a thirteenth-century version of his story: "vns grans sol-ers cauchies & vne courte cote vestue toute depecie si ot les kauels moult

114   *Chapter 2*

hirecies & la barbe moult grande & moult sambloit bien homme saluage"
(he wore big shoes and was clothed with a short coat, all crumbling, he had
very disheveled hair and a very long beard, and he looked a lot like a wild
man).[9] Merlin's thirteenth-century image, however, is based upon much more
ancient discourses.

Recently, Tova Rosen treated, with a pronounced Bakhtinian approach,
the "rich bundle of symbolical meanings" that the beard in *Achbor* may
symbolize.[10] For Rosen, the "preoccupation with beards and their signification echoes (and parodies) the accepted wisdom about the beard in Islamic
culture."[11] Accordingly, Rosen concludes with the suggestion that "Lemuel's
apprehension about beards might then be read as a symptom of a cultural
concern around the problem of Jewish appearance in the motley society of
thirteenth-century Iberia."[12]

The subsequent pages aim at showing that the overstatements regarding
Achbor's beard grant him an honorable position in a series of illustrious and
dubious fellows from various époques and places, also from Christian and
pre-Christian cultures, such as Emperor Julian, the Irish poet Moriuht, the
slave Geta, El Cid, and many more, all of whom stood out for their arrest-
ing bodily hair. I will discuss a variety of texts dealing with the subject of
the beard and with the beard as a subject, attempting to understand the possible significance of the beard as a cultural phenomenon, a *fait social total*,[13]
and an archetype. The subject begs not to be restricted by any traditional
boundaries of linear chronology, cultural or source history. I navigate freely
through time and themes, going backward and forward in the centuries and
the literary genres. This is a crucial point: This study is primarily a literary
analysis rather than a historical investigation.[14] Sometimes I juxtapose a text
with *Achbor*; at other times, I do not, trusting that the apparent affinities will
reinforce the prevalence of a topos. My intention is not to illustrate continuity
and change, draw historical conclusions about specific communities or meth-
ods of growing a beard, or determine specific sources of inspiration. Instead,
I aim to underscore the universalism of beards as a phenomenon, sometimes
in dichotomous and transcendent ways, without consideration for historical
and cultural fashions or modes of beard grooming that may present fundamental differences in different contexts. I argue that discussing the beard as
a symbol, or symbols, differs fundamentally from discussing the beard as a
practice within a specific community.[15] This idea finds support in Michael
Livingstone's remark regarding the pharaohs. They were, he says, "meticulous shavers of body hair in life, they consistently wore—and consistently
had themselves portrayed wearing—false beards, associating themselves with
the bearded god of the afterlife, Osiris, who in turn represented the regular
virility of the life-giving Nile."[16]

This chapter is divided into seven sections, providing various portraits of bearded protagonists. I begin with "Whiskers of Wisdom," a substantially informative account of the philosophical beard as it appeared in antiquity, primarily from the second century onward. Even in ancient times, philosophers were stereotypically portrayed as having unkempt beards, regardless of their school of thought. This stereotype was especially pronounced for the Cynics. However, ancient writers also noted the irony that merely having a beard was not sufficient to make one a philosopher. Following a brief discourse about bearded philosophers, I continue by discussing the religious pastor, or his reversed image, the impostor. This archetype transcends cultural boundaries, appearing in various religious traditions, and its portrayal as a bearded figure traces back to a distant, imagined past. Like the philosopher, the figure of a spiritual leader is characteristically adorned with an impressive beard, and like the vain philosopher who grows a beard so he may be perceived as a true philosopher, so does the fraudulent holy man. The prototype of the bearded spiritual pastor is not limited to specific churchmen but rather stems from a stereotypical cultural tradition that harkens back to legendary or biblical times.[17] In this section I will provide a few examples, attempting to demonstrate that the cultural ambivalence between the positive and negative images reflected by the beard, which is a leitmotif in *The Tale of Old Bearded Achbor*, is a constant that is discernible over generations, from antiquity to modern times. The section "The Misopogon" delves into the ludicrous portrayal of Achbor's beard as harboring all sorts of animals and insects. This comical caricature, which is repeated numerous times in the tale, is reminiscent of the *Misopogon*. Composed by Emperor Julian in the fourth century, the author admits that his rumpled beard swarms with lice. After providing a few other examples of human hair so filthy that it hosts imaginary and non-imaginary creatures, I examine whether this feature signifies another aspect of Achbor's heretic nature or inclination to assimilation, a topic to be explored further in section seven. The sections "Penis Erectus" and "Smooth Women, Bearded Men, or Vice Versa?" analyze sexual and gendered perceptions represented by the beard, and by extension by pilosity in general. This perspective may be the most relevant to the discussion of *The Tale of Old Bearded Achbor*. As the title indicates, in section "Penis Erectus," I delve into the portrayal of the overstated bearded man as a *Penis Erectus*, that is, a synecdochic depiction of the figure as a phallus. In another study, I demonstrated how this topos, which appears on three occasions in *Sefer ha-Meshalim*—besides the tale of our protagonist, Achbor, Birsha from Tale Five, and Cushan from Tale Six—can also be interpreted as embodiments of *pene erecti*, either reflecting the forbidden desires of their rivals or embodying the claws of social morals and order. Consistent with this book's methodological approach, here, leaning on a rich tradition of hirsute men embodying monstrous sexuality, my

116   *Chapter 2*

analysis primarily focuses on metaphorical-cultural depictions, particularly within the botanical realm, which assigned the metaphor of a branch to the penis. This part presents the beard as a cultural symbol imbued with pejorative connotations, associated with monstrosity, bestiality, and repressed desires. The section "Smooth Women, Bearded Men, or Vice Versa?" offers a correlating view of abundant pilosity. It emphasizes the obvious gendered disparity culturally constructed between men and women regarding the growth of bodily hair, based on the premise that it is not animalistic but rather extremely masculine. The section illustrates how medicine, philosophy, theology, and literary taste have promoted the notion that beards signify male superiority over female inferiority. I begin with a short overview of how culture expected women not to be bearded. While this may seem redundant, an analysis from a cultural perspective reveals that the issue extends beyond the proportion of women who suffered from hypertrichosis. Moreover, this chapter deals with the concept of women as bearers of a "pubic beard," which beauty standards encouraged them to remove. In this section, I suggest that such ideals stem from a conditioned gendered mentality, where the presence or absence of facial hair symbolizes dominance or submission. After illustrating this submissiveness with several sources depicting upper and lower bearded women, the section moves to examine the second side of the same coin, the perception of shaven or smooth-skinned men as effeminate. This section contributes to the broader understanding of how the punishment of beard plucking or shaving, the very punishment ultimately reserved for Achbor, serves as a metaphor for symbolic castration. This theme is the focal point of the section "Le Chastel des Barbes," which examines the phenomenon of the beard as an inherent symbol of male honor, a concept widely acknowledged by scholars such as Livingstone and Rosen.[18] After briefly mentioning two bearded national heroes celebrated for their battles against the Moors, the Frankish leader Charlemagne and the Castilian El Cid, both renowned for their beards, I examine this premise against the backdrop of the Celtic folkloric motif of a castrating giant collecting kings' beards to fashion a mantle for himself. This motif was somewhat cynically adapted in French romances, which incorporate the presence of a femme fatale into a struggle between two men vying for rulership. To demonstrate the humorous motif of beards, I include a short section titled "This Beard Was Meant for Kissing," which focuses on the humoristic aspects of beards, upper and lower, in "romantic situations" gone astray. Shlomo ibn Zakbel's "The Tale of Asher ben Yehuda," and Yehuda al-Harizi's "Tale of the Seven Virgins," deal with protagonists tricked by bearded men disguised as women, whom they wish to kiss. By drawing ideological parallels from classical literature, such as Aristophanes' "The Knights" and Apuleius' "Metamorphoses," as well as medieval narratives featuring characters like Lancelot, this section

Beardly Beloved 117

explores the symbolic use of beards and female sexuality across cultures. It also investigates the homoerotic subtext in medieval literature, focusing on intimate moments between men mistaken for women and the implications of these encounters.

Following, in the section "A Beard from Hell," I draw a parallel between Achbor's beard and the *barboir*, a facial mask depicting a dreadful bearded creature, which is designed to evoke fear by resembling the archetypal imagined look of the devil. The premise of this section is not that Achbor wears such a mask, but rather that his beard has the potential to function as one.[19] This association with such a mask allows us to consider another dramatic effect: Achbor as a frightening, demonized figure capable of causing harm. This concept paves the way to perceiving Achbor as a New Balaam. A profound and ancient apprehension surfaces in *The Tale of Old Bearded Achbor*: the dread of cultural and religious assimilation, a subject which will be explored in the following chapters.

WHISKERS OF WISDOM

. . . presence and a fine physical endowment should be among the attributes of a philosopher, and that above all else he should have a long beard that would inspire confidence in those who visited him and sought to become his pupils.[20]

You often see him, Cosmus, in the recess of our Pallas and by the threshold of the New Temple, an old man with staff and wallet. His bristling hair is white and powdery, his unkempt beard falls on his chest, a threadbare cloak, spouse to his bare pallet, covers him, and the crowd that comes his way gives him the food he barks for. Deceived by fake appearance you take him for a Cynic. He is no Cynic, Cosmus. What then? A dog.[21]

Greek and Roman writers and poets wrote abundantly on the external signifiers of the philosopher, whose commonly accepted characteristics were his facial hair, a cloak, a *pēra* (a bag or a wallet), and a stick.[22] This could apply to any philosopher, but the stream that was perhaps most associated with these features was Cynicism. The characteristic appearance—"disheveled hair, an uncropped and untended beard, a savage expression"—is considered "the Cynic uniform."[23] Philosophers persisted with the trend of growing beards, despite the fact that since the time of Alexander, both the Greeks and the Romans usually shaved their beards.[24] When drawing the portrait of Euphrates, the philosopher he admired, Pliny the Younger (first and second century) acknowledged that, although beards are not of real significance, they contribute to building a positive image: "He is moreover tall and distinguished to look at, with long hair and a flowing white beard, and though these

118 *Chapter 2*

may sound like natural advantages of no real importance, they help to make him widely respected."[25] The Greek philosopher Apollonius of Tyana (second century) noted that: "There is no wise elder in Athens, for no one at all has a bushy beard, since no one has any beard."[26] Simultaneously, an existing literary convention purports to doubt the external appearance of the sublimed figure. The saying "that having a beard and wearing a coarse cloak does not make philosophers," here quoted from Plutarch (first and second century), has been repeated in many variations.[27] Numerous anecdotes and satirical discourses abound concerning bearded men masquerading as philosophers in antiquity, their remarkable beards serving as a hallmark of their supposed wisdom or authority. As the examples are endless, let me examine a select few. Plutarch, who frequently spoke of beards, attempted to demonstrate the insignificance of the philosopher's beard and cloak by comparing students of philosophy to grains.[28] Grains are only appreciated by the farmers when they are heavy and thus are bent forward toward the ground. When they are empty and light, they can stand high and straight but are useless. By the same token, young students of philosophy can grow themselves beards, wear cloaks, and behave arrogantly, but still are not worthy of the title "philosopher." Only when:

> They lay aside their swagger and superficiality. And just as when empty vessels are being filled with a liquid the air inside is expelled by the pressure, so when men are being filled with the really good things, their conceit gives way and their self-opinion becomes less inflexible; and, ceasing to feel pride in their philosopher's beard and gown, they transfer their training to their mind, and apply their stinging and bitter criticism most of all to themselves, and are milder in their intercourse with others. They do not arrogate to themselves, as before, the name of philosophy and the repute of studying it, or even give themselves the title of philosopher.[29]

In his treatise about the way to recognize a flatterer, Plutarch exposes "the flatterer's chameleon-like promptitude in changing shapes according to the characters of his victims."[30] When his potential victim is "a scholarly and studious young man," the flatterer "is absorbed in books, his beard grows down to his feet, the scholar's gown is the thing now and a stoic indifference, and endless talk about Plato's numbers and right-angled triangles." When the victim changes into another type of man, a rich drinker, "off goes the scholar's gown, the beard is mowed down like an unprofitable crop."[31]

Aulus Gellius (second century) recounts the following anecdote:

> To Herodes Atticus, the ex-consul, renowned for his personal charm and his Grecian eloquence, there once came, when I was present, a man in a cloak, with

Beardly Beloved 119

long hair and a beard that reached almost to his waist, and asked that money be given him εἰς ἄρτους, that is, "for bread." Then Herodes asked him who on earth he was, and the man, with anger in his voice and expression, replied that he was a philosopher, adding that he wondered why Herodes thought it necessary to ask what was obvious. "I see," said Herodes, "a beard and a cloak; the philosopher I do not yet see. Now, I pray you, be so good as to tell me by what evidence you think we may recognize you as a philosopher." Meanwhile, some of Herodes' companions told him that the fellow was a vagabond of worthless character, who frequented foul dives and was in the habit of being shamefully abusive if he did not get what he demanded.[32]

Dio Cassius (second–third century) also writes that

Mucianus made a great number of remarkable statements to Vespasian against the Stoics, asserting, for instance, that they are full of empty boasting, and that if one of them lets his beard grow long, elevates his eyebrows, wears his coarse mantle thrown back over his shoulder and goes barefooted, he straightway lays claim to wisdom, bravery and righteousness, and gives himself great airs, even though he may not know either his letters or how to swim, as the saying goes.[33]

It would be worthwhile to end this overview of classical "philosophical beards" with Lucian (second century), who is perhaps the most fertile writer on this subject. In one of his mordant satires against philosophers, the beard becomes part of the plot. He tells of Hermes who, boarding dead people on Charon's boat, is responsible for stripping them of their earthly possessions and attributes. Menippus is the first to embark and takes a seat of honor near Hermes. We then read of a course of distinguished figures leaving behind their belongings when Hermes notices:[34] "But here's an august personage, to judge by his appearance, and a proud man. Who can he be, with his haughty eyebrows, thoughtful mien, and bushy beard?" Menippus then replies: "A Philosopher, Hermes, or rather an impostor, full of talk of marvels. Strip him too, and you'll see many amusing things covered up under his cloak."[35] Hermes demands that the philosopher strip off his clothes to reveal the other surprising traits that characterize philosophers: ". . . hypocrisy . . . ignorance, contentiousness, vanity, unanswerable puzzles, thorny argumentations . . . complicated conceptions . . . wasted effort . . . nonsense . . . idle talk . . . . splitting of hairs . . . gold . . . soft living, shamelessness, temper, luxury, and effeminacy, falsehood too, and your pride, and notions of your superiority over the rest of men."[36] When the philosopher sheds all of these traits, Menippus insists: "But he ought to take off that beard as well, Hermes; it's heavy and shaggy, as you can see. He has at least five pounds of hair there."[37] Hermes complies, while the philosopher worries: "Who will be my barber?"[38] It is then decided that Menippus will cut the beard off with an axe. When the

120 *Chapter 2*

anchor of Charon's boat is finally lifted, Hermes asks, "Why are you groaning like that, you fools, and you, in particular, the philosopher just despoiled of the beard?" The philosopher explains that he is crying because he thought his soul was immortal, but Menippus replies: "That he'll have no more expensive dinners, or go out at night, unknown to all, with his cloak wrapped over his head, and go the round of the brothels, and never again take money the next morning for cheating the young men with his show of wisdom. That's what grieves him."[39]

The criticism directed at the philosopher, intentionally left unnamed so that he may embody any and all philosophers, is reminiscent of the accusations against Achbor. Expensive dinners, debauchery, money earned by cheating, and a charade of wisdom—we have read that these are all part of Achbor's life. This should not be surprising, as these types of transgressions are archetypal. Gluttony, sexuality, and impersonation are all common deviations from social norms, and therefore prevail in stories and tales worldwide.

In some of the quotes presented in this section, the caricature of the bearded philosopher is understandable, given the significant role that erudite philosophers played in the second century. Their influence on community life, advising leaders, educating and mingling with aristocrats, and engaging in various forms of teaching and preaching, coupled with certain privileges such as tax exemptions, rendered them respected but also prime targets for satire.[40]

Gellius' description of the incompetent philosopher captures this authoritative role, akin to the influence exerted by spiritual and religious leaders. "I hate base men who preach philosophy. For he said that nothing could be more shameful or insufferable than that idle, lazy folk, disguised with beard and cloak, should change the character and advantages of philosophy into tricks of the tongue and of words, and, themselves saturated with vices, should eloquently assail vice."[41] We could easily replace the phrase "who preach philosophy" with "who preach morality" and receive a very similar portrait of the danger Achbor warns his congregation of: "lest those who bear beards of ignominies and impiety, blighted by evil, carry you astray, and branches of deception and dissimulation standing firm lead you close to them." He is referring, in other words, to tricks of the tongue and tricks of appearance, that is, disguised with the beard, aligning with archetypal perceptions of revered figures. In these instances, whether a real philosopher actually had a beard is inconsequential, as the literary and philosophical debate divorces the beard from its historical context and trends. The second-century philosopher Epictetus, for example, refused to surrender to fashion, because for him the beard represented his essence: "Come then, Epictetus, shave off your beard." If I am a philosopher, I answer, "I will not shave it off."[42]

In medieval Europe, pseudo-religious figures should be viewed through a similar lens. It is important, however, to differentiate between Western and Eastern Christianity, as they held contradictory views on the subject of beards for holy men. At the end of the Middle Ages, the beard was perceived as the religious mark of the Eastern Church priests or of a distant, somewhat exotic spiritual authority. As opposed to the Eastern Church, the Western Church considered *barba prolixa* (long beards) to be a sign of the inferior social and spiritual status of the "lay brothers," known as "*conversi barbati*" (bearded laymen).[43] Unlike the clerical monks who were educated in the monasteries from a young age, these religious men entered the monasteries at an age where they were old enough to have a beard, which they were obliged to grow and thus be distinguished from the shaven clerics.[44] Giles Constable showed "the beards of the lay brothers were considered a mark of their low status and menial occupations,"[45] and Leclercq demonstrated that it also symbolized their illiteracy. In the eyes of the Western Church, "beardliness was next to godliness," and though beards were originally grown so as to distinguish them from ordinary men, laypeople continued to grow beards because "shaving was a spiritual act for churchman but perverse in laymen," as stated by Christopher Oldstone-Moore.[46] As for the Jewish community, Elimelech Horowitz found that medieval Jews living in Christian Europe usually followed the Gentile custom and did not grow long beards, as did the Jews under Muslim influence in the Mediterranean countries.[47]

This overview is intentionally brief, for many studies have already delved into the history and cultural history of the various fashions, conventions, and regulations surrounding beards, both for laypeople and within different religious communities.[48] To understand the beard as a phenomenon, a fait social total, and as an archetype, I have chosen to focus on the universal conception of beards rather than the differences in beard styles across eras, cultures, and geographies. Therefore, I explore beards as an archetype transcribed into the human experience, echoing a mythological distant past. Earlier, we discussed Perceforest, who provided a sublime description of holiness residing in the momentous beard of a spiritual figure. Let me end with the opposite view that, although later than Achbor, shares similarities with him:

Vers la fin du quatorzieme siècle, on vit paroître, en France, la Barbe la plus vaste qui ait jamais existé: elle appartenoit à un certain Impostur, qui se disoit Patriarche de Constantinople, & qui, sous ce titre, se fit render divers honneurs dans plusieurs Cours de l'Europe. Il vint à Paris en 1329. Les Parisiens, toujours curieux, toujours étonnés, ne pouvoient se lasser de contempler cette Barbe immense. Cet Imposteur, graces à cet ornement respectable, reçut l'accueil le plus gracieux, et ne disparut qu'après avoir été comblé d'aumônes a de libéralités.[49]

122   *Chapter 2*

Towards the end of the fourteenth century, one noticed, in France, the vastest beard that had ever existed: it belonged to a certain impostor who presented himself as the Patriarch of Constantinople, and who, under this title, managed to receive many honors in several European Courts. He arrived in Paris in 1392. The Parisians are always curious, and always astonished, and could not stop contemplating this immense beard. This impostor, thanks to this respected ornament, received the most gracious welcome, and did not disappear until after he obtained many alms and donations.

Achbor is a preacher in an exotic Mediterranean city,[50] but in this case, his beard transcends, I contend, mere fashion or religious symbolism; it signifies his immoral character. His beard is not associated with any specific religion but rather serves as a manipulative tool. By projecting a positive, religious appearance through his beard, Achbor gains the trust of the public, only to betray it. In this way, his beard becomes a symbol of deception and abuse of trust, representing all impostors, regardless of their religious affiliation.

THE MISOPOGON

The magnificence of Achbor's beard is ambiguous. While it inspires reverence for an authoritative figure and appears etiological to a certain degree, as it is worshipped and feared as if it were a holy relic, we cannot overlook the comical, somewhat degrading description of its wildness. "A calf grazed there, it was sprawled there, destroying all its fronds. Its sight amazed and frightened all who looked at it," says the narrator introducing Achbor. A member of the audience in Achbor's sermon suggests that the beard is a place "upon each frond the whelps crouch." The topos comes to a climax when one of the four maidens describes Achbor's beard, whose "invigorated branches are a harbor for conies. From section to section, it is a refuge where foxes wander and the fleas, that had been there for a long time, fall asleep within it." She returns to the topos, stating:

In it, little animals march, and I had wondered: inside / are these apes that hide? / I have seen some creatures flying into it like birds, / and fleas have taken possession of it and set up their nests there, undeterred / I was answered: Achbor's beard is like a forest, / where [live] wild animals and little foxes. / There, the night-owl nested and laid eggs, / and there, it is also a refuge for the conies. / There they reside safely and with peace of mind, / each complacent under their vines. And each under their fig tree abound, / under Achbor's beard's shadow, invigorated and safe and sound!"

Beardly Beloved 123

The comical and exorbitant description of the disheveled beard, overwhelming readers with the chaotic impossibility that "innocent" animals, predators, and insects all live in the beard in perfect harmony, constructs Achbor's negative image. These themes appear in an ironic statement made by Emperor Julian in his *Misopogon* (Beard-Hater). In 361–362, the emperor stayed for several months in the city of Antioch, reputed to be quite corrupt. During his stay, he tried to restore the pagan cult in a city that was already Christian, as he believed that philosophy belongs to the gods. However, "his austere personality and mode of life repelled the Syrian populace and the corrupt officials of Antioch. They satirized him in anapaestic verses."[51] While these verses are no longer extant, according to the *Misopogon,* which is comprised of the emperor's derisive response to the allegations of the people of Antioch upon his departure, they mocked his physicality and especially his "philosophical beard."[52] As a reaction drenched in acidic irony, the emperor composed an alleged negative self-portrayal, sarcastically highlighting his deformed physical appearance. He begins by depicting his face, acknowledging that his deliberate choice to grow a beard serves as his personal form of retribution for not having been blessed with handsome features.

> For though nature did not make this any too handsome or well-favoured or give it the bloom of youth, I myself out of sheer perversity and ill-temper have added to it [his ugliness] this long beard of mine, to punish it, as it would seem, for this very crime of not being handsome by nature. For the same reason I put up with the lice that scamper about in it as though it were a thicket for wild beasts. As for eating greedily or drinking with my mouth wide open, it is not in my power; for I must take care, I suppose, or before I know it I shall eat up some of my own hairs along with my crumbs of bread. In the matter of being kissed and kissing I suffer no inconvenience whatever. And yet for this as for other purposes, a beard is evidently troublesome, since it does not allow me to press shaven "lips to other lips more sweetly."[53]

The image of flowing manes of hair accommodating living creatures is repeated in coarse narratives from the Middle Ages onward, sometimes exchanging the upper beard with the "lower beard."[54] The disgraceful portrait of Moriuht, a dubious fellow who will be presented in more detail below, shows him wearing minimalistic animal skins, through which his genitals can be seen in their entirety, his anus so wide that "Cattus ut ingrediens annum requiescere totum / Posset cum catta huc hiemando sua / Inguinis in silua nidum ciconia magna, / Vppupa uel proprium posset habere locum" (a cat could enter into it and rest (there) for an entire year, passing the winter in company with his consort cat, that in the vast forest of his groin a stork could build its nest and a hoopoe could have a place of its own).[55]

124   *Chapter 2*

An anonymous sixteenth-century comical parody that was strictly devoted to the way beards should and should not be worn, and to the men who should or should not bear them, emphasizes the difference between a well-kept beard, which is sublime, and "Qu'un hideux barbaux paysant / Qui tord la gueulle et fait la mine: / Sa barbe plaine de vermine, / De morpions, de poux et lentes / Sans repos et puces groulantes" (a hideous bearded peasant who sulks and pretends: His beard is full of vermin, with crabs, lice and restless lice eggs, and anxious fleas).[56]

The beard as a home for living creatures is also related to a medical condition, as any hirsute locus of the body is susceptible to harmful lice and insects capable of causing diseases, particularly transmitting sexual maladies. For this reason, it was common for prostitutes to remove their pubic hair. This practice, which was intended to minimize the chance of contracting sexual diseases, received ribald connotations. Studying the images of pubic hair in seventeenth-century Spanish erotic poetry, Manuel Montoya hypothesizes that one of the reasons prostitutes shaved their vaginas was "for hygienic reasons: a cleared of any hair pudenda gave the innocent client a healthier image and seemed to mean that there was no risk of finding 'ladillas' (pubic lice), as the pubic scruff could harbor a thousand beasties."[57] Nevertheless, read from an allegorical perspective, anecdotes about beasts and insects living in a person's hair could have conveyed the notion of the transmission of heretical religious ideas. Lemuel refers to Achbor's beard as unhealthy and to all the living creatures therein as sinful: "a beard so lengthy but not healthy, / in its sin, its inhabitants rot." In sum, we may deduce that literary descriptions of hair parasites, especially in pubic or rectal hair, rarely refer to actual medical conditions. Rather, they are euphemistic for the consequences of shameful actions and thus bespeak immorality.

PENIS ERECTUS

Long-bearded Hermes, why is your penis [pointing] to your beard and not to your feet?[58]

The lexical fields used to refer to beards in our tale combine the botanical with the anatomical,[59] providing a comical / caricatural and quite sexual image of their bearers. When Achbor warns against bearded seducers, he refers to their beards as "branches of deception and dissimulation standing firm," where "standing firm" is an interpretative translation of עלות בקנה אחד.[60] Although the sexual undertone is evident, I believe, in the translation, it should be noted that in Hebrew the phrase is even bawdier, with the verb "עולות" close to "erecting," while the stalk, like a branch, is a well-attested metaphor for

Beardly Beloved 125

the penis (קנה also means a limb, a hand, another euphemism). Several other images use both branches as limbs and their expansion portrays the image of the beard as a *penis erectus* or, even better, of the caricatural tree of *penes erecti*, as endless phallic branches spread out from Achbor's beard.[61] The description of Achbor's beard, divided into branches, is repeated on several occasions: "He had a beard and branches grew from it, and they were divided here and there, all its offshoots and sections and feathers and wings spread out"; "Its branches stretch to every part and sector"; and, finally, "Humble yourself before the length of his beard and the abundance of its branches." This description is reminiscent of Atlas' beard becoming a forest of trees during his metamorphosis into a giant: "Straightway Atlas became a mountain huge, as the giant had been; his beard and hair were changed to trees, his shoulders and arms to spreading ridges; what had been his head was now the mountain's top, and his bones were changed to stones."[62]

The horrific Cyclops Polyphemus in Ovid's *Metamorphoses* also creates an analogy between his beard and a tree. Deeply in love with the Nereid Galatea, she overhears him singing a love poem to her while she is lying beneath a rock in the arms of her mortal beloved, Acis. In this song, Polyphemus begs Galatea to love him, attempting to convince her that his hairiness (not to mention the one large eye positioned on his forehead; see also note 77 below) is a synonym for masculinity.

A wealth of hair overhangs my manly face and it shades my shoulders like a grove. And don't think it ugly that my whole body is covered with thick, bristling hair. A tree is ugly without its leaves and a horse is ugly if a thick mane does not clothe his sorrel neck; feathers clothe the birds, and their own wool is becoming to sheep; so a beard and shaggy hair on his body well become a man. True, I have but one eye in the middle of my forehead, but it is as big as a good-sized shield.[63]

Polyphemus' emphasis on his manhood, as reflected by his hairiness, facilitates the interpretation of his hirsute body as a phallus.

Stalks, stems, and especially branches (*ramus*), are well-established metaphors for erect phalluses since, as argued by J. N. Adams, Ausonius "imposed a sexual sense" on a Virgilian expression.[64] In Ausonius' (fourth century) *Nuptial Cento*, the new bride's defloration (note the word in Latin, *imminutio*, meaning mutilation) is described as the groom's branch (ramum, qui veste latebat, meaning the branch, hidden in his garment) violently penetrating her.[65]

In *Achbor*, when the third maiden declaims her disparaging poem, she is quite graphic in her invective strophe, using these archetypal metaphors: "The [facial] hairs reached the hairs of his limb, wing to wing they touched each

126   *Chapter 2*

other." It is hard not to see the duality that the word "limb" suggests here, as both the organ and the branch, the organ that is a branch. Achbor's beard is fused this way with his pubic hair, signifying a bold and explicit correlation.

To broaden the horizons of this discussion, I wish to present several case studies from medieval European literature.

Moriuht is a sordid satire written in the eleventh century by Warner of Rouen, a Norman satirist, about an Irish poet despised for his Otherness, being both Irish and a pagan, and, more specifically, for what the narrator considers a lack of talent and any poetic skill. The tale follows Moriuht throughout his astonishing adventures, which include repeated kidnappings, sexual assault, enslavement, and beatings, until he finally reunites with his wife, who had been abducted by Vikings and forced into servitude and prostitution, and their child. While the plot of this tale does not have much in common with the tale of Achbor, the substantial stratum is very close. Both Achbor and Moriuht are portrayed as the embodiment of abhorrence and transgression by the authors who created them. Warner fiercely denounces Moriuht's pretense of being a great erudite and poet, as he believes that Moriuht has distorted the art of classical poetry by changing its rules of metrics and versifying, which is deserving of contempt and should be eradicated.[66]

Yaakov / Lemuel sees Achbor as a false preacher. His enthusiastic sermon may repeat clichés and banalities, but as he himself does not follow its principles, he too is deserving of contempt and should be eradicated.[67] Notably, while Moriuht is not described specifically as bearded, he is depicted as a man-goat, animalistically hirsute (the goatee has become a particular word mocking philosophers' beards),[68] except for his bald head.[69] Specifically, his private parts are said to be dirty and wooded.

Warner did not spare his ink while depicting Moriuht as a walking penis of sorts, using the tree branch metaphor for his sexual organ. He created a metonymic bond between Moriuht and his penis, beginning with nicknaming him Mentula, which is a coarse term for the penis.[70] He then portrayed him as a bald man. When some nuns in Corbridge buy him as a slave: "Crispando risum detegit hec ueretum; / Qvid? dicam Moriuht cunctas ardere iuuencas / Ex coitu ramo tangere necne suo? Agnosei coepit cunctis ramoque pateri" (Grinning, this (nun) uncovers his dick [ueretum] (What? Shall I relate that Moriuht burned to touch with his penis [*ramo*] every young heifer in copulation or no? he begins to be recognized and to be available to all with his penis [*ramoque*]).[71] Later on, we hear of how Glicerium, Moriuht's wife, is constantly searching for "amare suum" (her own love), that is, her husband, even as a slave and a prostitute. While she provided sexual services to many others, she continued to search for her husband "Sicut uacca suum querit per deuia taurum / Sic hoc mancipium guasape uel ueretrum" (just as a cow seeks to find her bull through a remote

Beardly Beloved 127

place, so this creature—indeed cunt—(seeks for) a penis).[72] This may seem here as just another bawdy remark aimed at spicing up the already vulgar tone of the tale, while simultaneously reflecting the prevailing misogynistic tone. Yet, Warner engages this form of bawdiness to solidify his main argument. The Irish poet desacralizes poetry, and therefore he is attacked by poetry's defender, the referent, which represents the sharpest contrast to the refined intellectual activity, inspiration, talent, and humanity. Comparing Moriuht and Virgil, Warner concludes "Tv gratus domine pendentis munere coxe / Hic carus Rome carminis ex specie" (your mistress held you dear for the performance of your dangling hip bone. This man (Virgil) was valued in Rome for the beauty of his poetry).[73]

Elsewhere, Warner develops a synecdoche, suggesting that Moriuht's genitals define him: "Si quis adhuc audire cupit discriminia Scotti, / Perquirat enium corporis et uicium" (If anyone still desires to hear of the perilous situation of the Irishman, he should study in detail his penis and the violation inflicted on his body).[74]

Geta is a twelfth-century Latin comedy attributed to Vital de Blois. Based on the classical myth, it relates Jupiter's wish to possess Alcmena, Amphitryon's wife. Jupiter metamorphosizes as Amphitryon, while his son Archas metamorphosizes as Geta, Amphitryon's slave. Geta is charged with watching the door while Jupiter, posing as Amphitryon, makes love to Alcmena in the real Amphitryon's bedroom. When the real Geta returns home and finds all the doors closed, he hears Archas asserting that he, Geta, is already there. The confused Geta asks for proof that the person in the house is the same Geta as himself, while he is standing outside. Archas proceeds to describe himself, and it is this description that is relevant to us.

Archas then caricaturizes Geta-Archas through exaggerated stereotypes of alienation. He says that Geta is so very black: "Totus inaudita fedaque nigredine dampnor / Atque color membris omnibus unus inest; / Sum uelut Ethiopes aut quales India nutrit" (I am afflicted everywhere with an unheard-of and disgusting blackness, and my limbs are all the same color: I am the same as the Ethiopians, or the children of India). He is distorted and disproportionate: "Frons breuis et naris longa, reubentoculi . . . Collaque longa mihi sunt humerique breues . . . . Tibia curta mihi sed grossa pedesque recurui Ut pedibus solea nulla sit apta meis" (My forehead is low, my nose long, my eyes red; . . . my neck is long and my shoulders narrow . . . I have a short but fat leg, and my feet are so crooked that no sandal can fit them). He is fat: "Sic tumeo uentre quod dicor ydropicus esse, Et stomacus paruum neseit habere modum; Zonaque nulla potest hunc castigare tumorem Cum pane absortis dum tumet aluus aquis; Deest spatium lateri, deest renibus" (I have a belly so swollen that I am said to be hydropic, and my stomach does not know how to keep small measures; no belt can repress this swelling, When my belly is swollen with panade: my flanks lack room, my kidneys lack room). But most of all, he is hairy: "Hirsutum caput est et cinctum crine caprine . . . Menta genasque tegit et obumbrat silua pilorum . . . Hispida erura Sunt mihi que scabies ut sua regna tenet, Sed sic dum crebro singultu colligit iram Ad curtum muto tenditur usque genu" (My head is hairy and crowned with a goat's fleece, . . . a forest of hair covers my chin and cheeks with its shadow . . . I have hairy thighs, where scabies reign supreme, but, when with repeated palpitations it gathers its wrath, my virile limb elongates as far as my knees, which are low).[75]

Archas creates a reversed symmetry between facial ugliness and genital magnificence. The analogy, although reversed, functions precisely because of one common denominator, that is, the abundance of hair on both the head and face and the penis.[76]

The facial hair mirrors genital hair, the only distinction lying in public versus private presentation. While the face and the head belong to the public sphere, the lower body belongs to the intimate, unseen, private sphere. Similarly, what must be acknowledged as repulsive publicly can be confessed to be attractive privately. Hence, while women might be "socially" repelled by the hirsute, hideous, black Geta and are his enemies, they become his friends in the private zone: "Si qua meos uultus non amat, inguen amat: / Quas hostes uultus, inguen mihi, reddit amieas." (If some [woman] doesn't like my face, she likes my penis; just as my face provides me enemies, my penis brings me lady-friends.)[77]

This blurring between the head and the lower body, which is made possible because of the combination of genital and facial hair, also appears in *Achbor*.[78] Here, however, the movement is reversed. Achbor's "public" pilosity is at first socially admired. It is only when he is revealed as an impostor that it is compared to the hairs of the lower body, when one of the maidens complains that "[his facial] hairs reached the hairs of his limb, wing to wing they touched each other."[79] Seeing one is like seeing the other, and there is a fusion and confusion between the hairs to the point that the entire body becomes a big phallus and the man is melded into it.

Precisely like Moriuht, while Geta possesses a repulsive appearance, he is desired by women. Archas explains that "Ut uerum fatear, non Geta sed inguen amatur . . . Sic ut totus amer pars facit una mei" (to tell the truth, it is not Geta but his groin that is loved . . . hence a single part of me brings to love all of me). Both Moriuht and Geta are reminiscent of satyrs, mythological creatures with an "almost permanent state of erection . . . and always of exaggerated proportions"[80] (see Geta: "nunquam placata priapo Semper inest rabies, et modus absque modo." Never appeased, an amorous passion is always there in my phallus [priapo],[81] and its measure is beyond measure). In other words, as part of their dehumanization, alongside their "bestialization,"

Beardly Beloved 129

they are also objectified as phalluses. As such, they are not merely despised for their own animalistic desires, but also for their close and debasing association with women, culturally perceived as sexually unsatiable.[82] I have suggested earlier that the lewd analogy between Glicerium and a cow is in itself misogynistic but that it should be read in the global context, which is also misogynistic and reinforces the gap between women (or any "Other") and intellectual activity. Women, who are excluded from the domain of poetry, can enjoy Moriuht's "poetry" (i.e., sexual activity), which is more inspired by the Bacchae than the Muses. Moriuht is rejected as a poet because of his lack of talent. Yet, although throughout the tale Warner interweaves explanations about Moriuht's disastrous compositions, what captures the most attention and best illustrates his incompetence is the corruption of his body, both as a satyr of sorts with women and as a woman of sorts with men (not merely is he in the submissive position of penetration when he is raped but he also expresses pleasure from this position).[83]Achbor may be echoing, to a certain extent, men like Moriuht and Geta. Physically, he looks like them, as he is monstrous in his appearance and satyr-like in the way his hairiness is depicted. Achbor, however, is not an active "philanderer" who is fulfilling voracious feminine lust. His suggestive phallic image remains mostly in the narrative sphere. The metaphorical depiction of the beard gives the impression of Achbor's debauchery, influencing our perception of him as a lecher as we read that he is "bouncing from lap to lap" of the four maidens, or when hearing Lemuel's description of adultery as the fifth woman joins him, and when Achbor talks about his loin-ache and his desire for rotten figs. Nevertheless, besides bawdy verbal suggestions, not one real sexual episode occurs in the tale. Achbor falls asleep, or pretends to do so, in the middle of the lap dance, and thus it can be safely argued that, at the most, it was foreplay gone wrong. Since he is attacked the moment that the mistress enters the room, and Lemuel strips them of their clothes as a means of humiliation, we may deduce that they did not even have the chance to disrobe. This, perhaps, may not be surprising in a tale about a man whose beard is, in any case, a fictitious means, intended to camouflage his hypocrisy. The lack of fulfillment, however, in his hinted sexuality, unlike the previous sexually assertive protagonists, does not negate the juxtaposition between the sources. The underlying principle remains theoretically the same. Achbor is a parody of a lecher, and even though no sexual act is explicitly described, it intertwines with the other facets of his corruption.[84] Like Moriuht, who declares himself a poet and then acts non-poetically, Achbor declares himself a spiritual leader ("I beseech you, [my daughter], incline your ear, and listen, be chastised and succumb") and acts non-spiritually. Just like Geta, who abused funds given to him, "Fallo senem, minuo commissa, recondita furor, Furtiuisque opibus Thaïda pasco meam" (I deceive the old man, I plunder what is entrusted to

130   *Chapter 2*

me, I steal what is hidden, and from such stolen resources, I feed my Thaïs),
so Achbor abuses the alms he collects from his followers.

Perhaps Yaakov ben Elazar could not have penned a bolder text as opposed
to Warner, who depicted rape and sexual encounters audaciously. Yet the
way he utilized various symbols to demonstrate his point illustrates that, like
Moriuht, Achbor "comically represents the threat of aggressive sexual energy
in the grotesque figure of a hyperactive penis."[85]

Less comic is the portrayal of Archimbaut's hairiness in the thirteenth-
century Occitan romance, *Flamenca*. Following an outburst of anger leading
to his decision to imprison his wife, the narrator describes Archimbaut thus:

> Alas! Caitiu malaürat, / Engilosit, engratonat / Ar iest tu fols gelos affriz, /
> Ronos, barbutz, espelofitz: / Tiei pel son fer et irissatz / Que semblon flameir
> espirat / E coa d'esquirol salvage.[86]

> Alas! unfortunate miserable! Jealous, furious, now, you seethe with unsensed
> jealousy, scraggly, [heavily] bearded, hirsute, your hair ferocious and bristling,
> resembling a flaming torch and the tail of a wild squirrel.

The accumulation of metaphorical hints transforms Archimbaut's beard
into a menacing penis erectus. First, this portrayal emerges within the context
of a fantasy of sexual possession, emphasizing his determination to retain
sexual dominance over his wife or, more precisely, the notion that he refuses
to relinquish his sexual claim over her. Second, the unkempt appearance of
the sexual wild man, accentuated by five adjectives describing his hairiness,
serves as a symbol of bestial sexuality, as we've observed with Moriuht and
Geta. Third, the imagery of the flaming torch—an erect instrument burning with desire!—and a squirrel's tail, which is a common euphemism for
the penis in the fabliaux, for example, require little explanation to signify
their phallic connotations. Somewhat differently than Moriuht and Geta, this
depiction aims to evoke true fear of Archimbaut and demonstrates the consequences of his metamorphosis from a courtly aristocrat, possessing good
manners and elegance, into a wild man of sorts, resulting from his jealousy
toward his wife, the beautiful Flamenca. While jealousy is an inherently
human emotion, it is ideologically and socially rejected, since it manifests the
triumph of impulse (nature) over self-restraint (nurture). The abandonment
of courtliness signifies the acceptance of animality. This symbolic transition
from "human" to "inhuman," which in this case also translates as "inhu-
mane," is expressed in *Flamenca*, by the rejection of personal grooming.
Archimbaut ceases to bathe and groom himself, allowing his hair, beard, and
nails to grow untamed. This makes him somewhat reminiscent of Arthurian

Beardly Beloved   131

characters, who in a fit of madness, became wild men of the forest.[87] Archimbaut is "mad with jealousy," but his wild appearance is conscious, reasoned, based on a choice he has made. Archimbaut, it is revealed, chose to behave this way intentionally: "Major pavor aura mo donz / Si'm vez barbat e guinhonut. / Il non fara ges tan leu drut" (a greater fear, she will have, my lady, when she sees me bearded and mustachioed. Not quickly would she take a lover).[88]

A final example to conclude this section would be that of the fourteenth-century Welsh bard named Iolo Goch. Iolo composed a poem in which he complains directly to his personified beard, accusing "him" of being the reason that a beautiful woman he had been kissing fled. The repeated metaphors of width ("You were planted too thickly in place"), verticality ("You're a crop of gorse shoots!"; "like stubble on ice"; "without any covering, straight-tipped arrow-like bristles"), firmness ("Irish, harsh, black and sharp"; "it is no smoother, indisputable fact / than a stake's rough-ended tail"), sharpness ("there is on my cheeks, so they say, / material for a thousand little teeth"; Every bristle is sharp and tough"; "like—so harshly do they grow— / a thousand points of tiny thistles"), elevation ("a great crop on my flesh"; "harsh like a teasel on the skin"), violence ("steel goads goading a girl"; "hard heather stabbing a girl"), and pain ("painful bristles, harsher every day") used to signify the beard, blur it with his penis and make it a prominent phallus, to which we shall return in the section titled "This Beard was Meant for Kissing?" further below.[89]

SMOOTH WOMEN, BEARDED MEN, OR VICE VERSA?

The Argives enacted a law, the one which says that married women having a beard must occupy the same bed with their husbands![90]

Constable generalized the subject of beard symbolism, stating that "Almost the only universal and obvious meaning of beards was their association with masculinity, virility, and strength, and even this could, in the metaphorical sense, be applied to women."[91] That pilosity in general and beards in particular are a heavenly gift to men, granted as a sign of men's superiority over women, is a cultural construct. This premise is evident even in fable-lore, as seen in the case of members of the goat family renowned for their goatees, whether they are female or male. Even in matters of gendered hierarchy, the male goats complained to Jupiter about the beards of their females, as related in a fable by Phaedrus:

132   *Chapter 2*

When the she-goats had obtained, by application to Jupiter, the favour of a beard, the male goats were very unhappy about it and began to express their indignation that women had attained unto a dignity equal with their own. "Let them," said Jupiter, "enjoy their empty glory and usurp your badge of service, so long as they are not your peers in stoutheartedness. This example teaches you to endure it with patience when those who are inferior to you in merit wear the same uniform as yourself."[92]

Throughout history, medical treatises also emphasized the gendered aspect of beards.[93] Traditional medicine explained the growth of a beard with the theory of humors:

The natural moisture in a body past childhood hardens and is sharpened into bristles: that's why at that age the pubic area, the cheeks, and other parts of the body take on a coating of hair. But in a woman's body the warmth dries this moisture and results in a dearth of hair, and that's why the female body remains smooth and radiant.[94]

This approach was still popular in the fourteenth century:

Those who are naturally warmer have both a beard and, so to speak, loose and sparse hair on their shoulders. But those who are not warm, but have a colder constitution, do not have the same outward appearance . . . from the sex point of view, the men are of a warmer nature and therefore adorn themselves with a beard, while with the women the genetic part is the case, one can say that those who have no beard at all, insofar as they deviate from the nature of the men, approach the nature of the women and lie in the middle space between the two sexes.[95]

Bearded women were only classified as either a shocking natural phenomenon occurring in exotic unreachable places or as a lethal physical condition. In the fourth century BC, Hippocrates of Cos reported the following cases:

In Abdera, Phaethousa the wife of Pytheas, who kept at home, having borne children in the preceding time, when her husband was exiled stopped menstruating for a long time. Afterwards pains and reddening in the joints. When that happened her body was masculinized and grew hairy all over, she grew a beard, her voice became harsh, and though we did everything we could to bring forth menses they did not come, but she died after surviving a short time. The same thing happened to Nanno, Gorgippus' wife, in Thasos. All the physicians I met thought that there was one hope of feminizing her, if normal menstruation occurred. But in her case, too, it was not possible, though we did everything, but she died quickly.[96]

Beardly Beloved 133

The subordination of femininity to a masculine presence, grounded in medical discourse and symbolized by the growth of a beard in women in the absence of a husband, prevailed in European thought. In the sixth century, Gregory the Great dedicated a chapter to the story of Galla, who refused to remarry after her first husband died. "But because she had a passing high colour, the physicians told her that, unless she did marry again, that she would through abundance of heat, contrary to nature, have a beard like unto men: which afterward fell so out indeed."[97]

Galla resisted, entered a convent, and became a saint, her story becoming a topos. From the late fourteenth century through the sixteenth century, the bearded woman saint persisted in the story of Wilgefortis, who was crucified by her father after she took a vow of virginity, grew a beard, and consequently had her marriage canceled.[98] Her beard symbolized the glorious side of her cultural masculinization.[99] She grew a beard, that is, a masculine attribute, as it best represented her sanctity, spirituality, and authority, highlighting what separates her the most from femininity. Most importantly, it remained a sign of esteemed sexual abstinence. The medical argument was no longer relevant, for the beard now served as a reaction to these women's rebellion against undesired marriage.

Bearded women also appeared in medieval imagination as a perplexing marvel, a repulsive exotism. Chrétien de Troyes offers, for example, a fantastic description of a shocking woman who bears bad news. She bursts into King Arthur's court to tell Perceval that he has failed in his mission. She is black, has dense black braids with rat eyes, a cat's nose, donkey's ears "et si ot la barbe come un bos" (and she had the beard of a goat).[100] Almost at the same time, around 1188, Gerald of Wales (Giraldus Cambrensis) reported in his description of the Irish landscape that:

Duvenaldus, rex Limericensis, mulierem habebat umbilico tenus barbatam. Quae et cristam habuit a collo superius per spinam deorsum, in modum pulli annui, crine vestitam. Mulier ista, duplici prodigio monstruosa, non hermaphrodita tamen, sed alias muliebri natura tantum emollita, ad intuentium tam risum quam stuporem, curiam assidue sequebatur. In spinae quidem pilositate, neutri; in barbae vero prolixitate, morem gerens patriae[101] non naturae.[102]

Domnall, King of Limerick, had a wife, bearded down to her navel. She also had a crest on her neck, extending downwards along the spine, covered with hair like the main of a year-old foal. This woman, notwithstanding these two monstrous prodigies, was not a hermaphrodite, but rather she was completely delicate according to female nature, she constantly attended the court, provoking here laughter and here astonishment. The hairiness of her spine, [resembled] neither [the ways of her homeland or her nature]; The length of the beard resembled indeed the custom of her homeland, but not of her nature.

134   *Chapter 2*

In his scientific Encyclopedia, *De Natura rerum*, Thomas de Cantimpré (thirteenth century) noted that "Mulieres etiam sunt in quibusdam silvis Indiae, quae habent barbas usque ad mamillas."[103] (there are also women in some forests of India who have beards down to their breasts). This belief was developed by a late thirteenth or early fourteenth-century French translation by the Clerck of Enghien.[104] The translator-adaptor moralized this phenomenon of bearded women, which he deemed unnatural and uncultured, as the result of a scandalous conception ". . . ne sai pas se par pecié / Furent premiers si conceües" [105] (I do not know, if it was by sin, that they were initially conceived). He then describes them:

Barbes ont grans et estendues,
Longes, groses jusques al çaint.
Laide chose est, se Dius me maint;
Car barbe nos mostre briement
Que nus ne l'ait sans hardement.
Dont doivent bien iestre hardies
Celes qui les ont si trechies;
Hardies doivent celes iestre
Qui barbes ont par itel iestre.
Dont nos mostre bien ci endroit
Que feme hardie ne soit,
S'ele n'est del tout si barbue
Que la barbe au çaint li baulue.
Gart soi feme de hardement,
Se sa barbe au çaint ne descent
Feme ne doit iestre hardie,
Se barbe n'a, n'en dotés mie.
Por çou di, c'est contre nature
De femme hardie a droiture;
Car ne doit feme barbe avoir
Par droiture ne par savoir.
Por çou n'os dire par raison
Feme de hardement ait non

[They] have beards, large and spreading,
long, thick, going down the waist.
Ugly thing it is, may God forgive me;
for the truth about beard is
that none has it without boldness.
Therefore, they must indeed be bold,
these [women] who have braided them this way.
Bold must these be,
who wear beards in such a way.
Therefore, by consequence, it becomes clear to us

Beardly Beloved 135

that a woman is not bold,
unless she is so completely bearded
that her beard hangs on her waist.
Each should watch his wife, with boldness,
that her beard does not descend to her waist.
A woman should not be bold,
Therefore, she lacks a beard, doubt it not at all.
This is why it is righteous to say
that a bold woman, is against nature.
Because a woman should not have a beard,
not by nature nor by knowledge.
Therefore, I dare not say,
That a woman can be called "bold".

In cultural Europe, the phrase "a woman's beard" could only refer, euphemistically, to their women's pubic hair and was a rich source of bawdy discourses. The thirteenth-century fabliau "Li Jugemenz des cons" tells of three sisters who are asked who, amongst them and their genitals, is older. The elder sister says that her organ (the word employed in the text is "con," that is, cunt) is older, since "Il a la barbe, je n'en ai point" (he has a beard, I do not have one).[106] In the fifteenth-century *Cent Nouvelles Nouvelles,* Dutch women are described as heavily bearded "la barbe du devant de ladite femme estoit assez et beaucop longue, comme il est coustume a celles de Hollande" (the beard on the front of this woman was quite long, as is customary for Dutch women).[107]

The image of the female beard also contributed to the concept known in Freudian terminology as the *vagina dentata*. This notion imagines the vagina as a mouth replete with teeth, closing on whoever enters therein. The idea that above this mouth there is a beard, akin to men's beards (i.e., mustaches) above their mouths, is depicted in the horrific Castle of the Beards in the romance *Perlesvaus*. Here, the door leading into the castle of a deadly seductress is adorned with the actual beards of her countless victims.[108] In most cases, however, references to women's genital beards were derogatory. This reflects a historical trend where attributes typically associated with masculinity were used to ridicule or belittle women, often as a means of asserting male dominance or enforcing social norms regarding femininity. The first-century Roman poet Martial wrote about Vetustilla, who yearned for men even in her old age. He described her face and body in vulgar terms, culminating with the crude remark, "Your bony cunt would defeat an aged Cynic."[109] Bearing in mind the popular image of philosophers, including the Cynics, discussed at the beginning of this chapter, the metaphor here does not require further explanation, and it is clear that he is mocking both Vetustilla, who represents the social disgust for old women, and the common satire of the Cynics.[110] A

136   *Chapter 2*

similar description, this time comparing the bearded female genitalia of an old woman (probably a prostitute) with Epicurus, is to be found in the somewhat contemporary *Corpus Priapeorum*, poem 11: "barbato macer eminente naso, ut credas Epicuron oscitari" (Your bearded nose, raised high in the air, opens with a chasm so foul and enormous that it resembles an epicurean's yawn).[111]

The concept of the female pubic beard reached its apex in a notable episode from *Le Roman de Renart*.[112] This episode unfolds at the court of King Connin, where the cunning fox Renart has just arrived, seeking retribution against Brichemert the stag, Chanteclair the rooster, and Isengrin the wolf, all of whom have deceived him.[113] Connin's occupation, as his name crudely suggests, involves creating vaginas for women who, according to a topos, were made without them.[114] Using a spade, Connin makes enormous cavities in women's bodies,[115] a sight that repulses Renart. Renart suggests sewing the skin from Brichemert's neck in the middle of the aperture, dividing the opening into two smaller holes, and implanting Chanteclair's crest inside to create an endpoint, which, we will learn, "Les dames l'apelent landie" (the ladies call it clitoris).[116] Still, something is missing: "Barbe il faut: se barbe eüst, / Plus biaus et miauz seenz en fust" (A beard is needed; if it had a beard, it would be more beautiful and better appropriate). It is then suggested that Isengrin's mane be used for this purpose.

This sexist fantasy about the creation of the perfect vagina, whose one and only essence and purpose is to be at the service of men, takes an even more oppressive tone in manuscript M, where Renart first measures Connin's / Noble's penis in order to determine how big the vagina should be. Second, if it was not clear enough that the king's wife (representing all women) is no more than a love doll, an object designed according to men's whims, here Renart drugs the queen during her creation / mutilation, totally removing her from the decisions and discourses taken over her body. This is surely a distorted echo of the biblical Creation of Adam, where God puts Adam to sleep to fashion Eve from his rib. Renart, however, is not God, and upon awakening, the queen rebels against her defilement.[117] In any version, this episode is doubly misogynistic and probably homoerotic. The first aspect of misogyny, harking back to the concept of *vagina dentata*, is that female sexuality persists in its age-old stereotype as lethal and emasculating. Connin attains his skin, crest, and mane through three brutal actions carried out in the pursuit of the perfect vagina: slaughtering Brichemert, "castrating" Chanteclair, and flaying Isengrin. Men are thus sacrificed on the altar of the vagina. Outstanding among the three manly attributes of the vagina according to *Renart* is the beard, as it is externally noticeable and, much more than the other two, is deeply grounded in misogynistic discourses of castrating femininity. In the Jewish tradition, for example, "it was thought that during cohabitation the penis might become entangled in the woman's pubic hair."[118]

The second aspect of misogyny arises from the perpetuation of philosophical and theological concepts. Theological interpretations considered Eve to be secondary to Adam, given that she was created from his rib, with even her name suggesting derivation from a man. Aristotelian philosophy viewed women as flawed and imperfect, primarily due to the perceived inferiority of their genitals. According to *Le Roman de Renart*, women's genitalia suffered from three defects, for which Renart suggested three remedies. These are not just any defects nor just any remedies. The defects incarnate the prejudiced conception of the female genitalia as a wound,[119] odiferous because they are connected to the rectum, resembling a dark and endless abyss, and ugly: "Luciferian. It is *diaboli ianua*, a bottomless pit that devours everything."[120]

The remedies proposed by Renart all involve phallic attributes because, to use Pastoureau's words, these are all parts of the body that "form protuberances." This refers not only to the beast's hair,[121] but also, in our case, to the stag's neck—which swells during the rutting season—and the erect crest atop the rooster's head. [122]

Could it be argued that being comprised of these three phallic attributes—stimulus, erection, and hair—the vagina, in a sense, acquires a phallic quality of its own? Is there not a fantasy present in envisioning the vagina as possessing an anatomy entirely crafted from male genitalia, and longing for it is essentially yearning for what is male, with the beard epitomizing this desire? While it might be a stretch to suggest that Renart's idealized vagina is inherently phallic and conveys a homosexual fantasy,[123] the homoerotic atmosphere is much more explicit in manuscript M, in which Renart requests to see and measure the king's penis: "'Sire, or m'estuet veoir le vit, / Metez le ça tot a droiture; / Je vueil fere a vostre mesure'. / Li roi respont: 'si com toi plest.' / Tot maintenant le vit li trest / Entor en a pris la mesure / Puis le fent tant com le vit dure,[124] / Tant a fendu qu'a son point vient" ("Sire, now I must see the prick, place it here, straight ahead; I wish to make it [i.e., the vagina] to your measure." The king responds: "As you please." Immediately, he pulls out his prick, he takes the measurements all around it, then he cleaves [the vagina] vigorously, according to the prick, so much has he cleaved, until he reaches the goal).

The "vaginal beard" introduced by Renart raises intriguing questions about gender and sexuality. When the king asks: "Or me di donques que vaudroit / La barbe, qui or li metroit?" (well, now tell me, what good will come from the beard that now we shall put on her?), Renart justifies the beard as necessary to conceal the unattractiveness of the vaginal opening: "Sire, ele covreroit le con / C'on voit en mi tot a bandon / Et celle creste et cel coueinne" (sire, it will cover the cunt, which is visible and plainly exposed, as well as the crest and

138   *Chapter 2*

the stag's skin). This necessity to "conceal the truth" about the female body is then justified within the context of courtly and uncourtly. Renart implies that the beard will dissuade peasants from approaching, as they will perceive it as signaling a dangerous pit. In contrast, the men of the court, possessing knowledge about the beard, "Ja por barbe ne le hairont / Einz l'an avront assez plus chier / Clerc et borjois et chevalier" (They will never despise it for having a beard; rather, clerics, bourgeois, and knights will hold it even dearer).

The sublimation of the beard here contrasts with conventional aesthetic norms of female depilation. If there were a class distinction regarding pubic hair removal, it would likely be reversed. According to John Block Friedman, women's epilation was a sign of social status and differentiated between aristocratic and peasant women, whose hairiness was merely another sign of their coarse existence.[125] Regardless of rank, since antiquity, women were expected to remove body hair and acted accordingly. The belief that men be hairy, reflecting their superiority, and women smooth, reflecting their inferiority, forged a gap also in sexual perception. Since pilosity reflected virile sexuality, women were not to appear virile, and by a culturally accepted extension, their smooth bodies were a sign of their sexual passivity, submissiveness, and fragility. This gendered ideal of beauty and sexuality is also prevalent in Jewish thinking and in Islam.[126]

In *Le roman de la Rose*, the *vieille*, says: "Et comme bonne baisselete / Tiegne la chambre Venus nete; / S'ele est preuz et bien ensignie, / Ne laist entour nulle yraignie / Qu'el n'arde ou ree, arrache ou housse, / Si qu'el n'i puisse cueillir mousse" (and like a good girly, she should keep Venus' room clean. If she is wise and well educated, she should not leave there a single spiderweb which she will not burn, shave, pluck, or remove [literally: sweep away], so that she will not be able to catch moss down there, 13339–13344).[127]

Another illustrative example is the fifteenth-century farcical text known as *Sermon joyeux des barbes et des brayes*. This text is a comical guide for the wedding night, providing women with a thorough explanation of all they need to know about the inconveniences that their "barbes" cause their husbands, and, to a much lesser extent, explaining to men about the inconveniences that their "brayes" (codpieces) cause their brides. Both sexes are required to dispose of such nuisances: "se doivent si bien aproucher / Et de leurs jambes accrochier / Sans moyens de barbe et de braye / Que l'un autant de payne traye / Que l'aultre en leur labourage / S'ils veulent faire bon ouvrage" (if they want to get it right, they should come near each other, and join their legs together without the means of beards nor codpieces, since one causes as much pain as the other in their task!).[128] The cultural expectation for women to remove body hair corresponds with the perception that men who groom their bodies, interfering with their natural hairiness, epilating their genitals, or shaving their beards, are effeminate. Variations of these premises are extant

Beardly Beloved 139

in different cultures, discourses, and historical periods. In the second century, Lucian considered this question:

> ... he was pleased to have a beard and long hair, and not only he but all the other men of old too. For they were better men than you, and not a single one of them would have submitted to the razor any more than would a lion. For they thought that soft smooth flesh became a woman, but, just as they themselves were men, so too they wished to appear men, thinking the beard an ornament of men, as is the mane an ornament of horses and lions, to whom god has given additional gifts to grace and adorn them. So too has he given men the addition of a beard. These men of old therefore are the ones that I admire and should like to emulate, but the men of to-day I do not admire for the "wonderful" prosperity they enjoy in the matter of food and clothing, and when they smooth and depilate every part of their bodies, not even allowing any of their private parts to remain in its natural condition.[129]

Lucian's text was practically rewritten by the third-century Church Father, Clement of Alexandria: "For God wished women to be smooth, and rejoice in their locks alone growing spontaneously, as a horse in his mane; but has adorned man, like the lions, with a beard, and endowed him, as an attribute of manhood, with shaggy breasts—a sign this of strength and rule."[130] Later, in the fifth-century treatise *The City of God,* Saint Augustine claims that some features of the body were not created with the intent to serve any physical mechanism, but rather to adorn the body: "For example, a man's chest has nipples, and his face a beard. That the beard is no protection but a male adornment, is proved by the smooth faces of women, for since they are weaker, they should not be protected."[131] In another part of the world, a fourteenth-century Byzantine anonymous writer wrote a letter "To Andreas Lopadiotesn who in a letter to an acquaintance made fun of those who have a full beard." The writer explains scientifically that:

> Therefore, I can only make fun of those who shaved off their beard free-willingly and consider them as the authors of a pathetic act; Although they belong to the sex of men and are fully aware of their duties, although they know that they should avoid unmanliness, cowardice and feminine weakness and justify their name by being masculine, they do great harm to their sex and seek to become like women.[132]

The notion that the presence or lack of a beard, a signifier of virility, hinted at a person's sexual virility or impotence, thrived especially, though not exclusively, in comical literature. During the Middle Ages, texts mocking beardless men as sexually impotent were quite common. A cultural gap was thus created between the negatively bearded vagina and the positively pileous

140 *Chapter 2*

penis, a manifestation of potency and maleness. Étienne Wolff showed that for the Romans, male hair removal was a conventional practice, though it was supposed to be balanced and measured and performed only on the upper body: "The lower you go down the body, the risk of being seen as effeminate grows greater."[133] Medieval comedy also thrived on this topic, and I feel compelled to provide several notable examples. In a family quarrel regarding her coquetry and squandering, the wife in the twelfth-century *Le lai de Nabarez* denounces her husband to her relatives: "K'il face crestre sa barbe grant / e ses gernuns face trescher" (he should grow a long beard and braid his whiskers).[134] Rosanna Brusegan saw in this obscene repartee, referring to the husband's lack of beard, that is, (sexual) virility, "the confession of a certain impotence [. . .] because the hairs are a sign of virility [. . .] What does Nabaret's wife want, except that her husband should finally have enough beard hair to indicate that he is a virile man, as a husband should be?"[135] This interpretation was suggested by Brusegan based on what she identified as the "obscene equivoque" of the word "crestre," literally meaning "to grow" and frequently used in comic literature as a euphemism for an erection.[136] As for the second element of the pleasantry, "to braid the beard," after summarizing previous scholarship, Brusegan suggests understanding this cryptic line as if "The lady wishes her husband let his whiskers grow so much that he can braid them, that is to say that he turns into a coquettish gentleman, even more than she is."[137] Such an interpretation will indeed be appropriate revenge, as the wife not only refers to her husband's "poor sexual performance"[138] but also compromises his honor by wishing him to become feminine.

A fourteenth-century fabliau by Jean de Condé, *les tresces*, justifies a courtly lady's rejection of a certain suitor "car n'ot pas la barbe crenue / Poi de barbe ot, s'en ert eschieus, / Etant qu'as fames, en maint lieus" (because he did not have a dense beard. He did not have a beard at all, he was entirely hairless, like women are in certain places). Adding the superfluous comparison to women ensures that we clearly understand the reasons why this poor beau is clean-shaven. It is not because he is still young, nor because he is following the current fashion of not growing a beard. The aim here is to feminize him and mock his "non-maleness," that is, his impotence.[139] This concept is emphasized by a question he is asked while participating in a social game: Did he ever bear any children? The man naïvely answered, ". . . onques n'en oï nul, je croy" (I think I do not have any). What could have simply been the result of his young age, just like the lack of a beard, is presented as another sign of dysfunctional manhood.[140]

In a thirteenth-century *jeu parti*, the trouvère Gillebert de Berneville introduces the subject of the debate. Two young people have loved each other since childhood. The man had just been knighted after demonstrating his bravery. Nevertheless, "il ne poroit barbe avoir" (He cannot grow a beard).

It is then asked whether this disorder will prevent their love from lasting or being of any value. The debate unfolds between Gillebert and Amor, a pseudonym for a certain lady. Amor is of the opinion that the couple's love can last as long as there is true love. Gillebert, contrarily believes that:

Amors, je croy et sai de fi Que cil n'ait desir ne talent Ne cuer ki puist ameir celi; Par enfance a comancement, Sans cors tochier et per revel. On ne porroit un sec paxel Faire florir ne verdoier; Niant plux ne puet montiplier L'amor de lui, jel sai de voir, Ne il ne doit amie avoir.[141]

Amor, I believe, and know, that that man does not have neither desire nor lust, not the heart to love her. If something began between them, it was just childishness, a distraction, but without any carnal touch. One cannot make a dry stake flourish and blossom; no more can he (a man without a beard) manifest his love, this I can tell you, and he should not have a beloved.

LE CHASTEL DES BARBES

The irony, disdain, and comedic elements evident in the examples discussed in the previous section regarding short-shaven men can only be perceived as such within a context that views the beard as an inherent symbol of male honor and dominance. The most exemplary medieval character whose white beard is related to sovereignty and functions as a leitmotif is Charlemagne: "The fictional Charlemagne's manly virtues show themselves in his magnificent hair. When acting as a loving father, he is said to have a 'lovely beard,' when a warrior, a 'flowing beard,' and when a wise ruler, a 'white beard.'"[142] Another celebrated national hero, this time from Spain, is the Castilian Rodrigo Díaz de Vivar, famously known as El Cid. His magnificent beard, never trimmed nor plucked of a single hair, is consistently lauded. Its length and grandeur symbolize his virtues as a vassal and lord, his material success, his years in exile, and most importantly, his honor. As noted by P. A. Bly, "The beard, as a highly imaginable symbol, seems to preside over thematically important episodes in the *Poema*, alerting the audience to the state of El Cid's honour at a particular time."[143] The beard is so integral to the narrative of *El Cid,* symbolizing patriarchal honor, that the notion of its plucking represents an insurmountable humiliation and social degradation. This motif recurs throughout the poem, climaxing in the royal court of justice held in Toledo. There, El Cid's beard is mocked by Count Gracia Ordóñez. El Cid defends his beard's honorable status, reminding everyone present that while no one has ever been able to pluck a single hair from his beard, he had beard-flayed the count, and since that occurrence, some of the count's hairs cannot grow back.

142 *Chapter 2*

Drawing possibly from ancient Welsh and Celtic folklore, Arthurian literature, both in Latin and French, includes accounts of heroic knights fighting to preserve the integrity of their spectacular beards, in what is known as the "war of beards" topos.[144] They are confronted by a giant who demands their beards to fashion a mantle; given the giant's size, the mantle requires the beards of numerous valiant men. Since beards traditionally symbolize attributes such as virility, leadership, military prowess, and authority, their removal and voluntary surrender signify submission to the giant and acknowledge his absolute dominance.[145] This tradition is documented in the first half of the twelfth century through the chronicles of Geoffrey of Monmouth:

> *The History of the Kings of Britain*, wherein the giant Ritho had turned the beards of the kings he had slain into a cloak and had dispatched instructions to Arthur to shave off his beard carefully and send it to him, so he could place it above the rest, to reflect Arthur's preeminence over other kings. Otherwise, he challenged Arthur to a duel, to the victor of which would go the cloak together with the beard of the vanquished. Arthur won the duel and took Ritho's beard and the trophy. . . .[146]

This narrative was repeated during the twelfth and thirteenth centuries in various texts by several French narrators, including Wace's *Le roman de Brut* and the Merlin cycles.[147] Three notable sources that engage with this theme, particularly significant to us, are the thirteenth-century adaptation of the Grail myth, known as the romance of *Perlesvaus*, Thomas' twelfth-century rendition of Tristan, and the thirteenth-century *Le chevalier aux deux épées*. These texts propagate the misogynistic notion that even in supposedly all-male confrontations, castration is somehow associated with a dangerous woman.

In his version of *Tristan*, Thomas d'Angleterre situates the story within a specific context. To avoid excessive digression, I will refrain from delving into the intricate details leading to Tristan's departure from his beloved Iseut, who is wedded to his uncle, King Marc, and his subsequent marriage to Iseut of the White Hands, distinct from Queen Iseut. On his wedding night with Iseut of the White Hands, Tristan finds himself unable to consummate their marriage. Torn between nature (the sexual desire he has for his beautiful young wife, whom he does not love) and love (the devotion to his true beloved), Tristan is tormented by the dilemma of either yielding to his desires or abstaining. Each option—consummation or restraint—inflicts its own torment upon him, one physical and the other mental. Ultimately, love triumphs over nature and hinders Tristan from consummating his marriage, resulting in a moment of sexual impotence. Tristan implores his wife to keep what he is about to tell her a secret, explaining that he suffers from a debilitating injury on his right waist, which renders him unable to make love. The reference to

Beardly Beloved 143

the waist as a euphemism for the loins, and the notion of an injured waist as symbolic or literal castration,[148] underscores the embodiment of mental impotence through physical incapacity. Thus, the noble rationale for abstaining from sexual relations in order to remain faithful to true love is overshadowed by the embarrassment of a technical, physical limitation that must be concealed from others.

The focus now shifts to Queen Iseut, who is languishing for Tristan. By introducing Iseut at this precise moment, Thomas utilizes a digression to elucidate Tristan's impotence and associates it with the motif of the battle of the beards. For some time, Iseut has heard nothing of Tristan; the last she knew, he was in Spain, unaware that he had since been married in Brittany. Yet, this allows Thomas to recount how, during Tristan's time in Spain, he slew the nephew of the giant Orguillus ("the proud one"). Like Ritho, Orguillus fashioned a pelisse from the beards he had collected, demanding tribute even from Arthur, who ultimately fought and beheaded him. The pattern is repeated when Orguillus' nephew demands the beard of the King of Spain, leading Tristan to combat the giant on Spanish soil, resulting in his severe injury.

I believe that for Thomas, the disclosure of Tristan's waist injury within the context of his inability to consummate his marriage due to his longing for Queen Iseut clearly illustrates what is more implicitly suggested in earlier sources such as Geoffrey, Wace, and *Merlin*. The demand to surrender the beard has an emasculating dimension, as it relates to women symbolically castrating men, whether those women are desired or not.

While Tristan emerged victorious over the giant, permitting the king of Spain to keep his beard, he himself was wounded. This wound is only important on a symbolic level, as it provides the pretext for discontinuing his relations with Queen Iseut, who belongs to another man (she stopped receiving news from him right after the battle), a distancing that does not liberate him, but rather further castrates him, as he realizes on his wedding night.

In *Perlesvaus,* Lancelot is on his quest to find the Holy Grail when he encounters a most harrowing adventure. A severely wounded knight shares with him the following account:

> Il encontre Lancelot: "Sire fait il, por Dieu, retorneis ariere, car vos troverés ja le plus cruel passage del mont, la ou je fui navrés par mi le cors, se vos i aleis— Quieus trespas est cho dont? fait Lancelot.—Sire, fait il, c'est li trespas devant un chastel que l'on apele le Chastel des Barbes, et porcho a il non issi, qu'il covient chascon chevalier qui devant trespasse laissier sa barbe ou calengier. Si ai calengié la moie, fait li chevaliers en teil maniere que g'en criem morir.— Par mon chief, fait Lancelot, cho ne tien jo pas a couardie, puis que vos fustes hardis de metre vostre vie en aventure por vostre barbe calengier! Or me voleis vos enbatre en couardie, quant vos me voleis por cho faire retorner! Je voldroie

144   *Chapter 2*

mieus estre ferus par mi le cors par honor, que perdre un des peus de ma barbe par hunte! ..."[149]

He approached Lancelot: "Sir," he said, "for God's sake, turn back, for there, you will encounter the most atrocious passage in the entire world! [It is] Where I was wounded throughout my body, if you proceed." "What then is this passage?" Lancelot inquired. "Sir," he replied, "it is the passage leading to a castle that one calls the Castle of Beards, bearing this name because every knight that passes through must relinquish his beard or engage in a duel. I defended mine," said the knight, "in such a manner, that I fear I'm dying." "By my head," said Lancelot, "I do not consider that cowardice, you have been brave putting your life in jeopardy for defending your beard! Now you seek to provoke me into cowardice by urging me to turn back! I would rather be wounded through the middle of my body with honor, than to lose one single hair of my beard by shame!"

Upon arriving at the entrance to Le Chastel des Barbes (the Castle of Beards), Lancelot is amazed to see "le portal tot plain fichié de barbes, et i pendoient testes de chevaliers a grant plenté" (the gate completely adorned with beards, and there hung heads of knights in abundance). He is asked to pay the "entrance fee," which is his own beard, but as he had already sworn to the wounded knight, he refuses and engages in the duel. Lancelot emerges victorious and is welcomed as a guest by the lady of the castle, who attempts to seduce him. During the dinner service, Lancelot is astonished to discover that the food is served by chained knights who have been mutilated in five different ways. The first course is served by knights with their noses cut off, the second, those with their eyes gouged out, the third, those with amputated hands, and the fourth, those with one leg missing. Finally, for the fifth course, handsome knights approach the lady, offering their heads to be decapitated.

Both Armand Strubel, *Perlesvaus'* editor, and Francis Dubost, highlighted the connection between the Castle of Beards and the Arthurian War of Beards.[150] In this romance, however, the figure of the giant gives way to an explicitly castrating woman—a seductress and the ruler of the castle—who systematically "unbeards" and mutilates men, making them her servants. The entire episode's architecture is shaped according to the imagery of the *vagina dentata*. The dangerous passage, with an entrance that is embellished with beards, leads to a castle dominated by a beautiful woman who lures many men. Most will never return, while a few exceptional ones might manage to escape, albeit gravely wounded.[151]

Ironically, the beards that are not displayed on the castle portal are repurposed, not for luxurious fur but rather to fabricate haircloths or cilices, which were usually made from horse or goat hair and used by monks for mortification. Notably, sexual desires are among the primary reasons for the

Beardly Beloved 145

performance of mortification by hermits and monks.[152] It would thus seem that what Dubost identified as a "delusional fantasy of absolute power" is combined with the stereotypical image of the castrating woman.[153] Arthur, in all the versions recounting his story, as well as Lancelot here, remains triumphant, with their honor, synonymous with their virility and masculinity, never compromised. This resilience might stem from his primary engagement in significant tasks.[154] Tristan, on the other hand, overcomes the giant and saves the king of Spain's beard, but he is severely injured, and his wound symbolizes his weakness.[155]

Another source that underscores, to some extent, the feminine element in order to rationalize the symbolic castration inherent in the removal of beards is the thirteenth-century romance, *Le chevalier aux deux épées*. Here it is the powerful king Ris who has already amassed the beards of nine mighty kings to fashion a fur coat for his beloved lady. Arthur is then requested to deliver his beard, because Ris' lady desires to incorporate it into the coat's lining.

In the conflict between men over a masculine symbol, defending it from being seized entails a struggle against symbolic castration. This was sensed not merely by modern researchers, but also by some medieval writers.[156] Most significantly for us, these tales, which evidently captivated medieval audiences, consistently emphasize that a beard transcends a mere abundance of facial hair; rather, it embodies a cultural construct that, within a patriarchal society, revolves around stereotypical representations of virtuous and malevolent men. Achbor's dramatic downfall is finally that quintessential moment wherein, at the hands of women, he forfeits not only his beard but also any semblance of authority he once possessed, exhaling his final breath.

THIS BEARD WAS MEANT FOR KISSING?

"Was it you, beard, who scared off / the girl who was willingly kissing me?"[157]

As I near the conclusion of this chapter, I would like to highlight another comical pattern of the beard significant to the notion of gender identity. This time, it concerns the merging of social expectations of a beard-bearer and the creation of a homoerotic tone in a series of "comedies of errors."

In the fourteenth century, Iolo Goch, mentioned earlier, in his satirical poem dedicated entirely to the deficiencies of his beard, said, "A beauty has little desire for my lips, because of my beard." He may have found a thread of inspiration in Emperor Julian's *Misopogon* (and possibly also in *Moriuht*)[158] written a thousand years earlier. While acknowledging that he is not overly concerned with kissing, Julian noted that "a beard is evidently troublesome, since it does not allow me to press shaven 'lips to other lips more sweetly.'"[159] These two examples, separated by a thousand years, indicate a topos that is

146   *Chapter 2*

surprisingly well-established in medieval Hebrew literature, referring comically to the beard as a gendered obstacle for kissing.

In an extraordinary turn of events, Shlomo ibn Zakbel's "The Tale of Asher ben Yehuda," composed in twelfth-century Spain and recognized as the earliest extant maqama in Hebrew, describes how Asher finds himself alone in the company of a desirable woman. Yet, as he lifts her veil "ראיתי זקן ארוך והמוות עליו ערוך ופיו פתוח כסיר נפוח" (I saw a lengthy beard, death set all over it, a gaping mouth like a bloated cauldron). [160] In the thirteenth century, Yehuda al-Harizi provides an adaptation of this maqama in his "Tale of the Seven Virgins." Though the plot differs, the punchline remains the same: Heman, thinking he is partaking in a love adventure, asks a seemingly remarkable woman to unveil her face, but when she does "וארא והנה זקן ארוך כאילו הוא נחש כרוך" (I saw, lo! A lengthy beard wrapped around as if it were a coiled snake).[161] In both cases, an identical practical joke is in progress: the enticing woman is revealed to be the protagonist's best friend, aiming for a lighthearted laugh at the expense of a friend perceived as arrogant and overly confident in his romantic prowess.

What piques our interest most is this elusive moment when the beard is dramatically exposed, before the friend's identity is revealed. This moment, replete with sexual innuendo, is met with profound anxiety by both Asher and Heman. Neither they nor the readers were aware of the prank, so the discovery of a beard, on what was presumed to be the face of a beautiful woman, comes as a total surprise. In that short interlude, we must wonder: Do Asher and Heman still perceive the person in their company as a woman, albeit one with a beard (a possibility substantiated by numerous folkloric examples explored in this chapter), or do they realize they have been deceived by a man, yet to be identified? Here, the two texts diverge. Ultimately, the outcome will be the same, but they illustrate contrasting perceptions of the startling beard.

Heman repeats Asher's statement, "I saw a lengthy beard." Nonetheless, while Asher described the beard as "death set all over it, a gaping mouth like a bloated cauldron," Heman perceives it "as if it was a snake," continuing with "ויגלה מתחת בגדו חרבו שלופה בידו" (and he revealed beneath his garment his drawn sword!). The apparent contradiction arises from the divergent metaphorical imagery; a gaping mouth and a pot are clear metaphors for the vagina, whereas a snake and certainly a drawn sword are obvious metaphors for the penis. Consequently, Asher views the beard as vaginal, while Heman sees it as phallic.

Asher's statement is based on a common metaphor of the vagina as a pot: "not only the shape of the object which was suggestive, but also its heat."[162] In Aristophanes' play *The Knights*, it is said that Ariphrades "pollutes his own tongue with disgraceful gratifications, licking the detestable

Beardly Beloved 147

dew in bawdyhouses, besmirching his beard, disturbing the ladies' hotpots . . ."[163] Another relevant source is Apuleius' *Metamorphoses*. In Book II, Photis' lower body fuses with the pot in which she cooks, and her cooking gestures imitate, in Lucius' eyes, the movements of lovemaking: "She was turning the cooking pot round and round with her flowerlike hands, and she kept shaking it with a circular motion, at the same time smoothly sliding her own body, gently wiggling her hips, softly shaking her supple spine, beautifully rippling."[164] Lucious and Photis carry an entire conversation based on the pot as the signifier of her vagina. When Lucius compliments her "'How gorgeously, my Photis,' I said, 'and how delightfully you twist your little pot with your buttocks! What a delicious stew you are cooking! A man would be lucky—surely even blessed—if you would let him dip his finger in there,'"[165] she answers "Get away, poor boy; get as far away as you can from my oven, because if my little flame should blow against you even slightly, you will burn deep inside and no one will be able to extinguish your fire except me. I can season things deliciously, and I know how to shake a pot and a bed to your equal delight.'"[166] The two plan to meet that night to celebrate their love.

Many generations, languages, and cultures separate Lucious and Asher, but a unifying thread emerges in this moment as they find themselves alone in a chamber with a woman whom they desire. Both consider the woman's hair as an integral part of the game of love. Lucious dedicates a long meditation to the charms of women's hair, and Asher is eager to see the lady's hair "ופרשי" "עלי שערך (let your hair fall upon me).[167] For both, women's hair corresponds to their bodies. Lucious says: "what the cheerful colour of flowery clothing does for the rest of the body, its [i.e., hair's] own natural lustre does for the head,"[168] clearly differentiating between clothes and hair: "When most women want to prove their own real loveliness, they take off all their garments, remove their clothes: they wish to show their beauty naked."[169] Nonetheless, he perceives hair differently. He refers to Venus as the model of female beauty, but qualifies this by stating that no matter how beautiful she might be, "if she came forth bald she could not attract even her husband Vulcan.[170]"

Asher perceives the hair as a synecdoche of a woman's body. In the Oriental and oriental-influenced cultures of the twelfth century, which adhered to strict norms of modesty and concealment, women wore veils and turbans that covered their hair and much of their faces. Taken to the extreme, a woman's hair and face were considered as intimate as her body, making the exposure of the hair akin to undressing. Nevertheless, the synecdoche postulates a major difference between the part representing the whole. While aesthetic and even theological norms dictate that a woman's head should be adorned with abundant hair (though hidden by a veil or head covering), her pubic region, as we have seen numerous times in this chapter, was expected to be entirely smooth and epilated. Lucious is very explicit about how he is aroused by the

148   *Chapter 2*

dichotomy between the flowing hair, the naked body, and the hairless vagina: "She stripped herself of all her clothes, and let down her hair. With joyous wantonness she beautifully transformed herself into the picture of Venus rising from the ocean waves. For a time, she even held one rosy little hand in front of her smooth-shaven pubes, purposely shadowing it rather than modestly hiding it."[171] As opposed to Lucious, Asher is not so lucky; the "boiling pot" that *he* encounters when he lifts the veil of the mysterious woman is densely bearded.

The fierce image, which Asher describes as "I saw a lengthy beard, death set all over it, a gaping mouth like a bloated cauldron," resonates with Connin's court episode in the *Roman de Renart*, pointing to a misogynistic perception of monstrous female sexuality. This perception associates it with a deep cavity capable of castrating men, as evidenced by Asher's reaction to the sight ("I fell my full length," possibly a euphemism for the loss of his erection). It also highlights the threat posed by the female organ's ability to grow what is considered the quintessential signifier of manhood: the beard. The archaic, phantasmatic fear of such a dangerously masculine woman is realized in this paralyzing moment, as Asher discovers that the lady is, in fact, a bearded man. To sum up, there is something extremely bold in the "monstrosity" that Asher discovers under the covers of the lady, a manly female body, described as a lethal deformation with "death all over it," and truly dreadful. This depiction is striking because it is very rare to find a text in Hebrew literature where the female body is symbolically treated in such a manner. The female body is not just revealed to be a man in the end; it is a body that is not there, that has no place, that is rejected and alienated. The female body has been annulled. This portrayal remains noteworthy for its exceptional and symbolic representation.

Al-Harizi might have found the metaphor of the wide-open mouth and the hot cauldron too daring, as this dimension is absent from his version. Instead, the discovery of the beard immediately evokes phallic associations, as his protagonist, Hamen, perceives the beard as a snake and a sword discernible under the clothing.[172]

The two protagonists are deeply shocked by discovering something that should not have been there, representing a significant transgression. Both men are so frightened that they fall down (Asher: "I fell my full length"; Heman: "When I saw it, I fell on my face"). This is surely a comical moment that sparks a laugh.[173] The narrators indeed take advantage of the opportunities this practical joke affords, allowing them to create a homoerotic atmosphere. Like any moment of tension, the dangerous manifestation of the vaginal or phallic beard evokes a hidden enthusiasm, even if it is ultimately rejected. Such a homoerotic atmosphere is certainly present at the core of the entire maneuver, although it is manifestly repressed. The catharsis comes with the restoration of patriarchal heterosexual norms, as the masquerader is exposed. The gender-blurring charade concludes before any homoerotic encounter can occur. To underscore the supremacy of heterosexual thought and dominance, Asher is even entitled to his friend's daughter's hand in marriage following this episode.

Lancelot of the Lake is a renowned French hero who finds himself entangled in a similar comedy of errors, mistakenly embraced by another man. In the thirteenth-century Vulgate Cycle, we read that shortly after his release from the Chastel de la Charrette, Lancelot stumbles upon a pavilion in the forest. Inside, two candles are burning, yet no one is present. Lancelot assumes the pavilion is unoccupied, removes his clothes, places his sword beneath the pillow, snuffs out the candles, and settles into the bed.

Shortly later, the knight who owns the pavilion returns and, noticing that the candles have been extinguished, he assumes his wife is asleep. He undresses, enters the bed, and "se coucha erroment lés Lanselot et se traist pres de lui si l'acole et le commence a baiser" (quickly lay down beside Lancelot, drew him close, embraced him, and began to kiss him). This awakens Lancelot, who, believing it is a maiden or a woman who has joined him in bed, seizes her in his arms. The knight "s'aperçoit tantost si quida bien que ce soit li lechierres sa fem" (realizes right away [that it was a man], he believed it was his wife's paramour). He attacks Lancelot, who fights back, and the altercation ends with the knight's death.

To avoid digression, I will not delve too deeply into details here and will only highlight the similar kind of erotic atmosphere presented in the Hebrew texts. In the French source, this ambiance is achieved with three actions that are easily recognized as customary precursors to lovemaking: extinguishing the candlelight (ostensibly to facilitate sleep, but culturally perceived as dimming the light to conform to standards of decency and to permit intimate relations), undressing, and entering the bed. The difference between Lancelot and the knight lies in their intentions. Lancelot seems to have been preparing for sleep, whereas the knight was intentionally preparing for his wife. From a psychoanalytic perspective, however, Lancelot, perhaps unconsciously, was doing what any lover wishing to meet a beloved would have done.

In this homoerotic moment, the presence of two men in intimate seclusion distributes gendered roles between them. Lancelot is a universal hero, the symbol of manhood, the best of knights, and the beloved of all women (though he struggles to maintain his faithfulness to Queen Guinevere during his adventures). He is also the protagonist of the romance and therefore the narrator bestows on him the masculine role, giving the knight who owned the tent the effeminate one. In this overtly erotic moment, when the knight starts kissing Lancelot, Lancelot mistakes him for a woman. Simultaneously, the knight realizes that he has fondled a man. How he reaches this conclusion is

150   *Chapter 2*

too bold for the narrator to tell us. Knowing that the two men are naked in one bed in an intimate position, where physical contact has begun, does not require much speculation. Another image that supports the homoerotic tension is Lancelot's "naked" sword. He disarms himself before entering the bed and hence is somewhat vulnerable at the beginning of their interaction, but the knight is altogether unarmed. This detail is quite relevant, as when they begin to fight, after the first blow knocks him out of bed, Lancelot reaches for his sword "si le traist del fuerre toute nue" (and drew it from the sheath, entirely exposed). Lancelot holds the erect naked sword, and with it the masculine role. The knight, on the other hand, remains symbolically and literally "weaponless," and thus effeminate.

Two centuries later, Thomas Malory's rendition of this episode reveals that Lancelot was awakened because he "felte a rough berde kyssyng hym."[174] (source: Sir Thomas Malory, Le Morte D'Arthur, edited by P. J. C. Field, 2017, D. S. Brewer, Cambridge, 196). In this version, the knight's name is Belleus, and his beard, like the friends' beards in the Hebrew sources, serves as the informant that halts what is perceived as a lethal transgression, steering the text back to the sanctioned boundaries of heterosexuality. Again, it is beyond the scope of our discussion to delve into how Malory plays with gendered conceptions, painting Belleus, instead of Lancelot, in more virile colors. My point is that Malory used the beard euphemistically to convey the message that the Hebrew authors had written many years earlier and the French narrator would not say explicitly: A beard is not meant for kissing.

Returning to the beginning, we encounter Emperor Julian in his self-deprecating remarks about his own beard in his *Misopogon*, which may be one of the earliest sources to caustically point out the drawbacks of the beard in the matter of kissing. As mentioned above, Julian is aware that his beard hinders his ability to kiss. Although Julian does not explicitly specify the gender that he is unable to kiss, as both women and young boys are beardless, the evocation of Theocritus' account of the rite honoring Diocles, the lover of boys, imbues the atmosphere with homoerotic undertones. As we have seen, such homoerotic undertones continued to provide material for sassy episodes in medieval literature.[175]

A BEARD FROM HELL

A question persists. Why does Lemuel find Achbor's beard so dreadful upon their first encounter? "Its sight amazed and frightened all who looked at it. The entire city gathered to see it. People approached it, wanted to touch it, but they fear it."

Beardly Beloved 151

The passage navigates the complex fusion of admiration and fear evoked by the beard, illustrating the central idea that led this chapter, how it can simultaneously represent both positive and negative attributes. While the beard is commonly perceived as the ultimate symbol of manhood, it also holds deep-rooted associations with fear in medieval culture. Excessive hirsuteness, with the beard having a place of honor, is linked to notions of the unhuman and unmanly: the wild-beast, as we discussed above, and the diabolical.

We have seen earlier that Flamenca's husband Archimbaut's motives are self-serving, as he adopts a frightening appearance to exert control over his wife and dissuade her from betraying him. Danièle Alexandre-Bidon and Jacques Berlioz saw in his metamorphosed appearance an incarnation of a boogeyman. They demonstrated that one method used to deter medieval children from foolish behavior was to frighten them with a *barbo* (or "barboire" or "barbatoire"), a mask depicting a terrifying bearded figure, employed as a boogeyman not only to scare children but also to instill fear of hell in individuals of all ages.[176] This idea brings us to the concept that beards were deeply entrenched in the medieval human experience as diabolical symbols of fear.

As illustrated in Jeffrey Burton Russell's renowned work, the Devil embodies various forms, simultaneously enticing and terrifying.[177] When deliberately depicted in a monstrous guise, the Devil possesses several characteristic traits, one of which is his beard. Christian didactic discourses animated the diabolical through a fantasized black figure. The portrait of a typical devil can be drawn from an exemplum written in the thirteenth century by the French Dominican preacher and inquisitor, Stephanus de Borbone. The whole passage indicates:

> Or Qualis sit dyabolus. Igitur secundum quod in Passione beati Bartholomei legitur quod angelus uolens ostendere dyabolum illis quibus beatus Bartholomeus predicauerat, precepit eis in frontibus fieri signum crucis, et tunc ostendit eis ingentem Maurum nigriorem fuligine, facie acuta, barba prolixa, crinibus usque ad pedes protensis de oculis igneis scintillas emittentem, ex ore et naribus sulfureum ignem spirantem, uinctis retro manibus.

> Of what kind is the devil. So, following what is read in the Passion of the blessed Bartholomeus, that an angel, while wishing to show the devil to those to whom the blessed Bartholomeus preached, instructed them that the sign of the cross be made on their forehead and then displayed to them a giant Moor, blacker than soot, with a long beard, with hairs stretching all the way to his feet, while sending forth sparks from fiery eyes, while exhaling sulfurous fire from [his] mouth and nostrils, with [his] hands tied behind.[178]

Therefore, for example, medieval chroniclers, in their efforts to demonize the pagans fighting against the Christians under Charlemagne, depicted them

152   *Chapter 2*

adorned with these *barboires*, the diabolical masks. In the mid-thirteenth century, while reworking Latin chronicles, Philippe Mouskés described the Saracens on the battlefield as "Portèrent tabors et barboires, / Hideuses cornues et noires / Comme li diable d'infier" (bearing drums and *barboires*, hideous, horned, and as black as the devil from hell).[179] The dreadful noise they produced and their masks "Sanbloient diable cornut" (resembled horned devils). The fear instilled by these Saracens prompted the Christians to retreat during the battle. A fourteenth-century chronicle that reiterates Mouskés' account emphasizes the overwhelming fear evoked by the heathens, so intense that even Christians' horses could not withstand it:

> une grant tourbe de leurs gens à pie se mist devant les chevaux à nos combateurs, et avoit chascun en sa teste une barboire cornue noire et horrible, ressemblant à deable, et tenoist chascun deux timpanes en ses mains, qu'il heurtoit ensemble, et faisoit une noise et un tumulte grant et si épouventable, et les chevaux de nos combateurs eurent si grant paour, qu'ils s'enfouirent arrière, ainsi comme tout forsenés, maugré ceulx qui les chevauchoient.[180]

> An immense multitude of their footmen loomed before the horses of our warriors, each bearing atop his head a huge black and frightful *barboire* (i.e. a "barbo," the mask), resembling the devil, and each held in his hands two cymbals which he clashed together, making a great clamor and so frightful a tumult; the horses of our warriors were seized with such great fear that they bolted backward, entirely crazy, indifferent to those who rode them.

The *barbo* described above is black, whereas Achbor's beard is white. Setting aside the difference in color, could we argue that Achbor's beard is meant to evoke such a menacing figure? To delve further into this question, let us consider Birsha ben Mesha, a doubtful old man described in the fifth tale of *Sefer ha-Meshalim*, who is also densely bearded. Bursting into the enchanting scenery of the Land of the Lions, he seduces a beautiful he-gazelle, Sapir, who is the beloved of the hunter Shapir.[181] This tale presents a similar contrast to the one found in *Achbor*, between the possible positive yet delusional and negative yet true meanings of the beard.

Achbor and Birsha also share the same fate as both are eventually killed by their victims and receive the burial of the ass.[182] Their corpses are discarded and thrown shamefully into a pit, which, as a common metaphor for hell, may suggestively imply that their executioners wish for them to "go to hell." The phrase "thrown to hell" presents a degree of ambiguity. It could signify a punishment for the culprits' souls, if they indeed possess such, consigning them to err in the underworld. Alternatively, it might imply the expulsion of these demons to their rightful place.[183] I contend that, despite their opposing concepts, both options are correct. The main essence of the respective tales is

Beardly Beloved 153

to create a gloomy atmosphere, associating Achbor and Birsha, in one way or another, with the realm of the demonic.

We might wonder if Achbor and Birsha's beards are conceptually reminiscent of a *barbo*, intended to ideologically represent a devil-like creature, although they are entirely white. The *barbo*, as we have seen in the examples above, would usually be black, as the devil's beard is usually depicted in dark hues.[184] The white beard typically represents wisdom, but in parodical or satirical discourses aiming to expose a charlatan, the white beard is often used negatively, symbolizing hypocrisy. Conversely, a black beard could signify virility, but can also negatively embody bestiality and malevolence, aligning with the diabolical.

In essence, distinctly bearded men are subject to different clichés, which should be interpreted within their respective contexts. Nevertheless, in cases like *Achbor*'s, multiple meanings can converge into a single signifier, understood in its absolute value. Achbor's beard is simultaneously white and black. It is literally a white beard, as Achbor is eighty years of age, but ideologically it is a black beard. This is not merely because of his black mistress, who illustrates the transgression suggested by the beard, but also based on the maidens' verbal abuse, as they describe his beard as dirty, excremental, and unhealthy.

When the truth about Achbor's actions is revealed, his beard loses its symbolic whiteness. With such a black(ened) beard, Achbor resembles more of a diabolical creature than a preacher. It is in this sense that the already expansive range of symbolic possibilities inherent in the beard allows for an additional interpretation: Perceiving the beard beyond its mere physical presence, reminiscent of a *barbo* intended to instill fear of the devil.

A BEARDED EPILOGUE

Barba significat fortes

Everyone in *The Tale of Old Bearded Achbor* has something to say about beards. Lemuel wonders if Achbor's "beard is the beard of truth," in which case Achbor, so he believes, will inspire the crowd to renounce their sinful behavior. But when faced with the truth about Achbor, he composes a poem dedicated to beards, where it is implied that he is comparing Achbor to "men whose hoariness and beard look respectable, yet men painted upon the wall would be preferable." In a sarcastic contradiction, during his sermon, none other than the bearded Achbor raises the possibility that beards may convey abhorrent intentions and be physical signifiers of vice. His captivated audience is warned of "beards of disgrace and reproach" or "beards of treason and hypocrisy." The beard is mentioned once again by a man in the crowd, who

154 *Chapter 2*

asks: "Did you not know, this man has eighty years of age, he is old and venerable. Humble yourself before the length of his beard and the abundance of its branches." Later, the four maidens will view the beard as a leading symbol of Achbor's perversity in their exceptional tongue-lashing, referring to it as a site of dirt and excrement. They justify their initial attraction to Achbor by stating that they perceived his beard as respectable (e.g., "I have noticed that his beard engendered awe and reverence," "I did previously think that it was the beard of wisdom and reason," "I thought . . . that his beard's hairs were hairs of reason and righteousness"). Once the liaison with the black woman is revealed, however, they see the beard as a sign of transgression (e.g., "I call his beard the beard of villainy," "it has turned out to be the beard of shame and disgrace").

Thus, an examination of the theme of beards in *The Tale of Old Bearded Achbor* reveals its undeniable significance throughout the tale. Through a journey across different periods and cultures, we have uncovered the multifaceted symbolism associated with the beard, both in relation to Achbor and beyond. I have highlighted the constant dichotomy between positive and negative views of the beard, from its association with wisdom and honor to its depiction as a source of fear and disgust. Beginning with the figures of the philosopher and spiritual leader, I explored various interpretations of the beard, including its portrayal as a harbinger of beasts and insects, a signifier of sexuality and virility, and a symbol of dignity, I also delved into gendered perceptions of facial hair, discussing bearded women and smooth men.

NOTES

1. As a general rule, all translations of primary and secondary texts from Hebrew and French into English are my own. For Greek and Latin sources, I utilized published translations whenever available, acknowledging the translator in the note for the first occurrence, and in parentheses after the quoted text in subsequent occurrences. Due to the quantity of Latin and Greek quotes and their illustrative rather than deeply analytical nature, I opted to concede the original language in most cases. An exception was made for quotes from *Moriuht,* where I deemed it essential to include both the original and McDonough's translation (noting any slight modifications I made), given its pivotal role in this chapter. When no translation was available, I translated the text myself and included the original language. I am deeply grateful to John Levy and Ayelet Peer for their readings and comments on my translations. Any errors that may exist are entirely my own.

2. Yehuda al-Harizi, Yaakov ben Elazar's spiritual father, offered this description of the incompetent Khazan (cantor) in Sefer Takhkemoni (twelfth century). Here,

Beardly Beloved 155

as well as in *Achbor*, the beard is personified, therefore "she reached," and not "it." On the use of the feminine form for the personified beard, see Introduction.

3. A television series by Albert Barillé.

4. Jefim (Hayyim) Schirmann and Ezra Fleischer, *The History of Hebrew Poetry in Christian Spain and Southern France* (Jerusalem: Hebrew University of Jerusalem, 1995) [In Hebrew].

5. The colossal prose composition extant today was composed during the fifteenth century, but it is quite plausible to assume that the legend of Perceforest circulated earlier.

6. *Perceforest, première partie*, t. 1 edited by Gilles Roussineau (Genève: Droz, 2007), 195–96.

7. See Sebastian Coxon, *Beards and Texts: Images of Masculinity in Medieval German Literature* (London: UCL Press, 2021), 6. On Aaron and other biblical bearded men, see Giles Constable, "Introduction," 47–150, 77–85.

8. Jerome, *Select Letters*, translated by F. A. Wright. Loeb Classical Library 262 (Cambridge, MA: Harvard University Press, 1933), 119. Compare this with Achbor's warning: "lest those who bear hollow beards of ignomiany and impiety, blighted by evil, carry you astray, and branches of deception and dissimulation lead you close to them. Those who seduce with words of books and promises can easily soothe the pains of the daughter of my nation. They sigh and moan, and deliver [to my people] vain and delusive presages. Surely you know what is said of the beard of ignominy, which is blighted by evil."

9. *Die Abenteuer Gawains, Ywains und Le Morholts mit den drei Jungfrauen aus der Trilogie (Demanda) des Pseudo-Robert de Borron, die Fortsetzung des Huth-Merlin* nach der allein bekannten Hs. Nr. 112 der Pariser National Bibliothek herausgegeben, edited by von H. Oskar Sommer and Halle a. S., Niemeyer (Beihefte zur Zeitschrift für romanische Philologie, 1913), 47, 36.

10. Rosen, "The Beard as Spectacle and Scandal in a Thirteenth-century Hebrew *Maqāma*," 3.

11. Rosen, "The Beard as Spectacle," 7.

12. Rosen, "The Beard as Spectacle," 20.

13. Marcel Mauss, "Essai sur le don. Forme et raison de l'échange dans les sociétés archaïques," *L'Année sociologique*, 1923–1924, 30–186. Marie-Odile Géraud, Olivier Leservoisier, and Richard Pottier, "Fait Social Total," in *Les notions clés de l'ethnologie: Analyses et textes* (Paris: Armand Colin, 2016), 187–99.

14. For the history of hair and beard, see Bartlett, Robert, "Symbolic Meanings of Hair in the Middle Ages," *Transactions of the Royal Historical Society* 4 (1994): 43–60. See additional relevant references in note 43.

15. Issued as a scholar from French Studies, surely my natural inclination was to delve deeper into French literature, although Greek, Latin, Spanish, and Hebrew texts are also represented. As for medieval German literature, which is one of the richest to contribute texts dealing with beards, it is magnificently studied in Coxon's *Beards and Texts*.

156   *Chapter 2*

16. Livingstone, "Losing Face," 308–21, 310. See also his note "while the literary symbolism of the beard has seemingly remained steady, it is interesting to note that the actual cultural fashion of wearing beards has not been constant," 311 note 14.

17. This concomitance between the beard and the spiritual figure is universal. In his study of the legend of the hairy anchorite, Charles Allyn Williams noted that "The conception . . . of the holy man as a hairy man, at least with uncut hair and beard, is found among many peoples (cf. the Hebrew Nazirites and the Brahman vanaprastha, 'forest-hermit')." Charles Allyn Williams, *Oriental Affinities of the Legend of the Hairy Anchorite: The Theme of the Hairy Solitary in Its Early Forms With References to Die Lugend von Sanct Johanne Chrysostomo (Reprinted by Lother, 1537) and to Other European Variants* (Urbana: University of Illinois Press, 1925), 25. See also "The association of hairiness with holiness was also of great antiquity. Holy men, hermits, and recluses regularly had long beards both as a sign of their freedom and unworldliness and as a reward for their suffering" Constable, "Introduction," 66. See the portrait of the holy man in *Perceforest* above.

18. "Since men grow beards and women do not, an attack on the beard of a grown man is by extension an attack on his identity as a man—on his natural virility and self-identity, and perhaps ultimately his honor," Livingstone, "Losing Face," 310; "the measure of the beard is believed to correspond to authority, wisdom, power and judgment" in Tova Rosen, *Unveiling Eve, Reading Gender in Medieval Hebrew Literature* (Philadelphia: University of Pennsylvania Press, 2003), 153.

19. See commentary 144 about Achbor's beard as a mask.

20. Lucian, *The Eunuch*, translated by A. M. Harmon. Loeb Classical Library 302 (Cambridge, MA: Harvard University Press, 1936), 341.

21. Martial. *Epigrams, Volume I: Spectacles, Books 1-5,* edited and translated by D. R. Shackleton Bailey. Loeb Classical Library 94 (Cambridge, MA: Harvard University Press, 1993), 299–301. This statement is obviously ironic, as the dog is used here to criticize the hypocritical philosopher who pretends, by utilizing his beard, to be a Cynic. The word "cynic" itself nonetheless, derives from *kynikos*, "dog-like," a term that was linked to Diogenes, and therefore this epithet gave birth to the school of Cynicism.

22. See William Desmond, *Cynics* (London: Routledge, 2014), 78–82.

23. Diskin Clay, "Picturing Diogenes," in *The Cynics: The Cynic Movement in Antiquity and Its Legacy*, edited by R. Bracht Branham and Marie-Odile Goulet-Cazé (Berkeley: University of California Press, 1996), 366–88, 368; Desmond, *Cynics*.

24. Desmond, *Cynics,* 81.

25. "Letter to Attius Clemens," Book I, X in *Pliny the Younger. Letters, Volume I: Books 1-7*, translated by Betty Radice. Loeb Classical Library 55 (Cambridge, MA: Harvard University Press, 1969), 30–33.

26. Philostratus, *Apollonius of Tyana, Volume III: Letters of Apollonius. Ancient Testimonia. Eusebius's Reply to Hierocles*, edited and translated by Christopher P. Jones. Loeb Classical Library 458 (Cambridge, MA: Harvard University Press, 2006), 67.

27. Plutarch, "Isis and Osiris," in *Moralia, Volume V*, translated by Frank Cole Babbitt. Loeb Classical Library 306 (Cambridge, MA: Harvard University Press,

Beardly Beloved 157

1936), 11. See, for example, Apuleius (second century) "and someone with a long cloak, a staff, wicker sandals, and a goatee beard, pretending to be a philosopher." Apuleius, *Metamorphoses (The Golden Ass), Volume II: Books 7-11*, edited and translated by J. Arthur Hanson. Loeb Classical Library 453 (Cambridge, MA: Harvard University Press, 1989), 253.

28. See commentary no. 59, the juxtaposition of the impostor's beard with the ear of corn.

29. Plutarch, "How a Man May Become Aware of His Progress in Virtue," in *Moralia, Volume V,* 433. This metaphor resembles Achbor's use of the biblical symbolism of the good and bad corn ears from Pharaoh's dream (Gen. 41:6). See the previous note.

30. Silvia Montiglio, *From Villain to Hero: Odysseus in Ancient Thought* (Ann Arbor: The University of Michigan Press, 2011), 122.

31. Plutarch, "How to Tell a Flatterer from a Friend," in *Moralia, Volume I,* translated by Frank Cole Babbitt. Loeb Classical Library 197 (Cambridge, MA: Harvard University Press, 1927), 283.

32. Gellius, *Attic Nights, Volume II,* 155–57.

33. Dio Cassius, *Roman History, Volume VIII: Books 61-70,* translated by Earnest Cary and Herbert B. Foster. Loeb Classical Library 176 (Cambridge, MA: Harvard University Press, 1925), 283–85.

34. Hence, Charmoleos, Megara's lover, leaves behind him his beauty and kisses; Lampichus the tyrant, his wealth, vanity, and cruelty and his diadem; Damasias the athlete, his fleshiness, Craton his wealth and reputation; the army general, his armor and trophy.

35. Dialogue 20 in Lucian's *Dialogues of the Dead, Volume VII,* translated by M. D. MacLeod. Loeb Classical Library 431 (Cambridge, MA: Harvard University Press, 1961), 109.

36. Lucian, *Dialogues,* 111.

37. See 2 Sam. 14:26.

38. Lucian, *Dialogues,* 111.

39. Lucian, *Dialogues,* 115.

40. Dillon John, "The Social Role of the Philosopher in the Second Century C.E: Some Remarks," in *Sage and Emperor: Plutarch, Greek Intellectuals, and Roman Power in the Time of Trajan (98–117 A.D.),* edited by Philip A. Stadter and Luc Van der Stockt (Leuven: Leuven University Press, 2002), 29–40. Specifically on the privileges of the philosophers in the second century, 36.

41. Gellius, *Attic Nights, Volume II,* Book 13 viii, 431–33.

42. Epictetus, *Discourses, Books 1-2,* translated by W. A. Oldfather. Loeb Classical Library 131 (Cambridge, MA: Harvard University Press, 1925), I, 2, 23.

43. See Jean Leclercq, "Comment Vivaient les frères Convers," in *I laici nella "societas Christiana" dei secoli XI e XII, Atti della terza Settimana Internazionale di studio Mendola, 21-27 agosto 1965,* edited by Jean Chélini (Milano: Vita e Pensiero, 1968), 152–82. On the Barbati, see also James France, *Separate but Equal: Cistercian Lay Brothers 1120–1350* (Collegeville: Liturgical Press, 2012), 76–87. See also the ample discussion about how the medieval church came to perceive the

158 *Chapter 2*

beard (and hair in general) as a sign of sin, whereas shaving was a sign of holiness reserved for priests and monks, in Christopher Oldstone-Moore, *Of Beards and Men: The Revealing History of Facial Hair* (Chicago: Chicago University Press, 2015). On the beard as a subject of the twelfth-century religious dispute, see Giles Constable, *The Reformation of the Twelfth Century* (Cambridge: Cambridge University Press, 2002 [1996]), 195, as well as his classical study of beards in his "Introduction," 47–130. See also Leclercq, "Comment Vivaient," 156–57. It should be noted that the attitude toward laymen's beards varied over different periods and places in the Middle Ages, and it is not possible to make sweeping generalizations regarding their attitudes toward their beards. See also Laura Clark, "Fashionable Beards and Beards as Fashion: Beard Coats in Thomas Malory's *Morte d'Arthur*," *Parergon* 31, no. 1 (2014): 95–105, besides a general overview of beard's history, see her notes about how Christian clergy aimed to distinguish itself from the Jews by not wearing beards, 96. See also Coxon's "Beards as Texts, Texts as Beards" in his *Beards and Texts*, particularly 12–22.

44. Leclercq, "Comment Vivaient," 159; Constable, *The Reformation*, 100; France, *Separate but Equal*, 76.

45. Constable, *The Reformation*, 195.

46. Oldstone-Moore, *Of Beards and Men*, 87.

47. Elimelech Horowitz, "On the Meanings of the Beard in Jewish Communities in the East and Europe in the Middle Ages and the Beginning of the Modern Era," *Pe'amim* 59 (1993): 124–48 (Hebrew). On the beard in Islamic culture, see Hirsch Hadas, "Hair: Practices and Symbolism in Traditional Muslim Societies," *Sociology of Islam* 5 (2017): 33–35.

48. See the references mentioned in note 43.

49. Quoted from Augustin Fangé, *Mémoires pour servir à l'histoire de la barbe de l'homme* (Liège: J.-F. Broncart, 1774), 128 (my translation).

50. Decter noted that the author "largely shares the perspective of an author of Christian European literature who sends characters from Christendom to an unfamiliar and exotic Islamic world." Decter, *Iberian Jewish Literature*, 175.

51. Wilmer Cave Wright, "Introduction to Misopogon, or Beard-hater," in *The Works of The Emperor Julian, Volume II* (Cambridge, MA: Harvard University Press, [1913] 1998), 418–19.

52. Wright, "Misopogon," 419. All quotes are from this translation. See also Maud W. Gleason, "Festive Satire: Julian's Misopogon and the New Year at Antioch," *The Journal of Roman Studies* 76 (1986): 106–19, 107. See also from Ammianus: "Do you suppose that your beard creates brains and therefore you grow that fly-flapper? Take my advice and shave it off at once; for that beard is a creator of lice and not of brains," Ammianus, in *The Greek Anthology, Volume IV*, translated by W. R. Paton. Loeb Classical Library 85 (Cambridge, MA: Harvard University Press, 1918), 147.

53. Wright's translation, "Introduction to Misopogon," 423.

54. "Upper beard" and "lower beard" are terms from the Mishna regarding male puberty, which is determined "משיביא שתי שערות ועד שיקיף זקן, התחתון ולא העליון" "אלא שדברו חכמים בלשון נקיה" (from the moment he grows two hairs until a beard grows

Beardly Beloved 159

all around, the lower and not the upper), though the sages were speaking euphemistically. Sanhedrin, 8:1. I will further explore this theme in part four below.

55. McDonough, *"Moriuht,"* 89. Both the English translations of *Moriuht* and the Latin quotes are from his edition. McDonough emphasized a poetic means in *Moriuht:* "in obscene and academic language, the poem presents forbidden practices and repulsive subjects that aim to ridicule and humiliate the victim." *Moriuht,* 1. See also Rosen, "The Beard as Spectacle," 8.

56. Anonyme, "Blason des barbes de maintenant," in *Blasons, poésies anciennes des XV et XVImes siècle,* edited by Méon Dominique-Martin (Paris, 1809), 163–69, 164.

57. This passage is reminiscent of the words of La Vieille from *Le Roman de la Rose,* quoted below: *"Cunnus hortulus* ou du jardin de Vénus au verger planté de persil et de coriandre: figures et figurations du poil pubien dans la poésie érotique espagonole du siècle d'or," in Bertrand Lançon and Marie-Héléne Delavaud-Roux, eds., *Anthropologie, mythologies et histoire de la chevelure et de la pilosité, Le sens du poil* (Paris: L'Harmattan, 2011), 219–37, 222.

58. Musaeus Callimachus, *Aetia, Iambi, Hecale and Other Fragments. Hero and Leander,* edited and translated by C. A. Trypanis, T. Gelzer, Cedric H. Whitman. Loeb Classical Library 421 (Cambridge, MA: Harvard University Press, 1973), Iambus IX, 139.

59. Rosen referred to Achbor as a "humongous hybrid tree-beard!" Rosen, "The Beard as Spectacle," 5. The tree was also associated with the type of the Wild Man, who, as Philippe Walter has demonstrated, captivated the medieval imagination with his dichotomous representations: a monstrous creature yet also an embodiment of the "noble savage" who lives in harmony with nature, resisting social corruptions and temptations. He is depicted in symbiosis with trees, not only resembling them in appearance (with his beard and body hair) but also residing within them. As Walter explains, "Mythologically speaking, he seems to be part of the substance of the tree, blending into it . . . the wild man derives his existence directly from the tree, which is his natural matrix." Walter describes the theme as that of the "feuillu," a man covered entirely with leaves / hair, stating, "the man and the foliage are one, for this woodland man possesses the substance of foliage and merges with it." Philippe Walter, "Une ballade inédite du XVe siècle sur l'homme sauvage: éditions, traduction et commentaire," in *En quête d'utopies,* edited by Claude Thomasset and Danièle James-Raoul (Paris: Presses de l'université Paris-Sorbonne, Paris 2005), 313–22, 316. The fifteenth-century ballad that Walter edited (p. 314) in this paper portrays such a Wild Man, asserting that he prefers to eschew the trappings of society and instead "enc e creux ey fois mon herbergement" (made my dwelling in this hollow [of the tree]). The text in the manuscript faces a title page bearing the inscription "Ballade d'ung homme sauvaige estant ou le creux d'ung arbre" (A ballade of a Wild Man being in the hollow of a tree), and an ink on paper drawing of a naked man entirely covered with hair. The image can be consulted at https://gallica.bnf.fr/ark:/12148/btv1b9007630p/f5.item. The poem expresses his sentiment: "Je n'ai besoing de porter grant vesture; / mon poil me cuevre assez suffizamment" (I do not need to wear grand attire, my hair covers me sufficiently). Although this poem presents the Wild Man as a symbol of

160   *Chapter 2*

simplicity and a lesson in humility for the prince, the accompanying drawing reflects a phallic imagery of the Wild Man. The trunk of the tree resembles an erect penis (on the trunk as a sexual symbol see below), containing the hirsute man whose exposed organ is prominently displayed amidst his bodily hair, and in his hand, he is holding the phallic club. Compromising a triple series of erected elements, this pen drawing effectively captures the essence of the topos of the *penis erectus*.

60. On the decision to translate this segment in this way, see commentary 59.

61. The possible phallic image of Achbor's beard, suggesting his extraordinary sexual vigor, should not be confused with the medieval iconographic motif of the phallus tree. This motif refers to trees upon which erect penises grow in abundance, and women pick them at their leisure. These images, probably based on rites of fertility, illustrate the stereotype of women's sexual desire that is detached from any sentimental involvement. The tree is not a personification, as it would be in Achbor's case, of any particular man with sexual potency. On the contrary, the penises are offered to women to consume like fruit. Displayed specifically on trees, this motif is surely connotated on several levels with the forbidden fruit eaten by Eve, as it represents the stereotyped allegation of Eve's temptation, which brought sexuality into the world.

62. Ovid, *Metamorphoses, Volume I: Books 1-8*, translated by Frank Justus Miller, revised by G. P. Goold, Loeb Classical Library 42 (Cambridge, MA: Harvard University Press, 1916), 224–25.

63. Ovid, *Metamorphoses, Volume II: Books 9-15*, translated by Frank Justus Miller, revised by G. P. Goold, Loeb Classical Library 43 (Cambridge, MA: Harvard University Press, 1916), 289. It is notable that the last sentence of the Cyclopes' portrayal, with his hirsute body and the single large eye in the middle of his forehead, is extremely phallic. In his fourteenth-century courtly romance *Le livre du voir dit*, Guillaume de Machaut rewrites the story of the hirsute and cruel cannibal giant Cyclops, Polyphemus, who, despite his savage nature, falls in love with the delicate Galatea. Polyphemus is described in an erotic context through his beard: "La barbe est au corps afferans / Qui ressemble dens de cerens, / Qu'elle est poingnans et rude et grosse" (the beard suits the body. It resembles a hackle's teeth, as its hairs are thorny, hard, and thick). Guillaume de Machaut, *Le livre du voir dit*, edited by Paul Imbs (Paris: Lettres Gothiques, 1999), 620. Here Polyphemus is said to have sent Galatea his long love poem, which is practically a French translation of Ovid: "J'ai grant cosme que tout le vis / Aveuc les espaules me coeuvre. / Qui bien m'avient. Car c'est laide euvre / De cheval sans come et sans crins; / Les oisellés et les poucins / Doit couvrir la plume sans faille: / Let sont puis que plume leur faille; / Bien avient aus brebis leur laine; / Si est laide chose et villaine / Homme sans barbe; bien m'avient / Le poil qui en mon cuir se tient, / Qui est long et bien redrecié, / Ainsi com soies hirecié. [. . .] Pour ce, se le poil me redresse, / Ne me dois tu pas desprisier / Petit voit l'en l'arbre prisier / Quant il a perdue sa fueille" (vv. 7073–7096) (I have a long mane that covers my entire face, including my shoulders. This perfectly suits me. For a horse with neither a mane nor hair is an ugly, poorly crafted creature. Young birds and chicks must be completely covered by their plumage. They are hideous if they are missing a feather. Their wool fits the sheep perfectly. A man without a beard is an ugly, villainous thing. The hair that is planted on my skin perfectly suits me. It is long and well straightened, prickly

Beardly Beloved

161

like bristles [. . .] that is why you should not disdain me if my hair is erect. We can hardly see one praising a tree when it has lost its foliage).

64. Adams, *The Latin Sexual Vocabulary*, 28. See also Louise O. Vasvari, "Vegetal-Genital Onomastics in the 'Libro de buen amor,'" *Romance Philology* 42, no. 1 (1988): 1–29, esp. 19.

65. Ausonius, *A Nuptial Cento in Volume I: Books 1-17*, translate by Hugh G. Evelyn-White. Loeb Classical Library 96 (Cambridge, MA: Harvard University Press, 1919), 388–39. I slightly modified Evelyn-White's translation, in which "ramus" is translated as "rod" ("the rod within his garment"), though the metaphor for the penis does not require a second metaphor. The groom's branch is referred to explicitly as a terrible monster (monstrum horrendum, informe, ingens).

66. "As is evident in your verse, you, Moriuht, are an idiot. Why did you, a goat, boast that you were a great poet? It fills me with shame. Copy the practices of these renowned men! What will the Latins do? Horace, your poems are disappearing. Virgil, weep aloud! Look, a goat is driving you into exile. Let us depart from our native land! Now our writing is vanishing. Look, Ireland has brought into existence the very own art of grammar, inventing new He" (McDonough's translation, *Moriuht*).

67. The two tales share more common denominators. For example, Moriuht and Achbor both appear in a place that does not realize its potential because of the baseness of its inhabitants. Ireland is described in *Moriuht* as a place that "Vinceret Italaim fertilitate sua" (would surpass Italy in its riches), a place that is as beautiful as paradise, but those who populate it behave like beasts who "more cubant pecudum; Non braccas portant, ueneri quia semper adherent" (couple like animals; they do not wear trousers, because they are constantly locked in sexual activity) to the point that the narrator is even reluctant to write about them "Scribere quod nefas est quodque referre pudet" (It is immoral to record them and it shames [me] to recount [them]). In *Achbor*, Lemuel arrives at a city "whose inhabitants were rich, its merchants—princes, they do not spare their gold, and they squander their silver. This city pleased me, all my sorrows dissipated." Nevertheless, the following morning he decides "to observe its people, its inhabitants, its streets, and its fields. Lo and behold! They were all men of deceit and children of guilt!"

68. For example: "He was said to be one of those philosophers who talk rubbish to the boys, and in fact he had a regular goat's beard, excessively long." Lucian, "The Dream, or The Cock," in *Lucian, Volume II*, translated by A. M. Harmon. Loeb Classical Library 54 (Cambridge, MA: Harvard University Press, 1915), 161. See Coxon's note on the goat as a derogatory reference in the Middle Ages, inherited from late antiquity, Coxon, *Beards and Texts*, 11. And see below, Phaedrus' fable about the goats.

69. His baldness is a sign of his intellectual bareness and another aspect of his phallic appearance: "Because Moriuht represents lust, the bald head may also be emblematic of the penis." McDonough, *Moriuht*, 31. Birsha is also bald: "And it came to pass [right near Shapir], stood a tall and bald [man]." On Birsha's baldness, see Bibring, *The Patient*.

162   *Chapter 2*

70. McDonough translates it as prick: "as Moriuht's sobriquet, it focuses attention on his penis and sexual appetite. See there a list of the nine different terms used by Warner to refer to Moriuht's penis." *Moriuht*, 134.

71. McDonough's translation. Note that McDonough translated "ramo" (branch) as "penis," and "ueretum" as "dick."

72. McDonough's translation.

73. McDonough's translation with a slight modification, for "coxa" (hipbone) is used here metaphorically to denote the sexual organ in what seems to be an intended mockery, which is somewhat lost with "penis" used by McDonough.

74. McDonough's translation.

75. Etienne Guilhou, "Geta," in *La comédie latine en France au XIIe siècle*, edited by Gustave Cohen (Paris: Les Belles Lettres, 1931), 1–58. My English translation here is largely inspired by Guilhou's excellent French translation, facing the Latin in this edition.

76. Genitals are frequently presented as lower faces. In the fabliaux, for example, the urethra is commonly referred to as an eye, probably due to its graphic resemblance to the pupil, but also, and maybe mostly, thanks to the pun that the word "vit" (prick) forms with the word "vis" (saw). The image of the vagina as a mouth (teethed mouth, bearded mouth, speaking mouth) is quite commonplace.

77. On women's sexual fantasies, incarnated by the hirsute (metaphorical) beast, see Michel Pastoureau, *L'ours: Histoire d'un roi déchu* (Paris: Seuil, 2007), 269–74.

78. See Mikhail Bakhtin: "Substitution of the face by the buttocks, the top by the bottom. The rump is the 'the back of the face', the face turned inside out," Bakhtin, *Rabelais and His World*, 373. See also Rosen, "The Beard as Spectacle," 6.

79. See commentary 142.

80. François Lissarague, "The Sexual Life of Satyr," in *Before Sexuality the Construction of Erotic Experience in the Ancient Greek World*, edited by David M. Halperin, Forman Zeitlin, and John J. Winkler (Princeton: Princeton University Press, 1990), 55.

81. Priapus, the god of procreation, gave his name to objects considered to have an obscene, "priapic," shape.

82. See Joyce E. Salisbury, "Gendered Sexuality," in *Handbook of Medieval Sexuality*, edited by Vern L. Bullough and James A. Brundage (New York: Routledge, 2000). It is thus interesting to note that the men in these three cases, regardless of their theoretical potential as satyrs, are all involved with a single woman, albeit a notoriously infamous one. Moriuht is in love with his wife Glicerium, a consort nanny-goat (i.e., bestial) who was prostituted, just like him. The pseudo-Geta mentions "Est, quamuis turpis, Geta que gaudet amari. Scire uelis causam? Turpis et illa quidem" (Although he is repulsive, [there's a woman who] rejoices being loved by Geta. Would you like to know the reason? She is repulsive as well). Achbor is involved with a black woman who is, in the eyes of Lemuel and the four maidens, the incarnation of ugliness and lechery (as discussed in length in chapter 4).

83. "Svbditur obprobriis et tunc pro coniuge Danis / Coniugis officium cogitur esse suum . . . . Non tamen inuitus fit Rauola podice cuncis, / Percussus genio ingemuit . . ." (he is subjected to insults and then in place of a wife he is forced by the

Beardly Beloved 163

Vikings to perform the sexual services of a wife . . . . Yet not unwillingly does he play Ravola for everyone with his arse. Struck by a penis he groans . . .) McDonough's translation. McDonough links Ravola with "the name of a lubricious character," *Moriuht*, 137. On the perception of male penetration as "feminization," see Salisbury, "Gendered Sexuality."

84. It would seem that Yaakov ben Elazar played a little bit with the idea that Achbor, like Moriuht and Geta, would be portrayed as an active lecher. A certain ambiguity exists around his true relationship with the four maidens. I contend, however, that part of the parody in this tale consists of the ridiculous portrait of Achbor as a malfunctioning lecher, who does not even have intercourse once. When the time is ripe for an orgy with four beautiful women, he falls asleep, and when he is about to embrace the black woman, he is interrupted by a comical surprise with the invasion of an intruder. This perspective is, of course, my own interpretation and is based merely on the literal level of the text which, unlike the analogous sources, remains continually equivocal regarding what really happened and does not provide any explicit clues to actual copulation taking place. My arguments for this reading are given in chapter 6. If such arguments are plausible, they do not contradict the juxtaposition of Achbor with Moriuht and Geta. I think they could also easily be reverberated, as prototypes, in a parodical manner. Melamed and Rosen both read the text differently, as if Achbor had sexual relations with all five women.

85. Rosen, "The Beard as a Spectacle," 31.

86. *Flamenca*, edited by Valérie Fasseur (Paris: Librairie générale française, 2014), 202.

87. Returning to courtly life after a period of madness, Yvain, one of the most renowned Arthurian knights, is pampered by two women who help him regain his "human" form, providing him with a bath and a haircut: "Et sel font rere et reoignier, / Que l'en li poïst anpoignier / La barbe a plain poing sor la face" (and they made him be shaved and trimmed since one could fill his fist with the beard that he had on his face). Chrétien de Troyes, "Yvain ou le chevalier au lion," in *Œuvres complètes*, edited by Philippe Walter (Paris: Gallimard, 1994), 415. On madness in medieval literature, see Huguette Legros, *La folie dans la littérature médiévale* (Rennes: Presses universitaires de Rennes, 2013), specifically on the madman growing a beard see p. 157.

88. *Flamenca*, 228.

89. Iolo Goch, "The Poet's Beard," in *Poems*, translated and edited by Dafydd Johnston (Llandysul: Gomer Press, 1993), 102–04. Johnston's translation. See a similar "self-parody," to use Coxon's words, composed by Oswald von Wolkenstein and studied in Coxon, *Beards and Texts*, 160–61.

90. Plutarch, *Moralia, Volume III: Sayings of Kings and Commanders. Sayings of Romans. Sayings of Spartans. The Ancient Customs of the Spartans. Sayings of Spartan Women. Bravery of Women*, translated by Frank Cole Babbitt. Loeb Classical Library 245 (Cambridge, MA: Harvard University Press, 1931), 491.

91. Constable, "Introduction," 56.

92. Phaedrus IV:17 in Babrius and Phaedrus, *Fables*, translated by Ben Edwin Perry. Loeb Classical Library 436 (Cambridge, MA: Harvard University Press, 1965), 326–29.

164   *Chapter 2*

93. See Florent Pouvreau, *Du poil et de la bête. Iconographie du corps sauvage en occident à la fin du Moyen Âge (XIIIe-XVIe siècle)* (Chartes: Comité des travaux historiques et scientifiques, 2014), 47–48.

94. Macrobius, *Saturnalia, Volume III: Books 6-7,* edited and translated by Robert A. Kaster. Loeb Classical Library 512 (Cambridge, MA: Harvard University Press, 2011), 211.

95. I translate here the German translation of the Greek original from Gustave H. Karlsson, "Aus der Briefsammlung des Anonymus Florentinus (Georgios Oinaiotes)," *Jahrbuch der Österreichischen Byzantinistik* 22 (1973): 207–18, 217.

96. Hippocrates, *Epidemics 2, 4-7,* edited and translated by Wesley D. Smith. Loeb Classical Library 477 (Cambridge, MA: Harvard University Press, 1994), 274–375.

97. Gregory the Great, *Dialogues, Book IV, Chapter* XIII. Translation quoted from the Tertullian Project: https://www.tertullian.org/fathers/gregory_04_dialogues _book4.htm#C13. As noted by Coxon, Galla's story is central to Burchard de Bellevaux's *Apologia de barbis*. See Coxon, *Beards and Texts*, 9, which includes additional sources discussing bearded women.

98. A rich and scholarly literature exists on Saint Wilgefortis, spanning both art history and literature. These include Lewis Wallace, "Bearded Woman, Female Christ: Gendered Transformations in the Legends and Cult of Saint Wilgefortis," *Journal of Feminist Studies in Religion* 30, no. 1 (2014): 43–63; Ilse Friesen, *The Female Crucifix: Images of St. Wilgefortis since the Middle Ages* (Waterloo: Wilfrid Laurier University Press, 2001).

99. A groundbreaking meditation transcending the notion of the Saint's "masculinization" can be found in Hannah Skoda, "St Wilgefortis and Her/Their Beard: The Devotions of Unhappy Wives and Non-Binary People," *History Workshop Journal* 95 (2023): 51–74.

100. Chrétien de Troyes, "Perceval ou le conte du Graal," in *Œuvres complètes,* edited by Daniel Poirion (Paris: Gallimard, 1994), 799.

101. Gerald dedicates an extensive chapter to describing the ways in which the Irish men are uncivilized, barbaro (barbarous) one being the way of their "luxuriant beards" (barbis luxuriantibus). The pun is not unnoticed. We have already encountered fierce satire mocking the Irish and emphasizing their hairiness in the tales of Moriuht and Iolo.

102. Giraldi Cambrensis, *Topographia Hibernica, et Expugnatio Hibernica,* edited by James F. Dimock, Volume 5 of *Giraldi Cambrensis Opera*, Rerum Britannicarum Medii Ævi Scriptores (London: Longman, Green, Reader, and Dyer, 1867), Cap XX, Distinctio II, 107.

103. Alfons Hilka, "Liber de monstruosis hominibus Orientis aus Thomas von Cantimpré: De natura rerum. Erstausgabe aus der Bilderhandschrift der Breslauer Stadtbibliothek nebst zwei Seiten Facsimile," in *Festschrift zur Jahrhundertfeier der Universität Breslau am 2. August 1911,* herausgegeben vom Schlesischen Philologenverein (Breslau: Trewendt und Granier, 1911), 162.

104. On the "new character" of this French translation, see John Block Friedman, *The Monstrous Races in Medieval Art and Thought* (Syracuse: Syracuse University

Beardly Beloved 165

Press, 2000), 126 passim, where the theme of these bearded women is also commented upon.

105. Alfons Hilka, ed., *Eine altfranzösische moralisierende Bearbeitung des "Liber de monstruosis hominibus Orientis" aus Thomas von Cantimpré "De naturis rerum" nach der einzigen Handschrift (Paris, Bibl. Nat. fr. 15106)*, Abhandlungen der Gesellschaft der Wissenschaften zu Göttingen, Philosophisch-historische Klasse, 3. Folge, 7 (Berlin: Weidmannsche Buchhandlung, 1933).

106. Willem Noomen and Nico van den Boogaard, eds., *Nouveau Recueil Complet des Fabliaux (NRCF)*, tome 4, avec le concours de H. B. Sol (Assen/Maastricht: Van Gorcum, 1988).

107. Franklin P. Sweetser, ed., *Les Cent Nouvelles Nouvelles*, Nouvelle 12 (Genève: Droz, 1996), 90.

108. I will delve further into the relevance of this castle below.

109. Epigram III:93 in Martial, *Epigrams, Volume I*, 255.

110. The remark is directed toward the Cynic philosopher, since Cynicism typifies asceticism. On the subject of the diatribe against the Cynics, see James Uden, *The Invisible Satirist: Juvenal and Second-Century Rome* (Oxford: Oxford University Press, 2015), Chapter 5: "Satire 10. The Satirist among Cynics," 146–75.

111. Poem 11 is quoted from Priapeia sive diversorum poetarum in Priapum lusus, or Sportive Epigrams on Priapus by diverse poets, in English verse and prose translation by Leonard C. Smithers and Sir Richard Burton [1890] https://sacred-texts.com/cla/priap/prp11.htm. I have slightly modified his translation.

112. Quotations from "Comment Renart parfit le con," in *Le Roman de Renart*, edited by Armand Strubel, Roger Bellon, Dominique Boutet, and Sylvie Lefèvre (Paris: Gallimard, 1998), text 750–72, notes 1337–1347. Comparison from "Renart et le roi Connin," in *Le Roman de Renart, Volume 2,* edited by Jean Dufournet, Laurence Harf-Lancner, Marie-Thérèse de Medeiros, and Jean Subrenat (Paris: Champion classiques, 2015).

113. For a study of this episode in the larger context of the *Roman*, and especially the problem of rape and sexual violence, see Chapter 3 "Sexuality and Its Consequences": "The Rape of Hersent and its Renarrationsm" in *Animal Body, Literary Corpus. The Old French Roman de Renart,* edited by J. R. Simpson (Leiden: Brill, 1996), 33–85, especially 50–57.

114. Connin appears in manuscripts B and L, while the traditional name of the king and judge in the Renart, Noble the lion, remains in manuscripts C and M. For, in this episode dealing with the creation of the vagina, it is suitable for the king to be named accordingly, since like "cunnus" in Latin, "con" "was the basic obscenity for the female pudenda" Adams, *The Latin Sexual Vocabulary*, 80). The topos is found in the fabliau "Le con qui fu fez a la besche" where Satan complains that God only created one hole in Eve, and God thus permits him to create a second one. See *NRCF*, 13–21, 366.

115. According to Dufournet et al., *Le Roman de Renart,* the cavity was 60 cm deep! p. 63, note 4.

116. The word "landie" derives from the Latin Landica, which "in Classical Latin, was so indecent that Cicero alludes to it only by means of *cacemphaton*" Adams, *The*

166   *Chapter 2*

Latin Sexual Vocabulary, 97, see p. 98 for the use of Cresta (crest) to refer, in Latin, both to the clitoris and the penis.

117. Apparently, Renart put the two orifices backward, the vulva behind and the anus in front, which can strengthen the argument of the homosexual fantasy I subsequently suggest: "the perverse, sodomite Renart should have created a creature that cannot be approached naturally: she must either be approached legitimately from behind or sodomized from the front, making all sexual contact a sin." Simpson, *Animal Body,* 53.

118. Preuss, *Biblical and Talmudic Medicine,* 368. Preuss provides references to cases where unshaven pubic hair was the cause of tragic situations.

119. On the medieval perception of the vagina as a wound, see Simpson, *Animal Body,* 51.

120. Alexandre Leupin, *Fiction and Incarnation. Rhetoric, Theology, and Literature in the Middle Ages,* translated by David Laatsch (Minneapolis: University of Minnesota Press, 2003), 161. Ianua = door.

121. Pastoureau, *L'ours,* 272.

122. Although he is usually considered a spiritual emblem, the stag was known in medieval bestiaries for his sexual vigor. In medieval iconography, the stag's neck often appears disproportionately long, calling attention to it, maybe because he swallows while rutting.

123. Although "Among his many other crimes, Renart names himself as a sodomite . . ., stating that he has his way with everyone in the household, cutting across divisions of physical sex and social class," Simpson, *Animal Body,* 58.

124. The word "dure" here serves as an adverb describing the act of cleaving, but it is clearly intended as a pun with "dure," the adjective meaning "hard." "Com le vit dure" can thus be read "as the hard penis" or as "since he saw it (i.e. the penis) hard." This is compounded by the word "droiture," which, in this context, can also have a bawdy sense.

125. John Block Friedman, "Hair and Social Class," in *A Cultural History of Hair in the Middle Ages,* edited by Roberta Milliken (London: Bloomsbury Academic, 2018), 137–51, 198–202.

126. "Rabbinic literature generally assumes that female pubic hair should be removed because it was considered both unsightly and dangerous to the male during intercourse." Eliezer Segal, *From Sermon to Commentary: Expounding the Bible in Talmudic Babylonia* (Waterloo: Wilfrid Laurier University Press, 2005), 31, note 3.

127. The metaphor of the pubic hair as a spider web is somewhat reminiscent of the Misopogon motif discussed above, that is, that an unkept pilosity attracts flies and insects.

128. In: Jelle Koopmans, ed., *Recueil de sermons joyeux* (Geneva: Droz, 1988), 77–101, 100.

129. Lucian, *Cynicus,* translated by M. D. MacLeod. Loeb Classical Library 432 (Cambridge, MA: Harvard University Press, 1967), 403.

130. Clement of Alexandria, *The Paedagogus,* translated by William Wilson, in *Ante-Nicene Fathers, Volume II: Fathers of the Second Century: Hermas, Tatian, Athenagoras, Theophilus, and Clement of Alexandria,* edited by Alexander Roberts,

James Donaldson, and A. Cleveland Coxe (Buffalo: Christian Literature Publishing Co., 1885).

131. Augustine, *City of God, Volume VII: Books 21-22*, translated by William M. Green. Loeb Classical Library 417 (Cambridge, MA: Harvard University Press, 1972), 335.

132. I translated here the German translation of the Greek original from Karlsson, "Aus der Briefsammlung des Anonymus Florentinus (Georgios Oinaiotes)."

133. Étienne Wolff, "Martial et la pilosity," in *Anthropologie, Mythologies*, 209–18, 215 (in French, my translation).

134. Alexandre Micha, ed., "Le lai de Nabarez," in *Lais féeriques des XIIe et XIIIe siècles* (Paris: Flammarion, 1992), 342–47.

135. From: Rosanna Brusegan, "La plaisanterie dans la lai de Nabaret," in *Risus Mediaevalis: Laughter in Medieval Literature and Art*, edited by Herman Braet, Guido Latré, and Werner Verbeke (Leuven: Leuven University Press, 2003), 129–41, here 135 and 138 (French, my translation).

136. See the above discussion fn. 110 regarding the crest.

137. Brusegan, "La plaisanterie," 140. The perception of bodily pilosity as specifically reflecting pubic pilosity, and by abstraction male carnality, reaches an apogee in the sixteenth century in a sordid short theatrical play from the genre of the *sermon joyeux*, which includes the figure of Saint Vélu (Saint Hairy). This saint is an amalgamation of an object—a sex toy, and a human being—a horny churchman. He is "used" like a vibrator to cure frigid women and simultaneously gets them pregnant. Either way, human or object, the hairy Saint Hairy functions as nothing more than a sex machine.

138. Brusegan, "La plaisanterie," 139.

139. Perhaps even a possible hint of homosexuality. See Wolff's discussion of male genital and buttock epilation and the question of homosexuality, "Martial et la pilosity," 215.

140. In the sixteenth century, we see an opposite example, where a man's dense beard is a target for ridicule, implying that he is being cuckolded.

> Qui veult sçavoir de barbe non rasée
> Quel honneur faict à celuy qui la porte?
> D'autant qu'elle est au menton mal aisée,
> Et que Dames en ont fait leur risée
> Et la beaulte du visaige transporte,
> Conclure on peult, à tous je m'en rapporte,
> En ung brief mot, voire sans flaterye,
> Que le porteur, la portant en emporte
> Petit honneur, et grande moquerye.

Who would like to know, regarding an unshaven beard, what honor does it render to he who wears it? Since it is a nuisance on the chin, and the ladies made it the subject of their derision, and it takes away the beauty of the face, conclude we may, I am telling all of you in a brief word, and without any flattery, / That the bearer who carries it, gains little honor, and great mockery. Roger de Collerye, *Oeuvres de Roger de Collerye*, edited by Charles d'Héricault (Paris: P. Jannet, 1855).

168   *Chapter 2*

141. Gillebert de Berneville, "Jugement d'amour," in *Trouvères belges du XIIe au XIVe siècle. Chansons d'amour, jeux-partis, pastourelles, dits et fabliaux par Quenes de Béthune, Henri III, duc de Brabant, Gillebert de Berneville, Mathieu de Gand, Jacques de Baisieux, Gauthier le Long, etc.*, edited by Aug. Scheler (Bruxelles: Closson, 1876), 54–56.

142. In: Oldstone-Moore, *Of Beards and Men*, 81, and further on Charlemagne's beard, 79–83. And see on Charlemagne's beard also D. D. R. Owen, "Beards in the *Chanson de Roland*," *Forum for Modern Language Studies* 24, no. 2 (1988): 175–79; Clarck, "Fashionable Beards," 98–99; and Coxon, *Beards and Men*, 30–61.

143. P. A. Bly, "Beards in the *Poema de Mio Cid*: Structural and Contextual Structures," *Forum for Modern Language Studies* XIV, no. 1 (January 1978): 16–24, 21.

144. Clarck also makes a connection between El Cid and the "Fashionable Beards."

145. It would be worthwhile for future research to review this topos in the context of the *barbatoria*, a "rite [that] marked the young man's passage from childhood to adulthood . . . [and] was celebrated when the beard . . . of the young man was shaved for the first time" Yitzhak Hen, "The Early Medieval *Barbatoria*," in *Medieval Christianity in Practice*, edited by Miri Rubin (Princeton: Princeton University Press, 2009), 21–26, 22. Ceremonies of this kind conveyed that the shaved beard be offered to either the gods or the king, and postulated a connection of subordination between the boy and the person who shaved him. Thus "the barbatoria was a symbolic gesture that created a new social and legal order, by forming spiritual kinship and sponsorship" (Hen, "The Early Medieval *Barbatoria*," 23). In this context, the significance of offering the beard to the giant would be a signifier of their different hierarchical positions. See also Paul E. Dutton, "Charlemagne's Mustache," in *Charlemagne's Mustache and Other Cultural Clusters of a Dark Age* (New York: Palgrave Macmillan, 2004), 3–42.

146. Translated by Neil Wright in Geoffrey of Monmouth, *The History of the Kings of Britain*, edited by Michael D. Reeve and translated by Neil Wright (Woodbridge: Boydell & Brewer, 2007), 226. For the Latin text, Liber X, 95–105, 227, 229. For the much earlier Welsh origins of this folkloric theme, and its dissemination mostly in English literature, see Livingstone "Losing Face," 609. See also Coxon, *Beards and Texts*, 55.

147. In Wace, this episode is found in Vv. 11563–11600, for a translated edition, see, for example, *Wace's Roman de Brut: A History of the British*, text and translated by Judith Weiss (Exeter: University of Exeter Press, 1999). In the thirteenth-century continuation of the prose *Merlin*, the episode is found in chapter 71. See *La suite du Roman de Merlin*, edited by Gilles Roussineau, Textes littéraires français 972 (Genève: Droz, 2006). Also, see the Vulgate Version of the Arthurian Romances, volume II: *Lestoire de Merlin*, edited by Sommer Heinrich Oskar (Washington: Carnegie Institution of Washington, 1908), 412–13; On Thomas' Tristan, in vv. 668–730, see, for example, Thomas, "Le roman de Tristan," in *Tristan et Iseut: Les poèmes français, La saga norroise*, edited by Daniel Lacroix and Philippe Walter, Lettres gothiques (Paris: Librairie générale française, 1989). On the Knight of the

Two Swords, vv. 205–316, see *Le chevalier aux deux épées,* edited and translated by Gilles Roussineau, Texte courant 15 (Genève: Droz, 2022).

148. On Achbor's waist/loin disease, see commentary 132.

149. *Le haut livre du graal [Perlesvaus],* edited by Armand Strubel, Lettres gothiques (Paris: Librairie générale française, 2007).

150. Strubel, *Le haut livre,* note 1, 379. Francis Dubost, *Aspects fantastiques de la littérature narrative médiévale (XIIème-XIIIèeme sieclèes), L'Autre, l'Ailleurs l'Autrefois* (Geneva: Slatkine, 1991), 610–13.

151. On doors and paths as metaphors for female pudenda in classical Latin, see Adams, *The Latin Sexual Vocabulary,* 89.

152. To a certain extent, the fabrics made of beards are reminiscent of one of the maiden's allegations that Achbor's beard is like a cover, and see commentaries 143, 144, 145.

153. Dubost, *Aspects fantastiques,* 612. See his remarks on the lady's "castrating fantasies," 613.

154. Arthur, as a utopian king whose name is not often associated with love liaisons, and Lancelot, in his quest to find the Holy Grail, always rationalize the decision to defend the beard in terms of keeping honor, with the emphasis on the intrinsic humiliation of surrounding it. Lancelot is involved with King Arthur's wife, which is the reason why, according to one of the damsels of the Castle of Beards, he does not find the Grail. Nevertheless, Lancelot remains loyal to courtly love exigencies. Livingston noted that "Arthur's defeat of the giant thus underscores his position as the natural heir to the throne, and his ability to civilize the most barbaric corners of his realm," "Losing Face," 316. Tristan, on the other hand, transgresses them. Marrying Iseut of the White Hands is an act of self-restraint, as it is driven by jealousy and contradicts the foundation of the courtly game of sublime service and loyalty to one and only one lady. Perhaps his injury during the battle with the giant reflects this imperfection, and to a certain extent even serves as a punishment.

155. By marrying another woman, Tristan transgresses courtly love ideals that require him to remain faithful to his true beloved, even if it means deep suffering.

156. See Dubost, *Aspects fantastiques,* 610–13. And also Walter's commentary in his edition on the castrating giant in this episode, "Une ballade inédite," 373. And see Constable's remark on shaving representing "the equivalent of castration," "Introduction," 56.

157. Iolo Goch, "The Poet's Beard," 102, Johnstone's translation.

158. In his introduction and commentary, McDonough largely refers to the systematic reluctance toward Moriuht as an Irishman. Iolo also wrote a satire against the Irishman, featuring similar sentiments about the Irish as those of Warner of Rouen. See "Satire on the Irishman" in "The Poet's Beard," Johnstone's translation, 148–53.

159. *Misopogon,* Wright's translation, 423.

160. Shlomo ibn Zakbel, "The Tale of Asher ben Yehuda," in *Libavtini: Lovers' Tales from The Middle Ages,* edited by Yosef Yahalom (Jerusalem: Carmel, 2009), 59–71, 70 [in Hebrew].

170   *Chapter 2*

161. Yehuda al-Harizi, "Tale of the Seven Virgins," in *Tahkemoni or Tales of Heman the Ezrahite*, edited by Yosef Yahalom and Naoya Katsumata (Jerusalem: Ben Zvi, 2010), 235–41, 240.

162. Adams, *The Latin Sexual Vocabulary*, 87. The sources studied here as examples are all provided by Adams as examples in his chapter *Designations of the Female Genitalia* under the title "Household Terminology-," 86–87.

163. Aristophanes, *Acharnians. Knights,* edited and translated by Jeffrey Henderson. Loeb Classical Library 178 (Cambridge, MA: Harvard University Press, 1998), 391.

164. Apuleius, *Metamorphoses (The Golden Ass), Volume I: Books 1-6*, edited and translated by J. Arthur Hanson. Loeb Classical Library 44 (Cambridge, MA: Harvard University Press, 1996), 61.

165. Apuleius, *Metamorphoses*, 61.

166. Apuleius, *Metamorphoses*, 61.

167. Shlomo ibn Zakbel, "The Tale of Asher," 70.

168. Apuleius, *Metamorphoses*, 61.

169. Apuleius, *Metamorphoses*, 61–63.

170. Apuleius, *Metamorphoses*, 63.

171. Apuleius, *Metamorphoses,* 75.

172. These metaphors need no further explanation. For the sword see above, for the serpent see Adams, *The Latin Sexual Vocabulary*, 29–31.

173. I cannot but mention here the thirteenth-century *Frauendienst* by Ulrich von Liechtenstein. Dressed up as a woman playing the role of Venus, Ulrich has to pass the Kiss of Peace (a part of the Mass procedure) to the countess. For this, she tells him, "You'll have to move the veil aside." Ulrich obeys "The charming lady then began / to laugh and said, 'Why you're a man! / I caught a glimpse of you just now. What then? I'll kiss you anyhow.'" J. W. Thomas' translation from Ulrich von Liechtenstein's *Service of Ladies* (Woodbridge: The Boydell Press, 2004), 60; Coxon, *Beards and Texts*, 15–16.

174. Sir Thomas Malory, *Le Morte D'Arthur*, edited by P. J. C. Field (Cambridge: D. S. Brewer, 2017), 196.

175. "Always at the beginning of spring the lads gather round his [i.e., Diocles] tomb and compete for the prize in kissing; and whoever most sweetly presses lips on lips goes home to his mother loaded with garlands. Fortunate is he who judges those kisses for the boys." Theocritus, Idyll 12 in *Theocritus. Moschus. Bion,* edited and translated by Neil Hopkinson. Loeb Classical Library 28 (Cambridge, MA: Harvard University Press, 2015, 181). As noted: "The narrators report may even include a hint of promiscuity, as the boys are engaged in a competition of homosexual ardor, judged by a lucky judge, presumably an adult." Poulheria Kyriakou, *Theocritus and His Native Muse. A Syracusan Among Many* (Berlin: De Gruyter, 2018).

176. Danièle Alexandre-Bidon and Jacques Berlioz, "Le masque et la barbe. Figures du croquemitaine médiéval," *Le Monde alpin et rhodanien. Revue régionale d'ethnologie*, no. 2-4 (1998): 163–86. While beard (barba) gave this mask its name, it became integrated into language as a pejorative facial disguise, not necessarily featuring a beard. In the twelfth century, Reclus de Molliens refers to proud women

aspiring to the beauty ideal of a pale complexion, painting their faces in white tones to resemble marble (Se paint comme ymage marmoire). He admonishes this practice, asserting that the Lord loves faces as He created them, whether black or otherwise, rhetorically questioning these women: "mais volt de barbéoire / Cuidies qu'il l'aint ne qu'il le lot?" (however, faces like *barboire*, do you think He would love that or praise that?). *Li romans de Carité et Miserere du Renclus de Moiliens, poèmes de la fin du XIIe siècle,* edited by A.-G. Van Hamel (Paris: Vieweg (Bibliothèque de l'École des hautes études, Sciences philologiques et historiques, 1885), 61–62, 180. In a satirical vein, deeply influenced by Reclus' depiction of the proud woman in his *Miserere,* this sentiment recurs in the fourteenth-century satire *Les Lamentations de Matheolus* by Jehan Lefèvre de Resson. Jehan reverberates the more beard-like aspect of these masks, used as bogeymen, as he refers to the way such a proud woman looks like a mask of a demon that frightens children: "C'est la barboire des chetifs, / Paour fait aus enfans petis" (it is the devil's barboire, it frightens little children) *Les Lamentations de Matheolus et le Livre de leesce de Jehan le Fèvre,* de Resson (poèmes français du XIVe siècle), *Volume 1, Book II,* edited by A.-G. Van Hamel (Paris: Bouillon (Bibliothèque de l'École des hautes études, 1892), 95–96, 115. The word *"chetif"* typically refers to prisoners, captives, or the miserable, but by extension can also refer to a devil (Godefroy dictionary).

177. Jeffrey Burton Russell, *Lucifer. The Devil in the Middle Ages* (Ithaca and London: Cornell University Press, 1984), 68.

178. Stephanus de Borbone, Exempla, Tractatus de diversis materiis predicabilibus *Prologus—Liber primus. De dono timoris,* edited by J. Berlioz and J. L. Eichenlaub (Turnhout: Brepols, 2002), 101.

179. *Chronique rimée de Philippe Mouskes, évêque de Tournay au treizième siècle, Volume 1,* edited by Baron de Reiffenberg, Collection de chroniques belges inédites (Bruxelles: Hayez, 1836), 242.

180. *Les grandes chroniques de France, Volume III,* edited by Jules Viard (Paris: Librairie ancienne Honoré Champion, 1920), 233.

181. This tale was studied by Jonathan Decter, "A Hebrew 'Sodomite' Tale from Thirteenth-century Toledo: Jacob Ben Elazar's story of Sapir, Shapir, and Birsha," *Journal of Medieval Iberian Studies* 3, no. 2 (2011): 187–202, and Bibring, *The Patient,* and *Birsha,* which also provides the full translation quoted here.

182. On the Burial of the Ass in *Sefer haMeshlim,* see Bibring, *The Patient.*

183. On the idea of *Olam haba* in Achbor, see next chapter. Compare also with Lemuel's words to the black mistress, who is also demonized: "I shall say the word of the Eternal to every Cushitic maid: 'turn back, return to where you were made!'"

184. Black and red, symbolizing hell's flames (Russell, *Lucifer,* 69), although he is represented with a white beard or dark brown in paintings, as black was very expensive (le poil).

Chapter 3

A Prutah and a Prusa

Two Fables by Achbor

Achbor is a great orator and a gifted performer. The content of his message is secondary to the theatrical display. His otherworldly physicality, combined with extreme variations in body language, creates a total drama evoking what today we would call an "emotional roller coaster." Voice fluctuation ("He raised his voice . . . then said mellifluously"), gestures ("lifted his right hand and his left"), demagogy ("with tearful eyes"), and a perfect rhetoric that shifts from flamboyant reprimands to moralistic poetry, all contribute to this effect. The claim that the sermon's message is secondary to Achbor's show arises primarily from the dichotomy between the extraordinary (Achbor's appearance and performativity) and the ordinary (the moralistic ideologies, which are banal and refer to traditional recommendations of humility before God, purity, generosity, prayer, and equity). Despite their familiarity, these ideologies become interesting precisely because of the rupture between the philosophy and the practice, set aside from the artistry of the rhetoric. Understanding what Achbor says, beyond the poetic manner in which he says it, allows us to better appreciate the meaning of his hypocrisy and provides an opportunity to admire Yaakov ben Elazar's talent. Considerations of Achbor's discourses are dispersed throughout the chapters of this book, according to specific issues as they arise. This chapter consolidates the study of a particular moment of the sermon.

At the height of his sermon, Achbor shares two didactic exempla that deal with rich men who are unkind to the paupers who come to seek their charity, and the severe punishments they receive for their behavior.[1] As expected, these fables are concerned with the subject of charity, exemplified by the binary opposition of rich and poor. The theme of the fable, a request for charity on the doorstep of a manor or a church, and the refusal (or, in other

174   *Chapter 3*

cases, consent) followed by a punishment (or remuneration), is a popular component of sermonic discourses.[2]

A careful reading of the fables reveals two primary areas of interest. First, although they appear familiar superficially, one discerns only thematic similarities with Christian and Jewish sources, rather than direct parallels. Therefore, I believe it is worthwhile to study these fables detached from their contexts, as two supplementary accounts in a very rich corpus of anecdotes about charity, almsgiving, and the rich and the poor. Secondly, as "fables within the Fable," they should also be read in direct relation to the text, and more precisely, we should examine their role in its global binary structure. Upon a first reading, they seem to be connected to the tale's first part, as they illustrate Achbor's sermon. Nevertheless, they also hold a "prophetic role," as they actually illustrate Achbor's hypocrisy. Achbor declaims these fables to exhort people against corruption, but he himself turns out to be the incarnation of the corrupt man.

THE FABLE OF THE POOR MAN

The first fable illustrates two of the principles Achbor preaches in his sermon: "I adjure you in the name of the Most High, to pity the pauper and the indigent, and not scorn the name of God when you are adjured in His name by a beggar."

In the paragraph that follows, the phrase "סתר עליון" (seter elyon, the covertness of the Most High) appears five times, and a sixth synonymous time with the words "סתר אל" (seter el), the covertness of God.[3] Schirmann thought this could have been a common formula for oaths, and I concur, as I believe that Achbor was warning the people not to use such an oath in vain, which would be blasphemous. The literal translation of "ואני משביעכם בסתר עליון" is "in the covert of the Most High." Nevertheless, since "covert" here is metonymic to "name," the two words are interchangeable in the sense that they clearly indicate that the Lord should not be mentioned in vain. Thus, I believe that "in the name of the Most High" is a more appropriate translation of this passage.

Achbor implores his listeners to pity the poor and miserable in the name of the "covertness" of God. Although this may sound constructive, it is also perplexing: the message encourages positive moral values, yet it is also transgressive, using the name / covertness of the Lord in vain. This resonates with Maimonides' perception that swearing on a truth that is known and obvious should be considered an infraction of the principle of לא תישא.[4] In addition, these words will turn out to be ברכה לבטלה (a blessing recited for nothing, in vain). Achbor does not practice what he preaches and hence his

A Prutah and a Prusa 175

blessings, oaths, and castigations are entirely superfluous and the name of God (or the metaphor for it) is pronounced unnecessarily. This abominable behavior may explain the severity of Achbor's own punishment at the end of the tale. Achbor's admonishment to his audience to act in the name of God is contradictory to the poor man's plea to the landlord using the same diction and repeats the landlord's misuse of it. In a twist of the situation, our impostor will soon be discovered to be a reversed mirror image of the message that he is sharing with his audience.

The fable is shared with us in the following words:

> As in the fable of the pauper who, at the threshold, asked for bits of food. The Landlord gave him a *prutah* (penny). He adjured him, in the name of the Most High, "Add here a little wheat because I have young boys tormented by hunger and thirst." Then the landlord, in his own court, sinned and lied, and committed an act of heresy, as he said: "How dare you adjure me in the name of the Most High? Can you not see that I am a pauper and indigent?" And it came to be that even before he finished speaking, he was seized by pain and agony. His Creator struck him with blindness, madness, and annihilation. A voice passed over then: "So will be done to those who scorn the name of the Most High!" And you, my brothers, be warned. Perhaps on the day of [the Lord's] fury and wrath, you shall be protected in the shelter of the Most High.

We might wonder why the poor man asked for wheat if he had already received some money.[5] Based on a reprimand found in the book of Isaiah ״הלא פרוס לרעב לחמך ועניים מרודים תביא בית כי תראה ערום וכיסתו ומבשרך לא תתעלם״ (Is it not to deal thy bread to the hungry, and that thou bring the poor that are cast out to thy house? when thou seest the naked, that thou cover him, and that thou hide not thyself from thine own flesh? Isa. 58:7), Jewish tradition developed the concept that charity must be sufficient to fulfill the specific and immediate needs of the destitute. In this instance, the poor man came to ask for food for his starving children, and at that particular moment, money seemed almost useless. The Babylonian Talmud recounts a story about the sage Abba Hilkiah (grandson of Honi haMe'agel) who was asked to pray for rain. He and his wife prayed for mercy from different corners of their attic. First, a cloud appeared at the wife's corner, and then at Abba Hilkiah's. When he was asked why the cloud first appeared on his wife's side, he answered: ״משום דאיתתא שכיחא בביתא ויהבא ריפתא לעניי ומקרבא הנייתה ואנא יהיבנא זוזא ולא מקרבא הנייתיה״ (Since the woman remains at home and gives a morsel of bread to the poor, and his relief [literally: delight] is immediate, and I give small change [to the poor] and his relief is not immediate).[6] Abba Hilkiah and his wife constitute one household, each providing to the needy half of the charity their family gives the poor. This example shows that not merely does bread hold more meaning than money, as it directly addresses the urgent need for

176 *Chapter 3*

nourishment, but also that the two basic elements of charity, a *prutah* and a *prusa* (a penny and a piece of bread), are part of a single principle regarding charity, as the Mishna says "עני שנתן פרוטה לקופה ופרוסה לתמחוי—מקבלין אותה ממנו" (if a poor man gives a small coin [*prutah*] to the charity fund [*kupa*] and a piece of bread to the soup kitchen [*tamhui*] the prutah is accepted).[7] This Mishna refers also to people of modest means, not necessarily focusing on the rich. The landlord's initial act of giving the *prutah* is therefore not considered to be a full act of charity in any way. Being a בעל הבית (landlord) probably indicates that he is a man of means, surely more means than the poor man. While his claim of poverty is clearly fraudulent, according to the practice of charity, even if it was genuine, it would not have exempted him.

The landlord commits a number of infractions. He does not give the poor man what he requests and what he needs, he disregards the principle that giving should be done with a happy heart,[8] and that one need not be extremely wealthy to give to others. Most importantly, his claim to be "poor and miserable" is a lie that he utters while using God's name, and is therefore considered a desecration. His malfeasance toward the poor is doubled by his contempt for God. Medieval theologians perceived blasphemy to be an offense for which there is no repentance or *teshuva*.[9] Accordingly, divine intervention leads to the sinning landlord's death and a fierce warning about the Judgment Day. The repetitive use of the Lord's name, as mentioned above, supports the notion that we are not merely dealing here with the relationship between a man and his fellow man, but also between man and his Creator. This is dramatized in a baroque style, featuring supernatural forces such as the warning voice: "ויעבור קול: כה יעשה לבוזי סתר עליון" (A voice proclaimed: Thus will be done to those who scorn the name of the Most High), and the three catastrophes that signify direct divine punishment, "ויכהו בוראו בעורון ובשגעון ובכליון" (His Creator struck him with blindness, madness, and annihilation, Deut. 28:28).

As we will shortly discover, Achbor is the embodiment of this landlord. Not only is he a landlord, but he pretends to be poor, while he is, in fact, quite rich. A possible analogy may also be drawn between the rich man's *prutah* and Achbor's sermon. The prutah has a certain worth, yet, since the pauper asked for food for his hungry children, it has somewhat lost its essence. Likewise, the words that Achbor preaches are valuable and reflect a genuine traditional moral lesson, but they lose their strength as spiritual guidance and transform into a mirror reflecting the preacher's hypocrisy. Like the landlord, Achbor commits blasphemy, pretending to be a man of God, though he infracts all the religious principles he preaches about. The first fable is thus a small-scale version of the whole tale. Both contain the binary elements of a poor man and a rich man; sin and punishment; a tale and its moral. The exemplum—the fable—is echoed by the real case—Achbor's life.

A Prutah and a Prusa

THE FABLE OF THE TWO MEN WHO LIVED IN THE SAME DISTRICT

The second fable describes a rich man who refuses at first to give alms to the poor, but when the latter threatens him with divine anger, he mistakenly gives him all his fortune. If we read the text literally, it says that "the rich man rose early every morning" (משחר). Yet, understanding this sentence literally detracts somewhat from its comical effect. A person who rises early is usually perceived as an industrious and moral person, contrary to the rich man in this fable, who is described as a drunk. The author may be employing this verb here to mean "was awake until morning." It is also possible that this is intended as a pun, using the phonetic closeness between the words "שחר" (dawn) and "שכר" (inebriation or liquor) to indicate that at that point he was already "tipsy from wine," after having drunk all night until dawn.[10] This parodic image corresponds with the remaining events and the comical tone of the fable: The drunk rich man writes a promissory note for four hundred shekels instead of four, and thus loses all his wealth. The same pairs of opposites are present (rich / poor, sin / punishment, plot / moral, fiction / reality), with an additional element: the religious concepts of recognition of sin and repentance. Here the symmetry between the exemplum and Achbor's "reality" is broken. While the rich man understands his deeds and repents, Achbor will remain blind to his sins and will pay for this with his life.

As in the previous fable, here too Achbor illustrates two of the principles he preached in his sermon:

My brothers, why do you desire profit, and why do you harden your hearts?

So he spoke all that is innocent and pure, and no one replied. He then told them: "My brothers, why do you desire profit, and why do you harden your hearts? Have you not heard the fable about the two men who lived in the same district? One was rich and the other was poor. The rich man was a merchant, he used to [drink] every day till dawn. The poor man afflicted his soul with a three-day fast, sunrise to sunset. There was almost no breath left in him, from hunger and thirst. On the fourth day, in his distress, he took his stick in his hand and went, grieving and leaning upon the Lord's graces, until he arrived at the merchant's. He told him: 'Please comfort your servant's heart, do not tarry!' [The merchant] scolded him, and thought he was a good-for-nothing, because he was tipsy from wine. He told him: 'Why did you come here so early?' And he replied: 'Because my heart was starving.' He prostrated himself at his feet and went and sat on the other side. Then he scolded him again and told him: 'You are seeking but your own shame! I know your evilness! Why are you standing here? What are you plotting against me? What are you thinking about?' And the guest replied to him: 'Would I count on your fortune? It is the All-Mighty that I trust, He

178   Chapter 3

impedes the thoughts [of the witted], and He will turn your heart around.' While
the merchant was hearing this, God converted his heart into another. He had a
friend whom he made his clerk, who took care of all his treasure. He wrote an
order [for the clerk] to give the poor man four shekels, but his hand wandered
and his heart was inattentive. He meant to write to him: 'Give him four shekels
and nothing more,' but he wrote: 'Give him four hundred silver shekels.' The
pauper took the document from his hand and came to the clerk. The latter
weighed the money, and [the poor man] put it under his clothes and returned
home.[11] Then the merchant came [there] and demanded the money and the order
and said to the poor man: 'Is it not so that you inherit what your Lord bequeaths
you? He made my hand wander, to give you my fortune and fame. He is the
One who enriches and impoverishes, who sows and uproots, who preserves the
faithful and silences the [false] preachers. All are His lowly and haughty, He is
the Redeemer of all, the deceivers and the faulty.'"

Yonah David saw this fable as "a parodical story on the parable of the
poor man's sheep,"[12] referring to the parable extant in 2 Samuel 12. The
fable indeed begins with a citation from the prophet Nathan's introductory
sentence, "שני אנשים היו בעיר אחת, אחד עשיר ואחד ראש" (There were two men
in one city, one rich, and the other poor). After King David's sin of taking
Bat-Sheva and sending her husband Uriah the Hittite to die on the battlefield,
the prophet sent to him by the Lord tells the king a parable featuring a story
in which an unexpected guest arrives at a rich man's house. Although the
rich man possesses plenty of cattle, he is too miserly to give up one of his
animals and prepare it as a meal according to the hosting norms. He therefore
steals and kills the only sheep his poor neighbor possesses, one that he loves
as a daughter. King David, not recognizing himself as the parable's rich man,
sentences the latter to pay four times the value of the poor man's sheep.
The fable's themes are not the same as those of the parable. The conflict
in the parable is not about charity or giving but rather about usurpation.
Furthermore, the parable involves an essential third party (the sheep,
representing Bat-Sheva) who comes between the two rivals, and this is not
present in our tale. Achbor's fable does contain significant echoes from the
biblical text, including the somewhat burlesque ending of the fable, and here
lies the possible parodic resonance with the biblical source.

   When King David hears the parable, he rightfully applies a "fourfold fine"
(תשלומי ארבעה), which is the penalty for thieves of sheep and goats according
to Leviticus 21:37. By analogy, scandalized by the poor man's prophecy in
a manner similar to the way King David may have been by the prophet's
parable, the rich man in Achbor's fable could have been offering to the poor
man precisely the amount of four shekels as a hypothetical multiplication of
a hypothetical monetary unit, that is, the single coin he refused to give him
in the first place.[13]

A Prutah and a Prusa 179

The biblical parable ends with the prophet revealing to King David that he is the incarnation of the rich man. It is the real king, and not the parable's protagonist, who pays the fee for his sin, and a much higher one, with the death of his son. In our tale, at first, it is the fable's fictional rich man who pays a much higher fee than he intended. This fatal error may have a comical aspect, but the rich man, like King David, receives an instructive punishment, and like the king, he recognizes that he is at fault.[14] He goes to see the poor man and asks him "Is it not so that you inherit what your Lord bequeaths you?" This is a comical paraphrasing of the biblical source. Yiftach justifies his people's reign over the Gilead (previously the land of the Amorite, and before that, the Ammonite) as a godly inheritance, thus also justifying his refusal to surrender it to the king of Amon, who claimed this territory as his own. Without entering into the historical reasons for this dispute, let me just emphasize the demagogical statement Yiftach uses. First, he wonders, "אלהי ישראל הוריש את האמרי מפני עמו ישראל ואתה תירשנו" (the God of Israel hath dispossessed the Amorites from before His people Israel, and shouldest thou possess them? Judg. 11:23), and then concludes with, "הלא את אשר יורישך כמוש אלהיך אותו תירש ואת כל אשר הוריש ה אליהנו מפנינו אותו נירש" (Wilt not thou possess that which Chemosh thy god giveth thee to possess? So whomsoever the Lord our God hath dispossessed from before us, them will we possess, Judg. 11:24). The rich man in the fable uses the biblical verse ironically, accepting bitterly that the "poor man's God" bequeathed him all of the rich man's fortune. As for the demarcation "your God," based on the biblical source, this may be understood to be referring to an encounter between men of different religions since the rich man accepts the power of the poor man's God to interfere on his behalf. It can also be understood ironically, that is, the rich man's and the poor man's God is one and the same, and the rich man bitterly accepts His authority as being the only one that can decide on the (just) distribution of materialistic goods. The continuation of the rich man's discourse hints at the second option.

In comparison to the biblical parable, the transition from the imaginary character to the "real" one, that is, Achbor, is subtler. Achbor and the rich man both arrive at self-destruction through religious misbehavior. His abuse of wine causes the rich man to lose everything he has. First, he loses God's ways, as he denies charity to a starving man. This leads him to lose everything material as well. Similarly, Achbor also brings about his own destruction. He too seems to be fond of wine, and he too has forgotten the real meaning of worshipping God. Both in the parable and the fable, the punishment for wrongdoing is multiplied on two levels. The killing of the one sheep in the parable is deserving of a fourfold fine. The price that is actually paid is that of a life. The refusal to give charity in the fable brings about a promise of four shekels, which the rich man realizes he should give to the poor man instead of

180 *Chapter 3*

the one shekel that he could have given initially. Yet, although the price paid is one hundred times greater in the fable, ultimately Achbor (whom the rich man incarnates) will lose his own life. In the case of Achbor, what will occur is a reduction, rather than a multiplication. It is his immoral behavior, and not the punishment, that is now symbolized by the number four (the maidens) while the punishment is symbolized by the number one (the black Mistress). When Achbor remains with the black woman after being warned by Lemuel to recant his love for her, he is killed for choosing her over the four other women. Thus, in contrast to the fable, Achbor's misdeed and punishment involve a symbolic division by four.

Achbor's sermon consists of admonishments, teachings, praises of the Lord, poems, and—like any good preacher—exempla. The two fables about the men who refused alms to the poor are used to illustrate the perils of immoral behavior and to warn against blasphemy and drunkenness. Unfortunately, the tale's second part reveals that Achbor is the incarnation of the corrupt men described in his fables: a liar and drunk, abusive toward his congregation, and exhorting his listeners while using God's name in vain. It is this behavior that will ultimately bring him to ruin.

NOTES

1. This chapter constitutes an amendment and an amplification of my previously published Tovi Bibring, "The Fables within the Fable: Dualities in the Tale of Old Akhbor by Yaakov ben Elazar of Toledo," in *La sagesse en base de données. Sources, circulation, appropriation*, edited by Marie-Sol Ortola and Marie Christine Varol (Nancy: PUN-Editions universitaires de Lorraine, 2018), 379–91.

2. This is a vast topic that has already been extensively investigated. See, for example, Gregg E. Gardner, "Who Is Rich? The Poor in Early Rabbinic Judaism," *The Jewish Quarterly Review* 104, no. 4 (2014): 515–36.

3. It seems that here the phrase is used as a general epithet for God, rather than referring to the image of the divine and concealed shelter we encountered previously, commentaries 74 and 75. Among the six occurrences of the stanza "בסתר עליון תסתרו" in this paragraph, there is only one exception where it clearly refers to the hiding place.

4. Thou shalt not take the name of the Lord thy God in vain, Exodus 20:6.

5. It is worthwhile to distinguish between the case we have here and the discussions both in Judaism and Christianity regarding the "bad poor people," who claim to have less than they do, are too lazy to make a living, and prefer to receive easy charity, or are angry at being poor. An exemplum by Jacques de Vitry describes the distinction between the good and the greedy poor: While the former takes a small sack

A Prutah and a Prusa 181

when they go to collect alms, the latter takes a big one. The humble poor man returns with a sack full of grains, while the greedy poor man frightens the givers and returns with nothing. (The exempla of Jacques de Vitry, ed., CRANE, exemplum LXXVII, p. 35.)

6. Tractate Ta'a'nit, 23b.

7. Tosefta Peah 4:10, Gardner's translation, page 525–26, note 48.

8. "נתן תיתן לו ולא ירע לבבך" (Thou shalt surely give him, and thy heart shall not be grieved when thou givest unto him. Deut. 15:10).

9. A popular Christian exemplum, which has numerous variants in medieval books of exempla, tells of a rich tax collector who is extremely merciless toward the poor beggars, throwing stones at them instead of giving them charity. One day, one of the beggars makes a bet with his friends that he will succeed in getting something from the rich man. The latter, not finding any stone or other object, throws a piece of stale bread at the poor man (or some grains). Thus, the poor man wins the bet. The tax collector falls ill. He is brought to judgment before the Lord, and the demons pile his numerous crimes on one side of the scale. The angels on the other side cannot find anything to balance the scales. Finally, they use the stale piece of bread that he had thrown. Although it was not given as charity but rather meant to be an offense, he nonetheless gave something to the poor. The scales are balanced. Even a small and unintended act of giving surpasses his many sins. The collector repents and is spared. He returns to life and lives in poverty, giving everything he has to the poor. For different versions of this exemplum see Tubach, 3727. Unlike the case of the tax collector, no action, not even had he given the *prutah* to the poor man in the first place, can exonerate the landlord for swearing a false oath.

10. And note also the comical effect of the rich asking the poor why he has come to him so early.

11. Literally, the poor man is said to have returned to his master, but based on the biblical verse echoed here, "עד בא אדוניו אל ביתו" (until his master came home, Gen. 39:16) and on the fable's logic, it is more likely that he returned to his home with the money and that the merchant, once he regained his senses and realized what had transpired, went to the poor man's abode, as the continuation clarifies. "Master" here can thus either be a vestige of the abovementioned biblical phrase or, though less likely, imply that the poor man is a servant of another household.

12. See David, *The Love Stories of Jacob Ben Eleazar (1170–1233?)*, 149, note 168. For a thorough study of the biblical fable, see Uriel Simon, *Reading Prophetic Narratives* (Bloomington: Indiana University Press, 1997), 107–55.

13. The prutah in the first fable and the shekel in this one are biblical currencies that did not correspond to any specific amount in thirteenth-century Spain. Yaakov ben Elazar uses these anachronistic coins to convey an abstract idea about the value of charity. It is plausible to assume that the four shekels intended to be given may symbolize a multiplication of the monetary unit. In his revaluation of the situation, the rich man may have come to think about the sum of four shekels as a fourfold increase of what he would have given initially (i.e., one shekel). On the one hundred punishment,

182 *Chapter 3*

see commentary 71 in chapter 1. A shekel undoubtedly denotes a more considerable sum than the prutah, which has always been used as the smallest unit of currency.

14. The transition from rich to poor in this context is reminiscent of the idea of conversion. See Constance B. Bouchard, *"Every Valley Shall Be Exalted": The Discourse of Opposites in Twelfth-Century Thought* (Ithaca: Cornell University Press, 2003), 76–93.

Chapter 4

A Double Threat to Faith, or Is Achbor a New Balaam?

The Tale of Old Bearded Achbor deals with a substantial, archaic, and biblical fear: the fear of cultural and religious assimilation. In the biblical world, endlessly reconstituted in the tale by copious biblical references, this is expressed by the fear of paganism. In the medieval world, Jewish communities were also facing the dread of their members losing their Jewish identity through assimilation or forced conversion. The biblical echoes of idol worship are to be understood figuratively and interchangeably as indicators that allow for meditation on the danger of fusion with the culture of the "Other," who is dehumanized and degraded to minimize the danger they pose. I have already hinted at this with my comments in the previous chapters about the beard as a site for parasites, excrement, and diabolical horror, a sign of Otherness. This chapter serves as a venue to develop the discussion.

While there is a consensus about Achbor being a religious hypocrite, masquerading behind a facade of piety, reading his sermon on its own gives the impression that his teaching is valid. He develops basic notions of morals and faith: praise of the almighty, subordination to the words coming from the temple, almsgiving, and compassion to his fellow man and woman. Yet, if he himself fails to do all that, and instead transgresses the same pillars upon which he erects his moralistic monument, what value do his words have? Are they anything more than mere demagogical babble? Achbor labels the hypocritical man he has described as a charlatan, or an Other, who repeatedly vomits "the words of books and promises," or duplicitous words, allowing him to become rich and hold lavish feasts. The fine delicacies that fill his tables in the banquet episode are recognized for their symbolic meaning, seen already as the waste they will become, vomit and excrement. They are corrupt, representing perverted indulgence, in itself immoral, gained unlawfully by abuse and treachery. Indirectly, then, it is Achbor who is denounced with

184 *Chapter 4*

his own words. A different perspective, though not contradictory, from which
to view him is as what I will provocatively call "a figure of a new Balaam,"
meaning to see in him an embodiment of a magnet toward a different path.
The hypocritical aspect is more pronounced since the dichotomy between
Achbor's sermon and his lifestyle is flagrant and explicitly constitutes
the main plot. Conceiving Achbor as a false pastor requires a more subtle
reading.[1]

In his sermon in the city's plaza, Achbor treats his audience as a young
maiden whom he urges to maintain an unblemished life and warns her / them
of men bearing imposing beards: "Those who seduce with words of books
and promises. . . . They sigh and moan, and deliver [to my people] vain and
delusive presages."[2] The books used by the fearsome seducers are obviously
meant here as forbidden books, which we can imagine as full of charms and
magic, representing paganism. This might also be a reference to the New
Testament, representing Christianity.[3] The contents of these books promise
something that has the power, illusionary according to the "moralist" (i.e.,
Achbor), to lead the believers astray. Achbor warns his daughter / congregation
of their vanity: "You may think you found wheat, still you only found
thistle." Two biblical sources reverberate here to construct the image of a
hypocrite / false "pastor" whose appearance is discovered to be fundamentally
different from what it represents and his words to be fundamentally
misleading. These are Job's famous last words, which act as a curse of
sorts: "תחת חטה יצא חוח ותחת שעורה באשה" (Let thistles grow instead of
wheat, and noisome weeds instead of barley, Job 31:40), and Proverbs 26:9,
"חוח עלה ביד שיכור ומשל בפי כסילים" (As a thorn that cometh into the hand
of a drunkard, so is a parable in the mouth of fools). Medieval exegetics
suggested several possible meanings for the thorn metaphor, all reaching the
same conclusion: any supposed words of wisdom uttered by a fool are more
harmful than beneficial.[4]

The (religious) enticer of this kind is then portrayed as a voracious man
who "craves to eat the bread of the poor / he is avid to gorge himself on his
own vomit." The image Achbor describes is seemingly that of a grotesque
epicurean feast: "As a glutton dog he is avid to gorge himself with his
vomit." Here, too, we have two sources to consider. The first quote is also
from Proverbs 26, as the fool, whose mouth was described as emanating
"thorny words of wisdom," is now compared to a dog endlessly returning to its vomit, delighted to eat it again: "ככלב שב על־קאו כסיל שונה באולתו"
(As a dog that returneth to his vomit, so is a fool that repeateth his folly,
26:11).[5] The second quote resonates with Isaiah, where a parable about
drunken priests and prophets describes them symbolically seated around

A Double Threat to Faith, or Is Achbor a New Balaam?   185

"כי כל שלחנות מלאו קיא צאה בלי מקום" (. . . tables are full of filth and vomit, and no place is clean, Isa. 28:8).[6] Achbor's drunkenness, suggested by the thorn metaphor, is emphasized by another associative connection to transgressions committed by insobriety. He is not just any drunk man. He is perceived by the townsmen as a spiritual leader, a public spiritual position similar to that of the Jewish priests, to whom wine is altogether forbidden. Thus, the prophets referred to in biblical sources, some of whom become inebriated and deliver delusional prophesies, make a mockery of their position. In the two biblical sources, as well as in *Achbor*, vomit simultaneously embodies the two transgressions of the mouth. It is both the vicious thing that they eat or drink, which causes them to vomit (either because of excessive consumption or because the food or beverages are rotten),[7] and the vicious things that they utter, the words that they use to mislead their congregations. The moral lessons of a drunk man, even if he holds a spiritual role such as a priest or prophet, are no different than waste rejected by his own body and are damaging to those who consume them.

Later in the tale, when the four maidens condemn Achbor, they touch upon this problem, stating that they were initially drawn to him by his charismatic beard, perceiving him as a healer, pastor, and sage. When Achbor is revealed, one of the maidens declaims: "Achbor's beard is the beard of the fools' pastor."[8] It is hard to assess what the maiden means by this statement. In all likelihood, she is referring to a charlatan, a seer, a false prophet, one who misleads his followers. This statement suggests she could embody someone affected by his words—if not as a real follower, then as a representation of the potential consequences for those who do follow him, portraying herself as a victim of his influence. Both the phrase and the discourse, however, remain laconic; there is not enough information regarding the destination of the pastor leading his mob of fools. Is it toward a life of debauchery, or is it toward another religion?

Essentially, the maiden claims to have fallen victim to the same kind of seducer that Achbor mentioned in his sermon, one who blurs the lines between sexual and moral seduction. Perhaps she is even, symbolically, the "daughter of my nation" to whom the sermon was addressed. In other words, Achbor embodies two possible ideas. He is not only a hypocrite who exploits piety for personal gain, but also the incarnation of the very seducers / missionaries he warns against. Not only is he an impostor, but his being in general also represents somewhat of the "Other."

I would like to venture that Achbor himself may be representing Otherness, a somewhat distant, inconspicuous incarnation of a new Balaam, a title ascribed to Jesus, for the conception of religious rebellion.

186   *Chapter 4*

IS ACHBOR A NEW BALAAM?

"He rebelled against his sovereign"

So declares the fourth maiden in her encomium against Achbor. Indeed, the tale is full of examples denouncing rebellion against the Lord and His commandments. This claim is supported by the repeated biblical quotes from Jeremiah 2–5, a prophecy that describes how Jerusalem lost her moral virtue by assimilating to pagan ways. Lemuel, for example, refers to the city's elders as corrupt men who "had already broken their yokes, and had torn off their reins" (Jer. 5:5; Jer. 2:20 and Lam. 3:27). The biblical source compares the children of Israel to a beast of labor refusing to work. The yoke and the reins represent the burden of worshipping the Lord and His Torah, and we are told of the beast liberating itself from its master, forsaking Him in favor of idolatry.[9]

Another example occurs when Lemuel sees Achbor's wealth. He composes a poem about corrupt men characterized by their beards. One of the stanzas suggests that "men painted upon the wall would be preferable" to such beard-bearers. This is a sarcastic allusion to one of the harshest prophecies by Ezekiel, where Oholibah, a metaphorical name given to Jerusalem, is depicted as a fallen woman and an adulteress. One of the many images describing her misdeeds is her lust for "אנשי מחקה על הקיר" (men portrayed upon the wall, Ezek. 23:14), who are the Chaldeans, and Oholibah's desire for them demonstrates her pursuit of paganism.[10]

Although they are merely paintings, the Chaldeans in the Scripture represent an actual sin, idol worship, which is about to lead to destruction and exile. This substrate remains in consciousness even if Lemuel plays with this image, giving it another context, as he refers to the paintings as symbolizing vanity, implying that the minds of some beard-bearers are more vacant than inanimate drawings. Another way to interpret this setting is that some of the arrogant bearded men are so evil that even pagan men are better company and more reliable than them. This is reminiscent of Rabbi Tarfon's words on the subject of Christians: "If a murderer was running after me, I would enter into a house of idolatry but not their house, for idol-worshippers do not recognize Him and therefore deny Him, but they recognize Him, yet they deny Him."[11]

Being "of Mount Tabor" casts Achbor as a dubious figure from the outset. A verse from Hosea refers to the idolatry practiced on this mountain by the tribe of Ephraim. According to rabbinic tradition, this unholiness was the reason that God did not select it as the mountain for the giving of the Torah.[12] This mountain, situated in the vicinity of Nazareth, is traditionally identified as the mountain where the Transfiguration happened. Thus, the ascription of

A Double Threat to Faith, or Is Achbor a New Balaam?

Achbor to Mount Tabor is clearly a hint of his pejorative figure, as his words of wisdom are rooted in forbidden cults and cultures.

One of the most emblematic figures that threatened to lure the biblical Hebrews to paganism is Balaam.[13] Jesus has been alluded to as the "new Balaam" in some Talmudic writings.[14] While Balaam is associated with sexual perversity, Jesus is seen as arousing the rebellion against the Jewish authorities from which he was issued. Balaam, and Jesus as the new Balaam, are echoed in the tale, although never explicitly, since Achbor embodies perversity and rebellion.

For example, we have already evoked the connotation between excrement and hell in Christian and Jewish scriptures, excrement being an "ideal symbol," to use S. Morrison's words, of hell.[15] In Talmudic tradition, the two specific types of bodily waste, semen and excrement, appear also in two of the most atrocious punishments allotted to the souls of the criminals of Israel as they reach hell: "boiling hot semen" (*shichvat zera rotahat* שכבת זרע רותחת) or "boiling excrement" (*tzo'a rotahat* צואה רותחת). The first one is reserved for Balaam, who according to the sages of the Mishna and the Talmud sinned by trying to lure the Hebrews into assimilation, tempting them with pagan women. Though in some censured Talmud manuscripts the second punishment will befall all the "sinners of Israel" in general, it is traditionally reserved for Jesus Christ, for "whoever mocks at the words of the Sages is punished with boiling hot excrement."[16] As argued by Thierry Murcia, both received the deserved punishment for their misdeeds.[17] The tale does not aim to depict hell itself, and the discourse on excrement is employed as an external description of the transgressor rather than the punishment. Therefore, the evocation of such punishments here may seem a bit decontextualized. However, I contend that the closeness of the associative fields of the tales and the Talmudic descriptions, that is, transgressions, excrement, and hell, permit such a comparison. Furthermore, this brings us back to the initial idea. It is as an absolute value that I juxtapose Achbor with emblematic figures such as Balaam or even Jesus as the new Balaam. They are perceived as two of the most distinct representatives of the enemies of morality by Jewish moralists, as *symbolically* unfolds in *Achbor*. There are many direct and indirect allusions to the traditional Talmudic portrayal of Balaam. For example, both are lame,[18] both seem to have had a high spiritual potential that they misused,[19] both charge money for their "spiritual" services,[20] and both are sexually perverted.[21] Additionally, they embody the concept of heresy, leading others astray into sin. Such a person, according to Jewish tradition, has no place in the *Olam Haba* (the world to come, referring to Eden), a notion that is possibly hinted at by Achbor's unorthodox burial.[22] Despite the challenging juxtaposition between Achbor and Balaam, it would not be far-fetched to entertain the possibility that Achbor's essence was perhaps inspired by the

188   *Chapter 4*

model of Balaam, who is one of the four laymen whose names are specifically mentioned as prohibited from entering the world to come.[23]

The reference to assimilation is perceptible from yet another angle. The tale is imbued with the prejudice that a black person embodies the threat of religious or moral deviance, as reflected in various manifestations in medieval didactic and moralistic narratives. The Mistress in our tale does not really exist as an active character. Her fleeting presence swiftly elicits deeply engaged reactions, primarily related to Achbor's transgressions rather than her own. Thus, for a comprehensive understanding of *The Tale of Old Bearded Achbor*, it is imperative to underscore her symbolic role in contributing to the discourse on assimilation. This will be thoroughly addressed in the following chapter.

NOTES

1. On religious hypocrisy in medieval Hebrew literature, see Revital Refael-Vivante, "Beware of Hypocrites: Religious Hypocrisy in Medieval Hebrew Rhymed Prose in Spain," *Hispania Judaica* 6 (2008): 9–51.

2. "Come into the temple, and set your heart on the right path, purge yourself, purify yourself, defend yourself, safeguard yourself, lest those who bear beards of ignominies blighted by evilness, carry you astray, and branches of deception and dissimulation lead you close to them."

3. Medieval Jewish writers were probably dealing more with Christianity than idolatry, but the latter remained relevant theoretically through the study of the Torah (in which Christianity does not exist), and the Jerusalem Talmud, in which Christianity and its forbidden books, the Gospels, were perceived as worse than idolatry. See Rabbi Tarfon's quote above.

4. For Shlomo Yitzchaki (Rashi), the parable is stuck in the mouth of the fool and hurts as would a thorn stuck in the hand of the drunk. For Joseph Kimhi, the drunk cannot feel the thorn in his hand, just as the fool is unaware of the parable. Isaiah di Trani suggests that "the same way the drunk man holds in his hand a thistle, i.e. a thorn, and cannot discern whether it is the thistle or the flower, so are the parable and the [words of] wisdom coming out of the mouth of the fool[s]—he cannot discern whether it is a word of wisdom or a word of stupidity." Gersonides saw the drunk as one who, instead of taking things that can be useful to him or are benign, takes the thorn that harms him, "so is with the parable in the mouth of the fools, since from all the meanings that it can bestow, the fools will understand nothing and only be harmed." It is also extremely interesting to note the interpretation offered by Menachem Meiri (1249–1310, some decades after Yaakov ben Elazar), as he made the connection between the thorns mentioned in Proverbs and Job (Job 31:40), as suggested above:

עם היותו ברוב מקומות נאמר על מין מן הקוצים, נראה לי שהוא אמור הנה על מין חטה פחותה,
שנקראת בלשון תלמוד זונין, ובלע"ז גו"יל, וכמוהו תחת חטה יצא חוח. ואמר, שהשכור, כשיבא
לקצור את קצירו, יחשוב שיש בידו שבולת החטה, והנה היא שיבולת הזונין, והוא מחזיק בה כאלו
היא שבולת החטה, ולא ירגיש; כן הכסיל כשיראה המשל, הוא חושב שאין בו מכוון אחר, ויחזיק
בו כאלו הוא תכלית המכוון.

"Since it is widespread in numerous places, it was associated with a certain
species of thorns. It seems to me, however, that it describes a species of inferior
wheat, called in Talmudic language (see Mishna Kil'ayim, 1:1) zoonin [i.e.,
darnel] . . . just like "Let thistles grow instead of wheat" (Job 31:0). This means
that when he comes to reap his harvest, the drunk man will think that he has the
wheat's stalk while, in fact, it is the darnel's stalk, and he holds on to it as if it
were the stalk of the wheat and does not pay attention. So the fool behaves when
he sees a parable, he thinks that it does not contain any other meaning, and he
holds on to it as if it is the true meaning."

5. According to Moses Kimhi (1127–1190), as the dog returns to his vomit and
eats it for the second time, by abstraction, the fool is not ashamed to repeat deeds of
foolishness.

6. Some medieval exegetics, such as Joseph Kara (1065–1135), understood קיא
צאה as "filthy vomit," while others, such as Abraham ben Meir ibn Ezra (1089–1167),
understood it as vomit and excrement, that is, the table is filled with bodily wastes
"ממעל ומתחת" (from above and from beneath). These interpretations link the priests'
and prophets' excessive drinking and gorging to the criticized man in Achbor's poem.
Decades after Yaakov's lifetime, Joseph Caspi (1279–1340) will openly articulate this
idea: "שכל ענינם מאכל ומשתה גס, עד שיהיה כל שולחנם מלא קיא וצואה" (their whole interest was
eating and drinking coarsely until all their table was filled with vomit and excrement).

7. According to exegetics, the dog does not know that the food it ate is the cause
of its vomit, which is the reason that instead of keeping away from it, it returns to eat
it a second time.

8. See comment 136 for an explanation of this statement and its translation.

9. Chapter 5 examines two additional images from Jeremiah 2: drinking the
Nile's waters as symbolizing the absorption of pagan culture is extant in Jeremiah
2:18. Then, in 2:24, the prophet compares the transgressing Hebrews to an unsatiated
and unbridled female wild ass, who copulates with many males (i.e., worships many
idols) during her time of heat.

10. The repeated reference to Ezekiel 23 ("I shall judge you like adulteresses
are judged!"; "They judged him as adulteresses are judged!" (Ezek. 16:38, 23:45);
"nothing but adulteries" (Ezek. 23:43)), whose main subject is religious and cultural
assimilation, is intended to emphasize the *sous jacent* subject of the tale, which is
the same.

11. Yair Furstenberg, "The Midrash of Jesus and the Bavli's Counter-Gospel,"
Jewish Studies Quarterly 22, no. 4 (2015): 303–24, here 303.

12. "רבי יוסי הגלילי פתר קרא בהרים, בשעה שבא הקדוש ברוך הוא ליתן תורה בסיני, היו ההרים רצים
ומדיינין אלו עם אלו, זה אומר, זה אומר: עלי התורה ניתנת, וזה אומר: עלי התורה ניתנת, תבור בא מבית אלים וכרמל

190 Chapter 4

מאספמיא ... זה אומר אני נקראתי וזה אומר אני נקראתי, אמר הקדוש ברוך הוא: למה תרצדון הרים ... כולכם
הרים אלא כולכם גבנונים... כולכם נעשה עבודת כוכבים על ראשיכם, אבל סיני, שלא נעשה עבודת כוכבים
"עליו, ההר חמד אלוהים לשבתו

Said R. Yossi ha-Gelili—at the time when the Holy One Blessed be He came to give the Torah in Sinai, the mountains were racing and arguing these with these, this one says: 'the Torah shall be given on me,' and the other one says 'on me the Torah shall be given.' Tabor came from Bet Elim and Carmel came from Aspamia, this one says: 'I was called!' and this one says: 'I was called.' Said the Holy One Blessed be He: 'Why look ye askance, ye mountains of peaks?' (Ps. 68:17). All of you are mountains, but you are all humped; upon all of your heads, idolatry was practiced; but Sinai, on which idolatry was not practiced—the mountain which God hath desired for His abode (Ps. 68:17).

13. In her survey of how the Babylonian Talmud perceived the figure of Balaam, a perspective I follow here, Ronit Nikolsky argued that "Balaam should not be understood as a hard symbol, but a flexible one, allowing different interpretation according to need" (p. 224). Ronit Nikolsky, "Interpret Him As Much As You Want: Balaam in the Babylonian Talmud," in *The Prestige of the Pagan Prophet Balaam in Judaism, Early Christianity and Islam*, edited by George H. van Kooten and J. T. A. G. M. van Ruiten (Leiden and Boston: Brill, 2008), 213–30; In this tale, Achbor incarnates something universal that can be seen as a moralistic threat, though I believe multiple threats are actually implied here.

14. On this, see the works by Nikolsky, "Interpret Him," here 213–24; Thierry Murcia, "B. Gittin 56B–57A: L'épisode talmudique de Titus, Balaam et Yeshu en enfer—Jesus et l'insolite châtiment de l'excrément bouillant," *Revue des études juives* 173, no. 1–2 (2014): 15–40.

15. See Susan Signe Morrison, *Excrement in the Late Middle Ages: Sacred Filth and Chaucer's Fecopoetics* (London: Palgrave Macmillan, 2008), 26.

16. כל המלעיג על דברי חכמים נידון בצואה רותחת Tractate Gittin 57:1 (Maurice Simon translation https://halakhah.com/gittin/gittin_57.html) and Eiruvin 21:1 of the Babylonian Talmud. On the link between these two sources and an eye-opening study of this punishment, see Murcia, "B. Gittin."

17. Murcia, "B. Gittin," 21.

18. Nikolsky, "Interpret Him," 218.

19. Balaam's "prophetic abilities were originally quite high" (Nikolsky, "Interpret Him," 221) and Achbor's prophetic sermon seems quite just, and thus the prophetic abilities of both Balaam and Achbor are rhetorically impressive. But Balaam fails in all of his spiritual roles—prophet, son of a prophet, and then advice-giver—and becomes no more than a magician. Achbor, needless to say, also fails in his role as a spiritual guide.

20. Nikolsky, "Interpret Him," 223.

21. In rabbinic literature, Balaam was referred to as the prophet of the gentiles, and as such, he was mocked. In the Babylonian Talmud (Sanhedrin tractate 105), he is presented as a magician whose magic wand was his penis and whose mistress was his she-ass. "מר זוטרא אמר קוסם באמתו היה מר בריה מר דרבינא אמר שבא על אתונו" (Mar Zutra said: "He was practicing magic (or divining) with his member." Mar the son of Ravina said: "He copulated with his she-ass".

22. And compare the maidens' justification for killing Achbor: "Such a despicable man shall not be amongst us."

23. See Mishna Sanhedrin 10:2 שלשה מלכים וארבעה הדיוטות אין להם חלק לעולם" הבא. שלשה מלכים, ירבעם, אחאב, ומנשה....ארבעה הדיוטות, בלעם, ודואג, ואחיתופל וגחזי" (Three kings and four laymen have no part in the world to come [olam haba]. Three kings, Jeroboam, Ahab, and Menashe . . . . Four laymen, Balaam, Doeg [the Edomite], Ahithophel, and Ahithophel, Gehazi).

Chapter 5

"A Remnant of the Flame"

Achbor's Black Secret

"From the [other] room a woman exited, utterly Cushitic"—these are the words that Lemuel uses to describe what he witnesses from his hiding place in Achbor's palace, right after the decadent feast is over. We can assume that the prevailing skin color of the people of the ancient kingdom of Cush, situated on land that is part of present-day Ethiopia, Southern Egypt, and Sudan, was black, and therefore "Cushitic" is meant to be synonymous with the adjective "black." While it could have been used simply as an alternative term for the color black, without necessarily negative intent, in certain contexts, especially when referring to human beings, it carried pejorative connotations.[1] Blackness should be understood here initially as a notion that "is associated with everything that is considered to be negative in civilized society, including filth."[2]

The elasticity of the range of the negative symbolism associated with the color black in the tale is infinite. Derogatory designations, descriptions, and associations are used to enhance the references to the fifth woman as an "Other," such as black, blackish, fetid, heartless, dark, work of Satan, rotten figs, murky waters, coal, and darkness.

The emphasis on her Otherness—the insistent reference to her blackness—was somewhat simplified by Schirmann, who deemed it a reflection of Yaakov ben Elazar's probable racist tendencies. Originally, Schirmann believed that these tendencies must have derived from Christian discourses. Following B. Lewis' publication in 1968 concerning racism in Islamic literature, Schirmann later suggested that Arabic sources could also have been quite racist, and he no longer considered this episode to be convincing proof of a Christian influence.[3] Abraham Melamed was categorical about the exclusivity of Islamic influences, stating that "it is entirely clear that the black images used by ben Elazar stem from Islamic literature."[4] Nevertheless, it is

194   *Chapter 5*

sufficient to compare the representation of the Ethiopian or the Saracen as the incarnation of sin in medieval Christian exempla to the black mistress' attributes to conclude that such stereotyped representations had become archetypal in medieval discourses, both Christian and Islamic.

Epics, short and long romances, chronicles, and the varied corpus of edifying tales and anecdotes, known as *exempla*, served to fortify Christian morals and values, often through a binary representation of good and evil.[5] The abstract notion of "evil" thereby received an embodiment: The innocent Christians are constantly menaced by the threat of the Other, specifically the evil or demonized Other, who aspires to compel them to commit sins and lose their virtue. According to Jacqueline de Weeber, the origins of the European discourse against the symbolic black color are found in the Church fathers' and theologians' commentaries on the Song of Songs, and "Biblical exegesis has established that infidels and Ethiopians are black because of sin."[6]

Caesarius of Heisterbach, a German Cistercian monk and writer from the twelfth to thirteenth century, wrote of Saint Apollonius, who once trapped a "little Ethiopian" (*parvulo Ethiope*) while he was touching his neck, and buried him in the sand. The Ethiopian cried: "Ego sum, ego sum spiritus superbike" (I am, I am the spirit of Pride).[7]

His contemporary, the French Dominican preacher and inquisitor Stephanus de Borbone, recounts the temptation of Saint Anthony and his resistance to the sin of fornication. The saint had two visions, the first of a beautiful black woman. Then, similar to Saint Apollonius, he envisioned the embodiment of sin in the form of a tiny black figure. The sin Saint Anthony saw was that of fornication:

> Item, in Vita beati Anthonii legitur quod cum dyabolus temptaret eum, offerens ei ymaginarie speciem ornatissime mulieris, ipse semper opponebat meditationem infernalis incendii. Vnde dyabolus apparuit ei in similitudine paruuli et teterrimi Ethyopis, dicens se esse spiritum fornicationis uictum ab eo.

> In the Life of the Blessed Saint Anthony we read that the devil tempted him, presenting to him the image of a very beautiful woman during his meditation on hell's fire. Whence the devil appeared to him in the form of an Ethiopian, very small and very foul / black, telling him that he was the spirit of fornication who was vanquished by him.[8]

The devoutness of the saint reveals that beauty is a malfeasant illusion. Behind the beautiful woman lies an incarnation of the devil personified as a hideous Ethiopian, representing a deadly sin, the real essence of the devil's aims. This exemplum, showing the alternation between the devil and the woman, is an example of the medieval imagery often haunted by the fear of

"A Remnant of the Flame"   195

succumbing to maleficent powers and Satan. One interesting embodiment of this fear is demonstrated through the topos of marrying or falling in love with a black seductress of a demoniac nature who entices men to follow her toward an "Other" culture.[9] She is frequently a Saracen, a term used to denote the people of Arabia. In the Middle Ages, it became a reference, usually demeaning, to pagans or Muslims (all that are not Christian, except for Jews), and as adversaries of Christianity, they were also portrayed as black.[10]

One of the tales in *Vies de pères, Sarrasine* (The Saracen Woman) recounts the story of an Egyptian hermit who departs from his hermitage on a solitary voyage.[11] Arriving at a secluded place in a forest, he plans on living ascetically, but is attracted to a Saracen woman whom he sees bathing in the spring. He desires her and wishes to marry her, and in order to do so must sign a pact with the devil. On the verge of marrying her, as the hermit opens his mouth to profess his conversion to paganism, a white dove flies out. This experience humbles him, leading him to repent.

Like the vision of the woman in Stephanus' exemplum, the Saracen is a mere image.[12] They represent the forbidden desires of the protagonists, both holy men. As noted by Adrian P. Tudor, "As a symbol, the woman in *Sarrasine* [. . .] is in broad terms, quite insignificant as an individual and even as a representative of her sex."[13] I think that *Achbor* is based on similar patterns, only the tone is much less didactic than parodic. As an object of meditation and not an acting subject, the Mistress is the incarnation of Achbor's immorality, disclosing *his* depravation. Yet, while the Christian examples naturally treat the matter of redemption seriously, presenting devout men who resist temptation, Achbor is, at best, a fallen devout man who does not. It is merely in his eyes that the Cushitic is beautiful ("for me she is the light"). One of the maidens attributes this perception to the work of Satan: "Satan stood at his side, causing so that in his eyes, black is beautified."

The dichotomy between the beautiful and ugly strangers is merely a question of the narration's perspective. When the women are described as beautiful, the narrator adopts the transgressors' "blindness" to a demonic lure or illusion.[14] In cases where the women's hideousness is emphasized, the narrator remains at a distance from the erring protagonists.[15]

Being black is only one reflection of Otherness. A distorted face and abnormal corpulence are another. Lemuel gives an abbreviated portrait of the Mistress: "She had a lip similar to a firebrand, a remnant of flames, her eyes were like blazes and her nostrils were flared."[16] A more detailed description of a different spectacularly black figure appears in Tale Six of *Sefer ha-Meshalim,* that of Cushan the Cushitic:

> Lo and behold, to judge from his appearance, he was from a people of giants,
> . . . lo, he was black . . . . He was a man of colossal stature whose fingers and

196   *Chapter 5*

toes were six and six respectively, using them he could destroy fortified cities. His height concealed the hills, his width was of six cubits and a span. His face, a firebrand remnant of flames, his eyes, coals, he ran [rapidly], like a deer . . . from his throat he emits smoke, he cannot be but a malicious demon. . . . The Cushite Cushan approached, his face a furnace, smoke curling from his nostrils.[17]

Many of these attributes are borrowed from stereotypical descriptions of black demons or demonized human beings described in didactic and literary alienating discourses. We have encountered some instances of these references in the previous chapter, as they are often depicted through descriptions of a beard. Thus, one additional example will suffice here:

Tunc exierunt de flumine tres demones quasi Ethiopes, fuligine nigriories, magnis pedibus, terribilibus oculis et cruentis capilli totum corpus tegentes et per os et nares ignem sulphureum emittentes, loquendo uocem coruinam emittentes.[18]

Then, from the river, three demons looking like Ethiopians, black like soot, enormous feet, dreadful bleeding eyes [red like blood], covered by hair all over their body, and spitting fire through their mouth and nostrils, speaking in a croaking voice.

Describing a person as a repulsive monstrosity is a traditional means to convey what transcends their physical appearance, to give a concrete image of what they embody abstractly. In addition to blackness and a sinister countenance, the tale incorporates various elements that collectively contribute to the construction of Otherness, including odors, vociferousness, and promiscuity. When gathered and scrutinized for their significance, this demeaning discourse leads us to regard the black Mistress as yet another symbol of the threat of assimilation.

Insinuations regarding the Mistress as the embodiment of assimilation are only subtly presented or implied within the metaphorical language used by Lemuel as he castigates Achbor and by the four maidens during their tough condemnatory speeches against Achbor. When Lemuel bursts into Achbor's hall to attack him along with his Mistress, the two men debate the subject of love. Achbor advocates the holistic virtues of the love of black women, to whom he bawdily refers as "vile figs."[19]

The expression "vile figs," te'e'nim sho'a'rim, is a biblical phrase from Jeremiah. The inhabitants of Judea, unwilling to heed the true prophets, will encounter atrocities that will leave them as כתאנים השערים אשר לא־תאכלנה "מרע (vile figs, that cannot be eaten, they are so bad, 29:17).[20] The vivid imagery of the rotten fig is inseparable from its cause, namely the physical decay of the fruit (with all the associated connotations of nausea, stench, dryness, and blackening) and serves as a symbol of the moral decay of those who have forsaken the righteous path.

Treating black women as rotten figs may not directly relate to the biblical source. Consumable aliments are frequently used as metaphors for sexuality.[21] The statement "Evidently, the ardents' hearts are not drawn to vile figs" in a quarrel about women stands as a strong (misogynistic and racist) comment on sexual preferences, where the black color is likened to the dark hue of a putrid fruit. Leaning on the biblical phrase adds a layer of meaning, since it functions as a signifier of vice and moral scandal.[22]

However, the world is inverted here. For the scoundrel's palette, overly ripe figs are the better ones. "Vomited" from Achbor's mouth, the metaphor is ironic, rejecting the sense that Lemuel, the moralist derisively referred to as "ardent," would have given it. This inversion represents the socially accepted conception that Yaakov ben Elazar reconstitutes in this tale.

Lemuel then replies with a four-stanza poem that reaffirms several stereotypes, which I read as indicators of a warning against what the love of the Mistress, of the rotten fig, could incarnate in Lemuel's eyes: the threat of cultural assimilation and the danger of deviating from religious or moral norms.

What do they have in common, a [woman] who stinks and is dark-hued / and a maiden, who is with myrrh perfumed?

In the hand of a lover a lily so bright / to every eye, beauty and delight

But every black [girl] is heartless, / tantalizing, vociferous and devious.

I shall say the word of the Eternal to every Cushitic maid: / "turn back, return to where you were made!"

Malodor and perfume, with which the composition opens, serve as signifiers of socially accepted characteristics of the negative and the positive, respectively. Such metaphorical perceptions of good and evil are universal and are incorporated in the Judeo-Christian culture. They appear in the Scriptures and are developed in Christian thought, as summarized by Katelynn Robinson: "Medieval theology recognized two main types of odors, the sweet odor of sanctity and the foul stench of sin."[23] Víctor Rodríguez-Pereira also noted that they were frequent topoi utilized "by writers of the late antiquity who often made the connection between good smells and what is morally correct, and between foul smells and the opposite."[24]

In a thirteenth-century Cistercian exemplum, for instance, a monk recounts that he was once sent by an abbot on a forty-day journey to the desert to correct one of the convent's brothers who wished to forsake the ascetic

198 *Chapter 5*

life. Twenty days into his journey, the monk saw the devil, disguised as an Ethiopian woman. Because he was on a mission as the abbot's emissary, he was safe from the black devil-woman and was not seduced by her. Rather, he was disgusted by her stench.[25] The stench has several indicative folkloric purposes in this story, as it is concurrently associated with the devil, the feminine, and moral corruption, all fused into one representation wrapped up in the black skin of the Ethiopian woman. Another exemplum from a similar milieu tells of a pagan who was caught vandalizing St. Martin's church. He was punished for his actions by being turned into a statue, wearing the Saracens' dress, and exuding a nauseating smell.[26]

Lemuel answers the rotting fig metaphor with a metaphor of the bright lily and the cogent demarcation of their smells. The juxtaposition of the stench of rottenness with the fragrance of blooming serves as a clear reference to dichotomous negative and positive traits. Despite this, the olfactory symbolism employed in this context remains equivocal.[27] Read within the tale, the two women serve as two alternatives to erotic love. The first, promiscuous and ontologically foul,[28] is represented by the Mistress, and the second, the symbol of virtue, is represented by a bright maiden. Described as perfumed with myrrh, but also compared to the lily, renowned for its good fragrance, the fair-skinned woman is superior to the black woman on two levels, naturally and culturally. The two conceptual women naturally emit different smells. Being innately ambrosial like a lily, the fair-skinned woman overpowers the black woman, who is innately fetid. Being perfumed with myrrh, she undergoes a mindful, that is, a human, process. Although perfumes may be conceived as the tools of the seductress, here the conscious act of being perfumed is a sublimation of the virtuous maiden, emphasizing her sophisticated preparations for her meeting with the lover. She is "perfumed with myrrh" like the Shulamite from the Song of Songs, heading to meet her beloved (6:3).[29]

In an allegorical reading, the Shulamite symbolizes Israel and her beloved is God, and the myrrh is thus emblematic of the "scent of Israel's righteousness as wafting up to the divine."[30] The powerful metaphor of the black woman as a rotten fig versus white women as "good figs" used by Achbor still resonates here, as rotting is simultaneously synonymous with a bad smell, but also with promiscuity. Stench, in various forms, is a recurrent feature exemplifying the demoniac "Others," and the "equation of stench and sin" is "false religion."[31] It is a universal code for depicting religious Otherness, frequently found in various Christian writings against pagans and Jews, as well as in Jewish writings, where "foul odor is regularly used in the Hebrew Scriptures to describe the 'other.'"[32]

Lemuel continues by depicting the fair woman as "a lily so bright." Interestingly, in the Torah, the two words used here to construct the metaphor,

"A Remnant of the Flame" 199

namely the feminine form of the adjective ברה (bara, meaning pure or bright) and the noun שושנה in the singular form (shoshana, i.e., a lily), only appear twice in the same manner.[33] The double entendre of ברה כשושנה thus works simultaneously as an expression of the conventional beauty norms of bright maidens and hermeneutically as a metaphor for the spiritual congregation forsaken by Achbor. In Psalm 19:9, the word "ברה" describes God's commandment "מצות הברה, מאירת עינים" (the commandment of the Lord is pure, enlightening the eyes). The Song of Songs describes the Shulamite: "מי זאת הנשקפה, כמו שחר: יפה כלבנה, ברה כחמה" (who is the one that looketh forth as the dawn, fair as the moon, clear as the sun, 6:10). The two biblical descriptions, one referring to a devotional duty and the second to a sensual beauty, relate estimable qualities to brightness. Obeying the Lord's commandments is a source of spiritual brightness. The parallels between beautiful / bright and moon / sun suggest that just as the sun is superior to the moon, "bright" is a higher superlative than "beautiful." In fact, "bright" may well be implying a maiden's virtue.

"Bright as a lily" repeats the vacillation between the immediate meaning of the perfumed maiden as a "good" object of desire and a more researched one, where the maiden is a spiritual allegory. In the Song of Songs, the lily appears as an erotic metaphor for the beautiful Shulamite "כשושנה בין החוחים" (as a lily among the thorns, 2:2). As mentioned above, the beloved maiden of this biblical scroll also allegorizes the people of Israel who, by consequence, are correspondingly symbolized by the lily, such as in Hosea 14:6: "אהיה כטל לישראל, יפרח כשושנה ויך שרשיו, כלבנון" (I will be as the dew unto Israel; he shall blossom as the lily.)[34] Thus, "bright as a lily" may be referring either directly to the maiden's physical beauty or to the inner spiritual purity of the cultural community that Achbor is rejecting. Consequently, by the logic of contrasting elements, the Mistress embodies the adherence to the culture of the Other, demeaned by a long-lasting comparison to sexual promiscuity.

The Mistress is dichotomized with her reversed mirror image, the symbol of virtue, who is represented by a doubly fragrant bright maiden. This maiden is innately or naturally ambrosial like a lily, but she is also culturally or humanly perfumed, as she is covered with myrrh. As stated above, olfactory symbolism is somewhat ambiguous. Good-smelling perfume could have been associated with perverse sexual seduction and false luring,[35] yet this is not the case here.

Throughout the remainder of the poem, Lemuel continues to heap degradations upon black women, drawing from various biblical sources, particularly from the book of Proverbs. There, the foreign woman and the allegorical figure Folly, who entice innocent men to deviate from the right path by offering them sexual favors, are presented as heartless, noisy,

200   *Chapter 5*

vociferous, and devious prostitutes. In Lemuel's words, "But every black [girl] is heartless, / tantalizing, vociferous and devious." This stanza is constructed by combining three central biblical sources, each narrating instances in which a fundamental menace (paganism, deviation from divine wisdom, and sexual seduction) imperils the man who is lacking a heart (אין לב and חסר לב), that is, the fool devoid of reason.[36] The associative link forged between these sources and Achbor's Mistress bestows upon her the same ideas. She is the force that, with the recurring metaphor of negative sexual power, could draw Achbor's soul closer to assimilation. In that sense, it is actually Achbor who lacks a heart, according to the more common biblical idioms.

In his final stanza, Lemuel expresses his total rejection of black women by invoking their expulsion from society as a divine decree, reminiscent of exorcism.[37] He then ends his poem by asking: "Achbor, what is wrong with you? Why are you drinking from such murky water?" Literally, the words that Lemuel uses are "drinking from the water of the Shihor," Shihor being one of the names used in Hebrew for the Nile River. Lemuel thus juxtaposes the Nile and the black Mistress through a pun, as Shihor is graphically and phonetically close to the Hebrew word *Shahor*, black. Beyond the obvious additional defamation of the Mistress, the image of Achbor drinking from a blackened river illustrates the pinnacle of the fear of assimilation as embodied by the Mistress, for water commonly symbolizes a source of knowledge, intellectual or spiritual inspiration, while thirst is perceived as the desire for this knowledge.[38]

Chapter 2 in the book of Jeremiah deals substantially with the admonishment of Israel for having forsaken the worship of the Lord and shifting to idolatry. Jeremiah's flowery prophecies use numerous metaphors to refer to that transgression. In chapter 4, we saw Jeremiah 2:20, where the phrasing "to break the yoke, to burst the band" compares paganism to the rebellion of a beast against its master and its refusal to labor.

The metaphor of water as a source of culture is first introduced in verse 13, "For My people have committed two evils: they have forsaken Me, the fountain of living waters, and hewed them out cisterns, broken cisterns, that can hold no water." Jeremiah predicts that the Hebrews will receive a divine punishment in the form of total annihilation, causing them to seek help from people who will strike them instead. The prophet thus asks a somewhat rhetorical question, cited here also by Lemuel: "And now what hast thou to do in the way of Egypt, to drink the waters of Shihor? Or what hast thou to do in the way to Assyria, to drink the waters of the rivers?" (18). In the strict biblical context, these words refer to the futility of relying on and seeking assistance from pagan enemies, rather than trusting and adhering to the Lord's

"A Remnant of the Flame" 201

path. The prophecy emphasizes the essence of the chapter, admonishing the Hebrews for their idolatry.

In this context, Lemuel's words take on a second degree of meaning. Lemuel, it seems, is not only accusing Achbor of fornicating with the black woman, but also of adhering to or assimilating with a foreign culture, pejoratively labeled as a "blackened" culture.

Lemuel's fierce sexual implication, depicting Achbor as drinking from murky water, is met with Achbor's equally charged retort: "Surely, all those who like fair girls are riders of white she-asses." This is evidently a sarcastic statement, as according to Judges 5:10, those who ride white she-asses are rich and respectable people able to possess such an expensive and rare beast.[39] Here, the exquisite donkey serves as yet another unflattering metaphor for possessing women, countering Lemuel's taunt. The white she-ass replaces the murky water, and the euphemism "ride" supplants "drink," each serving as a euphemism with sexually suggestive undertones.

Lemuel reacts to this. His cry brings back the four maidens, with whom he shares all that he has learned about Achbor. He concludes with a second rhetorical question, this time addressed to the readers: "Who could restrain his lust for black women?" This rhetorical question holds several layers of meaning. Literally, Lemuel continues to express his repugnance toward what he perceives as morally corrupt and promiscuous sexuality. Furthermore, this statement may also be perceived as Lemuel's sophisticated reply to Achbor's wanton and defiant words about the riders of the white she-asses.

This echoes Jeremiah's accusation of the Hebrews in the same chapter. Idol worship is frequently paralleled to adultery and prostitution, and here the prophet went so far as to compare the Hebrews to פרה למד מדבר, באות נפשו נפשה שאפה רוח-תאנתה, מי ישיבנה; כל-מבקשיה לא ייעפו, בחדשה ימצאונה" (A wild ass used to the wilderness, that sniffs at the wind in her desire; In her time of mating, who can turn her away? All those who seek her will not weary themselves; In her month they will find her (Jer. 2:24)). Drawing a parallel between the transition to paganism and a sinful woman, usually an adulteress or a prostitute, is a frequent occurrence in the Scriptures. This mirrors an archetypal patriarchal principle whereby adulterous women are regarded as soiled, despised, reproachable, and deserving of execution, just as men who worship gods other than the Lord are judged. The comparison to the wild ass takes these tenacious metaphors a step forward. The female savage beast copulates with as many males as its nature dictates, and no reasoning can overcome this basic comportment. Comparing the transgressors to savage animals deprives them of any vestige of humanity or rationality.

In his rewriting of the biblical phrase, Lemuel omits the specific term פרה "wild ass," which he replaces with the word "black," but quotes the reference to the impossibility of interfering with bestial lust word for word, thus creating the association with the animal depicted in the biblical source and the interchangeability between the beast and the black mistress. It should be noted, however, that if the "black women" substitute the wild ass, it is Achbor, with his untamed sexuality, whose behavior is described as similar to that of the biblical female wild ass. By using conjunctions and connotations, Lemuel manages to create an implicit reversed and even more degrading analogy to Achbor's "white she-asses." It is precisely the omission of the word "wild ass" from the quote that recalls it to the conscience, and the word that replaces it (although not in the same syntactic function) draws, in the reader's mind, the image of "black wild asses." The common denominator is that both the white and the black, the domesticated and the wild, are used as bold, if not misogynistic, illustrations of the bestial and uncourtly aspect of sexuality.

Yet, as much as there is a major symbolic disparity between white and black, there is also a difference between a domesticated and wild animal, which symbolizes promiscuity to the extreme. As argued, it is Achbor's lust that is being referred to here, not the Mistress'. He is the one who is being compared to the despised way that the she-ass surrenders to its nature. The biblical phrasing of this issue is significant, as the animal's sexual excitement is dramatized with two depictions and the use of two terms, "desire" (אוות נפשו) and what seems to be "in heat" (תאנתה). In the tale, Lemuel reduced it only to one occurrence, using a form slightly different from the one in Jeremiah, תאוותו, meaning lust. I discuss the reading of this line in the context of the topos of assimilation in chapter 2. Here, I would like to suggest yet another level of possible interpretation for this line. It is the third quote from Jeremiah's reprimand against the children of Israel for their idolatry. So far, we have seen that the biblical source compares paganism to the rebellion of a beast against its master and its refusal to labor, and to drinking the water of the Nile. In this metaphor, the prophet compares the transgressing Hebrews to an unsatiated and unbridled female wild ass, who copulates with many males (likened to many idols) when she is in heat. I will return to this phrase in my commentary about Achbor's feminization.

The two rhetorical questions function in the same way. On a literal level, they reiterate the theme that has permeated the tale in various ways ever since the introduction of the black woman: Achbor desires black women, and black women are a reference, in Lemuel's mind, to an immoral, transgressive sexual inclination. Simultaneously, the echo of two major biblical images that refer to embracing the ways of the Gentiles and mingling with them hints at a deeper level, in which the black person represents the threat of assimilation. Thus, Lemuel could be condemning Achbor's love for the black mistress as morally dangerous (i.e., polluting waters by inciting or representing unbridled sexuality) and encouraging assimilation ("drinking" from the Other's culture).

With the wild she-ass provocation, the skirmish between Achbor and Lemuel has reached a dead-end. In his desperation, Lemuel cries out, and the four maidens return to commence the sensational scene of Achbor's shaming and execution. Their derogatory discourses mainly refer to Achbor and his beard, but the black symbolism resurfaces several times. The first maiden to take the floor accuses Achbor, saying that "he dug in the darkness." The first degree of the insult is immediately apparent: "darkness" is a self-evident derogatory reference to the Mistress' color, while "dug" is an established connotation for "screw." Given the background of all the arguments demonstrated above, a second level of interpretation can plausibly suggest that "digging in the darkness" could mean engaging in spiritual darkness.[40] In the same spirit, the second maiden says: "he made his bed in the darkness, he fornicated with the daughters of Ham, and he has worked in the coal mines." According to the biblical tradition, Ham's son is Cush, and thus this statement combines the Mistress' blackness and her dangerous paganism and perceives them as a threat of ethnic and religious assimilation. This is based on the fact that the statement is borrowed from Numbers 25:1, where the Hebrews fornicate with the daughters of Moab, which leads to the worship of their Gods.[41]

Even though she is not actively participating in the tale, the black Mistress, in her essence, incarnates the threat of assimilation. She is visible, and her Otherness, identifiable by the color of her skin, is palpable. Her short-lived presence in the story encapsulates a controversy: Achbor's illicit desire for a black woman, which translates into an essential transgression. The different discourses in the tale feed on the prejudiced notion that a black person could symbolize a threat to religious and moral integrity, a theme prevalent in medieval didactic and moralistic literature. The Mistress is portrayed through degrading stereotypes, reflecting social biases. Her depiction as silent and inactive further emphasizes her role as a projection of Achbor's immorality and corruption. She personifies his sins and serves as an allegorical figure in the broader meditation on assimilation.

NOTES

1. A common metaphor in the maqama for the beauty of a person's eyes embodies the pupil as a Cushite. See commentary n.118. Echoes of non-pejorative synonymity of Cushitic and black exist in modern Hebrew spoken in Israel. Leah Goldberg's most famous children's book, *Dira Le'haskir* ("An Apartment for Rent"), features a Cushite cat who is one of the neighbors seeking to rent the fifth apartment in their five-floor building: "בקומה השלישית חתולה כושית נקיה, מגונדרת על צוואר יש לה סרט"

(On the third floor, a Cushitic cat, clean, charming, with a ribbon wrapped on her neck). The emphasis on the cat's neatness may indicate that one should not expect her to embody the stereotypical portrayals of black characters as ugly or dirty. This is further supported by a pig who visits the flat and rejects it, stating: "השכנים אינם נאים בעיני. איך אשב אני לבן בן לבנים מימי בראשית בכפיפה אחת עם חתולה כושית? לא נאה לי ולא יאה לי" (The neighbors do not please me. How can I, white, son of whites, since the world began, dwell in direct proximity to a Cushitic cat? It does not please me and it does not suit me.)

While the pig was the third visitor refusing to rent the flat because of his dislike for one of the existing neighbors, he is the only one whose words provoke a fierce reaction from the neighbors: "לך, לך-לך חזיר, גם לנו לא נאה ולא יאה" (Leave, off you go, you pig! It does not please us and it does not suit us just as much.) This story, continuously published since 1948 and regularly performed as a children's play, is taught in every nursery school in Israel and uses the term "Cushitic." Likewise, the nursery rhyme "כושי כלב קט" (Cushi kelev kat, Cushi, you little dog) remains a cultural asset, with numerous modern renditions available on YouTube, contrary to Melamed's assertion that this song is no longer sung (see Melamed, *The Image*, 24). In another area, contemporary baking books and blogs continue to provide recipes for עוגה כושית ("ooga cushit," "Cushite cake"), a type of chocolate cake. However, these terms are considered offensive and politically incorrect when used to address human beings, and might even be grounds for a lawsuit. Abraham Melamed's *The Image* and Jacqueline de Weeber's *Sheba's Daughters* offer insightful studies of the pejorative symbolism associated with the color black.

2. Melamed, *The Image,* 13.

3. Schirmann, "A Tale of an Old Hypocrite," 375–78.

4. Melamed, *The Image,* 168, 169, and 263, no. 80.

5. The exempla, popular on Christian soil between the thirteenth and fifteenth centuries, were composed and preached by European preachers and addressed to a lay-Christian public. In her anthology of sermons, Joan Young Gregg maintains that ". . . the preacher attempted to articulate a clear, simple, and achievable set of core beliefs and behaviors that would distinguish the Christian, with his hope for life eternal, from the condemned Other." Joan Young Gregg, *Devils, Women, and Jews, Reflections of the Other in Medieval Sermons Stories* (New York: State University of New York Press, 1997), here 16. Gregg asserts that this "condemned other" refers to the devil, women, and Jews, defined as "an unholy trinity, of dark and distorted reflections of the orthodox trinity of Christian doctrine." Cf. Gregg 4. Their Otherness is established in "regular" oppressed groupings manifesting anti-Semitism, racism, and misogyny, and the fact that they belong to these groups facilitates their degradation and demonization.

6. de Weeber, *Sheba's Daughters*, xviii.

7. Hilka, *Die Wundergeschichten des Caesarius von Heisterbach*, t. I, no. 42 (Bonn: Hanstein, 1933), 82.

8. de Borbone, *Tractatus de diversis materiis predicabilibus*, here Livre I, IV, l. 1762/1767, 132. Les Tentations De Saint Antoine.

9. The culmination of this topic may be found about two hundred years after *Achbor*, in the French romance *Baudouin de Flandre*. Baudouin, Earl of Flanders, was led to marry the devil in the form of a woman. The text does not explicitly say that she is black, but several clues hint at this. For example, in a flagrant distortion of the theme of the hunt of the white boar after which a fairy (always characterized as being white) appears, the earl "trouva ung sanglier qui c'estoit endormy qui estoit grant et fourny et estoit plus noir que meure" (found a boar that was sleeping and was big and fat and blacker than blackberry. p. 52), after which a woman appears, riding a black horse. She presents herself as an Eastern girl, which is also a clue regarding her complexion. In the end, we learn that she is the devil incarnate, who has penetrated the body of a Saracen woman. Nonetheless, they fall in love, get married, and live together for thirteen years, having two daughters. On the occasion of a feast, "vint devant luy ung viel hermite qui s'apuyoit d'un baston et avoit bien cent ans de aage et request au conte en nom de Dieu que ce jour il luy voulsist donner son repas a sa court pour disner" (an old hermit came before him, who was leaning on a stick and was easily one hundred years old and requested, in the name of the Lord, that on that day, he [the earl] would kindly offer him a meal to dine in his court). When the devil-wife enters, the hermit "eust moult grant paour et comença tresfort a trambler et se seigna moult souvent et ne pouit boyre ne menger" (felt a great fear and started to tremble fiercely, crossing himself many times, and could not drink or eat) and proceeds with an exorcism ceremony: "Diable qui es ou corps de celle femme morte, jadis qui ne te chassa hors de son saint paradis et tous les mauvais angez qui avoyent mespris par le pechié d'orgueil que Lucifer eut prins, et des sept sacremens que Dieu a establis et de son grant pouoir qui tousjours durera, que tu te partez de cest compaignie!" (devil, you who are inside the body of this dead woman, in the name of He who chased you out of the holy paradise together with all the vicious angels who disdained, by the sin of pride that Lucifer led, both the seven sacraments that God established and His great power which will last forever, [I order you] that you shall leave this body!). Pinto-Mathieu, *Baudouin de Flandres*. See commentary n.126 on Exorcism.

10. Much before the emergence of Islam, according to popular lore, the Saracens were referred to by this term as a means of identifying them as the sons of Abraham's legal wife, Sarah, and not of the servant, Hagar: "This is the tribe which took its origin and had its name from Ishmael, the son of Abraham; and the ancients called them Ishmaelites after their progenitor. As their mother Hagar was a slave, they afterward, to conceal the opprobrium of their origin, assumed the name of Saracens, as if they were descended from Sara, the wife of Abraham." *Sozomen*, fifth century, Book VI, Chapter 38, translated by Chester D. Hartranft. *From Nicene and Post-Nicene Fathers, Second Series, Volume 2*, edited by Philip Schaff and Henry Wace (Buffalo: Christian Literature Publishing Co., 1890), revised and edited for New Advent by Kevin Knight, http://www.newadvent.org/fathers/2602.htm. See also Isidore of Seville's Etymologies, Book IX, 2, 57. Although this is probably not the etymological origin of the word, in medieval times it was an accepted one. Perhaps there is an ideological similarity between the term "Saracen" (conceived symbolically as the daughter of Sarah) and the daughter of Moab / Ham. In the epic texts, whenever Saracen women collaborated or assisted the Christian knight, they were depicted

206   Chapter 5

according to the European standards of beauty, having fair skin and blond hair, and could eventually become Christian themselves and marry the Christian knight. Yet, whenever they remained loyal to the Muslim faith or paganism, they were depicted as ugly, diabolical, and black. de Weeber, *Sheba's Daughters*.

11. A thirteenth-century French collection of hagiographic tales based largely on the ancient *Vitae Patrum*.

12. Based on the geographical area and the theme of the threatening black Saracen, the encounter between the Christian and the agent of the devil permits us to imagine that she is black, even if it is not explicitly indicated.

13. Adrian P. Tudor, *Tales of Vice and Virtue. The First Old French Vie des pères* (Amsterdam and New York: Rodopi, 2005), 67.

14. In a fourteenth-century exemplum by the Dominican Giordano de Pisa, we read of a man who was unfaithful to his wife. His mistress was an Arab woman. The exemplum mentions that he could not see her ugliness, both moral and physical. "TC0004, Esempi," Thesaurus exemplorum medii aevi, http://thema.huma-num.fr/collections/TC0004 (accessed May 6, 2019).

15. "Since the girl in *Sarasine* is not shown to convert, it is possible that she is here the personification of the devil," Tudor, *Tales of Vice*, 66. About the assumption that the Saracen is black, see ibid., n. 25.

16. See commentary no. 110 on this description.

17. My translation, forthcoming.

18. Stephanus de Borbone *Tractatus de diversis,* 165.

19. The Saracen princess Escorfine is described in *Maugis d'Aigremont* as "assez plus noire que more de morier" (she was much blacker than a ripe blackberry). More metaphors of the black Saracen in the epic *chansons de geste* include "blacker than ink" and "blacker than pepper."

20. On the adjective "שְׁעָרִים" (vile), see commentaries 126 and 128, on the vile figs versus the good figs, commentary 127.

21. On the fig's sexual symbolism, see commentary no. 126.

22. See also its resonance with Jeremiah 24:8.

23. Katelynn Robinson, *The Sense of Smell in the Middle Ages: A Source of Certainty* (London: Routledge, 2020).

24. Víctor Rodríguez-Pereira, "*Sabora Olor*: The Role of Olfaction and Smells in Berceo's *Milagros de Nuestra Señora*," in *Beyond Sight: Engaging the Senses in Iberian Literatures and Cultures, 1200–1750,* edited by Ryan D. Giles and Steven Wagschal (Toronto: University of Toronto Press, 2018), 31–44, here 32.

25. Jacques Berlioz and Marie Anne Polo De Beaulieu, eds., *Collectio exemplorum cisterciensis in codice Parisiensi 15912 asseruata* (Turnhout: Brepols, 2012), 59, no. 212 and 398, no. 212. The source for this exemplum is Vitae Patrum, V, Verba seniorum, 5, 23 (J.-P. Migne, éd., *Patrologiae Cursus completus [. . .] Series latina* [Paris, 1844–1864], 73, 879A-C); Miracula [De quibusdam miraculis], Paris, Bibliothèque nationale de France, ms. lat. 3175, f. 144v.

26. Berlioz and Polo De Beaulieu, *Collectio exemplorum cisterciensis,* 214, no. 661 and 499, no. 661. The source for this exemplum is Ps. Turpin, Historia Karoli Magni et Rotholandi (éd. C. Meredith-Jones, 1936, Appendix, Ms. A. 6, 246).

"*A Remnant of the Flame*" 207

27. As a general rule, good and bad smells represent the positive and the negative respectively, as "Medieval attitudes toward sensory perceptions were anticipated . . . by writers of late antiquity who often made the connection between good smells and what is morally correct, and between foul smells and the opposite." Rodríguez-Pereira, "*Sabora Olor*," 32. See also Katelynn Robinson, who stated that "medieval theology recognized two main types of odors, the sweet odor of sanctity and the foul stench of sin." Robinson, *The Sense of Smell*. Nevertheless, perfume could have been associated with sexual seduction: "rhetorical tainting of sweet scents as perfumes of deceit, with the admonition that Satan was as likely to be found in sweet odors as in fouls," Susan Ashbrook Harvey, *Scenting Salvation: Ancient Christianity and the Olfactory Imagination* (Berkeley: University of California Press, 2006), 203.

28. Stench is mostly associated with promiscuity, as noted by Patrizia Bettella: "Patristic writings with their deeply misogynistic stance mention the stench of the woman, particularly the prostitute in connection with lust. The prostitute, transgressive by definition, is depicted as a temptress of men, and the bad smell is symbolic of sin." Patrizia Bettella, *The Ugly Woman: Transgressive Aesthetic Models in Italian Poetry from the Middle Ages to the Baroque* (Toronto: University of Toronto Press, 2005), 23.

29. The idea of holiness is bolstered by the use of the particular verb describing the act of sacrifice using incense. On this verb and the holiness of the incense, see Green, *The Aroma of Righteousness*, 66–83. On its use in the Song of Songs, see 92.

30. Green, *The Aroma of Righteousness*, 64.

31. Harvey, *Scenting Salvation*, 207.

32. Green, *The Aroma of Righteousness*, 94.

33. Two important precisions are to be noted here. First, in this survey I do not refer to other possible forms of these words constructed from the same root and conveying similar meanings, but solely to the times that they appear in the identical form, as in Lemuel's words. Second, each of the two words "bara" and "shoshana" (although without the preposition "as"), appears a third time, but in a context irrelevant to our discussion. "Bara" appears in a quite enigmatic verse in the Song of Songs "ברה היא ליולדתה" English translations and commentaries do not seem to agree on the meaning of this term. Saint James translates this combination of words as "she is the choice one of her that bore her," which may be the closest translation to our text, as the Shulamite is also described as "black" and it could be understood as "brightest of the black" (similar to "I am black but beautiful"). Other translations include "the brightest of the one who gave her birth" (NCV) and "She is the pure child of the one who bore her" (NAS). As for the third appearance of "lily" in the singular form, the word appears in II Chronicles to describe the artistic craft of the huge bronze basin in Solomon's temple "ושפתו כמעשה שפת-כוס, פרח שושנה" (and the brim thereof was wrought like the brim of a cup, like the flower of a lily).

34. The same word appears once as a spiritual image, referring to the people of Israel, and then as a sensual image, seemingly referring to a woman, or to the people of Israel according to the allegorical reading of this scroll. The rare use of this identical formula to conjure these images in the Bible allows the reader to assume

208   *Chapter 5*

that they can be intermingled in Lemuel's words and create a credible combination. Medieval exegetics also saw the rapprochement between these sources. In his commentary on Hosea, Radak related this image, that Israel will bloom like a lily, to the quote from the Song of Songs: ״יפרח כשושנה אמר כשושנה לפי שנמשלה כנסת ישראל לשושנה, כמו שאמר ׳אני חבצלת השרון שושנת העמקים׳, ואמר, ׳כשושנה בין החוחים כן רעיתי בין הבנות״ (shall bloom *as a lily*—he said *as a lily* since the congregation of Israel was compared to a lily, as it is said 'I am a rose of Sharon, a lily of the valleys. As a lily among thorns, so is my love among the daughters' [Song of Sg 2:1-2]).

35. "Rhetorical tainting of sweet scents as perfumes of deceit, with the admonition that Satan was as likely to be found in sweet odors as in fouls," Harvey, *Scenting Salvation*, 203.

36. Hosea 7:8, where the tribe of Ephraim is mocked for its foolishness at having forsaken the ways of the Lord; Proverbs 9:13, where the prostitute Folly is the personification of foreign culture; and Proverbs 7:11, where the foreign woman entices men to join her in committing adultery, which can be understood in two semantical manners, sexual adultery and religious adultery. The particularities of the specific vocabulary, along with the possible interpretations they offer regarding the perception of the black Mistress, are thoroughly examined in commentary 135.

37. Compare with the words of the priest in *Baudoin de Flandre*.

38. See, for example, Proverbs: "The words of a man's (good) mouth are like deep waters, the source of wisdom is like a flowing stream" (18:4), and "drink waters out of thine own cistern, and running waters out of thine own well" (Prov. 5:15). The sage (*Tanna*, second to third century) Simeon ben Menasya commented on this verse: "Drink the water of your cistern," drink the water of your creator and do not drink any troubled water that will draw you to the things of heretics." This comment was still popular in the Middle Ages.

39. See Rashi, ״הסוחרים והשרים, שירכבו מעתה על אתונות לבנות החשובות מבלי יראה ודאג אויב״ (the merchants and the aristocrats who shall henceforth ride the distinguished white asses without fear or worry of the enemy). Joseph Kara shares the following anecdote: ״ומצאתי דברי אגדה: רוכבי אתונות צחורות—בני אדם המושלים על דברי תורה המחוורין כצמר צר. אתונות הן משניות וברייתא״ I found in the sayings of a parable: the riders of white she-asses—men who master the words of the Torah clear as pure wool. The she-asses are Mishnayot (Mishnah's chapters) and Baraitas (external Mishnahs))

40. A thorough examination of this phrase "dug in the darkness" appears in commentary 133.

41. See commentary 141.

Chapter 6

Transforming Maidens

Four Women, Three Episodes

As passionate as Achbor's sermon at the city plaza was, Lemuel is not fully convinced. He follows Achbor to his abode, where the signs of his corruption are revealed one by one. The splendid palace, the luxurious cutlery, the abundant food, the rich garments, the clear evidence of Achbor's robust health—now Lemuel knows for a fact that Achbor is an impostor. He composes a poem about wretched bearded men who have become wealthy by abusing the poor, which serves as the conclusion of the first part of the tale. Achbor's decadence, we will soon learn, has not yet achieved its apex, which is the subject of the second part. The apogee of Achbor's immoral self-indulgence is represented in a banquet where wine flows and food is abundant, and so are the women. The lasciviousness is embodied by the entrance of the feminine element: first, a group of four fair-skinned maidens, the subject of this chapter, and then a black woman, the subject of chapter 7, with all of whom Achbor has dubious interactions.

The four maidens enter the tale and remain integral to it until its conclusion, participating in three consecutive episodes. Their significant presence surely positions them as protagonists. Still, upon closer inspection, it is plausible to argue that they lack the personal agency and subjective depth typically associated with protagonists. Instead, they function as vessels for the transmission of ideologies. Initially symbolizing Achbor's decadence, they later transition into his accusers and then his executioners, before ultimately embodying courtly maidens in an orchard scene. Through these transformations, the maidens serve as a reflection of the author's evolving worldview, offering commentary on morality and social norms. Despite their consequential place, these women have not garnered much attention in scholarly discourse.

210 *Chapter 6*

In this chapter, I propose to explore their ongoing role in the three episodes in which they participate, positing that they serve as a poetic device, each time presenting a different facet of the author's message.

In terms of narratology, *The Tale of Old Bearded Achbor* presents some challenges due to its hybrid nature. It conveys an ambivalence regarding Lemuel's investment in this tale, as he adopts a mixed mode of narration. He begins with a lengthy, intimate prologue revealing his personal wanderings in the world, focusing on one particular adventure. While he initially takes on the role of a spectator when describing Achbor's sermon, he consistently emphasizes his subjective involvement in the unfolding events. He acknowledges the emotions stirred within him by Achbor, from the performance in the city plaza to the indulgent feast with the four maidens, and ultimately to the discovery of Achbor's affair with the black woman. These emotions drive him to action; he composes poems, follows Achbor, peers into his house, and engages in physical and philosophical disputes with him. At a certain point, precisely when Lemuel fails to dissuade Achbor from pursuing his love for black women, there is an elemental shift in the narration. Lemuel cries out in despair, which brings the four maidens back to the palace but also marks the end of his role as an active participant. From that moment on, Lemuel is no longer involved in what now has transformed from a firsthand account into the plot of a tale uttered from afar. The tale now evolves into the story of four maidens, who torment Achbor with words and deeds, ultimately leading to his demise. Put differently, determining who truly confronts Achbor—Lemuel in an autobiographical account or the four maidens in the realm of fiction—can be somewhat ambiguous. At first glance, it might appear as if they both do, separately and independently: Lemuel as an indecisive narrator who fluctuates in and out of his own story, and the maidens as central figures deeply intertwined in Achbor's fate. Nonetheless, I argue that while this certainly holds true superficially, the pivotal transition from Lemuel to the maidens suggests an ideological link between them.

Before delving into this argument, it is important to briefly discuss the significance of the number four in relation to the inseparable women. This abundance of women can be interpreted in two alternative ways. First, we can accept the number literally. Four beautiful women serving one wealthy man could be seen as reflecting a male fantasy of an exotic realm where men are indulged by multiple beautiful women. This is a satisfying explanation in a tale that is probably inspired by Arabic sources, where spicy stories about harems are prevalent. Furthermore, the four maidens appear as part of Achbor's feast, where they incarnate an element of corruption. They are a component in a series of dissolute manifestations, an exemplification of excessive wealth, existing within the backdrop of extravagant architecture, sumptuous clothing, and an abundance of food and wine.

Alternatively, the presence of multiple women can be viewed symbolically, as if the four maidens form a singular unit. From the moment they enter Achbor's hall, they function as a generalized group, executing an automatic series of completely identical tasks. It is almost as if there are four reflections of a single figure. They serve him together, attack him together, and kill him together. Finally, the four maidens reappear together in yet another role, this time as delicate courtly maidens.

Whether we consider the maidens literally, as four distinct individuals, or symbolically as a unified entity, their essence evolves from one episode to the next. They function, to a certain extent, as a deus ex machina, not possessing their own continuous story, but rather serving as auxiliary figures who guide the tale according to its thematic issues—the exposure of the corrupt impostor, his subsequent punishment, and the exploration of the true nature of love.

EPISODE 1: BACCHAE

In this episode, the four maidens take center stage as each of them crafts a poetic strophe which collectively forms an erotic wine poem about lovers who are on the verge of making love.[1] This theme reaches its climax when Achbor, in his turn, adds a fifth bawdy strophe, which ends when:

> He then rose up towards them and he regaled them, he seemed to be bouncing from lap to lap. They all rose to play, and in his heart's gladness he was dancing because he was burning like fire. And so it was until he became fatigued, and he laid down and closed his eyes, and covered his face, and fell into a deep sleep. The maidens exited towards the patio, and [he remained as if] he did not see, keeping silent and feigning [sleep].

The playful bacchanalia thus ends up with the preacher seemingly sound asleep, causing the maidens to leave before any sexual act explicitly takes place.[2] While Abraham Melamed interpreted the four maidens as Achbor's deserted mistresses, the entire tale, as I repeatedly argued in the commentary, deals with Achbor's lack of desire for fair-skinned women, and even his impotence in their presence.[3] The fake nap and the subsequent swift arousal with the black Mistress who will shortly make her appearance are just additional symbolic manifestations of their rejection. Furthermore, the final poem closing the culminating episode of the orchard, declaimed by one of the maidens, may suggest that they are virgins. This poem, as opposed to their song during the feast, does not invite listeners to indulge in free lovemaking, but rather encourages them to remain chaste until a chosen one is found and declared a wife.

212   *Chapter 6*

In essence, the banquet episode remains shrouded in ambiguity, leaving many unanswered questions about the four maiden-servant-musicians. Were they indeed, as Rosen suggested, "well-educated Andalusian court entertainers"?[4] Were they Achbor's mistresses? Were they regular staff members of the house, or was it their first visit? Were they brought there on Achbor's orders? Was their sole task to pleasure him? Was Achbor supposed to choose one, or was the gathering meant to be an orgy? In sum, do they, in this particular scene, have a story?[5]

These questions remain a mystery. What is evident is that the four women, regardless of whether or not they had had previous sexual interactions with Achbor, incarnate just another facet of Achbor's hedonism and materialism, starkly contrasting with the principles he preached during the public sermon and emphasizing his moral laxity.

EPISODE 2: AMAZONS

When the maidens re-enter the tale, right after Achbor's true nature is revealed by Lemuel, they present an entirely different standard, as now they echo social conventions about immorality, expressing social norms regarding sexual transgressions and social intolerance toward the transgressor. This is apparent in their respective discourses. In the previous episode, the leading tone and the central themes of the wine song strophes celebrate erotic love, blurring the boundaries between drinking and lovemaking. The erotic elements, nevertheless, do not render the poem personal or subjective in any way. It remains a piece modeled according to the poetic rhetoric and conventions of sensual love poetry, exempt from any pathos.

Upon discovering Achbor's proclivities, however, they become passionate, joining together to participate in a defamatory epideictic discourse. Here too, the maidens turn to their poetic talent: after each one hurls her colorful allegations at Achbor, focusing on his beard as an external symbol of his immorality, she doubles them with a new miniature poem. Like the wine poem, we can perceive the miniature poems as four strophes comprising a poem about Achbor's beard. Needless to say, here Achbor does not get the opportunity to add a fifth strophe of his own. He has already been castrated.

No longer submissive women who merely execute orders and silently exit the room, the maidens are now aggressors, and their sardonic discourses are followed by a violent execution.[6] Since they use the first pronoun when they speak, we get the impression that they are personally involved.[7] Each maiden reveals something of her own experience with Achbor in what seems to be more of an emotional reaction to the situation. I posit that this is mostly a rhetorical means and does not serve to reflect a distinct personality. It is only rhetorically that the maidens pass from objectified, emotionless characters (servants who serve food, sing, and dance with the protagonist and possibly also serve him physically) to "subjectified" characters who speak, seemingly express feelings, and act. This more engaged attitude dramatizes the scene, yet the maidens remain non-personalized and non-individualized. The first level of reading suggests that the maidens may be functioning here by mimesis, as a representation of rejected women whose femininity and honor have been bruised. I specifically use the word "mimesis" because I do not believe that there is a thematic continuity from the previous scene regarding the maidens. I contend that while the maidens participated in the feast, they were not presented as self-conscious mistresses but rather were "doing their duty." In this manner, Yaakov ben Elazar created a superficial link to the previous scene. On this superficial level, we can indeed accept that, for a moment, the maidens symbolically assume the role of betrayed women whose encounter with the black mistress, with the "Other" (woman), pierced their mechanized behavior and permitted the expression of emotions. It might appear that they are acting jealously according to the expected, schematic, stereotypical, and even somewhat comical conventions of the farce.[8] The specific sexual insults that are hurled at Achbor, as we will see in the commentary, address his lecherous behavior. From this perspective, it is indeed possible to look at the maidens as also being in a symbolic quest for self-liberation and identity definition. If initially, they were submissive women, some may say servants, they now rebel against their oppressor, eliminate him, and then, in the orchard, search for their proper fulfillment. Through this lens, they evoke, in an abstract sense, comparisons to Aristophanes' comedy *Lysistrata*, mostly for the ritualistic essence they embody.[9] Anton Bierl discusses the possible echoing in *Lysistrata* of "premarital rites of initiation for young girls," which prepare them for marriage.[10] Such rituals consisted of the preliminary seclusion of maidens in a place (the Acropolis, for example) where "by playing, dancing, washing, and woolworking, they receive a sort of symbolic education in sexuality."[11] The rite of Arrhephoria, which began in the autumn, culminated in the summer during a "festival at which the young people present themselves for marriage."[12] Without delving into whether Yaakov ben Elazar was familiar with the precise rite that Bierl is referring to, when we read *Achbor* with that example in mind, the common structure of women performing erotic rituals (the wine feast), involved in violence against a man (Achbor's beating and death), and then ready to marry (the meadow episode that concludes the tale of *Achbor*, during which the maidens are asked for their hand in marriage) may echo the mythological spirit of *Lysistrata* and should not be overlooked as a possible distant foundation.

More profoundly, I argue that the maidens embody here the prevalent social norms and the conventional reluctance to condone moral transgression.

214   *Chapter 6*

In fact, they amplify Lemuel's role. When Lemuel initially discovers Achbor's liaison with the Mistress, he erupts into the tale with a raging assault. He beats the lovers as if they were adulterous partners caught in *flagrante delicto*, and he is the cuckolded husband. Beneath the surface of this extremely dramatic staging, marked by an unprecedented blur of boundaries between the narrator and the protagonists, a sassy scene of voyeurism, and nudity, lies not a tale of sexual infidelity, but rather one of social rejection.[13]

The Mistress is an amalgamation of all of Achbor's wrongdoings, and Lemuel becomes somewhat of a preacher or moralist himself, merging and confusing the registers of the Hebrew meaning of the word he uses, קנאתי, between the "jealousy" of a husband for his wife, and the anger of the just toward moral and religious transgressions.[14]

Contrary to expectations, Lemuel refrains from taking further steps; his cry of despair reaches the maidens, prompting their return. They take matters into their own hands (and more, as we recall that they hurl insults at Achbor and later kill him), while Lemuel reverts to his role as a narrator and remains untainted by direct involvement in Achbor's death. This surprising move is a sophisticated narratological maneuver. I cannot help but notice a broad resemblance to the biblical figure of Yoav, who, upon seeing Absalom hanging from a tree by his hair, only wounded him with his darts, demanding that his men deliver the fatal blow that would end his life.[15] In this way, Yoav was not the killer of the king's son, although he desired his death.[16] Should we apply this analogy and suggest that Lemuel, as the narrator of all the tales in the book, desires Achbor's elimination, but refrains from being an actual murderer? If we do, it becomes easy to view the maidens' killing of Achbor as an extension of Lemuel's will.

Like Lemuel, the maidens perceive Achbor as a transgressor who threatens something fundamental, which they express through the more straightforward symbol of adultery. Lemuel refers to Achbor and the Mistress as "adulterers," while the maidens are said to "give him the judgment of the adulteress." These two cases, I believe, do not refer to a personal sexual betrayal, but a deeper concept. Achbor is more than a cheating husband or lover; he is the embodiment of transgression and immorality. The maidens here express and enact what Lemuel would have done. They even adopt a masculine demeanor, in stark contrast to their very feminine appearance in the first episode and later again in the third episode. In the carnivalesque setting of the present scene, where the world is topsy-turvy, the maidens play the role of symbolical "cuckold husbands" (as Lemuel did a minute ago), rather than "jealous rejected mistresses." The genders are entirely blurred when such "husbands" become judges (who are always male in medieval patriarchal societies), and when Achbor is feminized by having his beard removed and then being judged as an adulteress. The maiden's final words, "Such a despicable man

Transforming Maidens 215

shall not be amongst us, for the shame would be on us!"[17] clarify that, more than actual figures bruised by a disloyal lover or husband, the maidens are expressing a social norm of moral disgust and contempt.

Again, the story of the maidens presents a two-dimensional aspect, inviting an alternative interpretation grounded in the literal. If we confine our analysis to this realm, the motivation for the maidens to kill Achbor appears circumstantial. It is based upon the assumption that their actions were a crime of passion. Under this reading, the juncture where Lemuel yields his place to the four maidens can be perceived as a form of *denouement*, an event that propels the tale toward its resolution. Lemuel's cry conveniently summons the women who were already involved in the feast, establishing the circumstantial link that leads to their discovery of the black Mistress and, subsequently, Achbor's execution. While this interpretation aligns with the literal text, it prompts further investigation.

In their invectives, the four maidens proclaim that they were drawn to Achbor for his spirituality. At the palace, however, there are no traces of anything spiritual. Melamed even compared the feast with the maidens to an orgy. The dichotomy between the women's allegations and their behavior with Achbor raises some doubts. How could they not know that what they were doing with Achbor was wrong? Were they forced? Are they lying in the discourse? If we accept the "deux ex machina" theory, we can understand that although they appear to be the same maidens, they assume a different role with each entrance.

EPISODE 3: FAIRIES

In an extreme contrast to the previous part of the tale, Yaakov ben Elazar takes us from the macabre scene of Achbor's execution to an enchanting atmosphere of a fairy-like *locus amoenus* ("pleasant place"). The literary theme consists of a delightful outdoor scene, in which "minimum ingredients comprise a tree (or several trees), a meadow, and a spring or a brook. Birdsong and flowers may be added."[18]

This *locus* provides the perfect setting for courtly love adventures, which take place amidst abundant trees and flourishing gardens. Such landscapes are ambiguous, as they can function alternatively as a refuge and as a perilous place for a woman. They may provide an exquisite outdoor backdrop where women can either find spiritual comfort or hope for true love, hidden from the oppressing patriarchal restrictions. Yet, these landscapes may also represent an unsupervised wilderness, where any woman might find herself a potential victim of rape and violence. Surely there are endless episodes of courtly ladies who, just like the maidens here, are depicted as enjoying themselves

216 *Chapter 6*

by picking flowers, among other delicate activities of courtly damsels, and meeting their beloveds. But there are many other cases where women might be subjected to the misogynistic perception of their natural weakness and therefore find themselves assaulted. A recurring pattern in medieval French romances is the episode of the bathing maiden or fairy who is watched by an erring knight, hiding and waiting to seize the opportunity when she is most vulnerable so that he may attempt to rape her.[19] I believe that this is precisely the tension that Yaakov ben Elazar intended to transmit in this brief final episode. His description of the backdrop for this scene opens with a pastoral image of what seems to be innocent, refined maidens passing the time while dabbling in their favorite pastimes, singing, playing music, and, most importantly, bathing. Such diversions attract suitors, hiding and watching them covertly. Alas, it is unclear how the young men will behave: Will the lads behave as *fin'amants* or as beasts?, that is, will they be fine lovers, in control of their urges, complying with the courtly rules of love that encourage self-restriction, endurance, and their acceptance that they will have to suffer a certain amount of longing? Or will they act as bestial, untamed monsters, who abuse vulnerable maidens and defenseless fawns and does? This is the subject of the ultimate poem ending this tale, which offers insights about erotic love that differ greatly from the first love / wine poem recited at Achbor's feast.

The shift from the elaborate architecture of the palace into the open landscape for the tale's final chapter reflects the transition from the practical aspect of the tale, that is, the main scenario, to its philosophical outcome. The idealized setting, drawing elements from both the courtly *locus amoenus* and the sublime love poetry found in the Song of Songs, serves as the perfect backdrop for a contemplation on the subject of love.[20] Surprisingly, despite the enticing allure of the garden and the longstanding tradition of depicting amorous encounters in pastoral orchards, the author's perspective on love ultimately reverts to the traditional.

Here, too, the maidens convey the author's message in the quintessential poem sung by one of them.[21] Thus, they suppress the spontaneous impulse that might allow them, or even encourage them theoretically, to indulge in recreative physical love in favor of love governed by social and religious expectations.[22] In their final poem, the erotic instinctive desires expressed in their previous wine poem are replaced with a lesson on self-restraint, a didactic lesson for young boys. The previous invitation extended to the suitor, embodied here by Achbor, to "come drink" is supplanted by an order to restrain the instinct and desire of the suitor(s), now embodied by the four lads: "get up and hurry, accelerate / the reins of wandering you should amputate!" In order to reset the order and return to social conventions, the maidens appear accordingly. No more the sensual Bacchae of the first episode, nor the murderous Amazons of the second, now they appear under a new light, recalling the delicate and vulnerable fairies of courtly tales. I use these three mythological figures symbolically, as the maidens are reminiscent of all of them, but are really none of them. The feast's bacchanalia is a fiasco, as they are dismissed by a sleepy lover, and they are not real Amazons either, as they are not trained warriors but rather act in the heat of the moment. As for their comparison to fairies, this connotation is based on medieval French courtly fairy tales, where supernatural female creatures are watched naked (and vulnerable, as their power lies in their clothes) while bathing by knights, who then attempt and sometimes manage to violate them.[23]

The figures of the four maidens undergo a double metamorphosis during the tale, blurring gender expectations. From submissive maidens, they evolve to take upon themselves a dominant role, along with its virile characteristics. Not only do they speak up to severely reprimand Achbor, but they also use physical power as they beat him to death. Concurrently, Achbor undergoes a transformation, gradually becoming more effeminate, as he is judged as an adulteress, and his most recognized virile feature, his beard, is violently torn from his face in an act of symbolic emasculation. The maidens then return to play the role of pastoral young women, strolling and frolicking in an enchanted orchard.

Nevertheless, almost all the maidens' actions and words seem to be schematic and automatic. This is clearly true for their first appearance at the feast, and their last one in the orchard. On these two occasions, there is no personal, subjective, or emotional engagement with the plot, merely trite actions and flat poetical verses. A certain measure of involvement emerges in the confrontation scene as the maidens' discourses adopt a somewhat more intimate tone, each describing how she was hurt by Achbor. Finally, however, they ultimately return to the same allegation and conclusion, portrayed repeatedly as an exercise in rhetoric. Thus, I find it much more compelling to view the group of the four maidens as a poetical device, a prop within the tale that serves the narrator, who shapes it according to the fluctuations of his message.

NOTES

1. These four strophes gradually expose the effects of wine as paralleling the evolution of love, and the act of love is blurred with the act of drinking wine throughout the poem. A thorough analysis awaits these strophes in chapter 7, where they are studied in detail.

2. About the comical aspect of feigning sleep, see commentary 107.

3. Abraham Melamed refers to the maidens as nymphs and argues that they "participated willingly" in Achbor's adultery, which they "enjoyed thoroughly." Melamed, *The Image of the Black*, 165. I, however, do not find any support for that in the text.

218   *Chapter 6*

4. Rosen, "The Beard as Spectacle," 13.

5. The oriental topos of the khalif or emir selecting one beautiful woman out of the many that are paraded before him is familiar to medieval European literature through romances with Eastern antecedents such as Robert d'Orbigny's *Le conte de Floire et Blanchefleur*, edited by Jean-Luc Leclanche (Paris: Champion, 2003). An interesting variation appears in Tale Seven of *Sefer ha-Meshalim*, with the exotic "market of maidens," where Yoshpe chooses Yefifya, much to Yemima's disappointment. The likelihood that the maidens' procession ("walking light as the moon") and, more generally, their performance at the feast, was intended as a pageant for Achbor to select one is also hinted at, ironically, by the black Mistress.

6. On the literary theme of women manslayers, see Bibring, "Violent Women and the Blurring of Gender in some Medieval Narratives," 127–45.

7. Their first round of poems lacks any emotional or intimate commitment. They talk about lovers' deeds only in general terms and in the third person, except for the rhetorical (not personal) use of "I" in the riddle asked by the second maiden in her strophe.

8. Female jealousy is a topos in comic literature, contrasting with courtly literature, where a betrayed woman would usually express fierce heroic emotions and prefer suicide over an extroverted reaction (see, e.g., Dido or the Lady in *La chastelaine de Vergi*). Usually, jealousy arises from the shattered perception of the relationship's exclusivity. In our case, the four maidens accept their "sharing" of Achbor as a given, perhaps because the setting of the oriental city permits the image of harmonious bigamy, where all the wives live peacefully together. Another possibility, as I argued above, is that the four maidens should actually be seen as symbolic reflections of a single figure. Either way, the Mistress could be perceived as a detested concubine / mistress, that is, as another woman, with her skin color being secondary to her feminine essence. The point is that since the maidens overlap with Lemuel, they reflect his standards and are therefore averse to the Mistress because of what she represents, that is, Achbor's immorality. From this perspective, it is not a matter of her being another woman, but rather an "Other" woman. Her color is significant as an embodiment of all of Achbor's transgressions, including his liaison and his corruption, as repeatedly discussed in the commentary of this book. Melamed's perspective differs, as he argues that the four maidens join forces since "the white skin identity takes precedence over the feminine one," meaning they unite against the black woman's stereotyped sexual vigor, which they cannot compete with. Furthermore, since women are men's others, Melamed claims that in this tale, the black woman becomes "the other's other." He asserts that "they prefer to cooperate with white men like the author, against the black woman, rather than with her against the male group": Melamed, *The Image,* 167. Indeed, it is crucial to note that the maidens do not attack the black woman per se, as she has already vanished from the tale and the discussion. In their attack on the man who betrayed them, they do not refer to her as a distinct figure, but rather as a concept, that is, betrayed social morals. Again, as I see it, if they "cooperate" with Lemuel and, by extension, with Yaakov, it is merely because they

are their poetic representations (representing different concepts in different episodes) rather than independent figures.

9. *Lysistrata* tells of the Greek wives, led by Lysistrata, who go on a sex strike to restore peace in Greece. Although they do not exercise any physical violence, withholding sexual relations is also a form of violence, as it threatens the men's lives by preventing them from having legitimate heirs. I have juxtaposed *Lysistrata* and *Achbor* previously, in the context of a group of women exercising violence toward a man. Bibring, "Violent Women," 127–45.

10. Anton Bierl, "Women on the Acropolis and Mental Mapping: Comic Body-Politics in a City in Crisis, or Ritual and Metaphor in Aristophanes' *Lysistrata*," in *Crisis on Stage: Tragedy and Comedy in Late Fifth-Century Athens,* edited by Andreas Markantonatos and Bernhard Zimmermann (Berlin and Boston: De Gruyter, 2011), 255–90, here 269.

11. Bierl, "Women on the Acropolis," 269.

12. Bierl, "Women on the Acropolis," 269.

13. On the unusual interference of the narrator in the drama, see Decter, *Iberian Jewish Literature*, 172.

14. See commentary 112.

15. 2 Samuel 18:9-15.

16. David specifically asks Yoav to spare Absalom's life in the battle.

17. See Decter's comment about Lemuel's moral message in this tale: "touching upon leadership, sexual propriety, wine drinking, and the needs of the poor," all of which Achbor transgresses. Decter, *Iberian Jewish Literature,* 173.

18. Ernst Robert Curtius, *European Literature and the Latin Middle Ages,* translated by Willard R. Trask, Bollingen Series (Princeton: Princeton University Press, 1973 [1948]), 195.

19. This was also the case with Suzanna in the book of Daniel.

20. The multiple references to the Song of Songs in this excerpt only augment the erotic atmosphere and are commented upon in chapter 4.

21. Decter saw in the two different treatments of love (the feast scene and the orchard scene) a shift from the Arabic and Andalusian Hebrew values of love to the Courtly values. See Decter, *Iberian Jewish Literature,* 169–70.

22. Non-marital sex is a topic to which Yaakov ben Elazar returns several times in *Sefer ha-Meshalim,* usually condemning it. In Tale 6 *Maskil and Penina,* as the lovers are on the verge of becoming intimate, they are confronted by the black giant, representing repressed forbidden sexuality. After they manage to eradicate this urge, they can consume their love, but only after they get married. A similar occurrence is described in Tale 9 *Sahar and Kima.* The lovers live together, unwed, in Kima's marvelous castle, but they remain chaste until Kima's father gives his blessing to their union. The triumph of conjugal love is also manifested in Greek novels such as Longus' *Dafnis and Chloe* where, despite their freedom to indulge in free love, the protagonists end up consummating their love only after they have been legally wed. In the Middle Ages, Chrétien de Troyes endeavored to reconcile what the theorists of "fin'amor" perceived as conflicting notions of love and marriage. This is found in

220   *Chapter 6*

Chrétien's *Cligès,* for example, or *Erec et Enide,* in which the true lovers' goal is to be married. For the notion of medieval conjugal love, see Moshe Lazar, *Amour courtois et fin'amors dans la littérature du XIIe siècle* (Paris: Klincksieck, 1964).

23. It is possible that Yaakov borrowed the superficial feature of such tales (e.g., *Guingamor*) showing women as a vulnerable game for men, while simultaneously teaching that men should not abuse their power in such circumstances.

Chapter 7

"She Was a Fawn, She Is a Gazelle Now"

An Erotic Wine Song in Five Strophes

חַכְלִילִי עֵינַיִם, מִיָּיִן; וּלְבֶן-שִׁנַּיִם, מֵחָלָב. בראשית מט, יא-יב

His eyes shall be red with wine, and his teeth white with milk.
(Gen. 49:11-12)

Yaakov ben Elazar often resides in the shadow of more celebrated poets, leaving many of the poetic compositions in *Sefer ha-Meshalim* without the scholarly attention they merit. In *The Tale of Old Bearded Achbor*, one particular poem stands out. Having drunk wine and eaten delicacies, Achbor orders the four maidens to sing. Each plays an instrument and composes a short "miniature" poem.[1] I suggest these be read as gradually evolving strophes of one single piece, in the style of an erotic wine poem, a type of poetry that is deeply grounded in Arabic and Hebrew literary tradition.[2] The four strophes are followed by Achbor's reply, which may be considered the fifth and culminating strophe of the same poem. This poem captured my attention for its nuanced links to the themes explored in the tale. I therefore treated it somewhat differently than the other sections. Contrary to the typical structure of this book, the poem does not appear in the commentaries of chapter 1, but instead is examined here. To provide a comprehensive analysis and avoid redundancy, I follow the poem strophe by strophe to reveal the progression of themes and their interplay with biblical phrasing.

While the poem's strophes grow more erotic as we move from one maiden to the next, the central leitmotif remains the provocative blurred line between wine and physical love. This, like most of the themes and motifs cultivated in the maidens' poems, is a well-established feature of wine poetry. Yaakov ben Elazar was familiar with both Arabic and Hebrew poems, and it would thus be futile to enumerate all the borrowed elements, as they constitute practically the entire poem.[3] Nonetheless, as Levin noted, "A thousand faces has

222   *Chapter 7*

the wine poem," since such pieces are orchestrated by "An unlimited number of combinations."[4] The poem we have before us demonstrates the eminent scholar's observation: "Even when you are familiar with the elements of a particular poem, established by virtue of the 'rules' of its genre, it may often surprise you with an unexpected innovation, modifying the impression of its entire setting."[5]

FIRST STROPHE: GRADUS AMORIS

Wine's spark[6], like lightning, like a flame (Nah. 3:3) / shall ignite its drinkers' heart the same (Job 41:11).
　　Bitter yet sweeter than honey (Judg. 18: 14;18) that's true, / Its scent vivifies, like myrrh's his virtue[7] (Hosea 14:6).
　　Shall it find sorrow in any man's heart / it releases the regiment of joy to tear it apart.
　　It makes the miser's heart become like the heart of the grand / since (or cause) under its sway, the tight-fisted shall open his hand.

יין כעין ברק כעין להב / ידליק לבב שותיו בכידודו,
ימר, ואכן מדבש ימתק, / ריחו יחיה כי כמור הודו.
אם ימצאה יגון בלב כל איש, / ישלח גדוד משוש להשמידו,
ישית לבב כיליי כלב נדיב, / כי בו קפוץ-יד יפתחה ידו.

The erotic atmosphere is intensified by the presentation of wine as a substance that tantalizes the senses.[8] Just like wine, love also provokes the senses, and therefore we can attach a *sensual* meaning to any *sensitive* effect presented as resulting from drinking. While relying merely on the Arabic-Hebrew stock of figurative representations would have been sufficient to decipher the text, in this strophe I am specifically inclined to present additional analogies from the troubadouresque imagery. The conjunction of the senses' faculties with the erotic is reminiscent of the topos of the *gradus amoris*, metaphorically describing the steps, degrees, or successive stages of the love process from the first encounter until the ultimate act of love.[9] The five stages are *visus* (sight), *alloquium* (speech), *tactus* (touch, i.e., caress), *osculum* (kiss), and *factum* (the "act"). There is, of course, a "concordance between each gradus and a specific organ of sense perception."[10]

Wine's Spark: Sight

The imagery of the sources of illumination is closely connected to the sense of sight and suggests that the initial effect of wine is visual. The drinker's heart is aroused by the sight of the substance, depicted using terminology typically associated with beauty, even before it is tasted. By analogy, the

"She was a Fawn, she is a Gazelle Now" 223

first step of falling in love in the courtly tradition is the vision of the beautiful shining maiden (or the young lad). Thus, from the opening verse there is a fusion between wine, or the visual stimulation caused by its flaring, and a woman. Throughout the poem's analysis, this metaphorical blurring between wine and a maiden will be evident. Both sights ignite the heart, figuratively signifying extravagant sensual titillation.

Strictly related to wine, the interpretation likely leans toward drunkenness and the sensation of happiness and liberation that wine brings. Love, like wine, can be intoxicating and ignite the heart. In this case, "setting the heart on fire" conveys the emergence of desire, frequently depicted as an erupting fire whose flames burn in the lovers' hearts. David Kimhi (twelfth–thirteenth century) also employs this metaphor in his exegesis on Proverb 5:3, a source whose relevance will be explored in the fourth strophe. Kimhi relates this to a seductress who uses kisses היא עושה אותם להבעיר" "אש התשוקה בלב האנשים הנוטים אחריה (in order to light the fire of passion in the heart of the men that are drawn towards her).[11]

Bitter yet Sweeter: Taste and Smell

Evoking taste by contrasting bitterness and sweetness, this is the first of a series of three consecutive radical contradictions settled by wine, which also causes the sad to become happy and the miserly to become generous. These radical changes that wine, or more precisely inebriation, brings about, are also related to love. The pragmatic flavor of a bitter wine turns into the symbolic flavor of honey, which is used here conventionally as a metaphor for the sweetest item known to mankind.[12] The idea is doubled in the apodosis by calling forth the sense of smell, as the word indicating myrrh (מֹר) (mor) probably emanates from the bitterness (מַר) (mar) of its resin. The oil or powder made from it, however, emits a delicious scent, which, by the same symbolism as the taste of honey, is related to erotic love.[13]

In our context, the references to honey and myrrh work in two directions. If wine is just wine, it denotes its pragmatic sensorial effects on the drinker, describing its taste and aroma. If wine is love, honey and myrrh denote its metaphorical sensual effects as awakening sexual desire. The word "הוד" (hod, meaning splendor, beauty, vigor, but also sexual potency), describing the wine's power, further supports this reading, as we will soon see in the fourth strophe.[14]

The protasis "bitter yet sweeter than honey" recalls two biblical episodes of debauched feasts. The first is the sober prophecy "בשיר לא ישתו יין ימר שכר לשותיו" (They drink not wine with a song; strong drink is bitter to them that drink it, Isa. 24:9). This verse predicts that divine wrath shall destruct the land, bringing about the cessation of all joy when there will be no wine feasts and the

224   *Chapter 7*

taste of wine will become bitter. The second episode is from Judges 14:14-18, in which Samson provokes the Philistines with a challenge during his marriage feast. Since the Philistines were averse to his marriage with their kinswoman Delilah and disregarded the celebratory conventions, Samson declared that if they answer his riddle, "מהאכל יצא מאכל ומעז יצא מתוק" (Out of the eater came forth food, and out of the strong came forth sweetness, Judg. 14:14) he would provide them with thirty items of opulent outfits. If they could not solve the riddle, they would be indebted to him. The riddle refers to the corpse of a lion cub (the strong) that Samson had killed, in which bees had set up a hive and produced honey (the sweet). The Philistines used threats to get the answer from Delilah and replied: "מה מתוק מדבש ומה עז מארי" (What is sweeter than honey? and what is stronger than a lion? Judg. 14:18). The solution's reference to sexual desire was noticed by biblical research-ers, who posited that only love can simultaneously be described as מתוק (sweet) and עז (bitter),[15] thus interpreting the situation in the context of "a crowd of bachelors (בחורים) to a young bridegroom on the way to the nuptial chamber.[16] The thirteenth-century Spanish poet, Tadros Abu-l'afiah, incorporated a similar ribald interpretation in one of his sensual poems:

"מה מדבש מתוק ומה עז מארי? מחלה בעיניך ובשפתייך צרי" (What is sweeter than honey, stronger than a lion? Malady is within your eyes, the cure in lips).[17]

Both the riddle (the contrast between the robust and the sweet) and its solution (wine / love is sweeter than honey) are echoed in the strophe's erotic verse, which in itself is an introduction to a new riddle that the second maiden will soon ask.[18] At this stage, we are viewing a jubilant feast, but as the background echoes these two biblical episodes, this may be a hint at Achbor's forthcoming fall.

The biblical allusions to feasts getting out of control, along with Achbor's own words in the city plaza, are not only reminiscent of Samson's wedding scene but also expose Achbor's hypocrisy. Achbor himself was just criticiz-ing intemperance when he recounted the fable of the drunk miserly merchant who lost all his wealth. The latter's fall reflects two facets, which complete each other. On the one hand, there is an emphasis on the pragmatic aspect of the merchant whose hand is shaking and who is no longer the master of his two "wills" (his desire but also his heritage). Because of his drunkenness, he lost his sang-froid and wrote the mistaken sum on the banknote. On the other hand, this error is presented as the deed of God, avenging the desecration of His name. Not merely did the merchant lie about his financial situation and attempt to avoid giving alms to the poor man, which is in itself a condem-nable action, but he did this while committing perjury, falsely swearing on God's name. Therefore, God, and not merely wine, has caused his downfall. The miser who has transformed into a generous man exemplifies the positive outcome of wine within the framework of the strophe. This reverberates with the negative repercussions of wine described in the context of the tale, as it reanimates the fable about the miser who involuntarily, and just because he was drunk, also turned into a "generous man," a false generosity responsible for his undoing.

The troubling analogy between God's power and the power of wine, both able to modify people's nature and actions, is a cautionary sign of Achbor's fate. Even though in this strophe the two elements are meant to be positive, celebrating happiness and generosity while alluding to the joys of love, they do so within the framework of a wine poem performed at a lavish feast. However, when taken out of this context, they can be interpreted as subversive.

Regiment of Joy: Hearing

While sight, taste, and smell are explicitly elicited, touch and hearing are much more implicit. The association with hearing may lie in the subtext of the idea of "the regiment of joy" as the cure for grief. This may be associated with the tumult of war generated by the regiment and the sounds of musical instruments that are often associated with feasts, where the sound of wine being poured into glasses demonstrates that "inebriation is always to the sounds of 'music and song.'"[19] Another distinct blending is between the joy of wine and the joy of love, as the concept of joy also has clear erotic connotations, both in the Arabic and Hebrew traditions and the courtly tradition. In one of the wine poems produced by the great Arabic poet Abu Nuwas, joy is referred to as the offspring resulting from the copulation of pure wine (a feminine element) and the water (a masculine element) with which it is diluted in the preparation of the intoxicating beverage: "Rise and impregnate wine in water, indeed their offspring is joy."[20] The topos is also found in Shmuel HaNagid's (993–1056) poem: "The companion of grief, took for the son of waters, / a wife from the daughters of the grapevines. / Now gather them both in a cup, your mouth shall then become the grooms' chamber / they will conceive inside your head and will deliver / all of a sudden, joy is in your heart."[21] In troubadouresque vocabulary, the joy of love is a specific term describing "erotic pleasure derived from the verbally imagined physical union and the expected sexual gratification from the game of love."[22]

The Tight-Fisted Man: Touch

Touch may be hinted at by association, with the reference to the hand. Although it is discussed in the specific context of wine's ability to transform the miser into a generous man,[23] the movement of opening a hand is also connected introspectively to touching which, in an analogy to the game of love, symbolizes the third level, caressing. Generosity, however, is a notion that is

226   *Chapter 7*

also part of the *gradus amoris*, as the accordance of the ultimate grace, the grace of love, the *factum*, is the ultimate manifestation of pure generosity. True love and its ultimate tribute are the opposite of love that is sought for profit, and it is perceived as a present, the most exquisite present possible, given generously without any expectations.[24]

The nascent erotic atmosphere is also palpable in this first strophe through the references to the names of the body organs, even if they do not directly denote the physical body but are rather used proverbially. In four of the strophe's stanzas, the eye, כעין, is mentioned twice to create a comparison. The heart, too, is mentioned four times, as the center of sentiments: לבב, בלב, כלב. The hand is mentioned twice while describing avarice and generosity, but its depiction as being wide open cannot be dissociated, in the specific context, from the hand opening so as to caress, and the generosity to accord the ultimate grace. The eyes and the hands are perhaps the organs most associated with sensual love,[25] while the heart is the most emblematic organ of sentimental love, allowing the reader to understand that wine is both the cause of erotic love and its analogy.

SECOND STROPHE: RIDDLES

Wine that within the cups glows, / resembles deep waters that froze.

But its appearance *(Num. 11:7)* is not concealed by the cup, / revealing the spark through its covers *(Job 22:11-12)*.

I shall say when they despair of resolving the secret of the cup and the wine's glare, impenetrable *(Prov. 30:18)* to them.

Just as the sunbeams[26] glow, / and then hide *(Job 24:4)* under the clouds *(Ezek. 32:7)*.

יין אשר יאיר בעד כוסות / דמה עלי מים אשר קפאו
לא נסתרה עינו בעד הכוס / ושביב בעד סתר הראו.
ואומרה עת נפלאה מהם / סוד כוס אור ובם נלאו:
כאשר יאירון כוכבי חמה / ובעד שחקים הם יחבאו.

The second strophe deals with the wine's physical traits after it is already poured into glasses, which are presented in the form of a riddle and its solution.[27]

Stanzas 1 and 2 are the exposition of the riddle. They are two utterances of the same question. Stanza 4 provides the two with one answer correspondingly and by analogy. Hence, these three stanzas (1, 2, and 4) should be juxtaposed and read in parallel. Stanza 3 is a rhetorical intermission emphasizing the riddle-like nature of the baffling "secret" of the cup and the wine.

The apodosis of stanza 1, "*דמה* עלי מים אשר קפאו" (literally: resembles waters that have been frozen, i.e., the wine is the subject) appears in this orthography

"She was a Fawn, she is a Gazelle Now"   227

in the manuscript and was corrected by Schirmann and David in their respective editions to "דמ אלי מים אשר קפאו," thus maintaining that the stanza's subject is the cups, that is, the cups resemble frozen waters.[28] The manuscript's correction is strengthened by Achbor's further observation of the empty crystal cups, "כוסות בדולח מבלי יין." Nevertheless, it is possible to retain the manuscript reading, in which case the wine itself would be as resembling frozen waters. A poetic tradition viewed water as the masculine element and wine (surely present in the image, as the glasses are clearly wine glasses regardless of the subject of "resemble") as the feminine element.[29] We have seen earlier Abu Nuwas' and Shmuel HaNagid's poems regarding the copulation between water and wine.

Based on Arabic poetry, Hebrew poetry also incorporates references to pure wine, often personified as a pure virginal maiden. Thus, diluting wine with water, which was the usual way of drinking, becomes an erotic motif conveying symbolic coitus, reinforced also by the liquids' color symbolism. The white liquid refers by extension to semen, while the red liquid refers, by extension, to blood.

Leaning on such convention, a new possible interpretation appears. This is based on phonetics since the Hebrew word for "resembles," דמה, is a homophone of the word "her blood," דמה. "Her blood to the water" is surely an impossible way to translate this verse into English since it is a second-degree reading. The Hebrew reader, however, can appreciate the pun, which recalls stanzas such as those written by Shmuel HaNagid, and thus such a second-degree reading is possible, involving blood spilled in the process of sexual relations, chimeric as they are.[30]

By suggesting that it is the wine that vacillates between brightness and opacity, the notion that the crystal cups also contrast the wine's redness is clarified as well.[31] Furthermore, this translation decision creates symmetry with the apodoses in stanzas 2 and 4.[32]

The apodosis of stanza 2, as is the the manuscript's reading "ושביב בעד סתר הראו (revealing the spark through its covers) echoes, perhaps ironically, a leitmotif from Achbor's sermon. During his sermon in the city plaza, Achbor was very insistent that God's concealed shelter is forbidden to humans, as a dogmatic principle. This place will only be symbolically attainable by spiritual subordination and will be manifested as divine protection bestowed upon the true believers who follow God's commands wholeheartedly.

In the poem, however, the second maiden implies that that which is concealed (she uses the very specific word סתר, which was used to describe God's dwelling in Achbor's sermon) is attainable to drinkers, who can see the spark, though it is hidden, and perhaps even forbidden. This issue will be addressed again shortly.

Stanzas 1 and 2 both emphasize that the glowing character of wine is discernible through the cup.[33]

228   *Chapter 7*

By analogy, stanza 4 concerns the lighting properties of the sun in the sky. Marked by the word "כאשר", the analogy to the contrast of the sun's rays and the clouds, depicted in stanza 4, explains such a marvel. The sun and the clouds represent the wine and the cup, and like the rays of the sun, which at times shine bright and at other times are hidden by the clouds, the wine in the cup can both be seen and concealed.

What now remains to be clarified is how the wine, described as resembling frozen waters, parallels the idea that a spark can sometimes be seen through a cover and that the sunlight during the day is sometimes unremarkable since it is covered by clouds.

The answer to this is found in Zechariah 14:6, where the notion of light is juxtaposed, like in stanza 1, with the notion of freezing, understood as darkness "והיה ביום ההוא, לא יהיה אור יקרות וקפאון" (And it shall come to pass in that day, that there shall not be light, but heavy clouds and thick). Medieval exegetes understood this to mean that a day will come at the end of time when there will be neither "bright light" (אור יקרות) nor "dark, cloudy light," as the word "קפאון" was understood. Radak commented that אור קפאון (literally frozen light) was "והוא קפוא ועבה, שהוא כמו חושך. ופירושו, שלא יהיה יהיה היום ההוא כלו לא באור ולא בחשך" (frozen and thick, as it is like darkness, and its meaning is that this entire day will be neither in the light nor in darkness). Another relevant biblical source is Exodus 15:8, where the image of frozen waters is also associated with darkness and depth "קפאו תהומות בלב ים" (the deeps were congealed in the heart of the sea). Hence, if we understand stanza 1 as "Wine that within cups glows, resembles deep waters that froze," we have the missing piece, creating harmony between stanzas 1, 2, and 4. In stanza 1 the maiden asks about wine that glows bright but is also deeply frozen, and in stanza 2 she mentions wine that is seen but yet is covered. These paradoxes are resolved in stanza 4, which refers to the play of the sun and the clouds.

The strophe thus suggests two readings. A more conventional reading relies on the common image contrasting the cups, which are so transparent that they seem to be made of, and are as cold as, ice, and the red wine "burning like fire" (as described in the first strophe). This hints that the state of drunkenness may seem to be defying the forces of nature. Such dichotomies increase the notion that inebriation influences the senses, causing a person to perceive reality in an extraordinary, though distorted, manner. Perceiving the wine as non-perishable fire, a motif largely dealt with by Levin,[34] is reminiscent of the burning bush (הסנה הבוער), an additional extension of theological principles toward the general profanation. The dichotomy between the wine as hot and the cups as cold presupposes that the wine embodies the masculine elements and the cups the feminine ones, in a manner similar to the Humoral Theory, according to which men are hot and women are cold.[35]

"She was a Fawn, she is a Gazelle Now"

The second possible reading relies on the preconception that the wine embodies the feminine element, and the contrast is between two correlating aspects of the wine's consistency, that is, it is simultaneously transparent and opaque, a notion that will evolve in the fourth strophe to represent the teasing aspect of the cloth covering the maiden's naked body. In addition, it develops the image of the symbolic coitus between the wine (this time personified as a maiden) and the water, another tradition borrowed from Arabic love poetry. The possible symbolic intermingling of the blood and the water in an overwhelming jumble of picturesque allusions and puns (the word "dama," playing on "cried," "tear," "her blood," and "resembles") continue to evolve into erotic images in the following strophes since, as argued by Levin, in wine poetry "there are cases where the erotic language related to it is very extreme."[36]

Whether it is the cup or the wine that looks like frozen waters, the allegorical meaning returns to love. Both the wine and its cup symbolize young lovers. Thus, this strophe offers the first parallel of substances that alternate between luminescence and opaqueness, and the lovers (explicitly introduced in the third strophe) who simultaneously radiate and blush from love.

THIRD STROPHE: PARADOXES

A fawn covered her cheek with scarlet,[37] her hand holds a cup as if filled with the blood of the slain (Num. 23:24).

The redness of the two rendered everything red,[38] the beloveds' faces,[39] garments, and vessels (2 Kings 7:15).[40]

So much, that [even] the night is covered by [their] glow, the stars in the sky envy the radiance of their face.

With the fawn's apparel and her cup, the most obscure darkness lights up and the shadows flee.

ועופרה כסתה לחיה בשני / בידה כוס כאילו דם חללים

מאודם שתיהן אדמו כל / פני רואים, מלבושים וכלים

עדי ליל מרוב מאור יכוסה / מאורי רום פני אורם מחלים

ושית עופרה וכוסה באישון [ליל] / אזי יאור ונסו הצללים

This strophe develops the two elements introduced by the previous strophe: the connection between the wine and the glass that contains it, and the paradox of luminosity and darkness, transparency and opaqueness. It is divided into two central ideas. The first two stanzas present explicitly what was merely hinted at by the previous maiden, that the poem is about young lovers. In this strophe, we only hear of the fawn who stands with a cup of wine in her hand, but her beloved's presence may also be implied, hinting that we are actually witnessing a secret lovers' tryst. In addition, the reader learns of

230   *Chapter 7*

the symbolic significance of the color red as related to sensual love. The two
final stanzas evoke yet another paradoxical image, the simultaneously dark
and bright night.

Three interpretations can be offered for the emblematic protasis of the
first stanza, "A fawn covered her cheek with scarlet," as the scarlet on the
maiden's cheek can either be a natural blush or a sumptuous scarf.[41] Blushing from nascent sexual tension or attempting seduction by enhancing herself
with an enticing accessory are two opposite extremes of the idealized female
object of desire: adorned and feared, the virgin and the dangerous seductress.
Surely the maiden described here is a combination of the two. She is a shy
maiden whose blushing is eroticized since it externalizes her budding sexual
curiosity. It emphasizes the whiteness of her cheek skin, a symbol of her
innocence. Yet, she is also a seductress because she lures her desirers with
her tantalizing scarf (and beauty) and then metaphorically slays them with
rejection.

As depicted in the apodosis, "her hand holds a cup as if filled with the
blood of the slain," the maiden holds in her hand a glass full of דם חללים (the
blood of the slain). Schirmann, referring to Proverbs 7:26, sees in the metaphor a reference to "love casualties," which any beautiful and cruel maiden
would most probably leave behind.[42] Whether she is a shy or cruel maiden,
the correlation between the two states continues in the apodosis.

The metaphorical description of the blood-red wine in the gazelle's cup as
a reflection of the blood, that is, the suffering endured by the martyrs of love,
is only one approach to this sequence. The analogy, however, between the red
wine and the blood of rejected "desirers" does not correspond to the subject
of the poem, which deals with the mutual excitement of the two beloveds preparing (even if only chimerically) to taste wine, that is, love, for the first time.
Another hidden and bold subtext exists, relating more directly to the specific
subject of the poem. The ekphrastic image of the she-fawn holding the cup
indicates that she is offering something to her "desirer."[43] The gesture could
be metonymic, indicating the fawn's readiness to offer herself.[44] It could also
be analogous with Eve's apple, that is, a teasing temptation to consume something forbidden, or with the Courtly Lady's refined and sublime gift, that is, a
euphemistic invitation to the ultimate present of love. The utensil is plainly a
metaphor for a woman's body, while the "blood" in the transparent cup may
very well resonate with her virginity.

Levin records several occurrences of the metaphor of wine as an old aging
maiden, and the opening of the barrel as her defloration.[45] The boldest reference was penned by the Arab poet Abu Nuwas, who wrote that the wine is
"a peasant whose owner 'kept her innocence' while the blood of her menses
flowed, and who veiled herself (= in sealed jugs [*sic*]) for a lengthy period,
until her time came; then, when she was brought to the company 'they harried

"She was a Fawn, she is a Gazelle Now" 231

to crack her virginity with a sharp-tipped instrument—and the blood flowed from her like a stream from her nose.'"[46]

There is yet another way to construe the metaphor of the fawn holding a cup filled with wine. The glass could be the embodiment of the feminine, as any vessel is in metaphorical imagery, while the wine would represent the masculine,[47] as we have seen that it contains the male love-martyr's blood. The metaphorical blood as a liquid contained in a vessel thus has a double meaning. Previously, I noted its symbolic association with the maiden's virginity, offered on that occasion to her beloved. Here, the blood is associated with a man, not necessarily that of the victimized rejected desirer, but rather of the chosen beloved.[48] Thus, the cup filled with wine can be a preliminary sign of ejaculation, a possibility that is reinforced in the following verse. This provides the perfect metaphor for the equal roles that the two beloveds play in the love they share, incarnated in the glass and the wine. As noted above, this strophe does not explicitly present a man at the gazelle's side, but the symbolic blood associated with a "desirer" may be referring to him.

In the last two stanzas, the maiden suggests another possible solution to the riddle posed by her friend, or maybe even a new development. While the previous maiden compared the vacillation of the glow and the flush to the game of power between the rays of the sun and the clouds, this maiden refers to the kingdom of the night. The stars planted in the skies illuminate the dark night, just as love's radiance illuminated the reddened cheek, dress, and goblet of the maiden. This kind of radiance, however, surpasses the stars, who envy it. Again, grammatically, the entire strophe concerns the two signifiers of the girl herself (her cheek), she and her double, that is, the cup that she holds. Implicitly, though, they may also be alluding to the actual presence of the beloved, which will be revealed in the fourth strophe. Either way, the paradox is resolved by the idea that love changes physical appearances from white to red, just as the darkest night becomes bright from the radiance of the stars.

FOURTH STROPHE: IMAGES

When the vineyard's daughter is poured out / (together) with the tears of the graceful gazelle when her beloved sways,

she kills all worries at once, as if in her hand / she holds a sword, to put every [sorrow] to an end.

She turns a fearful heart into a lion's heart, / and by her splendor, she awakens lust.

Should you say: "How would her light / sparkle through the cup and all her secrets be in plain sight?"

Can you not see that a doe is charming under her mantle? / Similarly, imagine that the cup is her mantle.

232   *Chapter 7*

Now then, get up, as this is a time for drinking, find pleasure / my friend, in her bountiful treasure(s)! / my friend, in her bountiful treasure(s)!

ובת כרם בעת תורק בדמעות / צבייַת חן בהתנודד ידידה

דאגות תהרוג רגע, כאילו / להשמיד כל [כאב] חרב בידה.

ולב נמס כלב אריה תשיתו, / ותעיר אהבת דודים בהודה.

ואם תאמר: ואיך אורה ינוצץ / בעד הכוס ונגלה כל יסודה?

הלא תראה יפת גן יעלה תוך / רדידה—כן חשוב הכוס רדידה.

בכן קומה, הלא זה זה עת שתיה / והתענג, ידיד, מזיו כבודה!

This strophe, comprised of six stanzas instead of four like the others, is divided into three parts. The first three stanzas describe the traditional role of wine as blurring the borders of rationality. The strophe's second part presents a new attempt to solve the riddle. The maiden reformulates the question: "Should you say: 'How would her light, sparkle through the cup and all her secrets be in plain sight?').[49] She therefore compares the cup to a maiden: "Can you not see that a doe is charming under her mantle? the same way, imagine that the cup is her mantle." The maiden's imagined naked body is again on display and, by analogy, the wine riddle is entirely solved. The wine can shine through the cup not merely because the cup is made of transparent glass, but also by allowing viewers to fantasize about its content, tantamount to the way a maiden's body is fancied under her clothes, suggesting its curves. Finally, the last stanza returns to the feast and invites the listeners to imbibe.

First Part

Stanza 1: The Vineyard's Daughter

Schirmann corrected the manuscript and revised it to read "the grapevine's daughter" (בת גפן), noting that this is a well-established metaphor for the wine and commenting on this line as follows: "the wine blended with the tears of the girl mourning the separation from her lover."[50] In his edition, David returned to the manuscript's reading and re-edited it as "the vineyard's daughter" (בת כרם), but accepted Schirmann's note on the meaning of the text in general. According to this interpretation, "בהתנודד ידידה" would mean "when her beloved departs."[51]

The perplexity I feel regarding this interpretation, specifically here, is that it seems to be irrelevant to the poem's context. The lover's departure is not discussed in the poem nor the rest of the tale. I prefer the semantic "sway" for התנודד, a term that is much more compatible with the dazzling effects of wine and love.[52] My reading thus compares the two actions of "emptying": while the vineyard's daughter, that is, the wine, is being poured, the maiden cries, her tears pouring as her lover "sways." This may be interpreted as a poetic or even allegorical description of their first lovemaking, reflecting their

"She was a Fawn, she is a Gazelle Now"   233

excitement and their physical reactions. As we have seen, the poured wine can be metaphorical to both virginal blood and semen. The bold images that follow support this reading.

We cannot ignore the new nomination of the doe (עוֹפְרָה) from the last stanza, who has now grown into a "graceful gazelle" (צְבִית חֵן). The well-known biblical formula יַעֲלַת חֵן (graceful doe) appears only in the tale's final poem, in the closing orchard scene. Here and in Achbor's strophe, she is referred to as a gazelle, though a doe is mentioned later in this strophe. Both a gazelle and a fawn (and also a doe) are affective designations of an unmarried young maiden. Generally, they are synonymous, and I would not see much difference between them. However, the transition from the fawn of Strophes 2 and 3 to the gazelle of Strophes 4 and 5, that is, from a child to an adult, may be conveying a hidden symbolic meaning related to the path of sexual initiation. Further below, in Achbor's strophe, there is also a symbolic confrontation between the idea of inexperienced women (empty glasses) and experienced ones (filled glasses), as we will shortly see.

The metaphor of the "vineyard's daughter" equates wine to the grape and further blurs the boundaries between the wine and the maiden, who has now become a gazelle. In the Song of Songs, the vineyard appears several times as a metaphor for the beloved's own body (Song of Sg 1:6; 1:14). The little foxes plotting to raid the vineyards full of nascent fruit (Song of Sg 2:15) is a sassy general metaphor for female genitalia, coveted by the young men. It is reminiscent of a passage from Theocritus' first idyll:

> And but a little removed from master Weather-beat there's a vineyard well laden
> with clusters red to the ripening, and a little lad seated watching upon a hedge.
> And on either side of him two foxes; this ranges to and fro along the rows and
> pilfers all such grapes as be ready for eating, while that setteth all his cunning
> at the lad's wallet, and vows he will not let him be till he has set him breaking
> his fast with but poor victuals to his drink.[53]

Stanza 2: "She Holds a Sword"

The image of the maiden holding a sword is baffling because of its nearly oxymoronic nature. In the previous stanza, she was presented as vulnerable, tearfully crying, yet now she is depicted as a warrior, destroying any possible pain. We have already encountered this archetypal contrast in the previous strophe. It represents the fantasized ideal woman who is simultaneously a dangerous seductress and an innocent gazelle.[54] The seductress, who held a cup full of men's blood, which can be interpreted in a myriad of ways, now holds a preeminent phallic symbol in her hand, the sword.[55] As for what the maiden eliminates, this is not mentioned in the manuscript. David added "pain" (כאב), while I added "sorrow" in correspondence with the sorrow that

234   *Chapter 7*

is being eliminated (the use of the same verb) in the third stanza of the first
strophe.

Stanza 3: "A Fearful Heart . . . Awakens Lust"

This may be compared with Shmuel HaNagid's words: – "הבא בלב נדיב
"ויוסף נדיבות או בלב רך לב – ויגבר כלביא" (He who comes with the heart of the
generous, shall increase his generosity; he with a soften-heart heart, will be
strengthened like a lion).[56]

This is the second lion evoked in the wine poem. We implicitly
encountered Samson's lion in the first strophe, a lion that was killed, yet
honey was extracted from its corpse; hence "From the strong came forth
sweetness" (Judg. 14:14). In a reversed, though metaphorical way, love
renders a soft heart robust, that is, the timid heart of the desirer becomes brave
like the heart of a lion,[57] hence "from the tender came forth the strong." The
possible ideological connection between these two lions in the context of love
returns to the idea of gradation. The "slain" or drowsy lion is awakened, and
the foreplay (drinking bittersweet wine) forfeits its place to the next stage
(drinking love), as the bold images of this strophe reveal.

Holding such a sword awakens desire and permits two different readings
of the word closing the verse's apodosis. "בהודה" should, in all probabilities,
be read as "in *her* splendor," meaning that it is the maiden's magnificence
that stimulates her beloved, as we shall shortly see in much detail. However,
grammatically it is also possible to read here "in *its* splendor," that is, desire
is awakened in all of its vigor, a matching image to the sword being held in
the maiden's hand. The Hebrew permits these two meanings to coexist on
two different layers, while the English requires that a choice be made between
"her" and "its," and it is surely the more obvious interpretation that should be
retained for the translation, that is, "her splendor."

The maiden's splendor should be understood here as encompassing
all of her virtues. The sensual atmosphere recalls the Talmudic phrasing
"הוד שביופיה" (the splendor of her beauty), referring to a woman's breasts.[58]
It may also evoke her strength or her determination, as her image, standing
with the sword, implies.[59] It is worthwhile to note here a net of associations
related to the word used to designate the splendor, namely הוד (hod), also
meaning glory and heroism (both military and sacred), starting precisely with
the sword the maiden metaphorically holds in her hand.

The sword, the symbol and archetype of military bravery par
excellence, is related to the warrior's "hod," as, for example, in Psalm 45:4
"חגור חרבך על ירך גבור הודך והדרך" (Gird the sword upon thy thigh, O mighty
one, thy glory and thy majesty). But a derivative meaning of this strength
(hod) is male sexual potency, as we read in Proverbs 5:9, where men are
warned about following seductive foreign women "פן תיתן לאחרים הודך"

(Lest thou give thy vigor unto others). Could it be that the maiden's sword awakens here, metaphorically, the vigor of sexual desire? Let us be reminded that a similar question was asked in the first strophe, concerning the meaning of wine's "hod." As suggested above, there too the word implied the idea of the possible sexual vigor evoked by wine ("Its fragrance invigorates, as its splendor is like myrrh's").

The seductress mentioned in Proverbs is also depicted as a dangerous, fatal, and emasculating sword "ואחריתה מרה כלענה, חדה כחרב פיות" (But her end is bitter as wormwood, sharp as a two-edged sword, 5:4).[60] This Proverb is perhaps the earliest description of the theme of the *vagina dentata*, as it presents female sexuality as a double-edged sword, bringing the seduced man to his death: "רגליה ירדות מות, שאול צעדיה יתמכו" (Her feet go down to death; her steps take hold on the nether world, Prov. 5:5).[61] This source is particularly interesting in our context as it also presents two contrasts we dealt with in the poem: the antinomy of bitter and sweet and that of tenderness and harshness. The seductress' portrait depicts her as "כי נפת תטופנה שפתי זרה וחלק משמן חכה. ואחריתה מרה כלענה, חדה כחרב פיות" (For the lips of a strange woman drop honey, and her mouth is smoother than oil; But her end is bitter as wormwood, sharp as a two-edged sword, Prov. 5:3-4). The first set of opposites, the seductress' sweet lips and her bitter "end" (a euphemistic term designating where the sweet kisses of the lips lead to),[62] recalls the bittersweet wine discussed in Strophe 1. The medieval exegete Radak commented on this contrast: "Since in the beginning she ensnares the man with her lips' smoothness and their sweetness. *Bitter as wormwood* refers to the sweetness where the poison of death is hidden, killing those who drink it."[63] The second set of opposites, the smoothness of her mouth and the sharpness of her sword, is a clear reversed parallel of the maiden's portrayal at the beginning of the third strophe: she cries, but she kills (worries) with a sword.

While earlier we asked if the cup that the maiden holds in her hand is a dangerous or sublime "fruit of knowledge," we now ask whether the sword she holds is a heroic one supporting her beloved, or an immoral one, which will bring about his end. The answer is multi-layered. In the context of a sensual love poem sung at a joyful feast, there is no doubt that the image is a positive one. The maiden appears as the healer of all sadness related to the torments of love, and her sword is a metaphorical image of her courage, with which she inspires her desirer (bestowing on him a lion's heart). But just like the wine's capacity to change a man's heart and open the hand of the miser hints at Achbor's upcoming downfall, thus a woman holding a sword, a manly woman, hints at Achbor's fatal end, becoming a womanly man because of his love for a seductress. In addition, similar to the dichotomous wine, which has the potential to symbolize both the maiden and the boy, but is eventually a whole (the two beloveds share this moment equally), the sword, as we have

236

Chapter 7

seen, is a sexual referent of both genders, a phallic instrument and a *vagina dentata*. Thus, it conveys the same idea as the wine, that is, the maiden and her desirer are in it together.

Second Part

Stanza 4: "Plain Sight"

The word "יסודה" literally means "her essence" or her "foundation," based on Micah 1:6 (see also Ezek. 13:14). This is also associated with Psalm 137:7, where the idea of uncovering Samaria or Jerusalem respectively to "their foundation" is symbolically comparable to the undressing of a woman who is left without her garments. In other words, the idea conveyed here is a fantasized gaze on the maiden's "foundation / body," naked under her clothes. I chose the word "secret," סוד (sod), for the Hebrew word's phonetic closeness to "foundation," יסוד (yessod), and its compatibility with the riddle (the secret) and its answer (the body). In addition, in goliardic poetry "the word *secretum* . . . serves as a metonym for *secreta muliebria*: the female pudenda."[64] This is the first of four poetical images of the naked body contained in this strophe ("her splendor," "her secret," "charming under her mantle," and "her bountiful treasure"), which will soon be discussed. Imagining the beloved's body under her dress is also a common topos in the Arabic and Hebrew literary traditions and the troubadouresque love poetry.

Stanza 5: Charming Under Her Mantle?

Another bawdy image may be concealed here, if we are willing to bestow meaning on the formula יפת גן. This does not only relate to the gazelle's beauty, but also to the attractiveness of her intimate body, her garden, which her mantle discloses. While the combination "beautiful garden" is not found in the Bible, in the Song of Songs a garden is a recurring metaphor for the sensual body (e.g., 4:12; 16; 5:1; 6:2).[65]

Stanza 6: "Time for Drinking"

The maiden then concludes the third part of the poem with a vivid invitation to drink, thus returning to the conventional structure of a wine poem. Yet, the boundary between drinking and loving seems to be quite blurred once again.[66] With this final stanza, we achieve the climax of the blending between the wine, personified as the vineyard's daughter, and the maiden. The friend is thus invited by the poetess to "drink from the vineyard's daughter" in both

"She was a Fawn, she is a Gazelle Now" 237

its meanings, drinking wine and kissing, implying also the final stage of the *gradus amoris*, the *factum*, the ultimate act of consummation.

The phrase זיו כבודה may be compared to the phrase "her splendor," discussed above. In Aramaic the word "ziv" is synonymous with "hod" (splendor), and thus "ziv kevodah" (the brilliance of her virtue) creates an ideological continuation of "her splendor," both being, in this reading, superlatives for the vineyard's daughter. The phrase זיו כבודה is also composed of two subordinated nouns. The second, כבודה, literally means "her honor," and by extension can mean "her glory," "her praise," or "her virtue." In this specific context, it can also denote the treasures or favors of her substance and body, which were discussed and depicted throughout the entire poem. The meaning may also be adduced by the understanding of the word "זיו". Isaiah allegorizes Jerusalem as a nursing mother whose lovers will be fed to full satiation: "למען תינקו ושבעתם משד תנחומיה למען תמוצו והתענגתם מזיז כבודה" ("that ye may suck, and be satisfied with the breast of her consolations; that ye may drink deeply with delight of the abundance of her glory," 66:11). The English translation used here remains literal and euphemistic and ignores the nature of the allegory, relying probably on the amendment to זיו כבודה used in *Targum Yonatan,* the Aramaic translation of the biblical books of the prophets, for this verse. Several Bible translations translated זיז as breast or bosom.[67] Based on these sources, I was at first tempted to translate this line as "Now then, get up, as this is a time for drinking, and savor, my friend, from her bountiful nipple." But since the manuscript contains the word "ziv" (brightness, brilliance) and not "ziz" (nipple), I preferred to reproduce the ambiguity in the translation.[68]

Similar to the double entendre that the context conveys to "her splendor," this phrase is, in fact, an innuendo. A bland utterance such as "the brilliance of her virtue" seems a little misplaced in the poem's sensual atmosphere, and even more so as concluding words. Furthermore, the image of the drinker / lover suckling from the wine's nipple (or fantasizing about it) corresponds to the milk as a love elixir interchangeable with wine.[69]

With the mention of her splendor, her foundation, her body under the mantle, her suggested nipple, or her treasures / favors, the fourth strophe thus pays tribute to the fantasy of a woman's naked body.

THE FIFTH STROPHE: COLORS

The four miniature poems arouse Achbor's desire, and he is now ready to contribute his part: "Then Achbor said: 'lo, you very well used your mouth [to sing], your hands played admirably and by the quality of your poetry you accumulated the slain! As you have awakened my desire, I shall also reply with my part.'"

238   *Chapter 7*

Achbor resolves the main topics evoked by the four strophes, and therefore his can be read as the fifth strophe of the same poem. He starts with the contradiction between the wine's intense red color and the shimmering aspect that was at the heart of the servants' strophes, to which he adds yet another sexual layer.

Crystal cups empty of wine / are pure, and white and they do shine!
Once they are filled with the vineyards' tears / I see them [bloody] red and glowing.
Small sparks dance within them, / growing larger, into flames.
Did they glow or blush or did they not? / Is the appearance of the full the same as the appearance of the empty?
It is indeed the gazelles' way the moment they meet their beloved, / the faces and the cheeks with red are covered!
Reddened from the blood of the desirers' hearts / because they oppress and rob the love of the sweethearts.
Get up, graceful gazelle! Let me drink them all, / the big cups after the small.
Would that it be that my cup be the lip of a beloved, / as it is sweeter than any goblet.
For the way of the desirers is to sip / — these are their rules—from a beautiful gazelle's lip!

כוסות בדולח מבלי יין / צחות לבנות הן מזוקקות
יתמלאון דמעות כרמים, אז / אראם אדמדמות ירקרקות,
וירקדו תוכן בני רשף, / יתמלאו כמאזרי זיקות.
התבוששו או נכלמו או איך / לא עין מלאות היא כעין רקות?
כן חוק צבאות עת פגוש דודים / יתאדמו פנים וגם רקות:
יתאדמו מדם לבב חושקים, / כי לב ידידים גזולות עושקו.
קומי, צביית חן, והשקיני / כוסות גדולות אחר דקות
מי יתנה כוסי שפת רעיה / כי מתקה מכל כלי השקות!
כי-כן תעודת חושקים לשתות / בשפת צביית חן וכן חוקות.

Achbor begins with the contradiction between the wine's intense red color and the shimmering aspect that was at the heart of the previous riddle posed by the maidens. He first distinguishes between the glasses, those that do not contain wine and those that do, in a possible parallel to virgins and experienced women:[70] "Crystal cups empty of wine / are pure, and white and they do shine![71] / are filled with the vineyard's tears, / I see them [bloody] red and glowing" (Lev. 14:37). The emptiness of the cups / maidens is synonymous with innocence, which is traditionally conceived with the range of bright shades of transparency, whiteness, and radiance. This sublime image of such incorruptibility is extinguished by the act of pouring, once the cups / women are filled with the red shade of wine / love, as when they "are filled with the vineyard's tears, / I see them [bloody] red and glowing)."[72]

The blurring between the wine as simultaneously representing the male (ejaculation) and female (hymenal blood) liquid, which was introduced by the

"She was a Fawn, she is a Gazelle Now"   239

third and fourth strophes, achieves its climax. The empty cups are penetrated (by the "wine") and by that, they are no longer as white.

The leitmotif, consisting of the dichotomy between dark and light colors, goes a step further with the transition from metaphorical expressions of brightness, as we had so far, to an emphasized whiteness. It is no longer a question merely of contrasting tones. These tones are associated with moral virtues, embodied in the words "צחות" (tzahot) and "מזקקות" (mezakekeot).[73] Moreover, the name of the color, לבן (white), is explicitly articulated for the first time. It is revealing, because the tale's drama results from the protagonist's love for a black woman, representing repressed sexual desire, and contrasted to the pure love of a clear-skinned damsel. As we witnessed earlier, the poem's content is somewhat prophetical. Here is a culminating point of this mechanism, as the second verse hints at the fact that the stage of purity is not the one Achbor most prefers, an idea that will be developed once he is caught in the arms of the black mistress after dismissing the "white" servants.

Said differently, the wine poem is not a celebration of sexual modesty, but rather a laudation of filled cups! The following stanza relates already to the filled cups, which now take on a red tone, and that is the point when the fire of desire is ignited, starting with small sparks and culminating in a big flame: "Small sparks[74] dance inside them, / growing larger, into flames." The triumph of the filled, the red, and the ardent over the refined pure white will be echoed later in a vivid quarrel between Lemuel and Achbor regarding the love of white versus black women, and רשף (spark) will be used while painting the hideous portrait of the Mistress.

Achbor then asks a riddle of his own: "Did they glow or blush? (Gen. 2:25, also Isa. 5:16) or did they not? Is the appearance of the full the same as the appearance of the empty?" The stanza continues with the central contradiction between the full, that is, red, opaque, and hidden, and the empty, that is, glowing and transparent. The difficulty is with the two verbs התבוששו and נכלמו, which usually function as synonyms (ashamed, embarrassed). As such, it would be quite difficult to understand the meaning and purpose of this stanza, "they are either ashamed or embarrassed" seems incongruous to me here.[75] To my understanding, an essential distinction, justified by או (or) between these verbs, is required. I therefore suggest to read התבוששו as "glowing" based on the phonetic association of the verb התבושש with the word שש (white stone), and נכלמו as "blushing" by association with the prevalent notion that blush is the color of embarrassment and also the blush of love. We thus have here another parallel to the idea that like wine, the beloveds can simultaneously glow (or pale) and blush, that is, shine like the rays of the sun and be covered by clouds.[76]

The form רקות is mentioned in Achbor's poem three times in a sophisticated artistic wordplay and deserves special attention, as not merely do we have an

240   Chapter 7

identical graphic form conveying three different semantics, but also forming three couples. The first mention of the word is: "לא עין מלאות היא כעין רקות" (Is the appearance of the full the same as the appearance of the empty?), permitting the empty / full combination, in what seems to reply to the second strophe's main subject, the cups.

In the following stanza, we have "יתאדמו פנים וגם רקות" (the faces and the cheeks with red are covered!), where the word is used in its literal meaning, temples, though Schirmann maintains that it actually refers to cheeks,[77] a reference to the images conjured in the third strophe, the blood of the slain and the reddened faces.

The third occurrence is found two stanzas later, in "כוסות גדולות אחרי רקות" (the big cups after the small). Schirmann edited this to דקות , while David, following Brody, corrected it to רקות. The graphics of ר and ד are similar, making it nearly impossible to determine which form the scribe intended, especially since these two forms are entirely interchangeable. I think רקות would be a better reading precisely because of the artistic wordplay which I claim appears here, but again, the manuscript reading רקות is also entirely justified. The form דקות describes the seven emaciated cows in Pharaoh's dream "דקות בשר" (lean-fleshed, Gen. 41:3-4), whereas when recalling the dream to Joseph, he uses the form רקות בשר (Gen. 41:19-20). These cows are mentioned after the seven בריאות בשר (fat-fleshed, Gen. 41:2) cows. Achbor's new image rests on this contrast between the full-bodied and lean, "empty" cows, a parallel reference to the idea of the full and empty glasses.[78] Within the context of a feast, this stanza can convey a meaning such as "fill the cups once they are emptied," that is, replace the emptied glasses with full ones, acting as a simple expression of the joy of drinking wine. Another contrast to the word "big," which does not conflict with the biblical meaning, is "small." We have already seen the vacillation of the glasses between the vessel holding the wine and the embodiment of the maiden. From this perspective, the poem becomes extremely erotic. After drinking from "little glasses," that is, cups, Achbor asks the maiden to let him drink from "big glasses," that is, the maiden's lips, as he overtly says in the closing stanzas of his strophe: "מי-יתנה כוסי שפת רעיה / כי מתקה מכל כלי השקות // כי-כן תעודת חושקים לשתות / בשפת צבית חן וכן חוקות" (Would that it be that my cup be the lip of a beloved, as it is sweeter than any goblet. For the way of the lovers is to sip—these are their rules—from a beautiful gazelle's lip!). Achbor returns here to yet another familiar image from Arabic and Hebrew poetry, comparing the seductive maiden's lips to a cup, and kissing to drinking wine (or milk) from that cup. It seems that without the vowel signs, the meaning of רקות is subject to contextual interpretation.

BY WAY OF CLOSING

While a quick reading of the interspersed wine poem may give the impression that it is somewhat conventional due to its constant borrowings from the prevailing metaphors derived from Arabic and Hebrew poetry, the thorough decipherment presented above proves it to be quite a sophisticated piece. The five miniature poems construct a poetical world fascinated by the endless merging of wine and love, of man and woman. The fragile line between the metaphorical entity that wine embodies, at times the "desirer" and at times the beloved, referred to by the traditional word in Hebrew love narratives, חושק (literally "he who desires," or here "desirer"), or the maiden, referred to by the traditional words צביה (gazelle), עפרה (fawn),[79] or יעלה (doe), is well-represented in the first and fourth strophes. All the stanzas in the first strophe rhyme with the suffix "do," composed of the consonant "d" of the different elements and of "o." Three of the four stanzas use the singular masculine (in English neutral) possessive referring to wine: כידודו, הודו (his / its sparks, his / its vigor) or to its effect on the drinker: ידו (his hand). The singular masculine conjugation is used once, conveying the sadness that wine eliminates (להשמידו, to eliminate it). The rhymes in the stanzas constructing the fourth strophe are also based on words ending with "d," as if to pay tribute to the first strophe, but here the suffix becomes "da." Yaakov uses the singular feminine possessive and refers to wine as a maiden, the vineyard's daughter (ידידה, ידה, הודה, יסודה, רדידה, כבודה; her friend, her hand, her splendor, her secret, her mantle, her treasure).

The fourth strophe also responds to the first strophe by reutilizing similar vocabulary. The four elements, conjugated in the masculine in the first verse, are matched by a close feminine form in the fourth.[80] For example, by mirroring wine's / love's role to eradicate sadness: it releases the regiment of joy to stamp it out; she holds a sword, to put every (sorrow) to an end. It also brings full circle the idea of wine's capacity to arouse sexual desire, by repeating the word "hod" with its sophisticated semantic interpretations: its splendor (hodo) is like myrrh's[81]; "by her splendor (hoda), she awakens lust."

The transition from "do" to "da," from the wine as a masculine element to the wine as a feminine element, links all the maidens' strophes and prepares the reader for Achbor's words, where the wine is not merely a single desired woman, but all desired women.[82] The rhyming changes into the feminine plural (here the suffix is "kot"). On the symbolic level, this manipulation may reveal Achbor's lechery and corruption, as he disrupts the sublime balance between the feminine and the masculine in the first and fourth strophes in favor of the plural feminine. This echoes ideologically with his multiple relationships with the four maidens, which, as we know, are merely a charade.

242   *Chapter 7*

The first maiden's strophe ostensibly presents wine's good qualities while, as befitting good wine poetry, disregarding its negative aspects.[83] The wine arouses sensual love, which could also be perceived negatively, when the drunk desirer is no other than the preacher who, in his public life, advocates for a moral way of living. From here, through a gradual climbing of a sensual ladder, somewhat reminiscent of the *gradus amoris*, the strophe prepares the basis for the blurred boundaries between drinking and lovemaking. This is accomplished by a series of settled contrasts, as the bitter becomes sweet, the sadness transforms into joy, and avarice into generosity.

The second strophe also contains an element that the alert reader will perceive as undermining the sensual / positive atmosphere, and which is discernible only from the general context, that is, the idea that one can see, or perhaps imagine and fantasize (while intoxicated), those things that are not meant to be seen.[84] In our wine poem, the extremely erotic descriptions are subject to interpretation, as they are usually somewhat euphemistic. This is evident, for example, in the third strophe, where the two possible ways one might fantasize about a beautiful woman, as a virginal maiden or a dangerous seductress, are presented. It is the fourth strophe, however, that describes the culminating point in the fusion between wine and sensuality. This strophe seems to be boldly hinting at the act of love between the lovers through references to swaying and pouring and it is intensely preoccupied with the description of the maiden's body, proposing four possible euphemistic images of the intimate body in six verses: her splendor, her secret (or foundation), her charming body under her mantle, and her treasure.

The fourth strophe is the climax of the poem, symbolically containing more stanzas than the three strophes that precede it. It reiterates and expands the issues they evoked, often offering some correspondence with the previous ideas based upon semantic and phonetic interferences. The phonetic correspondences between the second and third strophes consist of the דמה (dama) and דמעות (dema'ot) and סוד (sod) and יסודה (yesoda). We have seen above the association of the fourth strophe with the first, but the fourth strophe also echoes the third strophe by overlapping words and sounds. The fawn (עופרה) has matured into a gazelle (צביה), and now holds a sword in her hand (חרב בידה) instead of a cup (בידה כוס).

While the fourth strophe marks the last of the maidens' contribution to the poem, the poem does not end there. Achbor joins in with a fifth strophe, directly continuing the semantic, metaphoric, and thematic connection.[85]

Achbor's strophe also anticipates forthcoming events, especially with the extension of the color symbolism. It begins with the dichotomy of red and transparent and then takes a step further with a new semantic field, expressions of the cups' white color. Embodying women explicitly this time, it cannot but prepare us for the tale's central drama, Achbor's love for the black woman. The white cups / maidens would thus be virginal, but after the act of drinking / loving, after wine / bodily liquids are poured, innocence (and whiteness) is lost. Again, detached from the entire tale, this could be construed as implying Achbor's attraction to his servants. After reading the entire text, we can see that this is an allusion to his favorite cup, the one that is already filled with wine, and therefore not white.

NOTES

1. The term is Israel Levin's, *The Embroidered Coat: The Genres of Hebrew Secular Poetry in Spain, Volume II* (Tel-Aviv: Katz Institute for the Research of Hebrew Literature, Hakibuz Hameuchad, 1995) [in Hebrew]. On the miniature poem, see 168.

2. The most complete survey clarifying the characteristics of medieval wine poetry and love poetry, frequently inseparable from one another, was written by Levin, *The Embroidered Coat,* 147–34. See also David Yellin, *Introduction to Hebrew Poetry of the Spanish Period* (Jerusalem: The Magnes Press, 1978), 29–31, 34–36 [in Hebrew]; Dan Pagis, *Poetry Aptly Explained, Studies and Essays on Medieval Hebrew Poetry,* edited by Ezra Fleischer (Jerusalem: The Magnes Press, 1993), 18–49 [in Hebrew], and Philipp F. Kennedy, *The Wine Song in Classical Arabic Poetry: Abū Nuwās and the Literary Tradition* (Oxford: Clarendon Press, 1997). The themes and images in both the maidens' and Achbor's poems are borrowed from and inspired by the classics, including the works of the most prominent Spanish-Jewish poets such as Yehuda Halevi, Shmuel HaNagid, Shlomo Ibn Gabirol, Moshe Ibn Ezra, Abraham Ibn Ezra, and Yehuda al-Harizi.

3. See also Decter's affirmation that, although familiar with such poetic genres, Yaakov ben Elazar "inverts their structures and themes in favor of a new mood and symbolic vocabulary." Decter, *Iberian Jewish Literature,* 172.

4. Levin, *The Embroidered Coat,* 222, 223. For further discussion of originality in wine poems and the poet's personal style, specifically those included in the maqama and influenced by its narratives and plots, see Pagis, *Poetry Aptly Explained,* 29.

5. Levin, *The Embroidered Coat,* 223.

6. Though כידוד is recorded to appear only in the plural form, Yaakov ben Elazar has constructed it here in the singular form.

7. On the word "הוד" as virtue or splendor, see the analysis of Strophe 4.

8. Levin frequently returns to his observation that "the delight of drinking is complete and wine pleasures all the senses." Levin, *The Embroidered Coat,* 178. See also Pagis, *Poetry Aptly Explained,* 30.

9. Lionel J. Friedman, "Gradus Amoris," *Romance Philology* 19, no. 2 (1965): 167–77. Moshe Lazar, "Carmina Erotica, Carmina Iocosa: The Body and The Bawdy in Medieval Love Songs," in *Poetics of Love in the Middle Ages: Texts and Contexts,* edited by Moshe Lazar and Norris J. Lacy (Fairfax: George Mason University Press, 1989), 249–78, here 258.

244   *Chapter 7*

10. Friedman, "Gradus Amoris," 170.

11. While there are many examples of the fire of love or the ardor of desire in courtly poetry and narrative, it is this one, from the *Roman de la rose,* that comes to my mind: "Et tout adés en regardant / Recouvertes le feu ardent / Qui ce qu'il aime plus regarde / Plus alume son cuer et larde" (vv. 2343–6) (and all along, while you gaze (at her), you are set on ardent fire. The more he gazes at the one he loves, the more his heart is rekindled and pierced).

12. From the endless possible examples, Petrarch best brings it to sublimation: "Cosi sol d'una chiara fonte viva / Move '1 dolce e l'amaro, ond'io mi pasco; / Una man sola mi risana e punge" (For me both sweet and bitter always come out of one clearly running fountainhead; a single hand heals and then pierces me). Text and translation by J. G. Nichols quoted from the latter's "Petrarch's Canzoniere 164: An Anthology of English Translations with a New Version by J. G. Nichols," *Translation and Literature* 5, no. 1 (1996): 71–80. See also, "'The Bittersweet' Convention of Finamor in Simon Gaunt," in *Gender and Genre in Medieval French Literature* (Cambridge: Cambridge University Press, 1995), 156.

13. Myrrh appears seven times in the Song of Songs in the context of the sensual descriptions of the beloveds and their preparations for their lovers' encounters. One biblical source that makes a pronounced symbolic connection between sensual love being tasted and inhaled like wine, love, honey, and myrrh is the Song of Songs 5:1 "באתי לגני אחתי כלה אריתי מורי עם בשמי אכלתי יערי עם דבשי שתיתי ייני עם חלבי אכלו רעים שתו ושכרו דודים." (I come into my garden, my sister, my bride; I have gathered my myrrh with my spice; I have eaten my honeycomb with my honey; I have drunk my wine with my milk. Eat, O friends; drink, yea, drink abundantly, O beloved). In this book, the garden is a recurring metaphor for the sensual body (e.g., 4:12; 16; 6:2), and thus the straightforward sexual hints of this biblical verse, describing indulgent drinking and eating of / from a metaphorical garden / body, need no further commentary. See more on the myrrh further below, and also in chapter 5. For a brilliant reading of the sexual metaphors of scents, including their euphemistic use as "bodily emissions" in the Song of Songs, see Green, *The Aroma of Righteousness,* chapter 3: "Election and the Erotic: Biblical portrayals of Perfume and Incense," 64–115 (here 89).

14. A common synonym for הוד (hod) is הדר (hadar), which often doubles it, and the words appear together as הוד והדר ("hod ve-hadar"). It is the word Achbor will use a little bit further in the tale, surely echoing the poem's thematic, to describe his black mistress in his attempt to elevate her status as a legitimate beloved.

15. In the Song of Songs, honey is used as a sensual metaphor "אכלתי יערי עם דבשי" (I have eaten my honeycomb with my honey, 5:1). The contrast related to sensual love also appears in the description of the foreign seductive woman mentioned in Proverbs 5, which will be studied in Strophe 4. The sexual symbolism of honey was studied by Claude Lévy-Strauss, *From Honey to Ashes,* translated by John and Doreen Weightman (London: Cape, 1973).

16. Philip Nel referring to Gunkel, "The Riddle of Samson (Judg. 14:14-18)," *Biblica* 66, no. 4 (1985): 534–45, 358. See also Arthur Quinn, *Figures of Speech: 60 Ways to Turn a Phrase* (Lanham: Scarecrow Press, 1993), 88; Azzan Yadin, "Samson's ḥîdâ," *Vetus Testamentum* 52 (2002): 407–26, 422.

"She was a Fawn, she is a Gazelle Now" 245

17. "עלמה בעיניה שנתי עשקה" (By her eyes the maiden stole my sleep) in *Gan Hammeshalim veHahidot: ben Judah Halevi Abulafia*, edited with notes and commentary by David Yellin (Jerusalem: Weiss Press, 1936), 48.

18. On the riddle in medieval Hebrew poetry, see Yellin, *Introduction to Hebrew Poetry*, 279–87.

19. Levin, *The Embroidered Coat*, 236. Moreover, sounds are closely linked to wine poetry, and some intertextual juxtapositions may be relevant here. For example, in a poem that Yaakov ben Elazar undoubtedly knew (as we shall see below), Yehuda Halevy tells of a feast where not only did he make an alliance with wine, which will dispel all that causes him grief, but he is surrounded by men who "ושרים אחרי נוגנים סביבי" (they shall surround me with song and play the music all around me); Yehuda Halevi, "נטה אל בית ידידך וייגו" (Hurry to your Friend's House and His Wine), in *An Anthology of Yehuda Halevi's Poetry: Hebrew Poetry of the Spanish Golden Age*, edited by Israel Levin (Tel-Aviv: Tel-Aviv University Press, 2007), 29. Another well-known example would be the poem "ידידי הזמן חדש" (Friend, the Season is Renewed) where Moshe Ibn Ezra uses onomatopes to describe the birds singing.

20. I translated Levin's Hebrew translation of the Arabic verse; see Levin, *The Embroidered Coat*, 224. More on the coitus between water and wine. See below.

21. Translated from Levin, *The Embroidered Coat*, 174.

22. Moshe Lazar, "Fin'amor," in *A Handbook for the Troubadours*, edited by F. R. Akehurst and Judith M. Davis (Berkeley: University of California Press, 1995), 77. See there his thorough discussion about the term and its uses in "Fin'amor and Joy," 76–83.

23. The miser becoming generous, and more generally bad dispositions turning into good as a result of drinking wine, is yet another conventional theme found in wine poetry.

24. Surely, not all of the troubadours or medieval songwriters applied such a sublimated vision of achieving the final step, as many of them were much more pragmatic. See Lazar, "Carmina Erotica."

25. In the following strophes, the heart and the hand will indeed appear in this metaphorical role. Moreover, they will reappear in Lemuel's reproving poem against Achbor. He will present the reversed image of the hand as a means of seducing a woman, as the man's hand holding a lily, the embodiment of an innocent maiden who is white. The black woman will be presented as heartless.

26. כוכבי חמה, Sukkah tractate, 22:2.

27. The themes developed here are significantly less evocative of courtly poetry than the previous strophe and rely mostly on Arabic and Hebrew imagery, although it is also quite common to encounter representations of young lovers' beauty as competing with the glow of the stars in medieval Christian narratives.

28. The image of transparent glass containing dark red wine is common in Arabic and Hebrew love poetry, as well as the concept that the glasses are cold (like ice, as suggested here within the previous text editions) while the wine is hot (like fire, as we saw in the first stanza of the strophe). The metaphor of the wine glasses as frozen water appears already in the eighth century, in a poem written by Abdallah ibn

246 *Chapter 7*

al-Mu'tazz: "Imagine that the goblets are water that have been frozen." I translated into English Levin's Hebrew translation of the Arabic verse. See Levin, *The Embroidered Coat*, 199.

29. Levin notes that viewing wine as female is mostly characteristic of Arabic poetry, while in Hebrew poetry it is represented in masculine form (224), however, it seems that our poem alludes to the marriage between the wine and the water, as I demonstrate here.

30. See Levin's interpretation of the erotic elements in this strophe in *The Embroidered Coat*, 175.

31. The two readings can be justified in medieval Hebrew and in the poetic expression that naturally promotes different possible correlating and complementary meanings. Making sense of these words only becomes a problem when attempting to translate them into a modern language, where a choice regarding verb conjugation is required.

32. For different possible materials and colors of the cups, see Levin, *The Embroidered Coat*, 178. In addition, the image of wine as frozen, although much less common, does exist; see ibid, 203. The emphasis on the color red in both of the following strophes and the contrast between the hidden and the revealed render it implausible to suggest that the wine under discussion is white. On the contrary, it is the deep color of the wine that this sequence alludes to.

33. On the correlation between the wine and the cup as two opposites attracted to one another, the wine is red and scalding and the cup is white and frozen, see Levin, *The Embroidered Coat*, 29.

34. Levin, *The Embroidered Coat*.

35. As we have seen, Levin noted that although in Hebrew poetry wine was more often personified as a man, wine embodied as a maiden, characteristic of Arabic poetry, is also detectable in the metaphor of the symbolic wedding between wine and water. Levin, *The Embroidered Coat*, 175–76.

36. Levin, *The Embroidered Coat*, 205.

37. The literal translation, "covered her cheek with scarlet," is somewhat heavy in English, but I chose to keep it, for the usual blushing metaphor of a reddened cheek may be doubled with the idea of artificial seduction. An intense referent to an intense idea, the strophe's first two verses contain four allusions to the color red, "the color of love, radiance, and beauty": scarlet, blood, redness, red. See Michel Pastoureau, *Red: A History of a Color,* translated by Jody Gladding (Princeton: Princeton University Press, 2017). The color of fire and blood, it is, by extension the symbol of sexual tension. It recalls both the flames of desire and the blood of lost innocence, along with the initial timidity of young lovers.

38. I intentionally reproduce the repetition אדמו / אדם, "redness / reddened," to maintain the textual intensity, but here the red is synonymous with a flush and a glow, thus explaining the sky metaphor that appears in the following stanza. The word "אדם" (odem), here redness, is homophonic with the word for ruby, known to be the most radiant-red stone, associated with love. See Pastoureau, *Red.* We can practically read in this protasis "they were both redder (or more glowing) than a ruby," though such a reading is incompatible with the apodosis.

"She was a Fawn, she is a Gazelle Now" 247

39. Literally "the *watchers'* faces," this voyeuristic reading implies that people are watching this lovers' rendezvous and also getting excited by the sensual tension. It can surely be a poetic parallel to the peripheral, as we know that Lemuel himself is watching the feast and hearing this song. However, I believe that this is not truly a reference to an external public, but rather is a reference to the two young sweethearts who are completely invested in this moment, and their entire selves, their faces, their clothing, and their goblets, all react to the presence of love. Hence, I offered my non-literal translation of this verse.

40. First, we must quickly note that while the word "כלים" here, by context, refers to a goblet, it can refer to any "tool," and thus also conveys an erotic meaning.

41. While it can also refer to a blush achieved by makeup, this is less likely in this context and hence will not be considered here.

42. The cruelty of a beautiful woman rejecting her suitors and thus symbolically slaying them is grounded in love poetry and narrative and is commonly found in such material. On this, see, for example, Levin, *The Embroidered Coat*, 181; 237. In our tale, the topos reappears both in Achbor's reply-poem and in the tale's closing poem, recited by one of the maidens, as a theoretical step in love. Achbor resolves this riddle, arguing that "לב ידידים גוזלות עושקות" (they oppress and rob the love of the sweethearts,) hence their cheeks are reddened. This is also the subject of the last poem, which is an almost didactic love poem explaining that partial suffering is a necessary part of seduction (see there for more examples) and "יום יצדקו" (a day shall come, their reward will be ample!)

43. The description recalls some iconographic representations of medieval "femmes fatales," such as Eve or Salome.

44. It is worthwhile to note that by the sixteenth century, an iconographical tradition depicting the prostitute handing a cup to her potential client had developed. See Peter Scott Brown, *The Riddle of Jael: The History of a Poxied Heroine in Medieval and Renaissance Art and Culture* (Leiden: Brill, 2018), 94; 120.

45. Levin *The Embroidered Coat*, 185; 187.

46. Levin, *The Embroidered Coat*, 217–18. The inner quotation marks refer to Abu Nuwas' poetry, translated into Hebrew by Levin.

47. See Levin's remarks that in Hebrew poetry the wine sometimes regains the status of the masculine. There is no contradiction in any case, since the same poem can contain different ideas, and different interpretations are possible. Levin, *The Embroidered Coat.*

48. Although "blood of the slain" appears in the plural form, I suggest perceiving it as a proverbial locution having a generalizing function and not relying on its grammatical plural.

49. On the decision to translate יסודה not literally as "her foundation," but rather as "her secret," see further below.

50. The tears shed by lovers due to the departure of their beloveds is a common theme, one of the numerous conventions of wine poetry mentioned by Levin in *The Embroidered Coat*, 177. See, for example, Shmuel HaNagid: "יין כדמעתי עלי פרוד," (wine [transparent] like my tear over the separation), quoted in Levin's *The Embroidered Coat*, 166. I claim here that it may not correspond to the context of this poem.

248   *Chapter 7*

51. "Wine as tears of the person who cries as his friends depart from him," is a convention, according to Levin, *The Embroidered Coat*, 177–78.

52. See Isaiah 24:20 "נוע תנוע ארץ כשיכור והתנודדה כמלונה" (the earth reeleth to and fro like a drunken man, and swayeth to and fro as a lodge).

53. Translation by J. M. Edmonds, quoted from *Greek Bucolic Poets, Volume 28,* translated by J. M. Edmonds. Loeb Classical Library (Cambridge, MA: Harvard University Press, 1912). Another hint rendering this a possible interpretation is found at the very end of the tale, when the four women will be liberated from Achbor and are described as entering the vineyards, where they are about to meet four suitable lads. In this ultimate scene, they can easily be called, metaphorically, the vineyard's daughters, and the sensual associations of the vineyard are studied there. The vineyard also appears as a *locus amoenus*, where the beloveds are free to make love.

54. Let us not forget that although the strophe is recited by a woman, it is based on male perspectives, not merely because she addresses this poem to please Achbor, but also because it was composed by a male author.

55. The sword is also an established phallic metaphor. See Warner's warning to some nuns of "the warrior" Moriuht: "Findende gladio ipsius ex rigido" (you are destined to be split apart by the stiffly erect sword of "Himself," McDonough's translation). See Adam, Latin Sexual Vocabulary, and Bibring "On Swords and Rings."

56. Levin, *The Embroidered Coat*, 173.

57. "The representation of the mistress and her beloved as a lion and a gazelle is common, highlighting the latter's timid and recalcitrant temperament," Kennedy, *The Wine Song in Classical Arabic Poetry*, 75. See also Levin, *The Embroidered Coat*, 179.

58. Rabbi Yosef ben Hananiah says that when the Shunammite woman grabbed prophet Elisha's feet, Gehazi pushed her, touching her in the splendor of her beauty, that is, between her breasts. Talmud Yerushalmi, Sanhedrin tractate, 10:2; 29:72, for the biblical episode see 2 Kings 2.

59. Another complementary biblical association of "hod" is also related to our framework: The maiden's beauty as covering the sky echoes a description found in Habakkuk, where such an idea is related to God "כיסה שמים הודו" (His glory (hod) coverth the heavens, 3:3).

60. A whore, according to Menachem Meiri (1249–1315).

61. Literally, this is the sword of two mouths. (See also Judg. 3:16.)

62. See Radak on this: אחרית האהבה שהיא מראה אל האדם (the end of the love she offers the man). The idea that the "end" is a euphemism is supported by its existence in his commentary regarding the "two-edged sword": "האהבה היא שחותכת מכל צד" (it is love that cuts from every side).

63. "כי בתחילה תופשת האדם בחלק שפתיה ובמתק מרה כלענה והיא מתיקות שבו טמון סם המוות הממית לשותיו"

64. Moshe Lazar, "Carmina Erotica," 274 n. 14.

65. See, however, beautiful "branch" (Ezek. 31:3) or beautiful "olive tree" (Jer. 11:16).

"*She was a Fawn, she is a Gazelle Now*"   249

66. Such energetic invitation (get up!) to drink is commonplace, see for example "לכן ידידי ... // ... קומה ! שתה בכוס, ושוב ושתה / בכד" (Therefore, my friend, ... rise! And drink from the cup, and return and drink from the jug ...), Shmuel HaNagid, quoted in Levin, *The Embroidered Coat*, 168.

67. For example, Holman Christian Standard Bible, God's Word Translation, Lexham English Bible, the Message Bible, and New American Standard Bible, to name but a few.

68. Could that be intentional or a scribal error? The close codicological graphics of the letters "vav" ו (v) and "zayin" ז (z) allow us to consider that it was an error. But then again, we have no way of knowing which version of scripture was available to the writer.

69. As found in some of the biblical references studied in the first strophe.

70. Achbor understands the riddle more traditionally, that is, the glasses resemble water that has been frozen, but as we have seen, there is no contradiction precluding that the two readings coexist.

71. While I manipulated this translation for the sake of a rhyme, a more literal translation would be: Crystal cups empty of wine, clear, white, they are pure! Semantically, the word "צח" means pure, clean, or radiant, and is also synonymous with the color white. Two specific sources come to mind in our context. The erotic atmosphere directs us toward the Shulamite's description of her beloved's beauty (white/clear faces with reddish cheeks) in Song of Songs: "דודי צח ואדום" (My beloved is white and ruddy, Song of Sg 5:10). The moralistic connotation directs us to Lamentations: "זכו נזיריה משלג, צחו מחלב; אדמו עצם מפנינים, ספיר גזרתם" (Her princes were purer than snow, they were whiter than milk, they were more ruddy in body than rubies, their polishing was as of sapphire, Lam. 4:7). This describes how the princes of the "daughter of my people" used to be. However, they became corrupt and transformed into "חשך משחור תארם" (Their visage is blacker than coal). This directs our attention to the fundamental dichotomy that will be the subject of the tale's second part, the debate about the love of white, "positive" women, as opposed to black "negative" women, whose color is compared to coal. The combination צחות לבנות can be read thus either as "radiant or shiny white," or as two subsequent independent equal qualificatives, "clear, [and] white." Either way, the notion of (sexual) purity is introduced into the equation and is reinforced by the following word, מזקקות (refined).

72. The direct biblical reference, naturally noted by Schirmann and David, is "והיה הנגע ירקרק או אדמדם" (if the plague be greenish or reddish, Lev. 13:49). The medical description may be referring to the light aspect of the colors, but this is not the meaning here. אדמדמות (which in modern Hebrew would be translated as reddish) takes the sense of dark red, as it was read by the sages and by medieval exegetes (Tosefta Negaim 1:5; Sifra 68:74; Rashi: "ירקרק—ירוק שבירוקין ... אדמדם—אדום שבאדומים" yerakrak [greenish]—the green of the greens ... adamdam [reddish] the red of the reds). Abraham Ibn Ezra perceived the duplication of the letters forming the names of the colors as toning down rather than emphasizing their hue, but acknowledged the opposite meaning, such as that given by Rashi: "ירקרק ... וזה כפול לחסרון, וכן שחרחורת (שה"ש א, ו) ויש אומרים הפך הדבר" (yerakrak [greenish] it is doubled for reduction, same as sheharhoret [blackish] (Song of Sg 1:6) and some say just the opposite). I believe ירקרק (greenish in modern Hebrew)

250   *Chapter 7*

should be read here in the context of Psalm 65:14, where it means the glow of gold: "כנפי יונה נחפה בכסף ואברותיה בירקרק חרוץ" (the wings of a dove are covered with silver, and her pinions with the shimmer of gold). Rashi based his commentary on Dunash he-Levi ben Labrat's tenth-century works, according to which:

"וירקרק החרוץ הוא הזהב אשר יובא מארץ החוילה ומארץ כוש טוב מאד מאד... לא הוא ירוק ולא הוא אדום, ולכן קראו ירקרק כמו לבן אדמדם (ויקרא יג מב) – שאינו לבן ולא אדום ולכן נכפל ירקרק, אדמדם"

  . . . the shimmer of gold is the gold brought from the kingdom of Havilah and the kingdom of Cush, a fine fine gold . . . it is not green and it is not red and therefore it is named yerakrak [greenish], just like "white-reddish" (Lev. 13:42), which is not white nor red and therefore it was doubled "yerakrak" ([greenish] "adamdam" [reddish]).

    In his commentary on Jeremiah 30:6, Abraham Ibn Ezra relates that "בירקרק—עין הזהב, כמו 'ונהפכו כלפנים לירקון' (יר' ל,ו) והטעם: מהרה תתנער מן השחרות ויראה הלובן" (in yerakrak [greenish]—the appearance of gold like "and all faces turn into paleness [yerakon]," and the meaning: shortly you shall shake off darkness and whiteness will be seen). It is also interesting to note that one of the adjectives describing the empty glass, מזקקות (pure), is associated with the essence of gold (e.g., Kings 3:3; 1 Chron. 28:18).

    73. This word is of particular interest, as it is associated both with the conventional beauty norms, describing in Song of Songs the clear faces of the beloved, contrasting with his red cheeks. More significantly, it appears in Lamentation (4:7), where it is used symbolically. The people's princes, who were once symbols of righteousness and depicted as צחות משלג (whiter than milk), became corrupted and חשך משחור תארם (blacker than coal, 4:8). As this appears shortly before the black mistress enters to replace the white maidens, the biblical connotation is revealing.

    74. The flowery locution בני רשף is a quote from Job 5:7, where it means "sparks." While literally this is translated as "sons of sparks," I translate it here as "small sparks," as I think that this is the image Yaakov intended to convey, specifically the sparks of love. The biblical locution מאזרי זיקות means "those who create a flame by assembling sparks together." It is based on the book of Isaiah, where those who refuse to hear the prophecy and correct their ways are compared to people setting fire: "הן כלכם קודחי אש מאזרי זיקות לכו באור אשכם ובזיקות בערתם" ("Behold, all ye that kindle a fire, that gird yourselves with firebrands, begone in the flame of your fire" Isa. 50:11).

    75. Unless the word "רקות" here is not meant as "empty" but rather as "cheeks," as Schirmann and David understood, and thus there are no paradoxes. I expand on this possibility below.

    76. Another interpretation by connotation, based on the physical metaphorical effects of these two verbs and not on their semantics, would be interesting to explore. The form התבוששו is associated with nakedness "ויהיו שניהם ערומים, האדם ואשתו ולא יתבוששו" ("And they were both naked, the man and his wife, and were not ashamed" Gen. 2:25). Before their transgression, Adam and Eve were not ashamed, even though they were unclothed. The nominal form of the second verb נכלמו (synonymous with

ashamed) frequently appears with the notion of a cover, as people are said to be covered by shame (כלימה). התבוששו could thus hint at "uncovered," not in the literal sense, but rather in the metaphorical sense, referring to the opposite effect of נכלמו. We can see the implied nuance between "shame's materiality" and its cover "נשכבה בבשתנו ותכסנו כלימתנו" ("Let us lie down in our shame, and let our confusion cover us," Jer. 3:25).

77. Schirmann, 279. And see also Song of Sg 4:3 or 6:7.

78. This is reminiscent of the use of Pharaoh's dream in the description of the beard.

79. עופר / ה is a common word used to designate young lovers (male and female) in Hebrew love poetry and narratives. It should be noted here that as the poem's erotic atmosphere grows, the fawn (Strophe 3) matures into a צביה, a gazelle (Strophes 4 and 5). This may represent yet another step taken in the game of love, from the initial timidity of still innocent lovers toward the consummation of their love. It is this reasoning that supplied the title of this chapter.

80. While there are two perfect pairs (its splendor and her splendor, and his hand and her hand), two other pairs are merely suggestive. כידודו (its spark) and ידידה (her beloved) share no semantic common denominator, though they are rather close phonetically and thematically, as the spark is characterized by its movement within the cup, repeated by the movement of the beloved, drinking from the cup. As we have seen, the form להשמידו (to eliminate it) does not return in a feminine form, but does return in the fourth strophe, maintaining the phonetic and thematic connection.

81. The myrrh is also one of the most emblematic oils used for sacrificial rituals, and it returns in this role in Lemuel's discourse about the white lily. See chapter 5 for further discussion. See also Green, *The Aroma of Righteousness*, 67–68.

82. The use of grammar to indicate gender and quantity also creates a symbolic heterosexual love affair since the first strophe represents the masculine, the second the feminine, and the third, the plural, the merging of the masculine and feminine.

83. On the general transgression of wine poetry, see Levin, *The Embroidered Coat*.

84. See the final poem, in which the maidens are angry that they have been watched while naked.

85. This is demonstrated in the following table, where the right column refers to Achbor's strophe:

כוסות דמו אלי מים (בית 2)	כוסות בדולח
בת כרם תורק בדמעות (בית 4)	יתמלאון דמעות כרמים
כעין ברק כעין להב (בית 1)	עין מלאות כעין רקות
גדוד משוש (בית 1)	חוק צבאות
אהבת דודים (בית 4)	פגוש דודים
ומאודם שתיהן אדמו כל פני רואים (בית 3)	יתאדמו פנים וגם רקות
בכן קומה, הלא זה עת שתיה (בית 4)	קומי צבייית חן והשקיני
מדבש ימתק (בית 1)	כי מתקה מכל

Bibliography

Adams, J. N. *The Latin Sexual Vocabulary*. London: Duckworth, 1982.

Alden, Maureen J. "The Resonances of the Song of Ares and Aphrodite." *Mnemosyne*, Fourth Series 50, Fasc. 5 (October 1997): 513–29.

Alexandre-Bidon, Danièle, and Jacques Berlioz. "Le masque et la barbe. Figures du croquemitaine médiéval." *Le Monde alpin et rhodanien. Revue régionale d'ethnologie*, no. 2–4 (1998): 163–86.

Allen, Danielle S. *The World of Prometheus: The Politics of Punishing in Democratic Athens*. Princeton: Princeton University Press, 2000.

Anonyme. "Blason des barbes de maintenant." In *Blasons, poésies anciennes des XV et XVImes siècle*. Edited by Dominique-Martin Méon, 163–69. Paris, 1809.

Apuleius. *Metamorphoses (The Golden Ass), Volume I: Books 1-6*. Edited and translated by J. Arthur Hanson. Loeb Classical Library 44. Cambridge, MA: Harvard University Press, 1996.

Apuleius. *Metamorphoses (The Golden Ass), Volume II: Books 7-11*. Edited and translated by J. Arthur Hanson. Loeb Classical Library 453. Cambridge, MA: Harvard University Press, 1989.

Aristophanes. *Acharnians. Knights*. Edited and translated by Jeffrey Henderson. Loeb Classical Library 178. Cambridge, MA: Harvard University Press, 1998.

Ashbrook Harvey, Susan. *Scenting Salvation: Ancient Christianity and the Olfactory Imagination*. Berkeley: University of California Press, 2006.

Augustine. *City of God, Volume VII: Books 21-22*. Translated by William M. Green. Loeb Classical Library 417. Cambridge, MA: Harvard University Press, 1972.

Ausonius. *A Nuptial Cento in Volume I: Books 1-17*. Translated by Hugh G. Evelyn-White. Loeb Classical Library 96. Cambridge, MA: Harvard University Press, 1919.

Babrius and Phaedrus. *Fables*. Translated by Ben Edwin Perry. Loeb Classical Library 436. Cambridge, MA: Harvard University Press, 1965.

Bakhtin, Mikhail. *Rabelais and His World*. Translated by Hélène Iswolsky. Bloomington: Indiana University Press, 1984.

Bartlett, Robert. "Symbolic Meanings of Hair in the Middle Ages." *Transactions of the Royal Historical Society* 4 (1994): 43–60.

Bayless, Martha. *Sin and Filth in Medieval Cultures: The Devil in the Latrine*. New York: Routledge, 2012.

Berlioz, Jacques, and Marie Anne Polo De Beaulieu, eds. *Collectio exemplorum cisterciensis in codice Parisiensi 15912 asseruata*. Turnhout: Brepols, 2012.

Berneville, Gillebert de. "Jugement d'amour." In *Trouvères belges du XIIe au XIVe siècle. Chansons d'amour, jeux-partis, pastourelles, dits et fabliaux par Quenes de Béthune, Henri III, duc de Brabant, Gillebert de Berneville, Mathieu de Gand, Jacques de Baisieux, Gauthier le Long, etc.* Edited by Aug. Scheler. Bruxelles: Closson, 1876.

Bettella, Patrizia. *The Ugly Woman: Transgressive Aesthetic Models in Italian Poetry from the Middle Ages to the Baroque*. Toronto: University of Toronto Press, 2005.

Bibring, Tovi. "A Medieval Hebrew French-Kiss: Analyzing the Love Story of Sahar and Kima by Yaakov ben Elazar Through Courtly Love Ideals." *The Jewish Quarterly Review* 109, no. 1 (2019): 24–37.

Bibring, Tovi. "Blood Matters, Matters of Blood—Fable 81 by Berechiah ha-Naqdan: Study and Critical Translation." In *'And Wisdom Shall Flow from the Wise:' Wisdom and Morals in Medieval Literature*. Edited by Tovi Bibring and Revital Refael-Vivante. Jerusalem: Misgav Yerushalayim, 2022.

Bibring, Tovi. "Fairies, Lovers, and Glass Palaces: French Influences on Thirteenth-Century Hebrew Poetry in Spain—the Case of Ya'akov ben El'azar's Ninth Mahberet." *The Jewish Quarterly Review* 107, no. 3 (2017): 296–321.

Bibring, Tovi. "Juif ou français? Berechiah ha-naqdan au carrefour culturel: Nouvelles considérations sur Souris et Grenouille." In *Berechiah ben Natronai ha-Naqdan's Works and Their Reception*. Edited by Tamas Visi, Tovi Bibring, and Daniel Soukoup, 29–50. Turnhout: Brepols, 2019.

Bibring, Tovi. *The Patient, the Impostor and the Seducer: Medieval European Literature in Hebrew*. Oxford: Legenda, forthcoming in 2025.

Bibring, Tovi. "Of Swords and Rings: Genital Representation as Defining Sexual Identity and Sexual Liberation in Some Old French Fabliaux and Lais." In *Genealogies of Identity*. Edited by Margaret Sönser Breen and Fiona Peters, 151–67. Amsterdam: Rodopi, 2006.

Bibring, Tovi. "Violent Women and the Blurring of Gender in some Medieval Narratives." In *Blurred Boundaries in Pre-Modern Texts and Images: Aspects of Audiences and Readers-Viewers Responses*. Edited by Dafna Nissim and Vered Tohar, 127–45. Berlin and Boston: de Gruyter, 2023.

Bierl, Anton. "Women on the Acropolis and Mental Mapping: Comic Body-Politics in a City in Crisis, or Ritual and Metaphor in Aristophanes' Lysistrata." In *Crisis on Stage: Tragedy and Comedy in Late Fifth-Century Athens*. Edited by Andreas Markantonatos and Bernhard Zimmermann, 255–90. Berlin and Boston: de Gruyter, 2011.

Bloch, R. Howard. *Medieval French Literature and Law*. Berkeley: University of California Press, 1977.

Bibliography

Bly, P. A. "Beards in the Poema de Mio Cid: Structural and Contextual Structures." *Forum for Modern Language Studies* 14, no. 1 (1978): 16–24.

Bodel, Jean. "Li sohaiz desvez." In *Nouveau recueil complet des fabliaux* (NRCF), publié par Willem Noomen, Assen et Maastricht, Van Gorcum, t. 6, 1991.

Bouchard, Constance B. *"Every Valley Shall Be Exalted": The Discourse of Opposites in Twelfth-Century Thought*. Ithaca: Cornell University Press, 2003.

Bragues, George. "The Market for Philosophers: An Interpretation of Lucian's Satire on Philosophy." *The Independent Review* 9, no. 2 (2004): 227–51, 245.

Brody, Saul Nathaniel. *The Disease of the Soul: Leprosy in Medieval Literature*. Ithaca: Cornell University Press, 1974.

Bromwich, Rachel, and D. Simon Evans. *Culhwch and Olwen. An Edition and A Study of the Oldest Arthurian Tale*. Cardiff: University of Wales Press, 1992.

Brusegan, Rosanna. "La plaisanterie dans la lai de Nabaret." In *Risus Mediaevalis: Laughter in Medieval Literature and Art*. Edited by Herman Braet, Guido Latré, and Werner Verbeke. Leuven: Leuven University Press, 2003.

Burrows, Daron. *The Stereotype of the Priest in the Old French Fabliaux: Anticlerical Satire and Lay Identity*. Lausanne: Peter Lang, 2005.

Callimachus, Musaeus. *Aetia, Iambi, Hecale and Other Fragments. Hero and Leander*. Edited and translated by C. A. Trypanis, T. Gelzer, and Cedric H. Whitman. Loeb Classical Library 421. Cambridge, MA: Harvard University Press, 1973.

Chrétien de Troyes. "Perceval ou le conte du Graal." In *Œuvres complètes*. Edited by Daniel Poirion, 799. Paris: Gallimard, 1994.

Chrétien de Troyes. "Yvain ou le chevalier au lion." In *Œuvres complètes*. Edited by Philippe Walter, 415. Paris: Gallimard, 1994.

Clarck, Elizabeth. "Fashionable Beards: Masculinity and Self-Representation in the Poema de mio Cid." In *Queering Iberia*. Edited by Josiah Blackmore and Gregory S. Hutcheson, 93–112. Durham: Duke University Press, 1999.

Clay, Diskin. "Picturing Diogenes." In *The Cynics: The Cynic Movement in Antiquity and Its Legacy*. Edited by R. Bracht Branham and Marie-Odile Goulet-Cazé, 366–88. Berkeley: University of California Press, 1996,

Clement of Alexandria. "The Paedagogus." Translated by William Wilson. In *Ante-Nicene Fathers, Volume II: Fathers of the Second Century: Hermas, Tatian, Athenagoras, Theophilus, and Clement of Alexandria*. Edited by Alexander Roberts, James Donaldson, and A. Cleveland Coxe. Buffalo: Christian Literature Publishing Co., 1885.

Cohen, Gustave, ed. *La comédie latine en France au XIIe siècle*. Paris: les Belles lettres, 1931.

Collerye, Roger de. *Oeuvres de Roger de Collerye*. Edited by Charles d'Héricault. Paris: P. Jannet, 1855.

Constable, Giles. "Introduction." In *Apologiae duae*. Edited by R. B. C. Huygens, with an introduction on beards in the Middle Ages by Giles Constable, 47–150, 77–85. Turnhout: Brepols, 1985. (Corpus christianorum. Continuatio mediaevalis, 62).

Constable, Giles. *The Reformation of the Twelfth Century*. Cambridge: Cambridge University Press, 2002 [1996].

256 *Bibliography*

Coxon, Sebastian. *Beards and Texts: Images of Masculinity in Medieval German Literature*. London: UCL Press, 2021.

Curtius, Ernst Robert. *European Literature and the Latin Middle Ages*. Translated by Willard R. Trask. Bollingen Series. Princeton: Princeton University Press, 1973 [1948].

David, Yonah, ed. *The Love Stories of Jacob Ben Eleazar (1170–1233?): Critical Edition with Introduction and Commentary*. Tel-Aviv: Ramot Publishing, Tel-Aviv University, 1992–93.

Decter, Jonathan P. *Iberian Jewish Literature: Between al-Andalus and Christian Europe*. Bloomington: Indiana University Press, 2007.

Desmond, William. *Cynics*. London: Routledge, 2014.

Dillon, John. "The Social Role of the Philosopher in the Second Century C.E: Some Remarks." In *Sage and Emperor: Plutarch, Greek Intellectuals, and Roman Power in the Time of Trajan (98-117 A.D.)*. Edited by Philip A. Stadter and Luc Van der Stockt, 29–40. Leuven: Leuven University Press, 2002.

Dio Cassius. *Roman History, Volume VIII: Books 61-70*. Translated by Earnest Cary and Herbert B. Foster. Loeb Classical Library 176. Cambridge, MA: Harvard University Press, 1925.

D'Orbigny, Robert. *Le conte de Floire et Blanchefleur*. Edited by Jean-Luc Leclanche. Paris: Champion, 2003.

Drori, Rina. "The Maqama." In *The Literature of Al-Andalus*. Edited by María Rosa Menocal, Raymond Scheindlin, and Michael Sells, 190–210. Cambridge: Cambridge University Press, 2000.

Dubost, Francis. *Aspects fantastiques de la littérature narrative médiévale* (XIIème-XIIIèeme sieclèes), L'Autre, l'Ailleurs l'Autrefois. Geneva: Slatkine, 1991.

Dutton, Paul E. "Charlemagne's Mustache." In *Charlemagne's Mustache and Other Cultural Clusters of a Dark Age*, 3–42. New York: Palgrave Macmillan, 2004.

Edmonds, J. M., trans. *Greek Bucolic Poets, Volume 28*. Loeb Classical Library. Cambridge, MA: Harvard University Press, 1912.

Elizur, Shulamit. *Hebrew Secular Poetry in Muslim Spain*. Tel-Aviv: Tel-Aviv University Press, 2004.

Epictetus. *Discourses, Books 1-2*. Translated by W. A. Oldfather. Loeb Classical Library 131. Cambridge, MA: Harvard University Press, 1925.

Fangé, Augustin. *Mémoires pour servir à l'histoire de la barbe de l'homme*. Liège: J.-F. Broncart, 1774.

Fantham, Elaine. "Commentary on Ovid: Fasti, IV:133." In *Ovid, Fasti Book IV*. Cambridge: Cambridge University Press, 1998.

Flamenca. Edited by Valérie Fasseur. Paris: Librarie générale française, 2014.

Fleischer, Ezra, ed. *Poetry Aptly Explained: Studies and Essays on Medieval Hebrew Poetry*. Jerusalem: The Magness Press, 1993.

Fox, Samuel J. *Hell in Jewish Literature*. Northbrook: Merrimack College Press, 1972.

France, James. *Separate but Equal: Cistercian Lay Brothers 1120-1350*. Collegeville: Liturgical Press, 2012.

Friedman, John Block. "Hair and Social Class." In *A Cultural History of Hair in the Middle Ages*. Edited by Roberta Milliken, 137–51, 198–202. London: Bloomsbury Academic, 2018.

Bibliography 257

Friedman, John Block. *The Monstrous Races in Medieval Art and Thought*. New York: Syracuse University Press, 2000.

Friedman, Lionel J. "Gradus Amoris." *Romance Philology* 19, no. 2 (1965): 167–77.

Friesen, Ilse. *The Female Crucifix: Images of St. Wilgefortis since the Middle Ages*. Waterloo: Wilfrid Laurier University Press, 2001.

Froissart, Jean. *Chroniques de J. Froissart, troizième livre, Volume 2 (1356-1388)*. Edited by Léon Mirot. Paris: Champion, 1931.

Furstenberg, Yair. "The Midrash of Jesus and the Bavli's Counter-Gospel." *Jewish Studies Quarterly* 22, no. 4 (2015): 303–24.

Gardner, Gregg E. "Who is Rich? The Poor in Early Rabbinic Judaism." *The Jewish Quarterly Review* 104, no. 4 (2014): 515–36.

Gaunt, Simon. *Gender and Genre in Medieval French Literature*. Cambridge: Cambridge University Press, 1995.

Gellius, Aulus. *Attic Nights, Volume II: Books 6-13*. Translated by J. C. Rolfe. Loeb Classical Library 200. Cambridge, MA: Harvard University Press, 1927.

Geoffrey of Monmouth. *The History of the Kings of Britain*. Edited by Michael D. Reeve. Translated by Neil Wright. Woodbridge: Boydell & Brewer, 2007.

Géraud, Marie-Odile, Olivier Leservoisier, and Richard Pottier. "Fait Social Total." In *Les notions clés de l'ethnologie: analyses et textes*, 187–99. Paris: Armand Colin, 2016.

Giraldi Cambrensis. *Topographia Hibernica, et Expugnatio Hibernica*. Edited by James F. Dimock. Volume 5 of *Giraldi Cambrensis Opera*. Rerum Britannicarum Medii Ævi Scriptores. London: Longman, Green, Reader, and Dyer, 1867.

Goch, Iolo. "The Poet's Beard." In *Poems*. Translated and edited by Dafydd Johnston, 102–04. Llandysul: Gomer Press, 1993.

Green, Deborah. *The Aroma of Righteousness: Scent and Seduction in Rabbinic Life and Literature*. University Park: Penn State University Press, 2011.

Gregg, Joan Young. *Devils, Women, and Jews: Reflections of the Other in Medieval Sermons Stories*. New York: State University of New York Press, 1997.

Guilhou, Étienne, ed. "Geta." In *La comédie latine en France au XIIe siècle*. Edited by Gustave Cohen, 1–58. Paris: Les Belles Lettres, 1931.

Hadas, Hirsch. "Hair: Practices and Symbolism in Traditional Muslim Societies." *Sociology of Islam* 5 (2017): 33–35.

Halperin, David M., John J. Winkler, and Froma I. Zeitlin, eds. *Before Sexuality: The Construction of Erotic Experience in the Ancient Greek World*. Princeton: Princeton University Press, 1990.

Hameen-Antitila, Jaakko. *Maqama—A History of a Genre*. Wiesbaden: Harrassowitz Verlag, 2002.

Hen, Yitzhak. "The Early Medieval Barbatoria." In *Medieval Christianity in Practice*. Edited by Miri Rubin, 21–26. Princeton: Princeton University Press, 2009.

Hilka, Alfons, *Die Wundergeschichten des Caesarius von Heisterbach*, t. I, no. 42, 82. Bonn: Hanstein, 1933.

Hilka, Alfons, ed. *Eine altfranzösische moralisierende Bearbeitung des "Liber de monstruosis hominibus Orientis" aus Thomas von Cantimpré "De naturis rerum" nach der einzigen Handschrift (Paris, Bibl. Nat. fr. 15106)*. Abhandlungen der

Bibliography

Gesellschaft der Wissenschaften zu Göttingen, Philosophisch-historische Klasse, 3. Folge, 7. Berlin: Weidmannsche Buchhandlung, 1933.

Hilka, Alfons. "Liber de monstruosis hominibus Orientis aus Thomas von Cantimpré: De natura rerum. Erstausgabe aus der Bilderhandschrift der Breslauer Stadtbibliothek nebst zwei Seiten Facsimile." In *Festschrift zur Jahrhundertfeier der Universität Breslau am 2. August 1911*, herausgegeben vom Schlesischen Philologenverein, 151–66. Breslau: Trewendt und Granier, 1911.

Hippocrates. *Epidemics 2, 4-7*. Edited and translated by Wesley D. Smith. Loeb Classical Library 477. Cambridge, MA: Harvard University Press, 1994.

Horowitz, Elimelech. "On the Meanings of the Beard in Jewish Communities in the East and Europe in the Middle Ages and the Beginning of the Modern Era." *Pe'amim* 59 (1993): 124–48. [In Hebrew].

Ibn Ezra, Moshe. *The Liturgical Poems of Moshe Ibn Ezra, A Critical Edition*. Annotated and introduced by Israel Levin and Tova Rosen. Tel-Aviv: Tel-Aviv University Press, 2012.

Jacquart, Danielle, and Claude Thomasset. *Sexualité et savoir médical au Moyen Age*. Paris: Presses Universitaires de France, 1985.

Jerome, Saint. *Select Letters*. Translated by F. A. Wright. The Loeb Classical Library. New York: G.P. Putnam's Sons, 1933.

Karlsson, Gustave H. "Aus der Briefsammlung des Anonymus Florentinus (Georgios Oinaiotes)." *Jahrbuch der Österreichischen Byzantinistik* 22 (1973): 207–18.

Karras, Ruth Mazo. *Sexuality in Medieval Europe: Doing unto others*. New York and London: Routledge, 2017.

Kennedy, Philipp F. *The Wine Song in Classical Arabic Poetry: Abū Nuwās and the Literary Tradition*. Oxford: Clarendon Press, 1997.

Koopmans, Jelle, ed. *Recueil de sermons joyeux*. Geneva: Droz, 1988.

Kucharski, Janek, and Przemyslaw Marciniak. "The Beard and its Philosopher: Theodore Prodromos on the Philosopher's Beard in Byzantium." *Byzantine and Modern Greek Studies* 41, no. 1 (2017): 45–54.

Kyriakou, Poulheria. *Theocritus and His Native Muse: A Syracusan Among Many*. Berlin: De Gruyter, 2018.

Lacrois, Daniel, and Philippe Walter, eds. *Tristan et Iseut Les poèmes français, La saga norroise*. Paris: Librairie générale française, 1989.

Lacy, Norris J., and James J. Wilhelm, eds. *The Romance of Arthur: An Anthology of Medieval Texts in Translation*. Abingdon: Routledge, 2013.

Lançon, Bertrand, and Marie-Héléne Delavaud-Roux, eds. *Anthropologie, mythologies et histoire de la chevelure et de la pilosité, Le sens du poil*. Paris: L'Harmattan, 2011.

Lazar, Moshe. "Carmina Erotica, Carmina Iocosa: The Body and The Bawdy in Medieval Love Songs." In *Poetics of Love in the Middle Ages: Texts and Contexts*. Edited by Moshe Lazar and Norris J. Lacy, 249–278. Fairfax: George Mason University Press, 1989.

Lazar, Moshe. "Fin'amor." In *A Handbook for the Troubadours*. Edited by F. R. P. Akehurst and Judith M. Davis, 76–83. Berkeley: University of California Press, 1995.

Bibliography

259

Le blason des barbes de maintenant. Edition accessible on Gallica. https://gallica.bnf .fr/ark:/12148/bpt6k83479q.pdf.

Le Roman de Renart. Édition bilingue établie, traduite, présentée et annotée par Jean Dufournet, Laurence Harf-Lancner, Marie-Thérèse de Medeiros et Jean Subrenat. Tome I (Branches I–XI); Tome II (Branches XII–XX). Classiques Moyen Âge. Paris: Honoré Champion, 2013–15.

Leclercq, Jean. "Comment vivaient les frères convers." In *I laici nella "societas Christiana" dei secoli XI e XII, Atti della terza Settimana Internazionale di studio Mendola, 21-27 agosto 1965*. Edited by Jean Chélini, 152–82. Vita e Pensiero, Milano, 1968.

Legros, Huguette. *La folie dans la littérature médiévale*. Rennes: Presses universitaires de Rennes, 2013.

Les grandes chroniques de France, Volume III. Edited by Jules Viard. Paris: Librarie ancienne E. Champion, 1920.

Leupin, Alexandre. *Fiction and Incarnation. Rhetoric, Theology, and Literature in the Middle Ages*. Translated by David Laatsch. Minneapolis: University of Minnesota Press, 2003.

Levin, Israel. *The Embroidered Coat: The Genres of Hebrew Secular Poetry in Spain, Volume II*. Tel-Aviv: Katz Institute for the Research of Hebrew Literature, Hakibuz Hameuchad, 1995. [in Hebrew].

Levin, Israel, and Tova Rosen, eds. *The Liturgical Poems of Moshe Ibn Ezra: A Critical Edition*. Tel-Aviv: Tel-Aviv University Press, 2012.

Lévi-Strauss, Claude. *From Honey to Ashes*. Translated by John and Doreen Weightman. London: Cape, 1973.

Lissarague, François. "The Sexual Life of Satyr." In *Before Sexuality: The Construction of Erotic Experience in the Ancient Greek World*. Edited by David M. Halperin, John J. Winkler, and Froma I. Zeitlin, 53–81. Princeton: Princeton University Press, 1990.

Livingstone, Michael. "Losing Face: Flayed Beards and Gendered Power in Arthurian Literature." In *Flaying in the Pre-Modern World*. Edited by Larissa Tracy, 308–21. Woodbridge: Boydell & Brewer, 2017.

Low, Peter Alan. "Translating Songs that Rhyme." *Perspectives: Studies in Translatology* 16, no. 1–2 (2008): 1–20. https://doi.org/10.1080/13670050802364437.

Lucian. *Dialogues of the Dead, Volume VII*. Translated by M. D. MacLeod. Loeb Classical Library 431. Cambridge, MA: Harvard University Press, 1961.

Lucian. "Harmonides." In *Lucian, Volume VI*. Translated by K. Kilburn. Loeb Classical Library 430. Cambridge, MA: Harvard University Press, 1959.

Lucian. *Soloecista. Lucius or The Ass. Amores. Halcyon. Demosthenes. Podagra. Ocypus. Cyniscus. Philopatris. Charidemus. Nero*. Translated by M. D. MacLeod. Loeb Classical Library 432. Cambridge, MA: Harvard University Press, 1967.

Lucian. "The Dream, or The Cock." In *Lucian, Volume II*. Translated by A. M. Harmon. Loeb Classical Library 54. Cambridge, MA: Harvard University Press, 1915.

Machaut, Guillaume de. *Le livre du voir dit*. Edited by Paul Imbs. Paris: Lettres Gothiques, 1999.

260   *Bibliography*

Macrobius. *Saturnalia, Volume III: Books 6-7*. Edited and translated by Robert A. Kaster. Loeb Classical Library 512. Cambridge, MA: Harvard University Press, 2011.

Malory, Sir Thomas. *Le Morte D'Arthur*. Edited by P. J. C. Field. Cambridge: D. S. Brewer, 2017.

Malti-Douglas, Fedwa. "Maqāmāt and Adab: 'Al-Maqāma al-Maḍīriyya of al-Hamadhānī.'" *Journal of the American Oriental Society* 105 (1985): 247–58.

Martial. *Epigrams, Volume I: Spectacles, Books 1-5*. Edited and translated by D. R. Shackleton Bailey. Loeb Classical Library 94. Cambridge, MA: Harvard University Press, 1993.

Mattok, J. N. "The Early History of the Maqama." *Journal of Arabic Literature* 15 (1984): 1–18.

Mauss, Marcel. "Essai sur le don. Forme et raison de l'échange dans les sociétés archaïques." *L'Année sociologique* (1923-1924): 30–186.

McDonough, Christopher J., ed. *"Moriuht": A Norman Latin Poem from the Early Eleventh Century*. Studies and Texts 121. Toronto: Pontifical Institute of Mediaeval Studies, 1995.

Melamed, Abraham. *The Image of the Black in Jewish Culture: A History of the Other*. Translated by Betty Sigler Rozen. London: Routledge, 2010.

Meyer, Paul, ed. *Daurel et Beton, chanson de geste provençale*. Paris: Firmin Didot (Société des anciens textes français), 1880.

Micha, Alexandre, ed. *Lais féeriques des XIIe et XIIIe siècles*. Paris: Flammarion, 1992.

Migne, J.-P., ed. *Patrologiae Cursus Completus: Series Latina*. Paris, 1844-1864.

Milliken, Roberta, ed. *A Cultural History of Hair in the Middle Ages*. London: Bloomsbury Academic, 2018.

Montiglio, Silvia. *From Villain to Hero: Odysseus in Ancient Thought*. Ann Arbor: The University of Michigan Press, 2011.

Morrison, Susan Signe. *Excrement in the Late Middle Ages: Sacred Filth and Chaucer's Fecopoetics*. London: Palgrave Macmillan, 2008.

Mouskes, Philippe. *Chronique rimée de Philippe Mouskes, évêque de Tournay au treizième siècle*. Edited by Baron de Reiffenberg. Hayez, 1836.

Murcia, Thierry. "B. Gittin 56B-57A: L'épisode talmudique de Titus, Balaam et Yeshu en enfer - Jesus et l'insolite châtiment de l'excrément bouillant." *Revue des études juives* 173, no. 1–2 (2014): 15–40.

Nemah, H. "Andalusian Maqamat." *Journal of Arabic Literature* 5 (1974): 83–92.

Nichols, J. G. "Petrarch's Canzoniere 164: An Anthology of English Translations with a New Version by J. G. Nichols." *Translation and Literature* 5, no. 1 (1996): 71–80.

Nikolsky, Ronit. "Interpret Him as Much as You Want: Balaam in the Babylonian Talmud." In *The Prestige of the Pagan Prophet Balaam in Judaism, Early Christianity and Islam*. Edited by George H. van Kooten and J. T. A. G. M. van Ruiten, 213–30. Leiden and Boston: Brill, 2008.

Noomen, Willem, and Nico van den Boogaard, eds. *Nouveau Recueil Complet des Fabliaux (NRCF)*. Tome 4. Avec le concours de H. B. Sol. Assen/Maastricht: Van Gorcum, 1988.

Bibliography

261

Oldstone-Moore, Christopher. *Of Beards and Men: The Revealing History of Facial Hair*. Chicago: University of Chicago Press, 2015.

Ovid. *Metamorphoses, Volume I: Books 1-8*. Translated by Frank Justus Miller. Revised by G. P. Goold. Loeb Classical Library 42. Cambridge, MA: Harvard University Press, 1916.

Ovid. *Metamorphoses, Volume II: Books 9-15*. Translated by Frank Justus Miller. Revised by G. P. Goold. Loeb Classical Library 43. Cambridge, MA: Harvard University Press, 1916.

Owen, D. D. R. "Beards in the Chanson de Roland." *Forum for Modern Language Studies* 24, no. 2 (1988): 175–79.

Pagis, Dan. "Alternating Faces: On the Rhymed Hebrew Story in the Middle-Ages." In *Poetry Aptly Explained: Studies and Essays on Medieval Hebrew Poetry*. Edited by E. Fleicher, 62–80. Jerusalem: Keter, 1993.

Pagis, Dan. *Change and Tradition in the Secular Poetry, Spain and Italy*. Jerusalem: Keter, 1976. [In Hebrew]

Pastoureau, Michel. *L'ours: Histoire d'un roi déchu*. Paris: Seuil, 2007.

Pastoureau, Michel. *Red: A History of a Color*. Translated by Jody Gladding. Princeton: Princeton University Press, 2017.

Paton, W. R., trans. *The Greek Anthology, Volume IV: Books 10-12*. Loeb Classical Library 85. Cambridge, MA: Harvard University Press, 1918.

Pellat, Charles. "Makama." In *The Encyclopedia of Islam, Volume 6*. Edited by Edmund Bosworth, Charles Pellat, and E. J. van Donzel, 107–15. Leiden: E. J. Brill, 1991.

Philostratus. *Apollonius of Tyana, Volume III: Letters of Apollonius. Ancient Testimonia. Eusebius's Reply to Hierocles*. Edited and translated by Christopher P. Jones. Loeb Classical Library 458. Cambridge, MA: Harvard University Press, 2006.

Pinto-Mathieu, Elisabeth, ed. *Baudouin de Flandres*. Paris: Lettres Gothiques, 2011.

Pliny the Younger. *Letters, Volume I: Books 1-7*. Translated by Betty Radice. Loeb Classical Library 55. Cambridge, MA: Harvard University Press, 1969.

Plutarch. *Moralia, Volume I*. Translated by Frank Cole Babbitt. Loeb Classical Library 197. Cambridge, MA: Harvard University Press, 1927.

Plutarch. *Moralia, Volume III: Sayings of Kings and Commanders. Sayings of Romans. Sayings of Spartans. The Ancient Customs of the Spartans. Sayings of Spartan Women. Bravery of Women*. Translated by Frank Cole Babbitt. Loeb Classical Library 245. Cambridge, MA: Harvard University Press, 1931.

Plutarch. *Moralia, Volume V*. Translated by Frank Cole Babbitt. Loeb Classical Library 306. Cambridge, MA: Harvard University Press, 1936.

Poos, L. R. "Sex, Lies, and the Church Courts of Pre-Reformation England." *The Journal of Interdisciplinary History* 25, no. 4 (Spring, 1995): 585–607.

Pouvreau, Florent. *Du poil et de la bête. Iconographie du corps sauvage en occident à la fin du Moyen Âge (XIIIe-XVIe siècle)*. Chartes: Comité des travaux historiques et scientifiques, 2014.

Preuss, Julius. *Biblical and Talmudic Medicine*. Translated and edited by Fred Rosner. Northvale: Jason Aronson, 1993.

262 *Bibliography*

Priapeia. *Priapum lusus or Sportive Epigrams on Priapus.* Translated by Leonard C. Smithers and Sir Richard Burton. [1890]. https://sacred-texts.com/cla/priap/prp11.htm.

Quinn, Arthur. *Figures of Speech: 60 Ways to Turn a Phrase.* Lanham: Scarecrow Press, 1993.

Refael-Vivante, Revital. "Beware of Hypocrites: Religious Hypocrisy in Medieval Hebrew Rhymed Prose in Spain." *Hispania Judaica* 6 (2008): 9–51.

Refael-Vivante, Revital. "Religious Hypocrisy in Medieval Hebrew Rhymed Prose." *Hispania Judaica* 6 (2009): 5–51.

Robert de Borron. *Die Abenteuer Gawains, Ywains und Le Morholts mit den drei Jungfrauen aus der Trilogie (Demanda) des Pseudo-Robert de Borron, die Fortsetzung des Huth-Merlin nach der allein bekannten Hs. Nr. 112 der Pariser National Bibliothek.* Edited by H. Oskar Sommer. Halle a. S., Niemeyer (Beihefte zur Zeitschrift für romanische Philologie, 47), 1913.

Robinson, Katelynn. *The Sense of Smell in the Middle Ages: A Source of Certainty.* London: Routledge, 2020.

Rodríguez-Pereira, Víctor. "Sabora Olor: The Role of Olfaction and Smells in Berceo's Milagros de Nuestra Señora." In Beyond Sight: *Engaging the Senses in Iberian Literatures and Cultures, 1200-1750.* Edited by Rayan D. Giles and Steven Wagschal, 31–44. Toronto: University of Toronto Press, 2018.

Rosen, Tova. "Eros and Intellect in the First Maqama by Jacob Ibn Eleazar." In *Studies in Hebrew Literature of the Middle Ages and Renaissance in Honor of Professor Yona David.* Edited by Tova Rosen and Avner Holtzman, 191–212. Tel-Aviv: Tel-Aviv University Press, 2002.

Rosen, Tova. "Love and Race in a Thirteenth-Century Romance in Hebrew with a Translation of the Story of Maskil and Peninah by Jacob Ben El'azar." *Florilegium* 23, no. 1 (2006): 155–72.

Rosen, Tova. "The Beard as Spectacle and Scandal in a Thirteenth-century Hebrew Maqāma." *Intellectual History of the Islamicate World* 9, no. 1 (2021): 1–24.

Rosen, Tova. "The Story of the Crooked Preacher by Jacon ben El'azar". In *'His Pen and Ink Are a Powerful Mirror', Andalusi, Judaeo-Arabic, and Other Near Eastern Studies in Honor of Ross Brann.* Edited by Adam Bursi, S. J. Pearce and Hazma M. Zafer, 231-258. Leiden: Brill, 2020.

Rosen, Tova. *Unveiling Eve: Reading Gender in Medieval Hebrew Literature.* Philadelphia: University of Pennsylvania Press, 2003.

Roussineau, Gilles, ed. *La suite du Roman de Merlin.* Geneva: Droz, 2006.

Roussineau, Gilles, ed. and trans. *Le chevalier aux deux épées, roman en vers du XIIIe siècle.* Geneva: Droz, 2022.

Roussineau, Gilles, ed. *Perceforest, première partie,* t. 1. Genève: Droz, 2007.

Salisbury, Joyce E. "Gendered Sexuality." In *Handbook of Medieval Sexuality.* Edited by Vern L. Bullough and James A. Brundage, 81–102. New York: Routledge, 2000.

Scheindlin, Raymond. "Love Stories by Ya'akov ben Elazar: Between Arabic and Romance Literature." In *Proceedings of the World Congress for Jewish Studies,* Division III, 16–20. Jerusalem, 1994. [In Hebrew].

Schirmann, Jefim. "A Tale of an Old Hypocrite." In *The History of Hebrew Poetry and Drama: Studies and Essays.* Jerusalem: Mosad Bialik, 1979. [in Hebrew].

Bibliography

Schirmann, Jefim. *Hebrew Poetry in Spain and Provence*. Jerusalem: The Magnes Press, 1997. [in Hebrew].

Schirmann, Jefim. *The History of Hebrew Poetry in Christian Spain and Southern France*. Edited and supplemented by E. Fleischer. Jerusalem: Magnes, 1997.

Schirmann, Jefim. "The Love Stories of Jacob ben Elazar." *Yedi'ot haMakhon leHeker haShirah haIvrit* 5 (5699 [1939]): 211–66. [in Hebrew].

Scott Brown, Peter. *The Riddle of Jael: The History of a Poxied Heroine in Medieval and Renaissance Art and Culture*. Leiden: Brill, 2018.

Segal, Eliezer. *From Sermon to Commentary: Expounding the Bible in Talmudic Babylonia*. Waterloo: Wilfrid Laurier University Press, 2005.

Sheehan, Sarah. "Boar-hunts, and Barbering: Masculinity in 'Culhwch ac Olwen.'" *Arthuriana* 15, no. 3 (2005): 3–25.

Shlomo ibn Zakbel. "The Tale of Asher ben Yehuda." In *Libavtini: Lovers Tales from The Middle Ages*. Edited by Yosef Yahalom, 59–71. Jerusalem: Carmel, 2009.

Simon, Uriel. *Reading Prophetic Narratives*. Bloomington: Indiana University Press, 1997.

Simpson, J. R. *Animal Body, Literary Corpus. The Old French Roman de Renart*. Leiden: Brill, 1996.

Skoda, Hannah. "St Wilgefortis and Her/Their Beard: The Devotions of Unhappy Wives and Non-Binary People." *History Workshop Journal* 95 (2023): 51–74.

Sommer, Heincrich Oskar, ed. *Lestoire de Merlin, Volume II* of *Vulgate Version of the Arthurian Romances*. Washington: Carnegie Institution of Washington, 1908.

Sozomen. "Ecclesiastical History." Translated by Chester D. Hartranft. In *Nicene and Post-Nicene Fathers*, Second Series, *Volume 2*. Edited by Philip Schaff and Henry Wace. Buffalo: Christian Literature Publishing Co., 1890.

Stephanus de Borbone. *Exempla, Tractatus de diversis materiis predicabilibus Prologus - Liber primus. De dono timoris*. Edited by J. Berlioz and J. L. Eichenlaub. Turnhout: Brepols, 2002.

Strubel, Armand, ed. *Le haut livre du graal [Perlesvaus]*. Lettres gothiques. Paris: Librairie générale française, 2007.

Strubel, Armand, R. Bellon, Dominique Boutet, and Sylvie Lefèvre. *Le Roman de Renart*. Paris: Gallimard, 1998.

Sweetser, Franklin P., ed. *Les Cent Nouvelles Nouvelles*. Nouvelle 12. Genève: Droz, 1996.

Theocritus. "Idyll 12." In *Theocritus. Moschus. Bion*. Edited and translated by Neil Hopkinson. Loeb Classical Library 28. Cambridge, MA: Harvard University Press, 2015.

Thomas, J. W. *Le roman de Tristan*. In *Tristan et Iseut Les poèmes français, La saga norroise*. Edited by Daniel Lacrois and Philippe Walter. Lettres gothiques. Paris: Librairie générale française, 1989.

Thomas, J. W., trans. *Ulrich von Liechtenstein's Service of Ladies*. Woodbridge: The Boydell Press, 2004.

Tracy, Larissa, ed. *Flaying in the Pre-Modern World*. Woodbridge: Boydell & Brewer, 2017.

Bibliography

Tubach, Frederic C. *Index Exemplorum: A Handbook of Medieval Religious Tales.* Helsinki: Suomalainen Tiedeakatemia, 1969.

Tudor, Adrian P. *Tales of Vice and Virtue: The First Old French Vie des Pères.* Amsterdam: Rodopi, 2005.

Uden, James. *The Invisible Satirist: Juvenal and Second-Century Rome.* Oxford: Oxford University Press, 2015.

Van Hamel, A.-G., ed. *Les Lamentations de Matheolus et le Livre de leesce de Jehan le Fèvre, de Resson (poèmes français du XIVe siècle), Volume 1.* Paris: Bouillon (Bibliothèque de l'École des hautes études, 9596), 1892.

Van Hamel, A.-G., ed. *Li romans de Carité et Miserere du Renclus de Moiliens, poèmes de la fin du XIIe siècle.* Paris: Vieweg (Bibliothèque de l'École des hautes études, Sciences philologiques et historiques, 61-62), 1885.

Vasvari, Louise O. "Vegetal-Genital Onomastics in the 'Libro de buen amor.'" *Romance Philology* 42, no. 1 (1988): 1–29.

Veenker, Ronald A. "Forbidden Fruit: Ancient Near Eastern Sexual Metaphors." *Hebrew Union College Annual* 70 (1999): 57–74.

Wace. *Roman de Brut: A History of the British.* Translated by Judith Weiss. Exeter: University of Exeter Press, 1999.

Wacks, David A. *Double Diaspora in Sephardic Literature: Jewish Cultural Production Before and After 1492.* Bloomington: Indiana University Press, 2015.

Wallace, Lewis. "Bearded Woman, Female Christ: Gendered Transformations in the Legends and Cult of Saint Wilgefortis." *Journal of Feminist Studies in Religion* 30, no. 1 (2014): 43–63.

Walter, Philippe. "Une ballade inédite du XVe siècle sur l'homme sauvage: éditions, traduction et commentaire." In *En quête d'utopies.* Edited by Claude Thomasset and Danièle James-Raoul, 313–22. Paris: Presses de l'université Paris-Sorbonne, 2005.

Weeber, Jacqueline de. *Sheba's Daughters: Whitening and Demonizing the Saracen Woman in Medieval French Epic.* New York: Garland Publishing, 1998.

Williams, Charles Allyn. *Oriental Affinities of the Legend of the Hairy Anchorite: The Theme of the Hairy Solitary in Its Early Forms With References to Die Lugend von Sanct Johanne Chrysostomo (Reprinted by Lother, 1537) and to Other European Variants.* Urbana: University of Illinois Press, 1925.

Wolff, Étienne. "Martial et la pilosity." In *Anthropologie, mythologies et histoire de la chevelure et de la pilosité, Le sens du poil.* Edited by Bertrand Lançon and Marie-Héléne Delavaud-Roux, 209–18. Paris: L'Harmattan, 2011.

Wright, Wilmer Cave, trans. "Introduction to Misopogon, or Beard-hater." In *The Works of The Emperor Julian, Volume II*, 418–19. Cambridge, MA: Harvard University Press, [1913] 1998.

Yadin, Azzan. "Samson's ḥîdâ." *Vetus Testamentum* 52 (2002): 407–26.

Yahalom, Yosef, and Naoya Katsumata, eds. *Tahkemoni or Tales of Heman the Ezrahite.* Jerusalem: Ben Zvi, 2010.

Yellin, David, ed. *Gan Hammeshalim veHahidot: ben Judah Halevi Abulafia.* Jerusalem: Weiss Press, 1936. [in Hebrew].

Yellin, David. *Introduction to the Hebrew Poetry of the Spanish Period.* Jerusalem: The Magnes Press, 1978. [in Hebrew].

Index

The Acharnians (Aristophanes), 106n89
Achbor's sermon, 2, 53, 54, 122,
173–74, 176, 180, 184, 209, 210,
227; "The Fable of the Poor Man," 5,
174–76; "The Fable of the Two Men
Who Lived in the Same District," 5,
55, 177–80
Adams, J. N., 125
adultery, 82, 102n47, 129, 214
Alexandre-Bidon, Danièle, 151
allegorical mode, 2
Apollonius of Tyana, 118
ardent, 69, 72, 197
Augustine, 139
Ausonius, 125

Balaam, 6, 187, 188, 190n19, 190n21
barba prolixa (long beards), 121
barbo, 151–53
beard, sign of community elder:
Aaron's beard, 113; beard as a home
for living creatures, 115. *See also*
"The Misopogon"; Chernomor's
beard, 113; motif of beards in
romantic mishaps, 116. *See also*
"This Beard Was Meant for
Kissing"; philosophical beard,
115, 119. *See also* "Whiskers of
Wisdom"; sexual and gendered

perceptions of the beard, 115–16.
See also "Penis Erectus," "Smooth
Women, Bearded Men, or Vice
Versa?"; symbolic significance of
beards, 153–54; symbol of male
honor, 116. *See also* "Le Chastel des
Barbes"; symbol of manhood, 117.
See also barba prolixa (long beards),
barbo, "A Beard from Hell", war of
beards
"A Beard from Hell," 117, 150–53
ben Elazar, Yaakov, 1, 2, 11, 12, 32–37,
46, 47, 49, 51, 53, 54, 61, 68, 70–72,
80, 85, 86, 92, 93, 98, 112, 126, 130,
173, 181n13, 193, 197, 213, 215,
216, 221, 241, 245n19
Berlioz, Jacques, 151
Berneville, Gillebert de, 140, 141
biblical phrasings (*shibutzim*), 13;
Achbor's preaching in city plaza,
43–60; black Mistress, 66–81; in
blame of the beard, 81–92; didactic
love poem, 95–98; a fairy tale
ending, 92–95; feasting with four
maidens, 60–66; prologue, 29–43
Bierl, Anton, 213
bitter as wormwood, 235
blackness, 2–7, 25, 56, 66–81, 133, 137,
151–54, 180, 188, 193–203, 210, 211,

265

213, 215, 228, 239, 242. *See also*
Cushitic; digging in the darkness
black wild asses, 202
Bly, P. A., 141
Bodel, Jean, 66
Book of Takhkemoni (al-Harizi), 86
"bright as a lily," 199
Brody, Saul Nathaniel, 50, 100n31, 240
Brusegan, Rosanna, 140

Caesarius of Heisterbach, 194
Cent Nouvelles Nouvelles, 135
Chrétien de Troyes, 133, 219n22
The City of God (Augustine), 139
Clement of Alexandria, 139
Condé, Jean de, 140
Constable, Giles, 47, 121, 131
conversi barbati (bearded laymen), 121
crushed testicle, 25, 71, 82, 105n87
Culhwch and Olwen, 87
cultural assimilation, 197; Otherness,
193, 195, 196, 198, 203; secret
black woman, 195–203; secret black
woman as a personification, 194–96
Cushitic, 24, 193, 195, 204n1
Cynicism, 117

Daurel et Beton, 90
David, Yonah, 12, 13, 32, 42, 46, 50, 53,
54, 56, 57, 60, 61, 64, 67, 70, 74, 79,
84, 96, 178, 227, 232, 233, 240
Decter, Jonathan, 4, 9n16, 10n23,
158n50, 219n21
d'Angleterre, Thomas, 142
de Cantimpré, Thomas, 134
de Lorris, Guillaume, 76
didactic pattern, 3
digging in the darkness, 82–83, 86, 202
Dio Cassius, 119
Dira Le'haskir ("An Apartment for
Rent") (Goldberg), 203n1
Dubost, Francis, 144, 145

El Cid, 141
Elizur, Shulamit, 102n54
Epictetus, 120

Epicurus, 136
evil, 17, 194
exempla, 180, 194

fin'amor, 95
flagrante delicto, 68, 102n48, 214
Fleicher, E., 8n4
four maidens as a poetical device,
209–11; Amazons, 212–15; Bacchae,
211–12; fairies, 215–17
Friedman, John Block, 138
Froissart, Jean, 87

Gellius, Aulus, 118, 120
generosity, 225, 242
Gersonides, 44, 77, 188n4
Geta, 127–29
Goch, Iolo, 145
Goldberg, Leah, 203n1
gradus amoris, 222, 226, 242; hearing,
225; sight, 222–23; taste and smell,
223–25; touch, 225–26
Gregg, Joan Young, 204n5
Gregory the Great, 133

HaNagid, Shmuel, 225, 227, 234
al-Harizi, Yehuda, 1, 86, 116, 146, 148,
154n2
Harmonides (Lucian), 35, 36
Hippocrates, 132
Horowitz, Elimelech, 121
Humoral Theory, 228
hypertrichosis, 116
hypocritical preachers, 4, 6; Balaam,
6, 187, 188; Jesus, the new Balaam,
186–88

Ibn Ezra, Abraham, 38, 57, 100n25,
249n72, 250n72
Ibn Ezra, Moses, 51, 37
ibn Zakbel, Shlomo (Solomon), 116,
146
idol worship, 33, 183, 201
ignominies, 101n34
Il était une fois . . . l'Homme (Once
upon a Time . . . Man), 111

jeu parti, 140
Julian, 35, 46, 84, 115, 123, 145, 150

Kalila and Dimna, 1
Kara, Joseph, 82, 100n23, 189n6, 208n39
Kimhi, David, 38, 189n5, 223
Kitab al-kamil (the Complete Book), 1
The Knights (Aristophanes), 116, 146
"Le Chastel des Barbes," 116, 141–45

Le chevalier aux deux épées, 142, 145
Leclercq, Jean, 121
Le lai de Nabarez, 140
Le livre du voir dit, 160n63
Lemuel ben Ithiel, 1–4, 6, 7, 13, 29–33, 35–42, 45–48, 53, 59–61, 67–69, 72–81, 114, 124, 126, 129, 150, 153, 161, 180, 186, 193, 195, 196–203, 209–10, 212, 214, 215
Le roman de Brut (Wace), 142
Le Roman de la rose (de Lorris), 76, 138
Le Roman de Renart, 136, 137, 148
Les Lamentations de Matheolus, 171n176
les tresces, 140
Levin, Israel, 221, 228–30, 246n29
Lewis, B., 193
Li Sohaiz desvez (the dream of pricks) (Bodel), 66
Livingstone, Michael, 114, 116, 169n154
locus amoenus, 92, 93, 215, 216, 248n53
Lucian, 35, 36, 119, 139
Lysistrata (Aristophanes), 213, 219n9

Machaut, Guillaume de, 160n63
mahbarot, maqama, 1, 4
Malory, Thomas, 150
Martial, 135
McDonough, Christopher J., 169n158
Melamed, Abraham, 103n58, 105n87, 193, 211, 215, 217n3, 218n8
Metamorphoses (Ovid), 125

Metamorphoses (Apuleius), 116, 147
mimesis, 213
Misopogon (Julian), 35, 46, 84, 115, 122–24, 145, 150
Montoya, Manuel, 124
Moriuht: A Norman Latin Poem from the Early Eleventh Century, 35, 85, 114, 123, 126–30, 154n1, 161n67
Morrison, S., 187
Most High, 18, 19, 48, 49, 56
Mouskés, Philippe, 152
Murcia, Thierry, 187
mythical style, 2

Nichols, J. G., 244n12
Nikolsky, Ronit, 190n13
non-marital sex, 219n22
Nuptial Cento (Ausonius), 125
Nuwas, Abu, 225, 227, 230

Odyssey (Homer), 102n48
Olam Haba (the world to come), 187
Oldstone-Moore, Christopher, 121
olfactory symbolism, 198, 199
Otherness, 45, 69, 183, 185, 193, 195, 196, 198

parodical encomium, 3
Pastoureau, Michel, 137
"Penis Erectus," 115, 124–31
Pentateuch, 42, 44
Perceforest, 112, 121
Perlesvaus, 135, 142–44
Phaedrus, 131
Plato, 35, 118
Plutarch, 118
Poema, 141
Polyphemus, Cyclops, 125
Prodromos, Theodore, 46
prutah (penny), 176, 181n13

Rashi, 32, 55, 67, 83, 95, 100n23, 188n4, 249n72
Remedia Amoris (Ovid), 103n59
Republic (Plato), 35
rhetoric-realistic style, 2

268   *Index*

rhetoric tales, 2
rhymed prose, 1, 11, 12, 31
Robinson, Katelynn, 197
Rodríguez-Pereira, Víctor, 197
romance-like tales, 2
Rosen, Tova, 114, 116, 159n59, 212
Ruslan and Ludmila (Pushkin), 113
Russel, Jeffrey Burton, 151

Saracen, 152, 194, 195, 205n10
scatological discourses, 87, 107n101
Schirmann, Jefim, 4, 12, 30–32, 42, 44,
    46, 49, 50, 56, 61, 64, 67, 69, 74, 79,
    84, 95, 96, 101n34, 111, 113, 174,
    193, 227, 230, 232, 240
Sefer ha-Meshalim (The Book of Tales),
    1, 29, 31, 115, 152, 195, 218n5,
    219n22, 221
Sermon joyeux des barbes et des brayes,
    138
she'ol, 106n88
"Smooth Women, Bearded Men, or
    Vice Versa?," 115, 131–41
stench, 198, 207n28
Stephanus de Borbone, 151, 194
Strubel, Armand, 144

"The Tale of Asher ben Yehuda" (ibn
    Zakbel), 116, 146
The Tale of Old Bearded Achbor, 5,
    8, 11, 12, 45, 87, 88, 111, 115,
    117, 153, 154, 183, 188, 210, 221;
    Achbor's preaching in city plaza,
    16–21; black Mistress, 24–25;
    in blame of the beard, 25–27; a
    fairy tale ending, 27–28; feasting

with four maidens, 21–24; prologue,
    13–16
Tale of Sahar and Kima, 31, 97
"Tale of the Seven Virgins" (al-Harizi),
    116, 146
Tarfon, Rabbi, 186
Targum Yonatan, 237
Theocritus, 150, 233
"This Beard Was Meant for Kissing,"
    116, 145–50
Thomas, J. W., 142
Tristan (d'Angleterre), 142
Tudor, Adrian P., 195

vagina dentata, 135, 136, 144, 235, 236
Vies de pères, *Sarrasine* (The Saracen
    Woman), 195. *See also* Saracen
vile figs, 71–72, 196
Vitalis de Blois, 127

Wace, 142
Walter, Philippe, 159n59
Warner of Rouen, 126, 127, 130
war of beards, 142, 144
Weeber, Jacqueline de, 194
"Whiskers of Wisdom," 115, 117–22
white she-asses, 201, 202
wild ass, 201, 202
Williams, Charles Allyn, 156n17
wine poem strophes: colors, 237–40;
    gradus amoris, 222–26; images,
    231–37; paradoxes, 229–31; riddles,
    226–29
Wolff, Étienne, 140

Yitzchaki, Shlomo. *See* Rashi

About the Author

Tovi Bibring is an associate professor and chair of the Department of French Culture at Bar-Ilan University. During the academic year 2021–2022, she was a Masada fellow at Worcester College, Oxford. Her fields of expertise include medieval and renaissance French and Hebrew literature and the possible correspondence between Christian and Jewish texts. She has been working on biblical adaptations, phrasings, and citations from a large number of Christian and Jewish narratives and has published extensively on medieval fables and exempla, drama and farces, courtly and popular literature, and on the trend of adopting and manipulating Christian themes into Hebrew compositions.

www.ingramcontent.com/pod-product-compliance
Lightning Source LLC
Chambersburg PA
CBHW032257160525
26794CB00002B/14